Bulmer Hobson and the nationalist movement in twentieth-century Ireland

Bulmer Hobson
and the nationalist movement
in twentieth-century Ireland

MARNIE HAY

Manchester University Press
Manchester and New York

distributed exclusively in the USA by Palgrave Macmillan

Copyright © Marnie Hay 2009

The right of Marnie Hay to be identified as the author of this work has been asserted by her in accordance with the Copyright, Designs and Patents Act 1988.

Published by Manchester University Press
Oxford Road, Manchester M13 9NR, UK
and Room 400, 175 Fifth Avenue, New York, NY 10010, USA
www.manchesteruniversitypress.co.uk

Distributed exclusively in the USA by
Palgrave Macmillan, 175 Fifth Avenue, New York,
NY 10010, USA

Distributed exclusively in Canada by
UBC Press, University of British Columbia, 2029 West Mall,
Vancouver, BC, Canada V6T 1Z2

British Library Cataloguing-in-Publication Data
A catalogue record for this book is available from the British Library

Library of Congress Cataloging-in-Publication Data applied for

ISBN 978 0 7190 7868 2 *hardback*
ISBN 978 0 7190 7987 0 *paperback*

First published 2009

18 17 16 15 14 13 12 11 10 09   10 9 8 7 6 5 4 3 2 1

The publisher has no responsibility for the persistence or accuracy of URLs for external or any third-party internet websites referred to in this book, and does not guarantee that any content on such websites is, or will remain, accurate or appropriate.

Typeset in Sabon by
Koinonia, Manchester
Printed in Great Britain
by MPG Books Group

For Ivar with love

Contents

List of illustrations	*page*	viii
Acknowledgements		ix
List of abbreviations		xi
Introduction		1
1 Early influences		6
2 Cultural nationalism in Ulster		23
3 Political nationalism in Ulster		42
4 The other Sinn Féin leader		66
5 Rising fortunes in the IRB		93
6 The struggle for control of the Irish Volunteers		122
7 A Quaker and an Irish Volunteer		153
8 The Easter Rising and its aftermath		183
9 Building a new life		216
10 Remembering 1916		236
Conclusion		250
Bibliography		253
Index		264

List of illustrations

1	Bulmer Hobson in 1912	*page* 3
2	Arthur Griffith, founder of the Sinn Féin movement	68
3	Countess Markievicz and Bulmer Hobson with Na Fianna Éireann	77
4	Tom Clarke, a veteran revolutionary and father figure within the IRB	95
5	Sean MacDermott, Hobson's one-time protégé turned rival within the IRB	107
6	Roger Casement	239

All photographs are reproduced with the permission of the Board of the National Library of Ireland.

Acknowledgements

This book began as a PhD thesis undertaken in the School of History and Archives at University College Dublin (UCD). Thus I would like to begin by thanking my thesis supervisor Professor Michael Laffan for his patience, wisdom, generosity and unfailing good humour.

I also wish to thank Professor Eunan O'Halpin and Dr Margaret O'Callaghan for their valuable feedback on the book manuscript and the funding bodies that made the research for this book possible: the Irish Research Council for the Humanities and Social Sciences, UCD and the Ireland Fund of Canada.

I am grateful to the directors, trustees and boards of the following libraries/archives for granting permission to cite manuscript material from their collections: National Library of Ireland; National Archives of Ireland; University College Dublin Archives; National Archives of the UK; Historical Library of the Religious Society of Friends in Ireland; Public Record Office of Northern Ireland; RTÉ Libraries and Archives; BBC Written Archive (Reading); and Belfast Central Library. Efforts have been made to trace the copyright owners of the various primary sources used, but in cases where this search has been unsuccessful, I offer my sincere apologies.

Over the years many people have provided assistance with my research in ways too numerous to mention. I wish to thank (in alphabetical order): Richard Aldous, Ross and Robina Chapman, Manus and Petra Coffey, Marie Coleman, Sean Connolly, Clara Cullen, Enda Delaney, Charlie Doherty, Tom Feeney, Diarmaid Ferriter, Garrett Finegan, John Gageby, Tom Garvin, Luke Gibbons, Richard S. Harrison, Roisín Higgins, Christine M. Hobson, Carole Holohan, Sandra Hynes, Michael Kennedy, Gerry Long, Christina Lowry, Tom and Joe MacDonagh, Dónal McAnallen, Joe McCullough, Bríd McGrath, Eoin Magennis, Peter Martin, Angus Mitchell, Catherine Morris, William Murphy, Cormac O'Callaghan, Margaret Ó hÓgartaigh, Tim O'Neill, James Quinn, Joe Rafferty, Susannah Riordan, Paul Rouse, Paddy Ryan, Roger Sawyer, Neville Scarlett, Mark Tierney, Valerie Wallace and Paul Ward. I am grateful to Des Gunning for generously sharing his Hobson archive with me. I also wish to thank Stephen McGrath, Ann Jones and Crystal Joseph in London and Anthony Malcomson and Bruce Campbell in Belfast for their warm hospitality during research trips.

The Hay family in Canada – my parents Harriet and Bill, my brother Shaun and my aunt Irene – deserve special thanks for their bemused interest in this project over the years.

Acknowledgements

Most of all I would like to thank my husband Ivar McGrath for his support, insight and general affability, especially when faced with my all-too-frequent musings about Bulmer Hobson and a cottage scattered with my books, papers and file folders.

List of abbreviations

ACS	*An Claidheamh Soluis*
AOH	Ancient Order of Hibernians
BBC	British Broadcasting Corporation
BH	Bulmer Hobson Papers
BMH	Bureau of Military History
CO	Colonial Office
CSB	Crime Special Branch
DCWTCC	Dublin Central Wolfe Tone Clubs Committee
DMcC	Denis McCullough Papers
DORA	Defence of the Realm Act
EMacN	Eoin MacNeill Papers
FHLD	Friends Historical Library (Dublin)
GAA	Gaelic Athletic Association
GA	*Gaelic American*
GPO	General Post Office
Hobson, *IYT*	Bulmer Hobson, *Ireland yesterday and tomorrow* (Tralee, 1968).
IF	*Irish Freedom*
IHS	*Irish Historical Studies*
II	*Irish Independent*
IJA	Irish Jesuit Archives
IN	*Irish Nation*
INP	*Irish Nation and the Peasant*
IP	*Irish Press*
IRB	Irish Republican Brotherhood
IRPEAL	*Irish Review of Politics, Economics, Art and Literature*
IT	*Irish Times*
IV	*Irish Volunteer*
JMcG	Joseph McGarrity Papers
n.d.	no date
NAI	National Archives of Ireland
NAL	National Archives of the UK (London)
NLI	National Library of Ireland
P	*Peasant*
PMcC	Patrick McCartan Papers

List of abbreviations

PRONI	Public Record Office of Northern Ireland
QUB	Queen's University of Belfast
R	*Republic*
RC	Roger Casement Papers
RIC	Royal Irish Constabulary
RTÉ	Radio Teilifís Éireann
ShSk	Sheehy Skeffington Papers
SP	*Sunday Press*
SS	Secret Societies
TCD	Trinity College Dublin
TD	Teachta Dála (deputy / member of the Irish parliament)
U	*Uladh*
UCD	University College Dublin
UCDA	University College Dublin Archives
UI	*United Irishman*
UIL	United Irish League
ULT	Ulster Literary Theatre
WS	witness statement

Introduction

Bulmer Hobson (1883–1969) was worsted in the political game of the Irish nationalist movement of the early twentieth century. He is one of the losers of Irish history.[1] Prior to the 1916 Easter Rising, Hobson was one of the key leaders of this movement. However, his opposition to an insurrection which had no hope of military success, combined with his evasion of arrest after the event, condemned him to the sidelines of the nationalist movement and scuttled a potentially promising political career in an independent Ireland. This is, perhaps, one of the reasons why a published study of his contributions to Irish nationalism has not appeared until now.[2] The history of the winners is usually written before the history of the losers.

The research for this book is based on a variety of primary sources. They include: Hobson's 1968 memoir *Ireland yesterday and tomorrow*; his contemporary journalism; his papers in the National Library of Ireland; the papers and memoirs of his nationalist associates; Bureau of Military History witness statements; police intelligence reports; contemporary newspapers and magazines; print and broadcast media interviews with Hobson and surviving nationalists; and interviews with individuals who knew Hobson and his associates.[3]

Born in Belfast to a Quaker family descended from Cromwellian planters, he was that rare combination of an ardent nationalist and an Ulster Protestant. His father supported Liberal Prime Minister William Gladstone's Home Rule bills of 1886 and 1893, while his mother was a suffragist. While he was in his teens, his neighbours, the poets Alice Milligan and Ethna Carbery, helped to instil in him an enthusiasm for Irish culture and a commitment to the non-sectarian and separatist aims of Theobald Wolfe Tone (1763–98) and the United Irishmen. Hobson left school with an aim 'to endeavour to bring the English occupation of Ireland to a timely end'.[4] From the ages of seventeen to thirty-three, he single-mindedly pursued this objective.

In the years 1900 to 1916 Hobson devoted his time to establishing and working for organisations engaged in furthering the cause of Irish nationalism. He played leading roles in the Gaelic League and the Gaelic Athletic Association (GAA) at a local level in Belfast, and, at a national level, in the Irish Republican Brotherhood (IRB), Sinn Féin, Na Fianna Éireann and the Irish Volunteers. He drummed up support (albeit limited) for nationalism in Ulster through his involvement in the Gaelic League and GAA, and through his establishment of Na Fianna Éireann in 1902, the Ulster Literary Theatre in 1904, and the first Dungannon Club and its newspaper, the *Republic*, in 1905 and 1906 respectively.

Hobson's focus later shifted from Ulster to the national stage. The Dungannon clubs amalgamated with Cumann na nGaedheal and the National Council to form Sinn Féin in 1907. Hobson was such a talented Sinn Féin propagandist that he, rather than the movement's founder Arthur Griffith, was invited to introduce the Sinn Féin policy to the United States in the same year. In 1909, under the patronage of Countess Constance Markievicz, Na Fianna Éireann was reincarnated as a national organisation to train boys (and some girls) for participation in a future war of liberation. Hobson helped to revitalise the IRB and rose through the organisation's ranks to become editor of its republican paper, *Irish Freedom*, and a member of its governing body, the Supreme Council. He joined Eoin MacNeill in taking the lead to establish the Irish Volunteers in November 1913. His currency within the IRB diminished, however, after he helped to ensure that the nominees of Irish Parliamentary Party leader John Redmond were co-opted onto the Provisional Committee of the Volunteers in June 1914 in order to avert an early split in the organisation.

Hobson deviated from the pacifism of his Quaker roots by displaying an ambivalent attitude toward the use of violence in order to gain political ends. In 1901 he began to link Wolfe Tone's goal of an independent Ireland to a policy that James Fintan Lalor had suggested during the Great Famine. This policy of 'moral insurrection' advocated the defensive, rather than aggressive, use of physical force, employing tactics that would be later labelled guerrilla warfare. It attracted Hobson, a voracious reader of Irish history, because it represented neither the 'abject surrender' of constitutional agitation nor the futility of past attempts at armed revolt.[5] Hobson's loyalty to this policy would later alienate him from influential members of the Irish nationalist movement. He was a man who was not afraid to stand by his convictions even when they offended other members of the nationalist movement or damaged his employment prospects. His open disapproval of the 1916 rising is a prime example.

Studies abound of leading nationalist figures of the time, such as Patrick Pearse, Roger Casement, Tom Clarke, Arthur Griffith, Eoin

Introduction

1 Bulmer Hobson in 1912

MacNeill, Countess Markievicz and Sean MacDermott.[6] Yet, to date, Hobson has not been the subject of a similar study. The need for such a work is underlined by Charles Townshend's 2005 book *Easter 1916: the Irish Rebellion*, which emphasises the importance of Hobson's role in the period leading up to the rising.[7]

It can be argued that this gap in the historiography arose because Hobson does not fit comfortably into the collective memory of the major events of the period. The Easter Rising became an essential element of an Irish myth. In making a heroic blood sacrifice, the leaders of the insurrection had redeemed the Irish people. As Michael Laffan has argued, this myth 'served to justify the state, the means by which independence had been achieved, and those who wielded power'.[8] Until F.X. Martin began the re-assessment of the Easter Rising in the 1960s, anything or anyone who did not fit neatly into this myth was in danger of being misrepresented or forgotten. Hobson is a good example. While some of his former colleagues within the nationalist movement branded him a traitor and a coward because of his misunderstood opposition to the rising, the general public forgot about his existence.

Hobson's career, both pre- and post-1916, provokes reflections on both Irish identity and the conscious forgetting of individuals who do not fit the dominant historical paradigm. The Easter Rising and the people associated with it became an important part of Irish identity. The significant contributions to the Irish nationalist movement of a Protestant Ulsterman who rejected this event have been, at most, forgotten or, at least, minimised in the collective memory of the early twentieth century.

During the 1966 commemoration of the Easter Rising Hobson questioned the hero status conferred on its leaders. In the same way, a study of his nationalist career challenges the construction of the Irish past that the so-called 'winners' of Irish history championed. Thus, this book seeks to offer a wider view of Irish identity and historical memory. It is as much about retrieving what has been forgotten, on purpose or otherwise, as it is about documenting what has been remembered. Ultimately, however, it aims to answer three key questions: firstly, why and how did Hobson become a leader of the Irish nationalist movement prior to 1916; secondly, why and how did he 'disappear' from the political scene after 1916; and finally, what did he do with the rest of his life? In so doing, this book will help to provide a better understanding of the whole spectrum of Irish nationalism in the early twentieth century.

Notes

1 Like his political contemporaries John Redmond, Edward Carson and James Connolly and one of his influences, James Fintan Lalor, Hobson could have merited an essay in Ciaran Brady's edited volume *Worsted in the game: losers in Irish history* (Dublin, 1989).
2 For an unpublished study, see Marnie Hay, 'Bulmer Hobson: the rise and fall of an Irish nationalist, 1900–16' (PhD thesis, UCD, 2004). This thesis built

upon F.X. Martin's work in reassessing the Easter Rising and the period leading up to that event, expanding upon his article 'McCullough, Hobson and republican Ulster', in F.X. Martin (ed.), *Leaders and men of the Easter Rising: Dublin 1916* (London, 1967), pp. 95–108. In addition, a brief article published in *History Ireland* makes a compelling case for a biography of Hobson. See Des Gunning, 'Bulmer Hobson, "the most dangerous man in Ireland"', *History Ireland*, no. 10 (Spring 2002), pp. 5–6.
3 I contacted Hobson's children Declan Hobson and Camilla Mitchell in 2002, but they declined to be interviewed.
4 Hobson *IYT*, p. 2.
5 Ibid., p. 3.
6 Some examples include: Denis Gwynn, *The life and death of Roger Casement* (London, 1930); Louis Le Roux, *Tom Clarke and the Irish freedom movement* (Dublin, 1936); Ruth Dudley Edwards, *Patrick Pearse: the triumph of failure* (London, 1977); Michael Tierney, *Eoin MacNeill: scholar and man of action, 1867–1945* (Oxford, 1980); Anne Haverty, *Constance Markievicz: an independent life* (London, 1988); Brian Maye, *Arthur Griffith* (Dublin, 1997); Gerard MacAtasney, *Seán MacDiarmada: the mind of the revolution* (Manorhamilton, 2004).
7 See Charles Townshend, *Easter 1916: the Irish rebellion* (London, 2005).
8 Michael Laffan, 'Insular attitudes: the revisionists and their critics', in Máirín Ní Dhonnchadha and Theo Dorgan (eds), *Revising the rising* (Derry, 1991), p. 108.

1

Early influences

As a young student at the Friends' School in Lisburn, Bulmer Hobson was punished for an offence that he did not commit. Although it was not fair, 'it was school life' and he accepted it. He would later find political life as unfair as school life. Again he would accept it. His teacher Charles Benington subsequently came to him and said, 'Bulmer, I punished you unfairly. I am sorry.' When Hobson recalled this episode shortly before his death in 1969, his 'great white head shook gently and [his] unseeing eyes registered vividly the distant event'. 'Just think,' said Hobson, 'that he should apologise to me, a mere slip of a lad!' He paused. 'You know, you learn things at school … things you never forget.'[1]

People do learn things at school that they never forget. People also learn things at home, in their religious community, and in their own neighbourhood that they never forget. This was certainly true of Hobson. At first glance his espousal of republican nationalism seems surprising in light of his comfortable middle-class Quaker background. But upon closer examination it becomes clear how exposure to key individuals and writings in his early life shaped his nationalist ideology and inspired him to become an unusually active participant in the Irish nationalist movement.

Family

John Bulmer Hobson, who was known by his middle name 'Bulmer', was born on 14 January 1883 in Belfast to a prosperous Quaker family. The Hobsons of Ulster are among the longest established Quaker families in Ireland. Partly of English and Scottish stock, they are descended from Cromwellian planters who received 'a grant of a small parcel of land' in the Moy region of County Tyrone during the Cromwellian settlement of Ireland in the middle of the seventeenth century.[2]

The Religious Society of Friends, also known as the Quakers, was founded in the mid seventeenth century in the north-west of England.

The first regular Quaker meeting in Ireland was set up in Lurgan in 1654 by William Edmondson, a former Cromwellian soldier.[3] Edmondson took the Quaker message on the road and among the first people whom he convinced were Francis and Laurence Hobson,[4] two of three brothers who had recently settled in Ireland. They became members of the first Quaker meeting in Lurgan. Bulmer Hobson was a direct descendant of Laurence Hobson.[5]

Hobson's parents were Benjamin Hobson Jr (1852–1927), a commercial traveller, and Mary Ann Bulmer (1856–1947), an English-born women's rights activist and amateur archaeologist. Benjamin Jr was the youngest son of Benjamin Hobson, a small farmer from outside Lurgan, County Armagh, while Mary was the daughter of John Bulmer, an architect turned engineer.[6] The couple were married in the Friends' Meeting House in Darlington, County Durham on 22 April 1880,[7] and first lived in Monasterevin, County Kildare, where their eldest child, Florence Fulton Hobson (affectionately known as 'Flossie'), was born in 1881. Shortly after her birth the family moved to Belfast, where they initially settled in a house close to what was then Queen's College. Living at 5 Magdala Street, where Bulmer was born, the Hobsons were surrounded by 'indisciplined and unruly' students living in digs.[8] By the time the youngest member of the family, Harold Benjamin Hobson, was born in 1884[9] they had moved to a larger house, with a garden suitable for children, at 6 Hopefield Avenue, which ran between the Antrim and Cave Hill roads in north Belfast.[10]

In these early years mother and children survived many serious illnesses, like scarlet fever. Of their Hopefield Avenue home, Mary Hobson recalled: 'We were on the verge of country lanes, where we went blackberrying and picnicking; and so, despite the illnesses, the children grew and thrived in the clean air of the Antrim hills.'[11] The family appear to have been avid picnickers, often indulging Mary's love of archaeology and history by eating al fresco at local landmarks such as the Giant's Ring and Helen's Tower.[12] Both parents took much pleasure in reading, a trait that they passed along to their eldest son. There were visits to the Free Public Library and an annual trip on Easter Tuesday to the old museum on College Square North to see the Egyptian mummy – 'a fearful delight'.[13] On rainy days the children dressed up Beppo, the family's Irish terrier, and staged pantomimes.[14] Perhaps this was the start of Hobson's interest in theatre – an interest that he shared with his mother, whose theatre attendance once led a wealthy Quaker to reject her as a suitable marriage partner.[15]

Mary took the children on annual trips to England to visit her mother, Ann Bulmer, until they were old enough to make the journey on their own. They would spend two months with their grandmother, often pottering around Darlington market spending their pocket money on gifts.[16] It is perhaps to these extended trips that Hobson referred when he told a republican colleague that he had lived in England and had 'found that England despised all Irishmen'.[17]

The Hobson family attended the Frederick Street Meeting in Belfast. The Friends' community was the centre of their social lives, with many Quaker families living in the Antrim Road area.[18] Mary Hobson once said of the Belfast Friends: 'No group of people could be more affectionate and hospitable whilst knowing one another's foibles and shortcomings as only a family can know its members.'[19] It was amongst this close-knit group of people that Hobson grew up to become an unusually confident young man: confident of his convictions, and confident of his ability to promote these convictions.

The Hobson children were educated at the Friends' School on Prospect Hill in Lisburn, a co-educational boarding school that had about eighty students in the 1890s. The few school records that are extant indicate that fees of £16 per year were paid for Hobson's education from 1894 to 1898. Quaker children, especially those from lower-income families, received a reduction in fees; some families, such as those who were not members of the Society of Friends, paid as much as £32 per year to send a child to the school.[20] Surviving records of fees paid suggest that Hobson attended the school from the ages of eleven to fifteen. In his own memoirs he stated that he left school in 1899 at the age of sixteen.[21]

Under the guidance of its English headmaster, Joseph Radley, the Friends' School 'found its identity as a small, semi-rural community in which children were helped to practise those Quaker virtues likely to make them decent men and women, and to learn enough practical skill and book knowledge to get them jobs when they were old enough'.[22] The curriculum included English, arithmetic, languages (French, Latin and Greek), science, art and music.[23] In Hobson's case additional money was paid to cover the cost of laboratory fees (3s 6d) in 1895 and music lessons (£1 10s) in 1897.[24]

Hobson's opinion of the school was mixed. Looking back on his time there, he recalled:

> In my day there was much reading from the Bible and many Moody and Sankey hymns. There was a free and easy atmosphere but not many lessons were interesting ... English literature was making us learn by heart a number of lines ... sometimes sixty. The teachers were a poor lot. Charles Benington was the only good one. But in Joseph Radley's day the school was like home. He was a bit slack, and we took advantage of him, and he knew we took advantage of him, but we all loved him.[25]

Considering Hobson's voracious appetite for researching topics that interested him, it is not surprising that he was critical of the school's slack academic standards. His positive attitude toward its home-like atmosphere, however, may have contributed to the decision to send his own children to a Quaker boarding school in Waterford.[26]

The Friends' School in Lisburn managed to maintain some Quaker traditions, such as plain dress, while losing others in the face of modernisation. In this period 'some old and distinctive Quaker customs were quietly disappearing'. Teachers were still addressed by their full names and without titles (for instance, Charles Benington, rather than Mr Benington), but it was difficult to get the students to use the old grammatical terms 'thee' and 'thou' when addressing an individual.[27] Both boys and girls wore plain, grey clothing. The boys sported waistcoats, knickerbockers fastened just below the knee over black stockings, and the wide, stiff, white Eton collar.[28] On Thursday and Sunday mornings the students attended the Meeting for Worship at the Railway Street Meeting House in Lisburn. On Sundays the boys had to wear bowler hats to the meeting. Hobson remembered 'playing football with them on the day their owners left school for good'.[29]

Hobson was already a committed nationalist by the time he left the school. Not surprisingly, his political viewpoint and subscription to the nationalist newspaper the *Shan Van Vocht* set him apart from his fellow students at the Friends' School. This viewpoint and the subscription were the result of influences absorbed through exposure to his parents and neighbours in the Antrim Road area.

Hobson grew up in a home where 'we argued everything, we discussed everything with good temper, and no opinion was barred'. Benjamin Hobson was a Gladstonian Home Ruler. His eldest son described him as 'a man who had strong opinions of his own', but was 'completely tolerant'.[30] Florence Hobson recalled that her father was the only member of the Belfast Meeting who supported Home Rule during her childhood, which was 'punctuated' by British Prime Minister William Gladstone's first and second Home Rule bills in 1886 and 1893. In her opinion, her father and brother Bulmer shared 'the same kind of moral courage' that enabled them to hold political views that went against the mainstream of their communities.[31]

Hobson's later devotion to the cultural, political and economic renewal of Ireland could be described as a 'concern', the Quaker term for 'an insistent internal spiritual imperative'.[32] In Florence's view, her brother expressed his spirituality through 'his passionate desire for justice and hatred of all oppression'.[33] Hobson himself asserted that it was from his father that he 'inherited a natural urge to take the weaker side in every quarrel and to resent injustice of every kind'.[34]

Although he did not acknowledge it, Hobson probably inherited the same urge from his mother, who was a prominent women's rights activist in Belfast. The roots of her activism could be found in the traditional Quaker advocacy of gender equality and her resentment that the women of her day were barred from attending university. The latter circumstance was particularly provoking as she grew up a mere sixteen miles from Durham University.[35] Mary Hobson belonged to suffrage societies; campaigned in 1896–97 for the election of Kate Megahy, the first female Poor Law Guardian in Belfast; served on the committee formed to administer the boarding out, or fostering, of children from the Belfast Workhouse in the community; and marched with the Irish contingent in the 1911 suffrage procession from Cleopatra's Needle to the Royal Albert Hall in London.[36] That her daughter Florence became Ireland's first woman architect must have been a particular source of pride for Mary Hobson.

As gender equality was a principle that Hobson would have absorbed through his Quaker upbringing, his mother's gender is not likely to have been a factor in his failure to acknowledge her influence. It is more likely that Mary's English background and negative attitude toward republican nationalism may be the reason why Hobson never acknowledged her as an influence either in interviews or in his memoirs. It is clear, however, that he shared his mother's passion for history and writing – as well as her activism.

Once she had packed her children off to boarding school, Mary was free to indulge her love of archaeology. She even got her eldest son to teach her how to ride a bicycle so she could transport herself to various sites in the north of Ireland.[37] Between 1904 and 1911 she published a number of abstracts and articles in journals.[38] On at least two occasions she attended the conference of the British Association for the Advancement of Science as a delegate from the Belfast Naturalists' Field Club.[39] To help ease her loneliness following her husband's death in 1927, she compiled a family chronicle of the Bulmers that she deposited in various archives in England and Ireland in 1937.[40] Ten years later she privately published an amusing memoir of six generations of her family. Edmond Cotter, one of Hobson's colleagues in the Irish Volunteers, suggested to him that he had inherited his mother's 'fine "hand"': 'You may get qualities from your father but a mother who writes like she does is bound to have left her impress on you.'[41]

Friends and neighbours

As Hobson grew older, he came into increasing contact with people outside his family and religious community. In the 1890s he was greatly influenced by two of his neighbours, the poets Alice Milligan (1866–1953) and Anna Johnston (who wrote under the pseudonym Ethna Carbery; 1866–1902). These women, closer to his mother's age than his own, provided him with nationalist reading material and later encouraged him to join the Gaelic League, which afforded him the opportunity to mix with people who shared his burgeoning views on Irish culture and politics.

The Milligans moved to the Antrim Road in 1893, the same year that Alice met Anna, who lived on a nearby side street.[42] At the same time Mary Hobson and Alice Milligan worked together in the Belfast branch of the Irish Women's Association, of which Milligan became president in late 1895.[43] The organisation's goal was to bring Protestant and Catholic women together.[44] Thus, even before he had been exposed to the objectives of Wolfe Tone, Hobson witnessed a project whose aim was to unite Protestant and Catholic. Many of his future nationalist projects would share the same aim.

Although Milligan and Johnston came from a similar social background, their families' political and religious affiliations were completely different, leading them to Irish nationalism by different paths. Milligan was the daughter of Seaton F. Milligan, a successful Methodist businessman who was also a noted antiquarian and fellow of the Royal Irish Academy. Alice grew up in a staunch unionist atmosphere and was formally 'educated without reference to Irish history or culture'.[45] As Catherine Morris notes, however, this upbringing 'was countered by an alternative political vision she encountered through songs, servants and graffiti'. One of Milligan's first flutters of nationalist sentiment was in response to the song 'The Wearing of the Green'.[46] As a child in County Tyrone, Milligan turned to a hired boy, 'the first native Irishman' with whom she recalled conversing, to decode the words 'Home Rule for Ireland' emblazoned on a stone wall.[47] When asked to explain her conversion to ardent nationalism, Milligan once said: 'Instinctively, since I was a child my heart went out to my own nation. In spite of all I heard, I knew that Ireland was my country and that its people were my people.'[48] In contrast, Johnston was born into the Irish nationalist tradition. She was the daughter of the veteran Fenian Robert Johnston, a timber merchant by trade and a Catholic by religion.

By the time they met, Milligan and Johnston were already published writers. Their poetry was 'enormously popular for a time', despite, in Terence Brown's opinion, its 'generally poor quality'.[49] The two women went on to collaborate on two newspapers. In October 1895 they became editors of the *Northern Patriot*, the organ of the Henry Joy McCracken Literary Society. As editors, they used the paper to promote Ulster's ability 'to contribute to the national cause, in order to encourage Northern nationalists, and to assure Southern nationalists about the "hard" North's ability to contribute to a national revival'.[50] The pair edited the paper for three issues before they left in acrimonious circumstances.[51] They then bounced back in January 1896 with a new, independent monthly paper, the *Shan Van Vocht*, which took a broader approach, linking revivalist initiatives all over Ireland and beyond.[52] The title of the paper was an anglicised spelling of the Irish words meaning the 'poor old woman', a common metaphor for Ireland.

In 1895, the same year that she established the Henry Joy McCracken Literary Society, Milligan began lending her young neighbour Bulmer books by Standish O'Grady, such as *The Coming of Cuchulain*. He was twelve years of age, 'old enough to take a serious interest in books'. These volumes 'opened up for [him] new ranges of hitherto unimagined beauty'.[53] The heroes of a great but neglected literature captured his imagination: 'Balor and Lugh and the Sons of Tuireann, Mananan and the De Danaan gods, Fergus MacRoy, Cuchulain and Ferdia became my constant companions and were to me far more real than the crude town in which I lived.' Hobson later admitted that 'at school I didn't pay much attention to what they tried to teach me' because he was caught up in 'a far more vivid and interesting world' in his imagination.[54] As an Irish boy, he found these tales more relevant than stories of Greek heroes ploughing through the waves of the far-off Aegean Sea. He was familiar with the haunts of his heroes, having seen Oisín's grave and Grania's Cairn,[55] possibly on one of his family's picnics. Richard P. Davis has surmised that 'Standish O'Grady's vivid prose rendering of the sagas may have weaned the young Quaker Bulmer Hobson from his ancestral pacifism'.[56]

Hobson was still at the Friends' School in 1896 when Milligan and Johnston founded the *Shan Van Vocht*, the first advanced nationalist paper of its time. He had to struggle with the headmaster, an Englishman, to release his pocket money so he could subscribe to it. The subscription 'caused quite a flutter in the school and definitely marked [him] as an eccentric', but this did not perturb Hobson. Obviously, from an early age he was content to follow his own path, armed with his father's moral courage. The *Shan Van Vocht* was significant because it put him 'for the first time in touch with the new forces that were beginning to stir in Ireland'.[57]

While Hobson was still at school, the centennial celebration of the 1798 rebellion took place, with Milligan serving as the secretary for the Ulster-based commemoration events and the *Shan Van Vocht* playing a key role in publicising the centenary. Many nationalists, including Milligan and Johnston, saw the 1798 centenary as a chance to fuse the various strands of the nationalist movement and foster 'a spirit of resolute patriotism by Irishmen who have hither stood apart, divided from each other by the supposed impassable lines of political differences' that had hardened since the fall of Irish Parliamentary Party leader Charles Stewart Parnell (1846–91) in 1890–91.[58] The political faction fighters remained steadfast, however, hindering the reunification of the nationalist movement and lessening the potential impact that a carefully co-ordinated commemoration campaign could make on a nationwide basis.[59]

The political wrangling of the commemoration organisers did not stop the centennial celebrations from raising awareness about the 1798 rebellion and the United Irishmen. Milligan communicated a message that hit home: the United Irishmen were the first to recognise that 'the future liberty of Ireland depended on the abolition of creed distinctions and the promotion of union amongst all those whose homes were in the land'.[60] Coverage of the centenary spurred on young people like Hobson and his future republican colleague Patrick McCartan (then a student at St Macartan's Seminary in Monaghan) to delve into history books to study the lives and ideals of the United Irishmen.[61] The personal significance of the United Irishmen's Belfast roots, coupled with the prominent involvement of Protestants, was not lost on Hobson. Here were some fitting role models for a Protestant boy brought up in the shadow of Cave Hill. Wolfe Tone, Thomas Russell, Samuel Neilson and Henry Joy McCracken became his heroes.[62] 'I got quite enthusiastic about them,' Hobson noted. 'I found myself living in a city enriched by their associations. The result was that I decided to spend the succeeding years of my life in trying to complete their task.'[63]

By the time he left school, Hobson was a disciple of Wolfe Tone, in full accord with his much-quoted declaration from August 1796:

> To subvert the tyranny of our execrable government, to break the connection with England, the never failing source of all our political evils, and to assert the independence of my country. These were my objects. To unite the whole people of Ireland. To abolish the memory of all past dissensions and to substitute the common name of Irishman in place of the denominations Protestant, Catholic and Dissenter – these were my means.[64]

Unlike some militant republicans or Ulster Protestants, Hobson equally embraced *both* aspects of this declaration: separatism and non-sectarianism.[65] Like other Irish republican nationalists, he espoused the combination of separatism and republicanism (as opposed to other varieties of republicanism promoted in the early modern period) that Wolfe Tone adopted over time.[66] To Hobson, the autobiographical writings of Wolfe Tone ranked as one of the 'two best books produced under the influence of the national idea in modern Ireland'; John Mitchel's *Jail Journal* was the other.[67] While the writings of O'Grady had provided Hobson with 'a very definite bias in a pro-Irish direction', the ideology and models of Wolfe Tone and the United Irishmen mapped out the course of his future.[68]

He left school with a self-confessed 'obsession': 'I was determined to devote what little talent I had to trying to upset the English government in Ireland and that was a very odd opinion to hold in those days.'[69] As it was time to start earning a living, he had to confine the pursuit of this unusual obsession to evenings and weekends. By day he was employed in the printers' trade, working for various Belfast firms. He soon found it difficult to maintain a post because, as he quickly discovered, 'if you didn't beat the Orange drum you didn't stay in the job very long'.[70]

His parents and siblings were more accepting of his obsession than were his employers. Hobson reported that his family found his views 'rather odd' and completely disapproved of them, but, for the most part, remained 'peculiarly tolerant'.[71] In 1905 McCartan revealed to Joseph McGarrity, a fellow native of Carrickmore, County Tyrone and a leader of the Irish-American organisation Clan na Gael, that Hobson's 'father goes a little way but his mother is an Englishwoman and shows it. He dare not discuss his plans with me in her presence. At least to avoid trouble he did not.'[72] Outlining a practical scheme to break the connection between Ireland and Britain, in front of an Englishwoman living in Ireland, was perhaps too much, even for a 'peculiarly tolerant' family. After Hobson's death his sister Florence expressed pride in his achievements: 'My judgement is that there has been no Northern Protestant who has done so much for the nationalist cause since John Mitchel and no man of his stature.'[73] Hobson's family may not have agreed with his political opinions, but they did not interfere with his determination 'to seek out people who held similar views and to endeavour to bring the English occupation of Ireland to a timely end'.[74]

At Anna Johnston's suggestion, Hobson joined the Gaelic League in 1901, which helped him to connect with like-minded people. Through the Gaelic League he met Denis McCullough (1883–1968), a Catholic from the Falls Road area who was the same age as he was. Educated by the Christian Brothers, McCullough was apprenticed to the musical instrument repair trade. Unlike Hobson, McCullough was born into the national movement. His father and grandfather were members of the

IRB.[75] Although his mother was raised in an area where there were no Catholics or nationalists for miles, she became the strongest republican nationalist and separatist that McCullough ever knew. She raised her four sons to believe that they had only two duties: one was to God and the other was to Ireland.[76] Hobson and McCullough formed a nationalist partnership similar to the one forged by Milligan and Johnston.

Another key individual whom Hobson met in this period was antiquarian solicitor Francis Joseph Bigger (1863–1926). It is unclear whether McCullough introduced them or they had met previously through the north Belfast Protestant social scene. McCullough described Bigger as 'a rubicund, genial, pleasant man', whose family enjoyed a positive reputation among both commercial and political circles.[77] Bigger had a passion for Irish art and archaeology and, as editor of the *Ulster Journal of Archaeology*, he published an article by Hobson's mother and sister in 1907. Bigger made friends with everyone who was important in the cultural and political movements of the time and had an extensive library with a noted Irish collection. He owned a large house just off the Antrim Road on the slopes of Cave Hill, overlooking Belfast Lough. He called it 'Ardrigh', which was Irish for 'high king', naming it after his mother Ardrie. There, he held gatherings attended by a range of people including diplomat, humanitarian and future martyr to the Irish cause Roger Casement (1864–1916), historian Alice Stopford Green (1847–1929) and numerous Irish and English politicians. McCullough was Bigger's favourite of all the young nationalists, and together they visited graveyards, seeking the graves of patriots and tracing genealogies.[78] Hobson may not have been Bigger's favourite, but he too became a member of the Ardrigh set, which provided him with the opportunity to mix with a variety of people who shared his enthusiasm for Irish nationalism.

James Fintan Lalor and 'moral insurrection'

By the age of eighteen Hobson was a committed separatist, starting to make his way in Belfast's nationalist circles. The question of how to break the link with England and to assert Ireland's independence was constantly on his mind. (Hobson always referred to England and English rule rather than Britain and British rule, perhaps suggesting sympathy for Scottish and Welsh nationalism.) It was a challenging question at a time when Britain enjoyed a comfortable power base and, aside from the odd protest, Irish people had abandoned the fight for complete independence. According to Hobson, the majority of Irish people, like his own father, 'were content to ask for a subordinate parliament with very limited powers, leaving all our most vital interests in foreign hands'.[79] Hobson, a voracious reader of Irish history, sought a middle road that represented neither the 'abject surrender' of constitutional agitation nor the 'futile insurrection' of past attempts at armed revolt.[80] He found that road in the writings of James Fintan Lalor (1807–49).

Lalor, a writer connected with the Young Ireland movement of the mid nineteenth century, had written a series of letters to *The Nation* in 1847 advocating a rent strike by small farmers. His policy of passive resistance was probably inspired by his father Patrick, even though their relationship was troubled. Patrick Lalor was a firm Daniel O'Connell supporter who rose to prominence during the Tithe War of 1830–33. At a meeting in Maryborough (Port Laoise) Patrick Lalor shocked the audience by declaring 'that he would never again pay tithes; that he would violate no law; that the tithe men might take his property, and offer it for sale; but his countrymen, he was proud to say, respected him, and he thought that none of them would buy or bid for it if exposed for sale'.[81] When twenty-five of his sheep were seized in payment of tithes, he branded them with the word TITHE so that they would not be sold in any Irish or English market.[82] Patrick did not see tithes as a morally binding debt, noting that 'there was every facility to avoid the payment of tithes, if the people were only unanimous, and acted peaceably, as the society called Quakers did'.[83] Boycott, or as Patrick put it, 'the non-dealing system', was the aim and result of this Quaker-influenced policy of passive resistance.[84] His son James advocated a similar system.

Hobson read Lalor in 1901 and took from his writings a two-pronged approach to defeating British rule. The first prong was a policy of passive resistance that was similar to Arthur Griffith's Sinn Féin policy.[85] The attraction of this policy to Hobson may have derived from his own Quaker upbringing. The second prong was to employ tactics that would later be labelled guerrilla warfare. Hobson's acceptance of such tactics indicates his divergence from the Quaker tradition of pacifism.

In an 1848 letter to the *Irish Felon* Lalor outlined his strategy for passive resistance followed by, if necessary, physical force. It involved the following steps: 1) a refusal to obey usurped authority; 2) resistance to attempts to exercise usurped authority and endeavours to enforce obedience; 3) taking quiet and peaceable possession of all the rights and powers of government, and then proceeding to exercise them; and 4) maintaining and defending the exercise of such rights and powers, in the event of an attack.[86] It was a strategy that Hobson was keen to follow, and he frequently mentioned it in the lectures and speeches that he delivered in the ensuing years.[87]

Lalor called his strategy 'moral insurrection'. He asserted that 'the right of moral insurrection is worthless without a military force to sustain it, and unless you are prepared and willing to use that force'.[88] The difference between moral and military insurrection lay in the defensive, rather than aggressive, use of physical force.[89]

In describing the use of defensive physical force, Lalor listed tactics that would later be labelled guerrilla warfare.[90] He advised:

> The force of England is *entrenched* and *fortified*. You must draw it out of position; break up its mass; break its trained line of march and manoeuvre – its equal step and serried array. You cannot organise, or train, or discipline your own force to any point of efficiency. You must therefore disorganise, and untrain, and undiscipline that of the enemy; and not alone must you *unsoldier* – you must *unofficer* it also; nullify its tactique and strategy, as well as its discipline; decompose the science and system of war, and resolve them into their first elements. You must make the hostile army a mob, as your own will be; force it to act on the *offensive*, and oblige it to undertake operations for which it was never constructed.[91]

These tactics appealed to the pragmatist in Hobson: 'With regard to physical force, I early realised the complete impracticality of insurrections on the model of 1798, but I found in Lalor a method ... which appeared to me to be the one form which physical force could take in a situation such as ours with the remotest chance of success.'[92] From 1901 onwards, Hobson aimed 'to win independence by a condition of passive resistance and by guerrilla warfare if the opportunity arose' because he was convinced that this was the only way that 'an armed insurrection in Ireland had any hope of military success against the highly trained and well organised armies of a powerful state' like Britain.[93]

Conclusion

Hobson's espousal of republican nationalism may seem surprising in light of his comfortable, middle-class Ulster Quaker background. Yet his home, meeting house, school and neighbourhood all exposed him to influences that helped to shape his nationalist ideology and inspired his involvement in the advanced nationalist movement. From his father he learned to fight injustice and to have the moral courage to uphold convictions even when they clashed with mainstream opinion. In contrast to his father's advocacy of Home Rule for Ireland, which called for the creation of a devolved Irish parliament to deal with domestic issues and the maintenance of Ireland's political connection with Britain, Hobson instead promoted separatism. His mother provided him with an example of activism. His neighbours Milligan and Johnston shared their enthusiasm for Irish cultural and political nationalism by lending him O'Grady's books and encouraging him to join the Gaelic League, where he could mix with like-minded individuals such as McCullough and Bigger. The *Shan Van Vocht* and its coverage of the centenary of the 1798 rebellion inspired Hobson to learn more about Wolfe Tone and the United Irishmen, whose ideology provided him with a political objective. Hobson's research into Irish history led him to Lalor's policy of moral insurrection, which offered him the means to pursue his objective. His upbringing and education within the Society of Friends taught him to 'live his own truth',[94] as he pursued his 'concern' for the cultural, political and economic renewal of Ireland.[95] The roots of his future career as a republican nationalist and the controversial choices that he made during that career can be found at 6 Hopefield Avenue, in the neighbourhood of the Antrim and Cave Hill roads, at the Frederick Street Meeting House and on Lisburn's Prospect Hill.

Notes

1 Neville H. Newhouse, *A history of the Friends' School, Lisburn* (Lisburn, 1974), p. 143.
2 Hobson, *IYT*, p. 1.
3 Sandra King, *History of the Religious Society of Friends, Frederick Street, Belfast* (Belfast, 1999), p. 1.
4 Maurice J. Wigham, *The Irish Quakers* (Dublin, 1992), pp. 18–19.
5 Mary Ann Bulmer Hobson, *Memoirs of six generations* (Belfast, 1947), p. 47.
6 Ibid., p. 28.
7 To maintain cohesiveness within the Irish Quaker community, Friends favoured endogenous marriages, either between two Irish Quakers or between an Irish Quaker and an English Quaker, as in the case of Hobson's parents (Sandra Hynes, '"Walk according to the gospel order": theology and discipline in the Quaker meeting system, 1650–1700' (PhD thesis, TCD, 2002), p. 72).
8 Mary Hobson, *Memoirs*, p. 46.
9 Birth register of the Lisburn Monthly Meeting (PRONI, MIC/16, Reel 22).
10 Mary Hobson, *Memoirs*, p. 51.
11 Ibid., pp. 51–2.
12 Ibid., p. 66.
13 Ibid., pp. 52–3.
14 Ibid., p. 52.
15 Ibid., p. 26. In the past Quakers had objected to 'fiction and drama as being untrue' and to 'musical and theatrical performances as leading to depravity and the neglect of pure religion' (Wigham, *Irish Quakers*, p. 107).
16 Mary Hobson, *Memoirs*, pp. 53–4.

Early influences

17 Patrick McCartan to Joseph McGarrity, 23 Dec. 1905 (NLI, JMcG, 17,457 (2)).
18 Mary Hobson, *Memoirs*, p. 49.
19 Ibid., p. 59.
20 Ross Chapman to Marnie Hay, 6 May 2003 (response to a query made to the archives committee of the Religious Society of Friends Ulster Quarterly Meeting; letter in possession of author). All reference to money is in pre-decimal £ s d.
21 Hobson, *IYT*, p. 2.
22 Newhouse, *Friends' School*, p. 63.
23 Ibid., pp. 67–8.
24 Chapman to Hay, 6 May 2003.
25 Newhouse, *Friends' School*, p. 81.
26 Conversation with Robina Chapman of Newry, Co. Down, a former classmate of Camilla Hobson (23 Apr. 2003); Declan Hobson to William Glynn, 19 Aug. 1969 (FHLD, Box 3A, No. 85).
27 Newhouse, *Friends' School*, p. 75. Traditionally, Quakers had used the terms 'thee' or 'thou' to address individuals and 'you' or 'ye' to address more than one person as a way of asserting their commitment to equality by not treating people with false respect. 'Thee' and 'thou' were terms generally used to address someone who was supposedly inferior. Being addressed as 'thee' and 'thou' often caused non-Quakers to feel outraged (Richard S. Harrison, *A biographical dictionary of Irish Quakers* (Dublin, 1997), p. 18).
28 Newhouse, *Friends' School*, p. 85.
29 Ibid., p. 83.
30 TV interview with Bulmer Hobson, by John O'Donoghue, and featured in 'Thursday Topics', broadcast on Telefís Éireann, 5 Dec. 1963 (RTÉ Libraries and Archives).
31 Florence Patterson (née Hobson) to William Glynn, 21 May 1972 (FHLD, Box 3A, No. 85).
32 Harrison, *Dictionary*, p. 17.
33 Patterson to Glynn, 10 Aug. 1969 (FHLD, Box 3A, No. 85).
34 Bulmer Hobson, draft memoirs (NLI, BH, MS 18,283 (1)).
35 Mary Hobson, *Memoirs*, pp. 68–9.
36 Diane Urquhart, *Women in Ulster politics 1890–1940* (Dublin, 2000), p. 137; Mary Hobson, *Memoirs*, pp. 69–70. It should be noted that there were two women named Mary Hobson active in Belfast in the late nineteenth century. In addition to Mrs Mary Hobson (Bulmer Hobson's mother), there was the 'formidable' Miss Mary Hobson, daughter of the rector of Connor, who established the Belfast Association for the Employment of the Blind in 1871. See Maria Luddy, 'Isabella M.S. Tod', in Mary Cullen and Maria Luddy (eds.), *Women, power and consciousness in 19th century Ireland* (Dublin, 1995), p. 200; Alison Jordan, *Who cared? Charity in Victorian and Edwardian Belfast* (Belfast, 1992), p. 97.
37 Mary Hobson, *Memoirs*, p. 64.
38 Mary Hobson published her work under numerous, inconsistent versions of

her name. Examples include: Mrs Benjamin Hobson, 'Some souterrains in Antrim and Down' (1904), pp. 213–4, 'Denholes and souterrains' (1906) pp. 425–7, 'Great burial mounds of Loughcrew' (1908), pp. 48–51, all of which were published in the *Belfast Naturalists' Field Club Proceedings*; Mary and Florence Hobson, 'Some rude stone monuments in Antrim and Down', *Ulster Journal of Archaeology* (May 1907), pp. 84–9; Mary Hobson, 'The great burial mounds at Loughcrew, Co. Meath', *County Louth Archaeological Society Journal* (Oct. 1910), pp. 247–53.

39 Mary Hobson, *Memoirs*, pp. 64–5; Mrs Mary Hobson, 'Sanctuaries for our native flora and fauna', *The Irish Naturalist*, Nov. 1908, p. 219 (PRONI, D/1831/14); Mrs Hobson, 'Report of delegate to the British Association', in *Belfast Naturalists' Field Club, Report and Proceedings, 1908–09*, pp. 181–5 (PRONI, D/1831/16).
40 Mary Ann Bulmer Hobson, 'Bulmer family chronicle from before 1050 to 1936' (NLI, MS 5220).
41 Edmond Cotter to Bulmer Hobson, 16 July 1917 (NLI, BH, MS 13,161 (3)).
42 Catherine Morris, 'Becoming Irish?': Alice Milligan and the Revival', *Irish University Review*, xxxiii (Spring/Summer 2003), p. 95; Robbie Meredith, 'The Shan Van Vocht: Notes from the North', in Alan A. Gillis and Aaron Kelly (eds), *Critical Ireland: new essays in literature and culture* (Dublin, 2001), p. 174. The Milligans lived at Greenwood on the Antrim Road while the Johnstons lived at Lisnaveane (or Lios na bhFionn) on Donegall Park (*Belfast and Ulster Directory*, 1894, 1896).
43 Sheila Turner Johnston, *Alice: a life of Alice Milligan* (Omagh, 1994), p. 81.
44 Mary Hobson, *Memoirs*, p. 69.
45 Morris, 'Becoming Irish?', pp. 82–3.
46 Ibid., p. 83.
47 Ibid., pp. 83–4.
48 *Irish Weekly and Ulster Examiner*, 7 Sept. 1940, qtd. in Morris, 'Becoming Irish?', p. 83.
49 Terence Brown, *Northern voices: poets from Ulster* (Dublin, 1975), p. 59.
50 Meredith, 'Notes from the North', p. 175.
51 Catherine Morris states that they resigned because the paper's sponsors opposed Johnston's editorship after they found out about her father's membership in the IRB, while Robbie Meredith suggests that they were asked to leave because of their support for Maud Gonne's amnesty campaign for Irish prisoners in England (Morris, 'Becoming Irish?', p. 95; Meredith, 'Notes from the North', p. 175).
52 Morris, 'Becoming Irish?', p. 80.
53 Hobson, *IYT*, p. 1; Ó Lúing, 'Talking to Bulmer Hobson', *IT*, 6 May 1961, p. 10.
54 Hobson, TV interview, 5 Dec. 1963 (RTÉ Libraries and Archives).
55 Hobson, *IYT*, p. 1.
56 Richard P. Davis, *Arthur Griffith and non-violent Sinn Féin* (Dublin, 1974), p. 95.

57 Hobson, *IYT*, p. 2.
58 *Shan Van Vocht*, 8 Jan. 1897, qtd. in Urquhart, *Women*, p. 89.
59 Urquhart, *Women*, p. 91. For an examination of the political wrangling within the centennial movement, see Timothy J. O'Keefe, 'The 1898 efforts to celebrate the United Irishmen: the '98 centennial', *Éire-Ireland*, no. 23 (Summer 1988), pp. 51–73.
60 *Irish Weekly Independent*, 21 Dec. 1895, qtd. in Morris, 'Becoming Irish?', p. 91.
61 Patrick McCartan, witness statement, 15 Dec. 1952 (NAI, BMH, WS 766).
62 Hobson, TV interview, 5 Dec. 1963 (RTÉ Libraries and Archives).
63 Ó Lúing, 'Talking to Bulmer Hobson', *IT*, 6 May 1961, p. 10.
64 Wolfe Tone, qtd. in Hobson, *IYT*, p. 2.
65 For discussions of how various groups within Ireland have commandeered Wolfe Tone to support their own viewpoints and Wolfe Tone's own conversion to separatism, see Marianne Elliott, *Wolfe Tone: prophet of Irish independence* (New Haven and London, 1989), pp. 411–19.
66 For a discussion of differences between republicanism and separatism, and Wolfe Tone's conversion to the latter, see Thomas Bartlett, 'The burden of the present: Theobald Wolfe Tone, republican and separatist', in David Dickson, Dáire Keogh and Kevin Whelan (eds), *The United Irishmen: republicanism, radicalism and rebellion* (Dublin, 1993), pp. 1–15.
67 Bulmer Hobson (ed.), *The letters of Wolfe Tone* (Dublin, 1920), p. 1.
68 Hobson, *IYT*, p. 2.
69 Hobson, TV interview, 5 Dec. 1963 (RTÉ Libraries and Archives).
70 Ibid.
71 Ibid.; Ó Lúing, 'Talking to Bulmer Hobson', *IT*, 6 May 1961, p. 10.
72 McCartan to McGarrity, 23 Dec. 1905 (NLI, JMcG, MS 17,457 (2)).
73 Patterson to Glynn, 10 Aug. 1969 (FHLD, Box 3A, No. 85).
74 Hobson, *IYT*, p. 2.
75 Denis McCullough, witness statement, 11 Dec. 1953 (NAI, BMH, WS 914).
76 Denis McCullough, Ulster TV interview transcript, 8 Sept. 1964 (UCDA, DMcC, P 120/34).
77 Ibid.
78 Ibid.
79 Hobson, *IYT*, p. 2.
80 Ibid., pp. 2–3.
81 *Leinster Leader*, 31 Mar. 1883, reprinted from *Redpath's Weekly*; qtd. in David N. Buckley, *James Fintan Lalor: radical* (Cork, 1990), p. 11.
82 *Leinster Leader*, 31 Mar. 1883; qtd. in Buckley, *Lalor*, p. 11.
83 *Second report of the Select Committee of the House of Lords appointed to enquire into the collection and payment of tithes in Ireland*, p. 248; qtd. in Buckley, *Lalor*, p. 11.
84 Buckley, *Lalor*, p. 11.
85 See Chapter 3.
86 James Fintan Lalor, 'To the Irish Confederate and Repeal Clubs', *Irish Felon*,

1 July 1848, reprinted in *The writings of James Fintan Lalor* (Dublin, 1895), p. 83; qtd. in Hobson, *IYT*, p. 41.
87 Bulmer Hobson, 'The Volunteers', *IT*, 19 Nov. 1963 (UCDA, DMcC, P 120/40).
88 Lalor, 'Clubs', p. 84.
89 Ibid., pp. 83–4.
90 Hobson, *IYT*, p. 41.
91 Lalor, 'Clubs', pp. 80–1; Hobson, *IYT*, p. 41.
92 Hobson, 'The Volunteers', *IT*, 19 Nov. 1963 (UCDA, DMcC, P 120/40).
93 Ibid.
94 William Glynn, graveside tribute to Bulmer Hobson, 11 Aug. 1969 (FHLD, MSS B. 3A-87).
95 Harrison, *Dictionary*, p. 17.

2

Cultural nationalism in Ulster

In late 1904 Hobson donned the flowing garb of a tenth-century warrior to play a young Brian Boru in an Ulster Literary Theatre (ULT) production of his play *Brian of Banba*. Described by one ULT colleague as 'a stormy petrel', Hobson was a co-founder of the theatre company, which tried to use drama to promote nationalism in Ulster.[1] On a dim stage draped with cloth and lit with flickering torches,[2] the play opened in the death chamber of Cennedigh Mac-Lorcan, King of Thomond and heir to the kingship of Cashel. His elder son, Mahon, knelt down to support his ailing father. Brian, the headstrong younger son, stood apart, almost seething with anger. Cennedigh bequeathed to Mahon the kingship of Thomond, advising him to make peace with the Vikings so that they would not lay waste to the kingdom. The king asked his younger son what gift he could bestow on him. 'One hundred men to fight the Northmen,' was the impassioned response. The king called Brian foolish and advised him to support his elder brother so that in time he would succeed Mahon in the kingship. But Brian refused to be a tributary king to the Vikings. He took to the hills with his men. At night they swooped down to burn, to slay and to carry off booty from the Vikings. And for every one of his men who was killed, several Vikings were slain. Brian returned home alone in the garb of a beggarman, the only surviving member of his band, in order to admonish the new king, Mahon, for not providing him with aid when he first set out. Fired by the tales of Brian's victories against the Vikings, Mahon and his warriors, with a rousing cheer, agreed to support his next campaign.[3]

Hobson's play reveals much about his early career as a nationalist, which began in the cultural arena. The plays written during the Irish Literary Revival influenced him and he in turn contributed to the Ulster branch of that revival. He emulated the Irish mythological play pioneered by W.B. Yeats and acknowledged the propagandistic potential of theatre first explored by Inghinidhe na hÉireann, the nationalist women's organisation founded by Maud Gonne in 1900. In writing about Brian Boru, he looked back to a time prior to sectarian division in Ireland – an attractive period for a young nationalist of the Protestant persuasion. From his own teenage experience he recognised how tales from Ireland's history could fire a youth to fight with voice, pen, hurley and even sword for the cultural, political and economic freedom of his people. Hobson may have identified with Brian himself. In his native Ulster he and his young nationalist colleagues defied parental advice to espouse views and engage in activities that went against the mainstream of Ulster society at the time. Like Brian, Hobson later advocated the physical force, rather than the conciliatory parliamentary, tradition in the struggle for Ireland's freedom.

During Hobson's teens and early twenties, the reverberations of the wider Irish cultural revival were felt in his native Ulster. With the foundation in 1895 of the Henry Joy McCracken Literary Society in Belfast, Milligan had spearheaded an Ulster literary revival that echoed the Dublin-based movement. The Northern revival was facilitated by a sense of unionist security that was fostered by the fall of Charles Stewart Parnell and the subsequent split in the Irish Parliamentary Party, the failure of the second Home Rule bill in 1893, and the Conservative election victories of 1895 and 1900. After all, the writings of Samuel Ferguson and Standish O'Grady showed that one could be nationalist in literature and unionist in politics. The year 1895 also saw the publication of Belfast-born Methodist James Cousins's book, *Ben Madigan and other poems*, which Terence Brown has suggested 'could have given offence to none in unionist Belfast'.[4] In 1898 Mary Hutton began translating the great Ulster epic *The Táin*, which was later published with illustrations by John Campbell, an Ulster artist of the revival period.[5] The cultural revival in Ulster extended into the first decade of the twentieth century and included the Irish language, sport, dance, music and art, as well as literature.

1900 to 1903

Hobson launched his propagandist career at the precocious age of seventeen, with the foundation of the Ulster Debating Club for boys in 1900. It attracted about forty members, some of whom were students at the local Christian Brothers' school, and held both private and public meetings and lectures in Belfast. Lecturers included Milligan, a Mrs Hobson (probably his mother), the poet Seumas MacManus, and the Rev. Richard Lyttle, a Unitarian minister of Moneyrea, County Down[6] whom Hobson described as 'a true spiritual descendant of those Protestant clergymen who worked and fought with the United Irishmen in

1798'.[7] The Ulster Debating Club was likely inspired by the Ulster Debating Society, to which Hobson's mother may have belonged.[8]

In September 1900 the club started an Irish language class. Two of the elder club members taught the class, using Fr Eugene O'Growney's books, which were the standard Irish language textbooks of the time. In conjunction with the establishment of the language class, members of the local Gaelic League were invited to a meeting of the club where a debate took place on the preservation of the Irish language. After much argument, a vote was taken that resulted in a twenty-six to six division in favour of the language revival. The Northern correspondent in the *United Irishman* commented that this result 'speaks well for the spirit of the society, which we hope will be able to influence other clubs in the same direction'.[9]

Inspired by *tableaux vivants* (living pictures) shown by the Belfast Gaelic League at its Ceilidh Shamhna (November Dance) in 1900, Hobson organised a similar enterprise with his own club.[10] As Johnston revealed to Seamus O'Kelly, secretary of Feis Uladh (Ulster Festival), a provincial cultural festival that was held in the following month,[11] 'it is evident that [Hobson] was anything but unobservant during our rehearsals, for he has drawn up half-a-dozen different series of episodes in Irish History, suitable for *tableaux*, in the cleverest way'.[12] The club exhibited its *tableaux* on 27 December 1900 at the Avenue Minor Hall, with the Gaelic League's P.J. O'Shea providing descriptions of the scenes.[13] Johnston enthused: 'Is [Hobson] not a grand boy to venture upon such an entertainment on his own initiative?' She was also impressed with his efforts to sell tickets to Feis Uladh and advertising in the event's programme to his employer McCaw, Stevenson and Orr, a stationery company.[14] The *United Irishman*'s Northern columnist pronounced the Ulster Debating Club's first public venture a success, noting that the venue was crowded.[15]

It was at Lios na bhFionn, Johnston's home in north Belfast, that Hobson met the local leaders of the Gaelic League, as well as notable nationalists such as Douglas Hyde, Maud Gonne and John O'Leary.[16] The first Belfast branch of the Gaelic League, which attracted both Catholics and Protestants, was established in 1895 as an outgrowth of the Irish language classes started by the Belfast Naturalists' Field Club in 1892.[17] In 1901, on Johnston's advice, Hobson joined the Tír na nÓg (land of youth) branch of the Gaelic League in Belfast, which met in a hall in Albert Street. At that time the members 'were all very young and very enthusiastic'. McCullough already belonged to the branch, and the two soon established a friendship that was to last throughout their long lives.[18] McCullough's eldest son, Domhnall, has described the pair as 'nationalist' friends rather than personal friends.[19]

In addition to teaching the Irish language, the Tír na nÓg branch of the Gaelic League sought to revive traditional Irish dances and games in Belfast. McCullough reported: 'although none of us posed as athletes or disciples of the dance, we then struggled manfully to master the *camán* [hurley] or grasp the mysteries of the *Rince Fada* [long dance] in order to enable us to impart it to others'.[20] Hobson participated in both of these activities.

Between 1901 and 1903 Hobson worked in a Belfast printing house from 8.30 a.m. to 6.30 p.m., leaving the evenings and 'sometimes a good part of the night' to participate in nationalist activities.[21] By January 1902 he was the representative of the Tír na nÓg branch on the district council of the Belfast Gaelic League,[22] which was 'composed of a group of charming men', most of them older than his father.[23] He also joined the organising committee of the Gaelic League's Feis Uladh held in December 1902.[24] He later became secretary of the district council, for which he was fired from his day job.[25] His involvement with the nationalist movement resulted in his dismissal from paid employment on several occasions. It was a pattern that was to dog him throughout his nationalist career.

Supplying teachers to the many Gaelic League branches in the district was a constant challenge, with Hobson spending 'most evenings going from class to class to see if they had teachers for the crowds eager to learn'.[26] People who had made it through Fr O'Growney's 'Third Book' were recruited to teach people working their way through the 'First Book'. One evening, on a visit to a branch that met in the school attached to St Paul's Church on the Falls Road, Hobson found his friend Peter Murphy attempting to preside over a large classroom containing a mob of about ninety small boys. Frustrated, Murphy announced that 'he was not coming back and that the boys would not be allowed in again'. Thinking this unfortunate, Hobson took over the class himself the following week. To restore and maintain order, he ejected any boy who made an unnecessary sound. Hating to be excluded, the ejected boys crowded around the closed door and begged to be re-admitted. The curate of St Paul's was astonished to find a young Belfast Quaker teaching the Lord's Prayer, in Irish, to a crowd of his young parishioners. With a cash injection from his friends, Hobson bought camáns for the boys so that they could channel their energy and high spirits into hurling. Soon a dozen boys' hurling clubs sprang up in the district.[27]

The Tír na nÓg branch of the Gaelic League had already established a team of hurlers in Belfast in July 1901.[28] The *United Irishman* reported that they could 'be seen most evenings at the Falls Park wielding the camán'. Their example spurred on the Red Branch, the John Mitchel and other hurling clubs, all of which had been established during the previous few years, to make an effort to restart the old game.[29] By mid August 1901 there were seven hurling clubs in Belfast.[30] The *Irish News* praised Hobson's performance in an August 1901 hurling match between Tír na nÓg and Red Branch, even though the latter trounced Hobson's team by eight goals to nil.[31] That same month the first meeting of the Belfast Hurling Committee was held, attended by two representatives from each of the seven clubs. Hobson, one of the Tír na nÓg representatives, became secretary of the new organisation.[32] In September 1901 the Belfast Hurling Committee decided to affiliate with the GAA as soon as possible and began calling itself the Belfast County Board of the GAA. It later became the first Antrim County Board of the GAA.[33] (Although there had been hurling clubs in Antrim previously, not enough clubs had existed to form a county committee.[34]) The committee intended to spare no effort to revive hurling in the North: 'All that can be done to start hurling clubs in Ulster, will be done, and it will not be long now till the old game will be a potent factor in making Belfast as Irish as in the past it has been English.'[35]

The contribution of the Tír na nÓg branch of the Gaelic League to the revival of hurling in Belfast was echoed elsewhere in Ireland.[36] After 1900 it became common for Gaelic League branches to establish their own hurling clubs and then affiliate with the local GAA county board if one existed.[37] The revival of hurling in the Belfast area was part of a general expansion of the GAA that took place nationally from 1901 onwards. Marcus de Búrca has linked this expansion of the GAA to a resurgence in political nationalism at the beginning of the twentieth century that was due to the 1798 centenary celebrations, nationalist support for the Boers in South Africa, the publication of Arthur Griffith's newspaper the *United Irishman* in 1899 and the reunification of the Irish Parliamentary Party in 1900.[38] It was a case of cultural and political nationalism reinforcing one another.

The Belfast County Board was hardly established when a controversy arose over new clubs whose membership included policemen. In 1887, shortly after the IRB had gained control of the GAA's executive, the GAA had introduced a rule excluding policemen from the organisation. With its popularity on the wane, the GAA revoked this rule in April 1893,[39] both in an effort to attract more players and as a response to easing pressure from Dublin Castle due to the Parnell Split and the prospect of another Home Rule bill.[40] With the improvement in its fortunes at the beginning of the twentieth century, the GAA nationally passed a rule in January 1903 that excluded police, soldiers and sailors from playing hurling or Gaelic football.[41] Prior to this decision, county boards could decide who could be barred.

After hours of argument over the membership of policemen, the meeting of the Belfast County Board was adjourned until the following evening, when only those who had not already spoken would be heard. At this next meeting Hobson was the only person present who had not yet spoken. He recalled: 'I came out very strongly against allowing members of the police force to have any part in our activities, on the ground that they were not only hurlers but, from the nature of their calling, would be compelled to act as spies and providers of information about the national movement.'[42] Hobson spoke persuasively, and it was unanimously decided that policemen and soldiers should be barred.[43]

On another occasion his powers of persuasion were less successful. Unlike adults who took up hurling, young boys 'had grace and acquired skill very rapidly', and Hobson thought that if Antrim were ever to have hurling teams that could compete with those in other counties they 'should concentrate on training the young boys and making first-class hurlers out of them'.[44] He proposed that the county board of the GAA should hold competitions for the junior clubs. The other board members had no interest in this proposal, so Hobson resigned from his position as secretary in September 1901.[45] On 22 June 1902, at the beginning of the hurling season, he called a mass meeting in the Catholic Boys Hall on the Falls Road, which was attended by nearly three hundred boys.[46]

At this meeting he proposed the formation of Na Fianna Éireann, suggesting that the organisation would help to revive 'this old Irish sport' and teach the boys 'to speak their own native tongue', which would enable them to do 'noble, and exhalted [sic] work for Ireland'.[47] In keeping with the organisation's name, each club took the name of one of the warriors in Fionn Mac Cumhail's old Fianna, such as Conan Maol or Goll Mac Morna,[48] and the playing field's name was changed from Klondyke to Cnoc Aluinn, the legendary home of the Fianna.[49] By July 1902 twelve hurling clubs belonged to Na Fianna Éireann.[50]

The tremendous excitement of the Fianna's inaugural meeting convinced Hobson that the fledgling organisation was something that could be moulded 'into a strong force to help in the liberation of Ireland'.[51] The *United Irishman* saw the organisation as an antidote to the Catholic Boys' Brigades[52] that had turned into recruiting grounds for the British Army: 'Twenty thousand Irish boys enrolled in national brigades North and South to-day would mean twenty thousand thinking and disciplined men to-morrow, and twenty thousand thinking, disciplined men, filled with one purpose – what might they not accomplish in a land like ours!'[53] When the seed of the Belfast Fianna was later replanted in Dublin in 1909, it grew into a national body that fulfilled its early promise. In the mean time, the Belfast Fianna held inter-club hurling competitions and classes on the Irish language and history, and later expanded to include Gaelic football.

Sport was not the only cultural activity absorbing Hobson's time. Theatre was also on the agenda. The *United Irishman* had published his play *Brian of Banba* in its 2 August 1902 edition. Then, at the 17 October 1902 meeting of the executive of the Belfast Fianna, Hobson announced that 'he intended to form a dramatic section from the various clubs' and asked each club's representative to provide him with a list of suitable members from that club. A meeting of boys who qualified for the dramatic section was to be held on 4 November 1902.[54] It is unclear whether these boys participated in Hobson's next cultural project: the first production of the Ulster Branch of the Irish Literary Theatre, the forerunner of the ULT.

Impressed by the work of the Irish National Dramatic Company, which had been founded by Inghinidhe na hÉireann, Hobson and his friend David Parkhill journeyed to Dublin in the autumn of 1902 in order to meet the company's members.[55] With the production talents of the Fay brothers and the help of W.B. Yeats and George Russell (known as Æ), the Dublin-based company was engaged in producing Irish plays in small halls. Máire Quin, one of the company's best actors, invited Hobson and Parkhill to stay with her at Maud Gonne's house in Rathgar, where Æ lived nearby. Quin and Dudley Digges, another leading actor, took the pair to the company's rehearsal hall at 34 Camden Street, where they 'met the whole crowd – Yeats, Æ, Cousins, the Fays, Seumas O'Sullivan, Fred Ryan, O'Neill, Russell and a lot more'.[56] The object of the visit was to gain permission to perform their plays and to solicit help from their actors. Hobson described everyone as 'most cordial and helpful except Yeats – haughty and aloof'.[57]

Yeats refused their request for permission to perform *Cathleen Ni Houlihan*. In addition to his alleged 'antipathy towards all things Ulster',[58] Yeats probably resented the pair's goal of bringing Ulster more fully into the Irish Literary Revival, because the project would be outside his sphere of control.[59] When Quin reported Yeats's refusal to Gonne, the latter remarked: 'Don't mind Willie. He wrote that play for me and gave it to me. It is mine and you can put it on whenever you want to.'[60] Despite Yeats's hostile attitude, the newly formed Ulster Branch of the Irish Literary Theatre staged his *Cathleen Ni Houlihan*, along with *The Racing Lug* by James Cousins, in November 1902 at St Mary's Minor Hall in Belfast, with Digges and Quin playing the lead roles. Annoyed that Gonne had encouraged them to perform his play without his permission, Yeats 'formally withdrew her right to license performances of a play she believed she owned'.[61]

Despite its small size, the hall was far too big for the audience who attended the two-night run of the fledgling company's first performances. Gerald Macnamara (a pseudonym for Harry Morrow) recalled this early production:

> On the morning of the first performance the members were carrying some old second-hand scenery up the stairs to the hall when they were stopped by the caretaker who ordered them to take it away. 'This hall,' said he, 'is used for a Sunday school, and we'll have none of your damned scenery here.' As there was no time to discuss the matter with the manager of the school, the young enthusiasts were obliged to hire curtains to drape the hall in lieu of scenery. The effect of these curtains was so novel at the time that the audience applauded the set as the curtain rose.[62]

Sam Hanna Bell noted that the Protestant National Society, a group founded by Hobson, was the force behind this first production.[63] As this society was not formed until early 1903, it is more likely that Hobson, Parkhill and William McDonald[64] later formed the Protestant National Society to provide a formal structure for their various efforts to propagate the ideology of Wolfe Tone and the United Irishmen. Such efforts probably included performances by the Ulster Branch of the Irish Literary Theatre.

The theatre group was part of 'the same cultural quickening' that fostered the formation of the Ulster Arts Club, which held its first meeting in November 1902.[65] The artist John Campbell, his poet brother Joseph, and painter and cartoonist Edwin Morrow were among its members. They contributed to the ULT and to *Uladh* and the *Republic*, two publications co-founded by Hobson. Edwin was one of eight sons of painter and decorator George Morrow, of Hanover House, Clifton Street, Belfast. Edwin's brothers George, Jack, Norman and Harry also contributed to Hobson's early cultural projects.

In addition to his theatrical activities, Hobson dabbled in poetry. Like his fellow (and better-known) Northern poets Carbery (Johnston), Milligan, MacManus and Joseph Campbell, Hobson published poetry in the *United Irishman*. As with his play about Brian Boru, Hobson mined Irish history for heroes to inspire his readers. 'The Flight of the Earls' called for the return of the 'Warriors of the North' from across the sea,[66] while 'Robert Emmet' asserted that 'Though Emmet fell, the flashing light / he lit lights strong men's souls to-day'.[67] Other poems took a metaphorical look at Ireland's fight for freedom from Britain. 'Dawn' predicted that Éire would rise once again like the sun at dawn,[68] while 'Freedom's sword' revealed that 'Freedom flasheth a keen, bright sword,

/ A keen, bright sword for the hand that dare' and urged readers to 'Take and unsheath its flaming brand / And place once more our native land / Unfettered and free and fair'.[69] The language and imagery of Hobson's poems in the *United Irishmen* are martial and blood-thirsty – not quite what one expects from a young man brought up in the pacifist tradition of the Quakers. Such quotations reveal that poetry was clearly not Hobson's forte.

In addition to his poetic dabbling, Hobson established his second propagandist society in 1903. The Ulster Debating Club's principal value to Hobson had been that it brought him into touch with a number of like-minded people, including William McDonald, who helped him to start the Protestant National Society[70] in February 1903 at a meeting in the Stephen Street rooms of the Pioneer branch of Cumann na nGaedheal, the nationalist umbrella group formed by Griffith in 1900.[71] The society's establishment was sparked by a suggestion made by MacManus in the *United Irishman* that a Young National Protestant Party should be formed to bring Protestants in line with the nationalist thinking of Catholics.[72] Inspired by the spirit of Wolfe Tone and the United Irishmen, the aim of this society 'was to try and convert young Ulster Protestants and to recruit them into a national movement'.[73] By April 1903 the society was up and running, with rooms at 135 Donegall Street, and had adopted unanimously 'the policy of the *United Irishman*, as the best and most national policy yet put before the Irish people'.[74] This referred to Griffith's call in 1902 for a policy of parliamentary abstention.

That same month MacManus visited the society's small room, whose walls were hung with portraits of Protestant patriots ranging from Henry Grattan to Douglas Hyde. The walls were in the process of being painted by some of the members with the coats of arms of the four Irish provinces, the Belfast School of Art having proved a fertile recruiting ground for the club. Other members were the sons of clergymen, and still others came from the commercial sector. On the night that MacManus attended a society meeting, about twenty young men were present. He estimated that about half of these were already members, while four others had come with the intention to join that night. Considering that the society started with about three members, he deemed this weekly increase in members promising.[75]

The society kept abreast of nationalist activities in Dublin. It unanimously passed a resolution in May 1903 to 'help and assist ... in any way possible' the newly formed National Council, which had been established to provide advanced nationalists with a focal point for opposition to King Edward VII's impending visit to Ireland, and continued in existence thereafter as a vehicle to promote Griffith's abstention policy.[76]

Nationalist connections between Belfast and Dublin went beyond supportive words. In August 1903 members of the Protestant National Society and Belfast Cumann na nGaedheal visited Dublin, where they attended a Sunday night *ceilidh* hosted by Inghinidhe na hÉireann.[77]

1904 to 1907

Having met with 'little noticeable success' in their quest to convert Ulster Protestants to nationalism, the Protestant National Society decided to try using theatre for propaganda purposes, which likely led to the next recorded production of the Ulster Branch of the Irish Literary Theatre. In early 1904, probably in the month of March,[78] the fledgling company revived Yeats's *Cathleen Ni Houlihan* and added George Russell's *Deirdre* to the bill, playing to 'sparse audiences' and harvesting 'poor receipts', possibly because the overt 'Irishness' of the plays did not appeal to a Belfast audience.[79] As Macnamara put it, 'The Belfast public were not taken by *Cathleen Ni Houlihan*. Ninety-nine per cent of the population had never heard of the lady – and cared less; in fact someone in the audience said that the show was going "rightly" till *she* came on.'[80] Macnamara's recollection is evidence of the challenges that Hobson and his colleagues faced in Ireland's northern bastion of 'English' culture.

These promoters of 'Irish' theatre were a young, idealistic band of Protestants and Catholics who naively believed that the problem of sectarianism could be conquered by 'reason and enlightened humanism'.[81] Some of their families and employers disagreed with their views, a circumstance that forced some members to participate under pseudonyms to protect their identities. As Dorothy Macardle later noted, 'they had been gaily treading the path to perdition for several years before even their parents knew who [they] were'.[82] Hobson obviously felt no need to use a pseudonym for his theatrical work: his family was well aware of his views and activities.

Russell's decision to allow Hobson and his colleagues to stage *Deirdre* was a further annoyance to Yeats. Russell soon regretted the decision, complaining to Lady Gregory that they were 'some nice boys who wanted to constitute themselves the Belfast branch of the [Irish National Theatre Society, which succeeded the Irish National Dramatic Society in 1903] and who never realised the lofty skyreaching dignity of the Theatre Society until they got an indignant letter from [the Society's Secretary, George] Roberts putting them in their "proper place"'.[83] This letter stated that the Belfast-based company had no right to use one of the society's former names (the Irish Literary Theatre) and demanded royalties for the production of its plays. It was later reported that

Hobson and his colleagues each 'had to stump up to the tune of £2,10s to pay off the debt'.[84] In response, the young company changed its name to the Ulster Literary Theatre and, as Hobson later declared, 'annoyed by Yeats we decided to write our own plays – and we did'.[85]

In keeping with its new mandate, the ULT staged its first plays written by Ulster playwrights, *Brian of Banba* by Hobson and *The Reformers* by David Parkhill (writing under the pseudonym Lewis Purcell), on 30 November, 1, 7 and 8 December 1904 in the Ulster Minor Hall.[86] *Brian of Banba* was divided into two scenes and took about twenty-five minutes to perform. As contemporary critics were quick to point out, it was derivative of Yeats's mythological plays. Christopher Morash has compared it to Milligan's *Last Feast of the Fianna* and James Cousins's *The Sleep of the King*: all three plays featured 'heroes wearing horned helmets [spouting] interminable purple prose'.[87] Hobson's performance in the title role provoked critic W.B. Reynolds to comment in the *Belfast Evening Telegraph* that Hobson's 'written conception' of Brian of Banba 'was certainly better than his acted one'.[88] The aspects of the production that attracted the most praise were Fred Morrow's direction and scenery and Jack Morrow's costumes.

The reviewer from the *Northern Whig* (probably James Winder Good) preferred Purcell's comedy to Hobson's play, noting that 'Mr Hobson has evidently read Mr Yeats assiduously, and has modelled his piece on the works of the new Irish School'. Although he conceded that Hobson 'treated the situation very cleverly', he felt there was 'something lacking' in the play: 'The characterisation was good, but the end, though effective, did not convince.'[89] In a review in the ULT's own magazine, Good noted that Hobson's characters Brian and Mahon were 'abiding types', but he did not think that Hobson had 'realised their possibilities to the full'. Good added that Hobson's work was 'hampered by the fact that it suggests, inevitably, a contrast with the plays of Mr Yeats; and there are few living poets who can bear the comparison unscathed'.[90] Hobson's playwriting needed a little more originality and a little less emulation.

The play garnered a more positive review from the *Irish News* critic, who reported that 'to a great many "Brian of Banba" appealed with far greater force than did "Lewis Purcell's" brilliant little work. Mr Bulmer Hobson has adhered very closely to historical fact in his playlet, and avoided all extraneous details. It is really a picture-play and a very beautiful one at that.'[91] The reviewer praised 'a *caoine* sung by three female voices at the close of the first scene' for being 'full of a sad haunting sweetness which lent the last requisite touch'.[92] Beauty is indeed in the ear of the hearer: the *United Irishman* considered the *caoine* to be the 'gravest' fault of construction in the play because it 'became a definite song, it refused to blend with the drama, and remained a thing apart'.[93]

In November 1904 the ULT launched its own quarterly literary and critical journal entitled *Uladh* (the genitive case of the word Ulster). It was modelled on Yeats's theatre journals *Beltaine* and *Samhain*, but differed from its inspiration in two ways: its wide range of cultural coverage and its Ulster focus.[94] Like the ULT, *Uladh* was designed as a propagandist vehicle to drive Ulster Protestants onto the road to cultural nationalism.

According to Hobson, the magazine's working capital consisted of five pounds subscribed by architect David Parkhill, journalist James Winder Good, artist John Campbell, music critic W.B. Reynolds and Hobson himself. They formed the nucleus of an editorial committee.[95] The magazine's contributors were unpaid, and only a few hundred copies of each issue were printed. *Uladh* published four issues of cultural criticism, poetry, prose and drama over the course of its year-long existence.

A review by Good in the second issue of *Uladh*, which appeared in February 1905, betrays the young company's concern with 'what Mr Yeats would think', and considers the inevitable comparisons of Hobson's play to Yeats's work. Although Good pointed out that Hobson's mythological play paled in comparison to Yeats's work, such as *The King's Threshold*, he ventured that the great man would have approved of the Morrow brothers' contributions to the production: '[Mr Yeats] would have admired their resolute preference for convention in place of a sham naturalism, the severe simplicity of the costumes, and the skill with which they composed their colour scheme.'[96] (The *Irish News* critic also suggested that 'the little piece was presented in a manner that would have gladdened the heart of Mr Yeats'.[97]) Good was keen to assert that the ULT's members had not 'sacrificed art for propaganda, as Mr W.B. Yeats, in "Samhain," hints some Irish writers have done'. He admitted, however, that 'in their plays you will find propaganda – all writers in new movements cannot hope for Mr Yeats's serene detachment from sublunary things – but it is so handled as not to obscure the main object of the pieces as studies of character'.[98] The spectre of Yeats loomed large over the ULT's (and Hobson's) early efforts on stage and page.

Hobson's play *Brian of Banba* was later presented along with Lewis Purcell's *The Enthusiast* at a *feis* (festival) in Toombridge, County Antrim in early August 1905. Recognising the importance of reaching out to audiences in the country and the smaller urban centres, the ULT wanted to see 'what the plays meant to the intelligent country Gaelic Leaguer, and the less intelligent countryman at present untouched by the League propagandism'. In September 1905 *Uladh* reported that although

The Enthusiast garnered a mixed reaction, *Brian of Banba* 'quite carried away the audience in all parts of the hall'.[99] The performances stayed in the memory of one thirteen-year-old member of the audience, future journalist Cathal O'Shannon: 'I was interested enough in *Brian of Banba*, because I knew the story ... but what really did impress me was *The Enthusiast*, because for the first time I saw the kind of people that I knew and lived among in County Antrim and County Derry were there alive and talking as they talked at home.'[100] Forrest Reid agreed with young O'Shannon's assessment of *The Enthusiast*'s superior merits. On a 'damp dark night' in early 1905 Reid had visited a house in May Street where, 'in a brightly-lit and extremely chilly back room upstairs', he watched Hobson and his ULT colleagues rehearse *The Enthusiast*. There, he came to the conclusion that the play was 'a genuine work of art – slight, imperfect, but vital'.[101] Based on their participation in the *feis*, however, the ULT concluded that 'the heroic play ... with actors like Messrs John Campbell and Gordon in the leading parts, is a sure popular success in the country'.[102] The opinions of Reid and O'Shannon, rather than the general reaction of the audience in Toomebridge, were better predictors of the ULT's future, which lay in contemporary plays with a regional accent, like *The Enthusiast*, rather than what Christopher Morash has called the cul-de-sac of the Irish mythological play.[103] As its commercial success grew, the ULT abandoned its derivative, propagandist roots, as exemplified by Hobson's play, in favour of works that promoted a blossoming regional identity.[104]

Hobson's written contributions to *Uladh* came in the form of four poems that are much softer in tone than his work published in the *United Irishman*. Perhaps he did not want to alarm an Ulster audience potentially hostile to his overriding theme of Ireland's struggle for freedom. Two of his poems appeared in the first issue of *Uladh*. One entitled 'Uladh' came directly after the first editorial: 'In the north is the strength of the wind, of the whirlwind; / In the south there are murmuring waters; / The east has a caoine for its song; / In the west is strengthless love.'[105] The poem suggests that Ulster is the wind whose strength is needed to blow the other three provinces of Ireland out of submission. Another entitled 'The Deluge' was inspired by the Irish mythological tale of Manannan Mac Lir.[106] A reviewer in the *United Irishman* noted that it showed 'a great advance in versification'.[107] F.M. Atkinson, the literary critic with the contemporary journal *Dana*, pronounced the poetry in the first issue of *Uladh* 'not very good, but not very bad, it derives from Mr Yeats and "Æ"'.[108] Here again Hobson's literary attempts were compared unfavourably to those of Yeats.

Poetry, for reasons made obvious by the dubious quality of the above quotations, proved (to borrow Christopher Morash's metaphor) a literary cul-de-sac for the young man. Hobson's poetry communicates his preoccupation with Ireland's political situation. It does not explore more personal themes, which one might expect from a budding poet in his late teens and early twenties. If he wrote any poetry that was personal in nature, it was not offered for public consumption. He may have viewed poetry as a propagandist vehicle, not a personal outlet. Such a conclusion is supported by McCullough's report that Hobson published poetry in weekly periodicals in order to raise money for his various nationalist projects.[109]

The final issue of *Uladh* appeared in September 1905. Its editorial gave no indication of its imminent demise: 'This number of *Uladh* ends our first year of publication. We can now stand on the four-cornered tower of our year's building and note the outlook, retrospective and future.'[110] Clearly, the editors expected the magazine to continue, but a proposed January 1906 issue never appeared. Lack of financial sustenance, lack of copy and lack of an editor have all been suggested as possible reasons for the magazine's eventual demise.[111] By 1906 Hobson was probably too busy with political activities to provide regular copy or editorial leadership. He contemplated a revival of *Uladh* in 1907, but it did not come to fruition.[112]

Conclusion

Influenced by Milligan and Johnston, the engines of the Ulster branch of the Irish Literary Revival, Hobson began his nationalist career by promoting cultural nationalism in Ulster. His earliest propagandist endeavours involved re-packaging the activities of his elders so that they would appeal to young people like himself. In some cases he gave the activities of Dublin nationalists a Northern spin in order to appeal to an Ulster audience. His first propagandist organisation, the Ulster Debating Club, appears to have been a junior version of the Ulster Debating Society. Imitating an event held by the Belfast Gaelic League, the club's first public venture was to produce an evening of *tableaux vivants*. In his volunteer work with the Gaelic League and the GAA in Belfast, Hobson was keen to ensure that young boys as well as adults had access to language classes and opportunities to play hurling and to compete in tournaments. Inspired by a suggestion made in Griffith's *United Irishman* newspaper, Hobson co-founded the Protestant National Society in 1903 in order to convert young Protestant Ulstermen to the nationalist cause. This group, in turn, used theatre as a vehicle for propaganda, imitating the efforts of Inghinidhe na hÉireann in Dublin. Even Hobson's poetry, which was concerned with Ireland's struggle for freedom, was influenced by the work of fellow Northern nationalist poets, Milligan and Johnston.

Language, sport, theatre and poetry were all ways to educate Ulster people about their Irish heritage and had the potential to spark support for cultural nationalism, at the very least, and political nationalism, at most. The efforts of Hobson and his colleagues, however, did not succeed in converting Ulster en masse to cultural nationalism, let alone political nationalism. Instead they fostered the latent nationalism of individuals, be they young hurlers from the Falls Road area or thirteen-year-old theatregoers like O'Shannon.

Poor choice of propagandist vehicle and bad timing probably contributed to Hobson's failure to reach out to a wider audience. For instance, *Uladh* promoted its brand of cultural nationalism with an Ulster accent through an artistic quarterly, which limited its appeal to a small, middle-class elite.[113] The unfortunate timing of the magazine's publication in the middle of the devolution crisis of 1904–5 may have contributed to its inability to attract a wider Protestant audience. The publications that featured Hobson's literary work and reported on his other cultural activities – the *United Irishman*, the *Irish News*, *An Claidheamh Soluis*, *Uladh* – had a pro-Irish bias, indicating that Hobson was preaching to the converted.

Tracing the length of time that Hobson's early propagandist groups, the Ulster Debating Club, the Belfast Fianna and the Protestant National Society, existed is difficult because they tended to open with a blaze of publicity and then fade into obscurity. Lack of members, money or leadership contributed to their demise.

Although the Fianna got off to a successful start in Belfast, the organisation later ran into difficulties due to lack of money and Hobson's increasing commitments to other propagandist activities. It 'continued to exist for many years with various efforts from time to time to infuse new life into it'.[114] Hobson himself believed 'it accomplished quite a lot for the national movement in Belfast'.[115] Remnants of Hobson's original Fianna were still in existence in 1909[116] when, with the help of Countess Markievicz, he resurrected the Fianna as a nationalist youth organisation in Dublin, where it flourished.

The Protestant National Society 'had neither a long nor an important existence', but it did succeed in bringing together a group of young people (including Hobson) who started the ULT. In Hobson's opinion, the ULT 'exercised some influence on the cultural development of the North of Ireland'.[117] As Ireland's first regional theatre company, it became the most important theatre group of its day based outside Dublin.[118]

The ULT's relative longevity – it lasted until 1934 – was due not only to the project's ability to continue attracting energetic and creative contributors as former participants (such as Hobson) moved on to new challenges, but because it abandoned its nationalist roots as its commercial potential grew. Its ability to develop 'a rich vein of comedy which helped to sweeten relations between unionist and nationalist in a period of bitter political strife' gave it 'legs' that Hobson's other cultural propagandist ventures lacked.[119]

During the period 1900–7 Hobson's energy, precocity and wide range of endeavours is impressive. The derivative nature of his activities in the area of cultural nationalism shows that he was a populariser, not an originator. His genius was not in conceiving new ideas, but in re-packaging the ideas of others in order to appeal to new audiences. These audiences, however, tended to have latent nationalist sympathies waiting to be activated by a fiery, persuasive preacher like Hobson.

Notes

1 'The Ulster Theatre – its origin and growth', *IT*, 28 Nov. 1936 (NLI, BH, MS 13,175). The colleague was actor and playwright Rutherford Mayne (a pseudonym for Sam Waddell).
2 *Northern Whig*, 8 Dec. 1904, p. 11; *Irish News*, 8 Dec. 1904, p. 4 (NLI, BH, MS 13,175).
3 *UI*, 2 Aug. 1902, pp. 6–7.
4 Brown, *Northern voices*, p. 64.
5 Norah Saunders and A.A. Kelly, *Joseph Campbell, poet and nationalist 1879–1944: a critical biography* (Dublin, 1988), p. 19.
6 *UI*, 29 Sept. 1900, p. 5.
7 Hobson, *IYT*, p. 24.
8 *UI*, 30 Mar. 1901, p. 5. The newspaper reported that a Mrs Hobson chaired a meeting of the Ulster Debating Society at which Seumas MacManus delivered a lecture. As Hobson's mother was active in local organisations such as the Belfast Naturalists' Field Club, it is possible that she belonged to this society as well.
9 *UI*, 29 Sept. 1900, p. 5.
10 *UI*, 10 Nov. 1900, p. 5.
11 *UI*, 6 Oct. 1900, p. 5.
12 Anna Johnston (Ethna Carbery) to Seamus O'Kelly, 11 Nov. 1900 (NLI, BH, MS 18,461).
13 *UI*, 22 Dec. 1900, p. 5; Hobson, *IYT*, p. 14.
14 Johnston to O'Kelly, 11 Nov. 1900 (NLI, BH, MS 18,461).
15 *UI*, 5 Jan. 1901, p. 5.
16 Hobson, *IYT*, p. 3.
17 Pádraig Ó Snodaigh, *Hidden Ulster: Protestants and the Irish language* (Belfast, 1995), pp. 83, 86.

18 Bulmer Hobson to Martin McCullough (son of Denis McCullough), 25 Nov. 1962 (UCDA, DMcC, P 120/24/19).
19 Qtd. in letter from Joseph McCullough (son of Denis McCullough) to Marnie Hay, 10 Aug. 2002 (letter in possession of author).
20 Denis McCullough, 'Bulmer Hobson's work', *GA*, 16 Feb. 1907, p. 1.
21 Hobson, *IYT*, p. 3.
22 'Belfast and district committee', *ACS*, 25 Jan. 1902, p. 764.
23 Hobson, *IYT*, p. 14.
24 'Feis Uladh notes', *ACS*, 29 Nov. 1902, p. 631; 'Feis Uladh', *ACS*, 6 Dec. 1902, p. 658.
25 Hobson, *IYT*, p. 3, 16.
26 Ibid., pp. 14–15.
27 Ibid., p. 15.
28 Con Short, *The Ulster GAA story 1884–1984* (Rassan, 1984), pp. 39–41.
29 *UI*, 13 July 1901, p. 7.
30 *UI*, 17 Aug. 1901, p. 5.
31 *Irish News*, 10 Aug. 1901, p. 7.
32 *UI*, 24 Aug. 1901, p. 5.
33 *UI*, 14 Sept. 1901, p. 5.
34 Marcus de Búrca, *The GAA: a history* (Dublin, 1980), p. 58.
35 *UI*, 28 Sept. 1901, p. 5.
36 De Búrca, *GAA*, p. 85.
37 Ibid., pp. 87–8.
38 Ibid., p. 87; Short, *The Ulster GAA story*, p. 39.
39 De Búrca, *GAA*, p. 63.
40 Ibid., p. 64
41 Ibid., p. 92.
42 Hobson, *IYT*, p. 14.
43 *UI*, 14 Sept. 1901, p. 5.
44 Hobson, *IYT*, p. 15.
45 *Irish News*, 18 Sept. 1901, p. 8.
46 Fianna minute book, 1902 (NLI, BH, MS 12,176).
47 Ibid.
48 Bulmer Hobson, 'The IRB and the Fianna', in F.X. Martin (ed.), *The Irish Volunteers 1913–1915: recollections and documents* (Dublin, 1963), p. 18.
49 *UI*, 24 Jan. 1903, p. 1.
50 'Belfast notes', *ACS*, 5 July 1902, p. 293.
51 Hobson, *IYT*, p. 15.
52 The Boys' Brigade was founded by William Alexander Smith in 1883 in Glasgow. The organisation provided boys with training in military drill and discipline.
53 *UI*, 24 Jan. 1903, p. 1.
54 Fianna minute book, 1902 (NLI, BH, MS 12,176).
55 Sam Hanna Bell, *The theatre in Ulster* (Dublin, 1972), p. 1.
56 Hobson to Bell, 2 July 1965, qtd. in Bell, *Theatre in Ulster*, p. 2.
57 Ibid.

58 Bell, *Theatre in Ulster*, p. 2.
59 Mark Phelan, 'The rise and fall of the Ulster Literary Theatre' (MPhil thesis, TCD, 1998), p. 49.
60 Hobson, qtd. in Bell, *Theatre in Ulster*, p. 2.
61 R.F. Foster, *W.B. Yeats: the apprentice mage, 1865–1914* (Oxford, 1997), p. 320.
62 Qtd. in Bell, *Theatre in Ulster*, p. 3. The original quotation came from *Enter Robbie John*, a documentary written and compiled by David Kennedy for BBC Northern Ireland Region, 25 Nov. 1954.
63 Bell, *Theatre in Ulster*, pp. 2–3.
64 Hobson referred to this young man as McDonald while McCullough referred to him as McDonnell.
65 John Hewitt, *Art in Ulster* (2 vols, Belfast, 1977), i, p. 66.
66 *UI*, 30 Aug. 1902, p. 3.
67 *UI*, 13 Dec. 1902, p. 3.
68 *UI*, 28 Feb. 1903, p. 6.
69 *UI*, 13 June 1903, p. 3.
70 Contemporary sources, including Hobson himself, shift between calling it the Protestant National Society and the Protestant National Association.
71 *UI*, 28 Feb. 1903, p. 4.
72 Ibid. This suggestion was probably made in the 10 Jan. 1903 issue of the *United Irishman*, which is missing from the NLI's collection.
73 Hobson, *IYT*, p. 3.
74 *UI*, 4 Apr. 1903, p. 7.
75 Seumas MacManus, 'A roomful of Protestants', *UI*, 2 May 1903, p. 5.
76 *UI*, 30 May 1903, p. 5.
77 *UI*, 22 Aug. 1903, p. 7.
78 Bell, *Theatre in Ulster*, p. 3.
79 Ibid.
80 Qtd. in *Enter Robbie John* (Bell, *Theatre in Ulster*, p. 4).
81 Hagal Mengel, 'A lost heritage', *Theatre Ireland*, no. 1 (Sept.–Dec. 1982), pp. 18–19.
82 *IP*, 10 Dec. 1931, p. 6.
83 Qtd. in Foster, *Yeats*, p. 320. The letter itself is not dated, but Foster indicates that it was written in Apr. 1904 (ibid., p. 591).
84 Bell, *Theatre in Ulster*, p. 4.
85 Hobson, qtd. in Bell, *Theatre in Ulster*, p. 2.
86 ULT ticket and programme, 1904 (NLI, BH, MS 13,175).
87 Christopher Morash, *A history of Irish theatre 1601–2000* (Cambridge, 2002), pp. 120–1.
88 *Belfast Evening Telegraph*, 9 Dec. 1904, p. 6.
89 *Northern Whig*, 8 Dec. 1904, p. 11.
90 *U*, Feb. 1905, p. 6.
91 *Irish News*, 8 Dec. 1904, p. 4 (NLI, BH, MS 13,175).
92 Ibid.
93 *UI*, 24 Dec. 1904, p. 1.

94 For an in-depth examination of *Uladh*, see Marnie Hay, 'Explaining *Uladh*: the promotion of nationalism and regionalism in Ulster' (MA thesis, QUB, 1999); Marnie Hay, 'Explaining *Uladh*: cultural nationalism in Ulster', in Betsey Taylor FitzSimon and James H. Murphy (eds), *The Irish revival re-appraised* (Dublin, 2004), pp. 119–31.
95 Hobson, qtd. in Margaret McHenry, 'The Ulster theatre in Ireland' (PhD thesis, University of Pennsylvania, 1931), p. 83.
96 *U*, Feb. 1905, p. 6.
97 *Irish News*, 8 Dec. 1904, p. 4 (NLI, BH, MS 13,175).
98 *U*, Feb. 1905, p. 5.
99 *U*, Sept. 1905, p. 2.
100 Qtd. in *Enter Robbie John* (Bell, *Theatre in Ulster*, p. 25).
101 *The Times*, Northern Ireland Supplement, 5 Dec. 1922, p. xviii.
102 *U*, Sept. 1905, p. 2.
103 Morash, *Irish theatre*, p. 120.
104 David Kennedy, 'Ulster unionism and the new nationalism', in Kevin B. Nowlan (ed.), *The making of 1916* (Dublin, 1969), pp. 74–5.
105 *U*, Nov. 1904, p. 3.
106 *U*, Nov. 1904, p. 13.
107 *UI*, 19 Nov. 1904, p. 5.
108 F.M. Atkinson, 'A literary causerie', *Dana*, Dec. 1904, p. 252.
109 McCullough, 'Hobson's work', *GA*, 16 Feb. 1907, p. 1.
110 *U*, Sept. 1905, p. 1.
111 Hay, '*Uladh*: nationalism and regionalism', pp. 31–2.
112 Roger Casement to Bulmer Hobson, 12 Aug. 1907, 2 Sept. 1907, 24 Oct. 1907 (NLI, BH, MS 13,158 (2)).
113 Kennedy, 'Ulster unionism', p. 75.
114 Hobson, 'IRB and Fianna', p. 18.
115 Hobson, *IYT*, p. 16.
116 Hobson, 'IRB and Fianna', p. 18.
117 Hobson, *IYT*, p. 4.
118 Robert Hogan and James Kilroy, *The modern Irish drama* (2 vols, Dublin, 1976), ii, p. 121.
119 Kennedy, 'Ulster unionism', pp. 74–5.

3

Political nationalism in Ulster

In December 1905 Joseph McGarrity forecast that 'Hobson may yet make Protestant Ulster Irish and national'.[1] The prediction did not come true, despite Hobson's best efforts. Although he failed to convert Ulster to the nationalist cause – a failure he shared with every other Irish nationalist – Hobson's early propagandist work did succeed in influencing several young nationalists in the North, who would later play a decisive role in the nationalist movement and the foundation of an independent Irish state in twenty-six counties. Thus, F.X. Martin has referred to the efforts of Hobson and McCullough as 'puny in their initial stages, yet so far-reaching in their effects'.[2]

Good communication and organisation skills, a thorough knowledge of one's subject and the ability to devise creative and effective ways to reach one's target audience are essential for success as a propagandist. Hobson had these skills at his disposal. He was a noted public speaker and a prolific writer. He has been described as 'a widely read man, who combined imaginative realism with conceptual daring'.[3] McCullough called Hobson 'a very persuasive character' and credited this trait for their success in convincing future 1916 insurrectionist Sean MacDermott (1883–1916) to join the IRB and the Dungannon Club.[4]

The number and variety of propagandist activities that Hobson initiated attests to his organisational skills and creativity in trying to reach a mainly youthful audience. He participated in existing organisations such as Cumann na nGaedheal and the IRB; founded new nationalist groups, like the Protestant National Society[5] and the Dungannon clubs; produced and distributed propagandist publications; and promoted an advanced nationalist message through speaking engagements in Ireland and abroad. Hobson's initial platform for these activities was Ulster.

Cumann na nGaedheal and the IRB

In 1901 Hobson and McCullough joined the Pioneer Branch of Cumann na nGaedheal and became officers on the Belfast district council. Cumann na nGaedheal, which was founded by Dublin journalist Arthur Griffith (1871–1922) in September 1900, was an umbrella organisation for literary, athletic and political groups advocating advanced nationalism. Its main goal was the de-anglicisation of Ireland. Focusing on cultural endeavours, the promotion of Irish industries, and the creation of an Irish foreign policy, it was the forerunner of the later Sinn Féin (literally, 'we ourselves') self-reliance movement. Although Griffith had hoped that each member society would not lose its individual character, these separate clubs turned into branches of Cumann na nGaedheal.[6]

Hobson soon became a prominent member of Cumann na nGaedheal in Belfast. During 1903 he was called upon to undertake a number of high-profile tasks. These included presiding over the inaugural meeting of the Henry Joy McCracken Branch of Cumann na nGaedheal[7] and delivering a lecture on Peter O'Neill Crowley 'in grand style' to 'a large gathering of the Gaels of Belfast' at a meeting of O'Neill Crowley's namesake branch.[8] Although Hobson quickly became a leading light in the local organisation, he, like McCullough, was soon frustrated with its limitations.

At this time there were several active branches of Cumann na nGaedheal in the Belfast area which, according to McCullough,

> were mostly composed of irresponsible young publicans and grocers' assistants, with little or no national tradition behind them, from their home environment. Their activities degenerated into Sunday night 'ceilidhes' and as most of them had easy access to liquor, some unedifying scenes occurred, from time to time.[9]

This behaviour disgusted Hobson and McCullough, who were both 'dead set' against drink. Hobson's Quaker background influenced his views, while McCullough had a passion against liquor because his father had drunk the family into poverty.[10] The belief that alcohol impaired the ability to engage in effective work within the nationalist movement would also impact on Hobson and McCullough's involvement with the IRB.

McCullough had been born into the IRB tradition. His father and grandfather were Fenians and his family's home at 12 Divis Street in Belfast was an IRB meeting place. In 1901, when he was nearing the age of eighteen, McCullough agreed to his father's suggestion that he join the IRB. The experience of being sworn in was a let-down, however:

> [My father] brought me to the side door of a public-house, owned by a man named Donnelly – it was afterwards called 'The Republican Bar', on the Falls Road, and I was duly sworn in by a large, obese man, a tailor by trade, named Ibbotson, evidently a good and steady customer of Donnelly's. I was disappointed and shocked by the whole surroundings of this, to me, very important event and by the type of men I found controlling the organisation; they were mostly effete and many of them addicted to drink.

McCullough responded to this disappointment by organising one or two new IRB circles made up of young men like himself. With their support he managed to force the older men into retiring from the organisation, which, he claimed, 'had been split up into about three factions, by their personal squabbles'.[11]

Although McCullough was keen to recruit active young nationalists to the IRB, he was initially reluctant to bring Hobson into the organisation. In light of Hobson's rising profile within nationalist circles in Belfast, McCullough was concerned that police detectives from the G Division of the Royal Irish Constabulary (RIC), or 'G men' as they were known, would put the word out that the movement was being led by Protestants. These detectives kept an eye on prominent nationalists and reported their activities to the British authorities based at Dublin Castle. McCullough himself had been shadowed by G men ever since he had joined the IRB. Even though the IRB was non-sectarian and 'had quite a good number of young Protestant men in the movement at the time', he feared that these detectives might play upon 'the anti-Protestant and pro-Catholic' idea.[12] In the end McCullough decided to take the risk and introduced Hobson to the IRB in 1904.[13]

McCullough is generally acknowledged as the main instigator of the reorganisation of the IRB in Ulster, with Hobson and veteran Fenian Robert Johnston playing supporting roles in this endeavour. In reviving the IRB in the North, they purged anyone who was too fond of drink, including McCullough's own father. The triumph of the young and sober over the old and often alcoholic in the Ulster IRB was secured when McCullough succeeded Neil John O'Boyle of Randalstown, County Antrim, as Ulster centre and representative on the Supreme Council of the IRB in 1908 or 1909.[14]

The Supreme Council was the main governing body of the IRB. It consisted of eleven members, seven of whom were elected by the centres, who were the chairmen of local IRB circles, in their province or region to represent the following electoral divisions: Leinster, Ulster, Munster, Connacht, North of England, South of England and Scotland. These seven members in turn co-opted four other honorary members.

Members of the Supreme Council elected an executive, consisting of the president, secretary and treasurer, who held the ultimate power to govern: a decision made by two out of three members of the executive was binding on all.[15]

The IRB soon infiltrated Cumann na nGaedheal. As members of the Belfast district council of Cumann na nGaedheal, Hobson and McCullough attended the annual conventions of the umbrella organisation in Dublin. According to McCullough, the IRB attempted to have Major John MacBride elected as vice president of Cumann na nGaedheal and Maud Gonne excluded from this office at the November 1905 convention, following the couple's separation. McCullough reported: 'Attempts were made to "nobble" Hobson and myself on our arrival at the Mansion House, where the convention was being held, by P.T. Daly – the IRB leader in Dublin – by giving us "orders" to vote for MacBride and against Maud Gonne. We refused to accept these "orders".'[16] The pair's refusal to vote against Gonne suggests that they were supportive of women within the nationalist movement, and that they did not take the IRB orders seriously. In the end MacBride and Seumas MacManus were elected as the two vice-presidents.[17]

Hobson's promotion of advanced nationalist views resulted in his growing notoriety, which led to invitations to speak all over Ireland as well as in Great Britain and the United States, and brought him to the attention of the RIC's Crime Special Branch, which began tracking his activities for Dublin Castle, the seat of British authority in Ireland.[18] During the day a detective followed him everywhere and at night another kept vigil outside his home. When he took the train anywhere a detective would ask the ticket-checker where Hobson was going and ensure that he was intercepted and followed at the other end of his journey. Hobson ignored the G men who trailed him and claimed that it was not difficult to evade them.[19] Although he thought that detectives started trailing him because of his membership in the IRB, contemporary police reports suggest that detectives were uncertain about his IRB connection and instead were more concerned about his public propagandist work in support of the Sinn Féin movement and the anti-military enlistment campaign.

The Dungannon clubs and Sinn Féin

The year 1905 is commonly credited as the start of the Sinn Féin movement. Griffith was the main instigator of this self-help movement, which promoted political and economic nationalism. The movement's policies were generally based on Griffith's 1904 pamphlet *The resurrection* of Hungary: a parallel for Ireland, which was inspired by Hungary's achievement of a dual monarchy with Austria in 1867. Griffith first cited this example in a speech at the 1902 convention of Cumann na nGaedheal. Hoping to reconcile Ulster Protestants, Griffith advocated a dual monarchy under the British crown in which Ireland was an equal partner with Great Britain. He also recommended a policy of economic protectionism influenced by the German economist Friedrich List. As a way of achieving political equality he endorsed a policy of passive resistance. Irish MPs were to abstain from sitting in the Westminster parliament and instead were to set up their own governing assembly in Dublin. The Irish people were to withdraw their co-operation with British institutions, such as the police force and the justice system, and instead were to turn to home-grown Irish alternatives. Griffith recommended investment in Irish resources and industry and protection of the Irish economy through high tariffs. The ultimate goal of these political and economic policies was Irish self-sufficiency.

Meanwhile Hobson was developing a similar policy of passive resistance to British rule based on his reading of Lalor, whose writings he had first encountered in 1901.[20] Hobson later described Griffith's Hungarian policy as 'Lalor's policy of 1847 come home with a foreign dress and with a foreign prestige'.[21] In an attempt to point out that Griffith did not deserve all the glory for the policy that contributed to the achievement of Irish independence, Hobson asserted that 'the Sinn Féin idea took shape at nearly the same time in Dublin and Belfast'.[22] Although Hobson acknowledged that Griffith's newspaper the United Irishman, which superseded the Shan Van Vocht in 1899, 'was read by all the younger nationalists and profoundly affected them',[23] he was reluctant to concede that Griffith was one of his own influences. Instead he viewed himself as Griffith's equal rather than his disciple. This viewpoint helped to fuel the rivalry that developed between the two men. Throughout Hobson's career as a Sinn Féin propagandist, tension existed between the periphery (Belfast) and the centre (Dublin), represented by Hobson and Griffith respectively.

In March 1905 Hobson and McCullough established a new organisation, the Dungannon Club, 'which would do some serious national work and which [they] could control in Belfast'.[24] This new nationalist organisation reflected their frustration with the drunken conduct of some of their fellow Belfast Cumann na nGaedheal members and their disillusionment with the limitations of Griffith's Dublin-centric National Council. Founded in 1903, the National Council was conceived as a vehicle to organise opposition to Edward VII's forthcoming visit to Ireland, but continued as an association dedicated to promoting nationalist representation on elected bodies.[25] Hobson and McCullough were disappointed by 'the Dublin people who could think of nothing except winning a few seats in the Dublin Corporation'.[26] Thus the Dungannon Club had a dual purpose: to promote the Sinn Féin policy, particularly in Ulster, and to drive the Dublin crowd back onto the advanced nationalist track.

The Dungannon Club's name was designed to attract Protestant as well as Catholic members. It recalled the Volunteer convention held in Dungannon in February 1782, which led to the final, successful thrust toward Irish legislative independence. The Volunteers were a part-time military force that had been raised in 1778–79 to protect Ireland at a time when the regular army in Ireland had diminished in size, due to the demands of the American War of Independence. They eventually took on a wider political role providing extra-parliamentary support for policies and goals, such as free trade and legislative independence, promoted by the 'Patriot' interest within the Protestant-dominated Irish parliament.[27] In addition, Hobson and his colleagues hoped to see Ulster return to the spirit of the non-sectarian United Irishmen, whose initial advocacy of parliamentary reform later shifted to republicanism in the 1790s. As Hobson optimistically asserted, 'Protestant Ulster is awakening to the fact that its grandfathers dreamed a dream, and its fathers tried to forget it – but the call of it is in their ears.'[28]

Hobson chaired the Dungannon Club's first meeting, which was held at 109 Donegall Street in Belfast on 8 March 1905. McCullough, the poet Padraic Colum and six others were present.[29] The majority of these men were connected in some way with the Protestant National Society, the ULT or *Uladh*. For much of the first Belfast Dungannon Club's history, Hobson served as president and McCullough as secretary. The list of members in the club's minute book later swelled to seventy-one names, many of which were linked to Hobson's other propagandist ventures, but Hobson himself estimated its active membership at thirty to forty individuals.[30] Among the Protestant members of the club were Ernest Blythe, a future minister for finance in the Irish Free State government, and Sean Lester, the future Irish representative to the League of Nations.[31] The club became a recruiting ground for the IRB.

At its first meeting the club showed the influence of Griffith in outlining its goals as being the restoration of the Irish constitution of 1782, the conservation of the Irish language and traditions and the encouragement of Irish industries.[32] By the time the club issued its constitution and manifesto in late August 1905, the restoration of the 1782 constitution had been dropped in favour of 'the political independence of Ireland', while its other stated objective was now to build up Ireland intellectually, materially and physically. The club planned to educate people through classes, lectures, publications and libraries, to foster Irish industry though the 'exclusive use of Irish manufactures and produce' and to popularise physical culture through the spread of Irish games and the training of boys.[33] This concern with building up Ireland physically was also inherent in Hobson's earlier project, the first incarnation of the Fianna.[34]

Hobson and McCullough sent the manifesto to 'all the press offices in Belfast' and to 'leading people of all shades of opinion in Ulster'. Although McCullough claimed that it created 'quite a furore' and sent them 'off to a flying start', Hobson countered that 'it was ignored by everyone, except a unionist labour leader who roundly denounced the garbled version of it which he quoted'.[35] A trawl of the *Belfast Newsletter* and the *Irish News* for the summer and early autumn of 1905 bears out Hobson's assertion that the manifesto was ignored in the Belfast media. The police took more interest in the Dungannon Club's pamphlets, describing their first two publications – an anti-military enlistment pamphlet and the manifesto – as seditious.[36]

In keeping with Hobson's and McCullough's belief that alcohol impaired the ability to do serious work, the Dungannon Club advocated temperance. The club's manifesto also pointed out that decreasing the consumption of liquor in Ireland would help to deprive Britain of a significant source of tax revenue.[37] Although temperance was the official line, it seems that Hobson was not adverse to a drink on rare occasions. Years later he recalled spending 'a riotous day in Portaferry with McGrath getting too drunk to speak at a meeting [he] was addressing in the evening'.[38]

Dungannon Club member Patrick Carbery, who had been purged from the IRB because of his fondness for alcohol, was responsible for supplying Hobson and McCullough with a notable new recruit. He is reputed to have come to McCullough and said: 'Well, if you won't have me, would you have a promising young fellow from the country who doesn't drink?' 'Found to be of the right stuff', the young fellow from Kiltyclogher, County Leitrim joined the Dungannon Club and the IRB in 1906.[39] His name was Sean MacDermott. When Hobson and McCullough met him, MacDermott was a member of the Gaelic League and the Ancient Order of Hibernians (AOH). Many years and several betrayals later, Hobson would dismiss MacDermott as a 'bloody old Hib', whose membership in the AOH had given him a taste for intrigue that he never lost.[40]

At first MacDermott, who was reputed to be 'an extremely religious man at the time', was suspicious of Hobson and McCullough because the IRB was a secret society. MacDermott was unco-operative and would not have much to do with the pair until Hobson put his noted powers of persuasion to work and convinced him that they were not after his soul. Despite this assurance McCullough later joked that they cured MacDermott of his extreme religiousness.[41]

The first Belfast Dungannon Club engaged in a number of propagandist activities. These included an anti-enlistment campaign; weekly lectures and debates; open-air meetings in the summer; the publication of pamphlets, postcards and a weekly newspaper called the *Republic*; and the foundation of other Dungannon clubs and Cumann na Cailíní, a nationalist women's group. For example, the first Dungannon Club became a wholesale manufacturer and distributor of anti-military recruitment posters and leaflets to nationalists all around the country.[42]

The club's weekly meetings featured lectures on topics such as Sinn Féin versus parliamentarianism, as well as debates on topics such as 'Could Ireland given independence maintain it without foreign guarantees?' Hobson and McCullough tried to book speakers who would attract an audience, such as labour leader Jim Larkin or literary critic Robert Lynd. 'They'd all collect a good crowd and we'd get enough money to pay for the men for a few weeks,' McCullough explained. 'We lived from hand to mouth ... Mostly mouth.'[43] Meetings often ended in a nationalist sing-song led by McCullough, who was musically inclined. In contrast, Hobson, MacDermott and McCartan were tone deaf, which made it difficult to tell whether they were singing 'God save Ireland' or 'God save the King'.[44]

In order to raise money and to educate people about Irish nationalism and history, the club produced and sold a series of postcards. These postcards frequently featured political cartoons (generated by the Morrow brothers and Lynd) or scenes from the era of the United Irishmen, which were produced with a view to promoting the need for Protestant and Catholic to work together.[45] Funding the Dungannon Club's various activities was a constant headache for McCullough, its secretary, because Hobson, despite being a Quaker, had 'no sense of money': 'He'd give the last shilling he had to anybody.'[46] Lack of funding was a recurring problem with Hobson's Belfast propagandist activities.

More Dungannon clubs were soon formed, both in Ulster and beyond. In August 1905 Hobson presided at a meeting to form a second Dungannon Club in Belfast.[47] Members of this second club referred to one another as 'Citizen', showing the influence of the republican tradition of the French Revolution.[48] In September 1905 a third Dungannon Club was established in Derry with an initial membership of 'a dozen young men'.[49] Dungannon clubs were also formed elsewhere in Ulster, particularly in County Tyrone, where McCartan had contacts in places such as Carrickmore, Ardboe and Dungannon itself. In October 1905 a London Dungannon Club was established. Among its membership were four Cumann na nGaedheal members: P.S. O'Hegarty, George Gavan Duffy, Lynd and Jack O'Sheehan, the last of whom went on to organise the Irish hospitals' sweepstakes.[50] IRB member Dan Branniff started a branch in Newcastle-upon-Tyne. McCartan also participated in a Dublin-based student branch, which had been started by IRB members Dan Sheehan and John Elwood.[51] Another branch was formed in Glasgow. Hobson described the Dungannon clubs as 'a loose confederation' with no central force formally organising them. The various clubs, however, did look to the first Belfast Dungannon Club, headed by Hobson and McCullough, as the heart of the movement.[52]

In November 1905 Hobson wrote to McCartan, who had recently returned from a stint in Philadelphia, asking him whether he would be interested in starting a Dungannon Club in his native locality, Carrickmore, County Tyrone.[53] McCartan assumed that McCullough, whose uncle had known him in Philadelphia, had given Hobson his name and address.[54] Presuming (wrongly as it happened) that the local priests would not oppose the action, McCartan decided to help Hobson in his bid to 'blend orange and green'. Due to the efforts of the Dungannon clubs, the Gaelic League and the Independent Orange Order, McCartan believed that this task would not 'after a short time be very difficult' as there was 'undoubtedly a new Ulster springing up'.[55]

During Christmas-time in 1905 McCartan attended a Belfast Dungannon Club meeting where he met young, enthusiastic men committed to working for the cause of Irish nationalism.[56] Prior to the meeting McCartan called on Hobson for a long chat. Expecting to meet a man of about forty, he was surprised to discover that twenty-two-year-old Hobson was close to his own age. He described Hobson as 'an enthusiast with plenty of brains and a good worker', who was 'constantly thinking and planning'. Hobson was working out a scheme for the Dungannon clubs to perform the functions of a national government, with committees on sectors like industry and agriculture that would correspond to ministries in the American government. For instance, the committee or ministry of industry would 'make special inquiry in every district where there are clubs to find out what industry could be started there'. He also envisioned a beneficial fund in which imprisonment would render members worthy of benefit. He gave McCartan the impression that he had 'many influential Protestants at his back who yet remain in the dark'.[57]

Roger Casement was probably one of these influential Protestants. Hobson first met him in June 1904 when they were both staying 'in a charming old house at Cushendun in the Glens of Antrim' while attending the Feis of the Nine Glens held in Waterfoot. The house probably belonged to Ada MacNeill, a Gaelic League enthusiast and one of the *feis* organisers. Wandering about Glendun, the pair discussed the cultural revival that Ireland was undergoing.[58] Despite a nineteen-year age difference they quickly forged a friendship, with Casement taking an avuncular interest in Hobson's activities and Hobson often serving as a conduit for Casement's contributions to the nationalist movement.

In 1905 the Dublin-based Irish Unionist Alliance was so disturbed by the message and growing number of Dungannon clubs that it published a pamphlet alerting 'Englishmen and imperialists' to the danger presented by this youthful 'new Irish political force'. It described the Dungannon clubs as not only 'intensely hostile to England and the Union', but 'utterly opposed to the parliamentary policy' directed by Irish Parliamentary Party leader John Redmond. The pamphlet predicted that in a short time English statesmen would have to deal 'not with Mr Redmond and his frothy rhetoricians, but with this newer, younger force, whose policy is frankly an independent Ireland, and a sharp cutting of all connection with England'. Readers were urged to say no to an Irish policy of 'instalments' leading up to Home Rule before it was too late.[59]

During the summers of 1906–8 Hobson and McCullough took the Dungannon Club to the streets of Belfast, where they held open-air meetings, mostly in the Falls Road area. 'We acted on the principle that if the people did not come to our halls to hear us we would carry our republican message into their midst,' Hobson explained.[60] Before their first outdoor meeting, they admitted to one another that they were frightened out of their lives – with good reason.[61] Although some of these street meetings were successful others were stormy, with Hobson and McCullough often being 'attacked and mobbed'.[62] At one meeting club member Sean McGarry managed to catch an egg (which he subsequently ate for his breakfast) that was thrown at them.[63] A Fenian coal merchant lent them his four-wheel cart but not his horse, fearing that the animal would be injured, so they had to pull the cart themselves to the meetings. After convincing Bigger to lend them his magic lantern, they prepared slides listing statistics on subjects such as emigration, industry and the occurrence of venereal disease among British soldiers, and interspersed these with cartoons drawn by their artist friends. They set up the lantern at one end of the cart and a screen at the other, showed the slides, and spoke about these subjects.[64] As most of the audience did not give 'a tinker's hoot' about imports and exports, 'the lantern was often battered with stones thrown by hostile crowds, but was never put out of action'.[65]

Between May 1906 and May 1908 Hobson addressed at least ten open-air meetings in Belfast.⁶⁶ One audience member reported that Hobson appeared 'to have been born on the platform': 'There is something fascinating about his delivery which ... is even more noticeable when addressing large, open air meetings than when speaking in a hall.' It was not so much what he said, but how he said it that struck a chord with an audience.⁶⁷

In attempting to establish and expand Dungannon clubs in rural Ulster, Hobson, McCullough and MacDermott met with opposition, facing 'bitter hostility' from the sectarian AOH in particular.⁶⁸ Hobson and McCullough 'preached open republicanism' at a Dungannon Club meeting in Carrickmore on 7 October 1906, attracting forty new members. At the next meeting, however, there were only a dozen IRB men in attendance, the 'all powerful' AOH having warned off most of the new members.⁶⁹

In January 1907 Hobson and McCullough appointed MacDermott as the Dungannon Club organiser and in the following month sent him off to organise new clubs around Ulster. Blythe was impressed by the way in which the pair did not let a mere bagatelle like money interfere with their plan: 'They simply got thirty members of the Dungannon Club to agree to pay a shilling a week each ... into the organising fund and without more ado Sean went on the road.'⁷⁰ MacDermott was provided with a bicycle⁷¹ and a weekly salary of thirty shillings, which were contributed, as McCullough joked, 'by those members who could afford it (and most of us couldn't!)'.⁷²

A scheme to insure members of the Dungannon clubs and other Sinn Féin groups against incarceration by the British authorities was announced in late January 1907. Hobson noted:

> The Irish people have never shrunk from sacrificing themselves in the service of any national movement that they had faith in ... but we cannot expect many men who have women and children depending on them to leave these defenceless and unprovided for, or dependent on the charity of the more fortunate of their countrymen. And even those who are practically independent need to have some fund on which they can fall back, to enable them to start life afresh after they escape from the clutches of 'the law'.

Hobson expected only 2 per cent of the membership to be jailed at any one time.⁷³ Members of the scheme could insure themselves for the amount of their weekly income, up to a maximum of £2 10s per week. Anyone insured under the scheme would pay an annual registration fee of sixpence for every ten shillings insured.⁷⁴

From their inception in 1905 the Dungannon clubs were open to Irishmen of all classes and creeds.⁷⁵ Provision for women was not made until two years later, when Cumann na Cailíní (Society of Girls) was launched in early 1907. The women's clubs were to be 'similar in all respects to those of the men, subject to the same government, and have an equal representation on the executive and at the conventions'.[76] Cumann na Cailíní offered classes in Irish language, history, lace-making, dancing and physical culture, and started a library for the use of its members.[77] The establishment of an affiliated women's group implies that either a majority of Dungannon Club members were not in favour of opening up the club's membership to women or Belfast women preferred to have a separate club of their own.

The *Republic*

Plans to publish a Dungannon Club newspaper were under way by May 1906 when McCartan sent a copy of the prospectus to McGarrity. The directors were to be Hobson, McCullough, Jack Morrow and McCartan himself. McCartan deemed it important to note that the directorships were evenly divided between Protestants (Hobson and Morrow) and Catholics (McCullough and himself). Hobson was to be editor, and they hoped that the paper would make its debut later that year. McCartan asserted that the paper would represent 'no half measures'.[78] Upon reading the prospectus McGarrity became concerned that McCartan and his colleagues were running the risk of ending up in jail. McCartan optimistically responded that there was little danger of that because the Liberal government, which had returned to power in 1906, thought of 'giving nothing but sympathy'. The prospectus needed to be 'a bit hot', he insisted, in order to 'awake the enthusiasm of the young' because they were working for 'something noble'.[79]

Hobson's supporters had put forward the *Republic* as an appropriate title for the new paper. The members of the London Dungannon Club plumped for the *Irishman* or *Young Ireland* as more suitable. Hobson, however, continued with the initial suggestion, although he admitted to Gavan Duffy that he did not consider the *Republic* as the perfect title for the publication.[80] Despite this, the name *was* catchy and 'republicanism was a relatively popular idea, especially in the North where some Protestants feared a Catholic separatist monarchy'.[81]

The Dungannon Club launched the *Republic* in December 1906. Hobson, as editor, announced that

> We stand for an Irish republic, because we can see that no compromise with England, no repeal of the Union, no concession of Home Rule or devolution will satisfy the national aspirations of the Irish people nor allow the unrestricted mental, moral, and material development of our

country. National independence is our right; we ask no more; and we accept no less.[82]

Although the *Republic* preached a republican brand of nationalism, the leaders of the Dungannon clubs, like Griffith, realised that 'outside the IRB there were few republicans'. McCartan admitted: 'We were mere propagandists and we realised it.'[83]

The *Republic*'s office was located at 114 Royal Avenue in Belfast. The ten-page weekly paper, which was priced at one penny, lasted twenty-three weeks. The main contributors were Hobson, Good (who had to write anonymously because he was on the staff of the loyalist *Northern Whig*), Lynd and O'Hegarty. The latter two were based in London. Hobson wrote articles under his own name, as well as under the pseudonyms Fergus MacLeda and Curoi MacDare, two minor characters from the *Táin Bó Cuailnge* (Cattle Raid of Cooley), the central tale of the Ulster cycle. Good, in particular, stamped the paper with 'his skill in controversy and his ironic humour', and acted as editor while Hobson was on a speaking tour to introduce the Sinn Féin movement to America in early 1907.[84]

The *Republic* covered meetings of the Dungannon clubs and other nationalist organisations, promoted an anti-enlistment message and published essays on politics and economics, often with an Ulster slant, and articles on the nationalist movements in India and Egypt. Of particular note are the political cartoons contributed by Lynd, John Campbell and the Morrow brothers.[85] The paper included a very small amount of cultural content, including poetry, a short story and a review of a novel. Almost every issue included an article written in Irish. In addition, Hobson and Good delighted in detailing the antics of the police detectives who watched the paper's office[86] and in commenting on negative coverage of the Dungannon clubs in the mainstream and unionist media.[87]

Blythe later described the *Republic* as a 'vigorous weekly organ' that 'made a stirring appeal to young Sinn Féiners'.[88] Just as Milligan, Johnston and their nationalist newspaper the *Shan Van Vocht* had influenced a teenage Hobson, the *Republic* and the Dungannon clubs influenced Cathal O'Shannon as a young schoolboy: 'I had seen the paper the previous Christmas and it was what I had found in it that made me some months later seek out the club in its room in Royal Avenue.'[89] O'Shannon later recalled the pride he felt 'as a youngster in Belfast when Bulmer asked me to write one of the articles on Wolfe Tone he was assembling for some special number of the *Peasant*', a paper for which Hobson later worked.[90]

The *Republic* suffered from financial difficulties due to limited subscribers and advertising revenue. Hobson admitted to McGarrity that 'advertisements won't come in no matter what we do'[91] and told Casement that he had 'lost £3 or £3–10–0' during the paper's existence.[92] The financial difficulties were resolved when the Dungannon clubs and Cumann na nGaedheal decided to amalgamate immediately as the Sinn Féin League at a meeting in Dundalk, which was probably held on 7 April 1907.[93] This amalgamation led to the *Republic* being subsumed into the *Peasant*, W.P. Ryan's Dublin-based unofficial organ of Cumann na nGaedheal. The *Republic*'s writers began to contribute articles to the *Peasant*. As part of this merger deal, Hobson was to become sub-editor of the *Peasant*. As he did not move to Dublin until March 1908, Hobson either worked from his northern home or did not take up the position until his move south.

After the demise of the *Republic* in May 1907, Hobson kept busy with his writing and voluntary Sinn Féin League activities, which included secretarial work, meetings around the country and Charles J. Dolan's by-election campaign in North Leitrim.[94] Hobson was also engaged in research on agricultural co-operation and a revival of *Uladh* that never came to fruition. He was so busy that he was unable to keep his promise to write something for Francis Sheehy Skeffington's new paper, the *National Democrat*.[95]

The Sinn Féin League and the National Council amalgamated at the end of August 1907.[96] The first Dungannon Club held its annual meeting shortly afterwards: Hobson and McCullough were elected president and vice-president respectively.[97] A month later this Dungannon Club merged with the West Belfast Branch of the National Council, retaining the name of the latter organisation. The amalgamated executive consisted of: McCullough, chairman; Peter Burns, vice chairman; McGarry and Hobson, secretaries; and William Downey, treasurer.[98] In December 1907, when new officers were selected for the forthcoming year, Hobson was not on the list, presumably because he was no longer based in Belfast.[99]

Political and personal economics

Flann Campbell, the son of poet Joseph Campbell, criticised Hobson and the Dungannon clubs for missing an excellent opportunity to undermine unionism when they failed to provide active support to the workers during the Belfast dock strike, which was led by Jim Larkin in the summer of 1907.[100] Campbell commented that 'only Patrick McCartan seems to have appreciated the wider significance of involving Protestant workers in the struggle against the unionists'. Seemingly unaware of the *Republic*'s dire financial straits, Campbell found it surprising that

Hobson 'closed down [the paper] when the strike was beginning to gather strength'.[101]

The Dungannon Club's manifesto reveals the reasons behind this missed opportunity. The club put what it saw as the interests of the nation before the divisive interests of religion or class: 'It is not that one sect or one class may obtain the upper hand that we strive, but that all sects and all classes may be equal.'[102] The manifesto also referred to Irish trade unionism as 'a mean tail to an English Democracy' that 'must be reorganised and nationalised, and made to play its great and proper part in the upbuilding of the country'.[103] Hobson praised the strike for 'bringing orange and green together in fine style', but criticised it for 'damaging trade'.[104]

The manifesto of the Dungannon Club noted that the organisation favoured nationalised co-operative industries.[105] Hobson enlarged on the theme of co-operation in a number of articles in print. He advocated co-operation as 'the key to the industrial side of … nation-building' in Ireland. He cited the need for co-operation for both the production and distribution of agricultural and manufactured products. Although he applauded the establishment of the co-operative banks for farmers by the Irish Agricultural Organisation Society, which was founded in 1894 by Horace Plunkett, he emphasised that such banks should not only lend money, but teach their members to use their loans to best effect. Economics and education must go hand in hand to make the most of the land, thus helping to avert emigration.[106]

Hobson's involvement with the nationalist movement had had an adverse effect on his career in paid employment. It appears that for much of 1907 he was unemployed, which left him with plenty of time for his nationalist activities.[107] In 1907 McGarrity gave Hobson £50 to help support him while he concentrated on nationalist work, expressing the hope that things would improve in the coming months so that Hobson would not 'have to apply to anti-Irish Irishmen for a position from which to secure a livelihood'.[108]

Casement, while on holiday in Gortahork, County Donegal, in September 1907, expressed concerns about Hobson's personal future in avuncular tones:

> I don't like to think of you idle and without a personal occupation of your own. It is good for no one to be without a purpose of one's own in life and whatever you may be able to do for Ireland will be better done if you have your own private life and cares and worries to fight out too. I want to see you fixed up in some suitable work in Ireland, which while occupying your head, heart and time, should leave you with free hands to work for Ireland and Sinn Féin.

Casement suggested that Dublin would be a better base than Belfast if work could be found there. He could get Hobson well-paid work abroad, but 'it is just what none of us want you to do – unless it were for a time only'. Casement was adamant that Hobson needed to find employment beyond his nationalist activities: 'otherwise you are being seriously handicapped in life and grievously injured too – you are very young and have all your life before you and it is a great shame that these irreparable years should be lost to you for the future'.[109]

By the following month Casement, who was then staying in Cushendall, County Antrim, had figured out how to assist his young friend. He would help him gain the inside track on employment as the manager of the town's co-operative poultry society. The Irish co-operative movement, which began in the 1890s, focused on the processing and marketing of agricultural goods. Casement advised Hobson to outline in his letter of application that he would only ask a salary of £50 per year (although the current salary for the position was £65), that he would go to Dervock, County Antrim to 'acquire technical instruction in testing, grading, sorting, and packing the eggs', and that Casement would provide him with a surety for £100. Having put in a good word for Hobson with two influential local people, Barbara McDonnell and St Clair Dobbs, Casement felt there was little doubt that the committee would choose Hobson for the position.[110]

When he received news of Hobson's success, a delighted Casement responded that in the Cushendall job 'the truest patriotism and truest spirit of Sinn Féin' would be allied in work and not speech: 'Speech is silver – but silence *is* gold.' Casement felt that if Hobson could get this co-operative society on its feet, he could do more for his country in the next twelve months than he could foresee. Casement added: 'By steady work, too, you can prove to unionist and parliamentarian alike that Sinn Féin means what it says – the material uplifting of our country by her own effort.' By working hard in Cushendall for one year, Hobson would 'be *twice* the man this time next year' – and perhaps would be able to see 'a little bit of regenerated Ireland'.[111]

Casement's letter implies that Hobson had been accused of being all talk and no action. For instance, one unidentified critic, though an admirer of the idealism of Hobson's writings, suggested that he should be engaged in 'more profitable work ... for Ireland than devising schemes for insurance against arrest of Sinn Féinidthe', one of his pet projects.[112] Employment in the Cushendall Poultry Society would give Hobson a chance to prove his accusers wrong.

In a subsequent letter Casement expressed his hopes that Hobson would be able to dissipate all the problems of 'Miss McD's poor wee society'.[113] He had had a dream in which he and Hobson's father 'had a long chat' about Bulmer. Although he could not remember the details of their conversation, he had the feeling that Mr Hobson 'was quite happy in the dream' – probably relieved that his elder son finally seemed to be settling down to gainful employment.[114]

In February 1908 Hobson told McGarrity that he had accepted the job as manager of the 'almost bankrupt' poultry society because he wanted 'to get more in touch with the conditions in the rural districts, and one cannot really study rural Ireland from a town'. He added that he had done a little towards putting the society on its feet and had succeeded in getting in touch with rural conditions. In contrast with Casement's hopes that he would spend a year in Cushendall, Hobson was planning to leave in a week or two 'to get back to civilisation and more active politics' by moving to Dublin. Hobson admitted: 'I never quite thought rural Ireland was so bad as it is. I have always lived in the towns, and the towns have a habit of reckoning without the country. I have certainly learned a lot.'[115] This remark reveals that Hobson was an urban animal at heart, though he often took refuge in rural areas.

Hobson also had plans to get his insurance scheme 'permanently on its feet', believing that providing insurance for nationalists who had lost their livelihood because of their beliefs would help to fight coercion by Britain and its unionist supporters. He explained that it 'sounds egotistical, but I believe we can knock the bottom out of coercion. The only two weapons left England are bribery and coercion. If we could upset the first as easily as the second, one would feel more confident.'[116] Hobson had first-hand experience of losing employment because of his nationalist beliefs: 'One firm dismissed me because I was secretary to the Gaelic League, another because I was holding public meetings in support of the Sinn Féin movement.'[117] An insurance scheme for nationalists would help others who found themselves in the same position.

Hobson did not reveal to McGarrity the real reason why he was leaving Cushendall, which was due to differences between himself and McDonnell. In March 1908, while in Paraguay, Casement received 'an extraordinarily rude letter from Miss Barbara', which threatened him with legal proceedings if he attempted to subscribe anything to the Cushendall society. The 'terms of bitter rudeness' employed in the letter convinced Casement that she and Hobson were at odds. Casement wondered where Hobson was: Belfast, his favourite island getaway in Strangford Lough, or elsewhere?[118] Casement received the story of Hobson's Cushendall departure from McDonnell and Stephen Clarke, who had been arrested in 1905 for disseminating the Dungannon Club's anti-enlistment leaflets. Casement claimed that the cause of Hobson's departure lay not with Hobson himself but with McDonnell's 'impossible theories of control and interference'.[119] Considering Hobson's characteristic insistence on doing things his own way, it was not surprising that he and McDonnell had clashed.

In March 1908 Hobson moved to Dublin, informing McGarrity that 'we cannot move Ireland from Belfast how ever hard we work there and I am going to try and move the Dublin men into doing some work'. Hobson believed that the nationalists in Dublin 'ought to do six times the work they do'. In his opinion, only Dublin could provide the leadership needed to move the rest of the country. 'There are great opportunities for progress if Dublin would only wake up and give a lead,' he asserted. The letter included the admission that 'sometimes the people make one despair all together but we have just got to stick at it and make them national in spite of themselves. That is really what has to be done, and we are progressing even though there are many failures and progress is slow.'[120]

Conclusion

In December 1905 McGarrity had forecast that 'Hobson may yet make Protestant Ulster Irish and national', adding that 'if he achieves the conversion of Ulster to nationalism his name will be cherished by generations of Irishmen to come'.[121] Despite his best organisational, journalistic and oratorical efforts, Hobson, like every other Irish nationalist, failed to make 'Protestant Ulster Irish and national'. His name is not cherished by Irish people today. His relative obscurity, however, is a result of his later falling-out with the IRB rather than his failure to convert Ulster to the nationalist cause.[122]

This monumental task had little chance for success. As McCullough pointed out, they 'were a minority of a minority. Three-quarters of the population had no sympathy with the nationalist movement.'[123] Such a small audience was likely to result in the financial difficulties that dogged so many of Hobson's early propagandist activities, including the first incarnation of the Fianna, *Uladh*,[124] the *Republic* and the Dungannon clubs. Such financial difficulties often contributed to the demise of these ventures.

There are parallels between Hobson's activities in the area of cultural nationalism and his ideas about political and economic nationalism. He was a propagator, not an originator. He traced his Sinn Féin message to Lalor rather than to Griffith. He looked to the co-operative movement as the economic saviour of rural Ireland. His anti-enlistment endeavours had precedents within the Irish nationalist movement, such as the Irish

Transvaal Committee during the Boer War. He disseminated nationalist propaganda through clubs, lectures, debates, open-air meetings, pamphlets, posters, postcards and newspapers. Although his message was not particularly original, he was certainly an energetic propagandist and an extremely talented speaker. As one listener recalled, 'he may not say anything new or remarkably striking, but it seems to reach the heart of the audience'.[125]

A commentator writing in the *Peasant* in 1907 suggested that Sinn Féinism had taken less hold in Ulster than in any of the other provinces because 'there are so many conflicting elements in Ulster life that it is very difficult to find two parishes in the same district thinking in the same way, believing in the same policy and doctrine'. He or she went on to point out that although Sinn Féin had 'a formidable array of lecturers and speakers', they were rarely heard in Ulster: 'At the opening of a new branch of the National Council or the Sinn Féin League we hear Mr Bulmer Hobson but with the exception of Belfast and one or two other Ulster places, none of our towns hear Sinn Féin addresses in any number.' And in these cases it was 'largely a matter of "preaching to the converted"'.[126] Although both Catholics and Protestants participated in and provided an audience for Hobson's various propagandist ventures in Ulster, these Protestants, who were based mainly in Belfast, were receptive because they already held liberal views.[127]

In November 1905 McCartan had been confident that 'a new Ulster was springing up', explaining that the Independent Orangemen saw 'that the interests of Ireland and those of England are opposed to each other; that the interests of Irish Protestants and Irish Catholics are identical. They appeal to join hands across the Boyne. They are democratic. But they are yet unionists.'[128] He credited the Independent Orange movement, the Dungannon clubs and the Gaelic League for this new spirit in Ulster, which he predicted would make it easier to bring Protestants and Catholics together. Such optimism was short lived. While membership in the Independent Orange Order peaked in 1907, 'increasing division within the leadership deprived the order of talent and the capacity to grow in any other than a conventionally Protestant direction'.[129] By late 1909 the first Dungannon Club was in such low water that McCullough and Hobson had to stage a revival of the organisation.[130] Blythe blamed the decline of the clubs on the Liberal Party victory of 1906, 'which made so many think that an all-Ireland parliament was as good as established'.[131] This complacency was short-lived, as disillusionment with the Liberals soon spread. The Liberal victory also made unionists increasingly nervous and less likely than ever to be receptive to Hobson's attempts to blend orange and green.

Hobson's propagandist activities in Ulster did help to foster the nationalist beliefs of MacDermott, Blythe, O'Shannon and Lester, among others. That said, Hobson, like so many other Ulstermen who held 'dissenting' views, was forced to find his fortune outside of his native province.[132] Yet the move to Dublin allowed Hobson to shift his propagandist activities to an all-Ireland stage with a larger and potentially more receptive audience for his nationalist message. These activities sowed nationalist seeds that later blossomed in the other three provinces of Ireland.

Notes

1 McGarrity to McCartan, 25 Dec. 1905 (NLI, JMcG, MS 17,458 (1)).
2 Martin, 'McCullough, Hobson and republican Ulster', p. 96.
3 Michael Tierney, *Eoin MacNeill: scholar and man of action* (Oxford, 1980), p. 113.
4 McCullough, BBC interview transcript, 1964 (UCDA, DMcC, P 120/36).
5 See Chapter 2.
6 Davis, *Arthur Griffith and non-violent Sinn Féin*, p. 17.
7 *UI*, 7 Feb. 1903, p. 7.
8 *UI*, 16 May 1903, p. 7.
9 McCullough, statement, 1957 (UCDA, DMcC, P 120/29).
10 McCullough, BBC interview transcript, 1964 (UCDA, DMcC, P 120/36).
11 McCullough, witness statement, 11 Dec. 1953 (NAI, BMH, WS 914).
12 McCullough, BBC interview transcript, 1964 (UCDA, DMcC, P 120/36).
13 Hobson, *IYT*, p. 35; Hobson, witness statement, 17 Oct. 1947 (NAI, BMH, WS 30). For a discussion of the debate over when Hobson joined the IRB, see Hay, 'Bulmer Hobson', pp. 49–50.
14 Hobson, witness statement, 17 Oct. 1947 (NAI, BMH, WS 30).
15 See IRB constitution, 1873 (NLI, BH, MS 13,163).
16 McCullough, answer to questionnaire, 1952 (UCDA, DMcC, P 120/24 (9)).
17 'Cumann na nGaedheal', *UI*, 18 Nov. 1905, p. 7.
18 See Précis of information received in the Crime Special Branch (NAL, CO 904/117–118), and Précis of information received relative to secret societies, etc., in the Dublin Metropolitan Police district (NAL, CO 904/11).
19 Hobson, *IYT*, p. 35.
20 See Chapter 1.
21 Hobson, *IYT*, p. 19.
22 Ibid., p. 42.
23 Ibid., p. 4.
24 McCullough, statement, 1957 (UCDA, DMcC, P 120/29).
25 Davis, *Sinn Féin*, pp. 19–20.
26 Hobson to Martin McCullough, 25 Nov. 1962 (UCDA, DMcC, P 120/24 (19)).
27 'Volunteers', in S.J. Connolly (ed.), *The Oxford companion to Irish history* (Oxford, 1999), p. 581.

28 Bulmer Hobson, 'The new Ulster', *The Nationist*, 30 Nov. 1905, p. 169.
29 Dungannon Club minute book, 1905 (NLI, BH, MS 12,175).
30 Hobson, *IYT*, p. 8. Many of the names listed in the minute book were cut out of the pages at a later date, perhaps because these individuals dropped out of the club or did not want their names in a document that could be seized by the police.
31 Cathal O'Shannon, 'Denis McCullough', *Evening Press*, 20 Sept. 1968 (UCDA, DMcC, P 120/76 (8)). For a discussion of Lester's involvement with the Belfast Dungannon Club, see Douglas Gageby, *The last general secretary: Sean Lester and the League of Nations* (Dublin, 1999), pp. 3–5.
32 Dungannon Club minute book, 1905 (NLI, BH, MS 12,175); Davis, *Sinn Féin*, p. 26.
33 'Constitution of the Dungannon Club', qtd. in Hobson, *IYT*, pp. 23–4. See also Bulmer Hobson, *To the whole people of Ireland: the manifesto of the Dungannon Club Belfast* (Belfast, 1905), which is reprinted in *IYT*, pp. 93–8. A copy of the manifesto can be found in NLI, BH, MS 13,166 (4). A handwritten note on this copy states that it was first published around the end of August 1905.
34 See Chapter 2.
35 McCullough, statement, 1957 (UCDA, DMcC, P 120/29); Hobson, *IYT*, p. 24.
36 Précis, CSB, Oct. 1905 (NAL, CO 904/117).
37 Hobson, *The manifesto of the Dungannon Club*, in Hobson, *IYT*, p. 97.
38 Hobson to McCullough, 1 Sept. 1965 (UCDA, DMcC, P 120/17/4). Hobson was probably referring to Henry McGrath of Portaferry, whom the police considered a 'suspect' (Précis, SS, Mar. 1905 (NAL, CO 904/11)).
39 O'Shannon, 'Denis McCullough', *Evening Press*, 20 Sept. 1968 (UCDA, DMcC, P 120/76).
40 McCullough, BBC interview transcript, 1964 (UCDA, DMcC, P 120/36); Hobson, *IYT*, p. 8.
41 McCullough, BBC interview transcript, 1964 (UCDA, DMcC, P 120/36).
42 Terence Denman, '"The red livery of shame": the campaign against army recruitment in Ireland, 1899–1914', *IHS*, xxix (1994), p. 219. For a more detailed discussion of the club's anti-recruitment activities, see Hay, 'Bulmer Hobson', pp. 60–3.
43 McCullough, BBC interview transcript, 1964 (UCDA, DMcC, P 120/36).
44 Ibid.
45 Dungannon Club postcards (NLI, BH, MS 13,166 (3)).
46 McCullough, BBC interview transcript, 1964 (UCDA, DMcC, P 120/36).
47 'Dungannon Club, No. 2', *Irish News*, 29 Aug. 1905, p. 6.
48 'Dungannon Club, No. 2', *Irish News*, 6 Sept. 1905, p. 7; 12 Sept. 1905, p. 7; 20 Sept. 1905, p. 3; 28 Sept. 1905, p. 8.
49 Précis, CSB, Sept. 1905 (NAL, CO 904/117).
50 Davis, *Sinn Féin*, p. 28.
51 McCartan, witness statement, 5 Apr. 1948 (NAI, BMH, WS 99; NLI, BH, MS 13,170). The Dublin Students' Dungannon Club, which was founded

in October 1902, predated the first Belfast Dungannon Club, but affiliated itself with the organisation founded by Hobson and McCullough. See Dublin Students' Dungannon Club, *Manifesto to the whole students of Ireland* (Dublin, 1906).
52 Hobson, *IYT*, p. 21.
53 McCartan to McGarrity, 12 Nov. 1905 (NLI, JMcG, MS 17,457 (2)).
54 McCartan, witness statement, 5 Apr. 1948 (NAI, BMH, WS 99; NLI, BH, MS 13,170).
55 McCartan to McGarrity, 12 Nov. 1905 (NLI, JMcG, MS 17,457 (2)).
56 McCartan to McGarrity, 12 Jan. 1906 (NLI, JMcG, MS 17,457 (3)).
57 McCartan to McGarrity, 23 Dec. 1905 (NLI, JMcG, MS 17,457 (2)).
58 Hobson, *IYT*, p. 80.
59 Irish Unionist Alliance, *The Dungannon Clubs and a separate Ireland: a view of what 'Young Ireland' is doing* (Dublin, 1905), pp. 3–4.
60 Ó Lúing, 'Talking to Bulmer Hobson', *IT*, 6 May 1961, p. 10.
61 Hobson, *IYT*, p. 9.
62 Hobson to Martin McCullough, 25 Nov. 1962 (UCDA, DMcC, P 120/24 (19)).
63 McCullough, BBC interview transcript, 1964 (UCDA, DMcC, P120/36).
64 Hobson, *IYT*, pp. 9–10; McCullough, BBC interview transcript, 1964 (UCDA, DMcC, P120/36).
65 McCullough, BBC interview transcript, 1964 (UCDA, DMcC, P120/36); Hobson, *IYT*, p. 10.
66 Police reports (NAL, CO 904/11, 118) and reports in the *Peasant* (8, 15, 22 June 1907) indicate that Hobson spoke at meetings on the following dates: 29 May 1906, 5 June 1906, 12 June 1906, 28 May 1907, 4 June 1907, 11 June 1907, 22 Apr. 1908, 4 May 1908 (abandoned due to small audience), 5 May 1908 and 12 May 1908 (abandoned because audience would not listen). These meeting were held in Barrack, Clonard and Derby streets.
67 O'Neill, 'Sinn Féin', *GA*, 2 Feb. 1907, p. 1.
68 Ó Lúing, 'Talking to Bulmer Hobson', *IT*, 6 May 1961, p. 10.
69 McCartan to McGarrity, 22 Sept. 1906, 19 Oct. 1906 (NLI, JMcG, MS 17,617 (1)); McCartan, witness statement, 5 Apr. 1948 (NAI, BMH, WS 99; NLI, BH, MS 13,170).
70 Earnán de Blaghd (Ernest Blythe), 'An outstanding leader of genuine nationalism', *IT*, 13 Sept. 1968 (UCDA, DMcC, P 120/76 (2)).
71 McCullough, lecture notes, 10 Jan. 1964 (UCDA, DMcC, P120/33).
72 McCullough, statement, 1957 (UCDA, DMcC, P 120/29).
73 Hobson, 'The English government and Irish national movements', *R*, 31 Jan. 1907, pp. 3–4.
74 Dungannon Club insurance scheme (NLI, JMcG, MS 17,612).
75 Dungannon Club minute book, 1905 (NLI, BH, MS 12,175).
76 'Cumann na cailíní', *R*, 7 Mar. 1907, pp. 2–3; Rules for the first conference of Dungannon clubs (NLI, JMcG, MS 17,453). It is unclear whether a conference of Dungannon clubs was ever held.
77 'Cumann na cailíní', *R*, 7 Mar. 1907, pp. 2–3; 'Cumann na cailíní', *R*, 14 Mar. 1907, p. 2.

78 McCartan to McGarrity, 23 May 1906 (NLI, JMcG, MS 17,617 (1)).
79 McCartan to McGarrity, 26 June 1906 (NLI, JMcG, MS 17,617 (1)).
80 Davis, *Sinn Féin*, p. 29.
81 Ibid.
82 *R*, 13 Dec. 1906, p. 4.
83 McCartan, witness statement, 5 Apr. 1948 (NAI, BMH, WS 99; NLI, BH, MS 13,170).
84 See Chapter 4.
85 Some of these cartoons are reprinted in Hobson, *IYT*, pp. ii–viii.
86 'The old game', *R*, 21 Feb. 1907, p. 2; 'Quis custodiet ipsos custodes?', *R*, 28 Feb. 1907, pp. 3–4; 'The era of conciliation', *R*, 16 May 1907, pp. 1–2.
87 'For English consumption', *R*, 21 Mar. 1907, pp. 2–3; 'Yellow journalism and Sinn Féin', *R*, 11 Apr. 1907, pp. 6–7.
88 De Blaghd, 'An outstanding leader', *IT*, 13 Sept. 1968 (UCDA, DMcC, P 120/76 (2)).
89 Cathal O'Shannon, 'Memories of 50 Years Ago', *IP*, 20 July 1956 (UCDA, DMcC, P 120/37).
90 O'Shannon to McCullough, 25 Mar. 1958 (UCDA, DMcC, P 120/15 (3)).
91 Hobson to McGarrity, 30 Apr. 1907 (NLI, JMcG, MS 17,453).
92 Hobson to Casement, 19 May 1907 (NLI, RC, MS 13,073 (46/x)).
93 'Sinn Féin League', *R*, 11 Apr. 1907, p. 1.
94 See Chapter 4.
95 Hobson to Francis Sheehy Skeffington, 5 July 1907 (NLI, ShSk, MS 21,618 (iii)).
96 This amalgamation is sometimes reported as dating from September 1907. The conference at which the merger took place was held at the end of August, while newspaper coverage of the event was published in early September.
97 'Dungannon Club, Belfast', *P*, 14 Sept. 1907, p. 8.
98 'Dungannon Club and West Belfast Branch', *P*, 26 Oct. 1907, p. 8.
99 'West Belfast Branch', *P*, 14 Dec. 1907, p. 8.
100 Flann Campbell, *The dissenting voice* (Belfast, 1991), pp. 389, 398–9. For more on the strike, see John Gray, *City in revolt: James Larkin and the Belfast dock strike of 1907* (Belfast, 1985).
101 Campbell, *The dissenting voice*, p. 389.
102 Hobson, *The manifesto of the Dungannon Club*, p. 7.
103 Ibid., p. 3. Hobson excised this reference to Irish trade unionism when he reprinted this manifesto in *IYT* (p. 95).
104 Hobson to McGarrity, 21 July 1907 (NLI, JMcG, MS 17,612).
105 Hobson, *The manifesto of the Dungannon Club*, p. 3.
106 Bulmer Hobson, 'On co-operation', *R*, 9 May 1907, p. 9. Hobson enlarged on his belief in the need for co-operative banks to provide education as well as loans in an article entitled 'On tillage societies' (*P*, 15 June 1907, p. 6).
107 Hobson to McGarrity, 17 Feb. 1908 (NLI, JMcG, MS 17,453); Hobson to

Casement, 19 May 1907 (NLI, RC, MS 13,073 (46/x)).
108 McGarrity to Hobson, 22 Mar. 1907 (NLI, JMcG, MS 17,612).
109 Casement to Hobson, 2 Sept., 1907 (NLI, BH, MS 13,158 (2)).
110 Casement to Hobson, 24 Oct., 1907 (NLI, BH, MS 13,158 (3)).
111 Casement to Hobson, 29 Oct. 1907 (NLI, BH, MS 13,158 (3)).
112 K, 'The Tairngirie', *P*, 12 Oct. 1907, p. 7.
113 Casement to Hobson, 8 Nov. 1907 (NLI, BH, MS 13,158 (3)).
114 Casement to Hobson, 15 Nov. 1907 (NLI, BH, MS 13,158 (3)).
115 Hobson to McGarrity, 17 Feb. 1908 (NLI, JMcG, MS 17,453).
116 Ibid.
117 Hobson, *IYT*, p. 16.
118 Casement to Hobson, 27 Mar. 1908 (NLI, BH, MS 13,158 (4)).
119 Casement to Hobson, 20 Aug. 1908 (NLI, BH, MS 13,158 (4)).
120 Hobson to McGarrity, 17 Feb. 1908 (NLI, JMcG, MS 17,453).
121 McGarrity to McCartan, 25 Dec. 1905 (NLI, JMcG, MS 17,458 (1)).
122 See Chapter 6.
123 McCullough, RTÉ interview transcript, 8 Mar. 1965 (UCDA, DMcC, P 120/35).
124 Hay, '*Uladh*: nationalism and regionalism', pp. 31–2; Hay, '*Uladh*: cultural nationalism', p. 128.
125 O'Neill, 'Sinn Féin', *GA*, 2 Feb. 1907, p. 1.
126 S.A., 'Propaganda Work in Ulster', *P*, 24 Aug. 1907, p. 2.
127 McCullough, Ulster TV interview transcript, 8 Sept. 1964 (UCDA, DMcC, P 120/34/2).
128 McCartan to McGarrity, 12 Nov. 1905 (NLI, JMcG, MS. 17,457 (2)).
129 Alvin Jackson, 'Independent Orange Order', in Connolly (ed.), *Oxford companion*, p. 257.
130 'Sinn Féin – Dungannon Club, Belfast', *INP*, 16 Oct. 1909, p. 8. See Chapter 4.
131 De Blaghd, 'An outstanding leader', *IT*, 13 Sept. 1968 (UCDA, DMcC, P 120/76).
132 Flann Campbell cites the artist Paul Henry, the poet Joseph Campbell, the musician Herbert Hughes, and the journalists Lynd and Good as examples (*The dissenting voice*, pp. 380, 393–4).

4

The other Sinn Féin leader

In August 1906 the inhabitants of Finea, a village on the borders of counties Westmeath and Cavan, were poised for an onslaught of invaders intent on commemorating Myles 'the Slasher' O'Reilly, a soldier slain during the 1641 rising.[1] Hobson and Lynd were among the invaders because local supporters of the Sinn Féin movement had engaged the former to preach the gospel of national self-reliance at the meeting.

Lynd felt himself in the presence of a newly awakened Ireland. The village thrummed with the sound of fife-and-drum bands while green flags and portraits of great Irish heroes waved in the air. He described Hobson standing on the platform as 'a young man, at once curiously boyish and curiously Napoleonic in appearance'.[2] A local priest and Laurence Ginnell, MP, spoke first, but neither caught the mood of the crowd of about five thousand. Then it was Hobson's turn to address the gathering. Lynd recalled:

> He stepped forward to the bar in front of the platform with an air calm and resolute and almost indolent. No sooner had he spoken his word, 'Men and women of Ireland,' however, than you knew that he had the crowd in his grip. He reminded them that they were faced by the same enemies whom Myles the Slasher had died fighting ... I shall never forget their joy when the speaker held up before them, as the only ideal worthy of a brave man's striving after, the establishment of an independent Irish nation. Every hat was lifted; every throat was shouting; arms were thrust up and forward toward the platform, as though the crowd longed to take the speaker to its bosom.[3]

Hobson encouraged his listeners to rely on themselves instead of looking to a foreign parliament for salvation, to support Irish industries, to speak Irish, to stop drinking alcohol in order to deprive Britain of tax revenue, and not to enlist in the British army or police force. According to Lynd, 'it was the first time the Sinn Féin policy had been expounded in the midlands of Ireland, and the midlands drank it in as the earth after a long drought drinks in rain'.[4]

Reports of the success of this speaking engagement reached Clan na Gael leader and *Gaelic American* editor John Devoy in the United States. As a result, Devoy decided to invite Hobson instead of Griffith to preach the Sinn Féin message on an American tour. In comparing Hobson and Griffith as speakers, McCartan had informed Devoy that 'Hobson's delivery was more effective' though he conceded that 'Griffith's matter was much better than Hobson's'.[5] It looked as if the young Belfast man, a devotee of Lalor's strategy of 'moral insurrection', was poised to eclipse Griffith, twelve years his senior and the father of the more famous policy of passive resistance based on the Hungarian example.

American tour

Hobson needed no second bidding to accept Devoy's invitation. En route to Cork to catch a steamship to America, Hobson stopped in Dublin. While there he was surprised by Griffith's 'coldness and hostility'. After discovering that Griffith had wanted to undertake a speaking tour of the United States, Hobson regretted inadvertently spoiling the older man's chances.[6]

On the same day that Hobson set sail for America, Griffith voiced his disapproval on the front page of his newspaper *Sinn Féin*. He noted: 'The executive wishes it to be clearly understood that [Hobson's visit to the United States] is not authorised by the National Council, nor undertaken on its behalf.'[7] His words imply that the National Council held a monopoly on the Sinn Féin 'brand', despite the fact that the Dungannon clubs and Cumann na nGaedheal were engaged in propagating the Sinn Féin message and would soon merge forces as the Sinn Féin League.

In 1907 Griffith was acknowledged as the 'primary exponent' of the Sinn Féin policy of self-reliance. He was considered to be most at home, and at his most effective, in the editorial chair, serving as 'an encyclopedia of useful and practical ideas'. Hobson was recognised as being the next most prominent exponent of the ideology of Sinn Féin. In contrast, he was in his natural element on the speaking platform.[8] Hobson's superior public speaking skills earned him the chance to introduce the Sinn Féin movement to America.

A reception committee met Hobson on the dock when he arrived in New York on 9 February 1907.[9] Clan na Gael organised and funded the tour but did not take public credit for its efforts, presumably because Devoy and his colleagues hoped to attract a broad spectrum of Irish Americans to Hobson's speeches. Clan na Gael's organ, the *Gaelic American*, published advance publicity, much of it written by McCullough, McCartan and Lynd,[10] that hailed Hobson as an accomplished nationalist propagandist despite his youth. The paper went on to provide extensive coverage of the tour.

Hobson's American tour in February and March 1907 took him to New York, Brooklyn, Philadelphia, Cleveland, Indianapolis, Chicago, St. Louis and Boston.[11] He received invitations from at least twenty other cities but, due to his editorial and public speaking commitments

2 Arthur Griffith, founder of the Sinn Féin movement

in Ireland, he could not prolong his visit further.[12] In all of the cities that he did visit, he addressed packed halls, often with as many as a hundred people being denied admission. In Indianapolis, for example, he attracted an audience of more than 2,500 people.[13] Local newspaper coverage of his tour ranged from a small article at the bottom of page two of the *Chicago Daily Tribune* to a series of at least eleven articles in the *Boston Post*.[14]

Hobson's first public appearance in the United States was on 15 February 1907 at Grand Central Palace on Lexington Avenue in New York City. The meeting featured addresses by Hobson on the objectives of the Sinn Féin movement and by social economist S.L. Joshi on India's Swadeshi movement, in order to show the growing solidarity between Ireland and India, and ended with a selection of Irish music. It was expected to result in the formation of a Sinn Féin organisation in the city.[15]

Hobson responded to the applause that greeted his entrance on stage with a modest bow and 'a bashful smile' that lit up 'his shy boyish countenance'. Upon taking his seat, he 'dropped his head between his shoulders and sized up the audience'. Hobson's appearance surprised McGarrity, who had gone to New York to hear him speak. He had pictured Hobson as 'robust' and not as he was – 'tall and determined in appearance'. Colonel Robert Temple Emmet, a descendant of Thomas Addis Emmet, introduced Hobson to the audience. Only one sentence had escaped Hobson's lips before McGarrity was convinced that the young man was 'master of the situation'. Hobson's talents as an orator triumphed over concerns about his obvious youth: 'Whatever doubt might have been entertained by the audience as to his ability to handle the subject proposed they were soon shattered.' At the end of his speech, the entire room resounded with cheers.[16]

In his speech Hobson described how the 'English government' had shifted from using 'the pitch-cap' and 'the prison ship' to crush the Irish nation, to using the economic and educational systems. He accused the Irish Parliamentary Party of betraying Ireland by taking their seats in the Westminster parliament, thus recognising the right of a foreign government to rule their nation. He assured the audience that a new generation, dedicated to bringing the 'people of Ireland, North and South, Catholic and Protestant' together as 'Irishmen', was engaged in combating this situation. He also then outlined the Sinn Féin movement's policy of passive resistance.[17] He delivered similar versions of this speech throughout his tour.

Hobson's tour stirred up tensions within the Irish-American community, especially because it coincided with Irish Parliamentary Party MP

Thomas Kettle's visit. A few days before Hobson's speaking engagement in Boston, Kettle addressed a United Irish League (UIL) meeting in that city to celebrate the anniversary of Robert Emmet's birth. The UIL provided local organisational and fundraising support to the Irish Parliamentary Party. Kettle asserted that Hobson 'misrepresented the attitude and wishes of the Irish people' and accused him of harming the Irish cause.[18] The *Gaelic American* reported that there was more talk of Hobson than of Emmet at this meeting, where Hobson was criticised for being only twenty-four years old (ironically only 'one year younger than Emmet at the time he was hanged'), a Quaker and 'neither a member of parliament, a county councillor, nor a member of any board or corporation elected through the machinery of English law in Ireland'. The *Republic* suggested that Hobson's real sin was not asking John O'Callaghan, the national secretary of the UIL of America, for permission to visit the United States.[19]

The UIL clearly sensed the hidden hand of their political rivals Clan na Gael. As Hobson did not charge admission to his speeches or ask for donations, leading members of the UIL queried the financial side of his tour. They demanded – to no avail – answers to three questions: who invited Hobson, whom did he represent and who arranged his tour?[20] O'Callaghan denounced Hobson as

> an interloper, a disturber, a man who, under the profession of extreme rationality, is willing to do his share toward disrupting and destroying the influence of the Irish race in America at a critical period in the history of the Irish movement and when Irish unity and Irish patriotism should counsel every man doing his share in helping the national cause.[21]

While the organisers of Hobson's visit defended him in the *Boston Post*,[22] Hobson himself made no reference to the accusations during his speech in that city.

Hobson stopped off in Philadelphia before returning to New York to catch his ship home. During both of his stays in Philadelphia, he and McGarrity enjoyed 'a few good nights and a few very interesting talks' at the latter's home.[23] McGarrity was impressed with his new acquaintance, describing Hobson as 'a very sincere fellow' who was not afraid of declaring himself. McGarrity was satisfied with the newspaper coverage of Hobson's visit,[24] and hoped there would be 'no disagreement between [Griffith] and Hobson as there is more than enough work for both to do and for many more like them'.[25]

Hobson set sail for Ireland on 23 March 1907.[26] His tour to promote the Sinn Féin policy was considered a success (at least by Sinn Féiners), with the *Republic* naturally praising his achievements: 'He has outlined for the Irish in America the essential principle of the new movement, he has cleared away the doubts and suspicions so assiduously fostered by the parliamentarians, and set the issues between contending forces in this country in their true light.'[27]

Sinn Féin amalgamation

A central issue that emerged during the course of Hobson's tour was the refusal of Irish-American nationalists to provide financial aid to the Sinn Féin movement unless its component organisations merged. The existence of three different organisations (Cumann na nGaedheal, the National Council and the Dungannon clubs) advocating a Sinn Féin policy, two different leaders (Hobson in Belfast and Griffith in Dublin) and two different visions of what Ireland should strive to achieve (republic versus dual monarchy) proved problematic. Advanced nationalists in both London and the United States urged their colleagues in Ireland to strive for unity of purpose and a rationalisation of resources.[28]

Hobson and McCullough had already tried to bring about an amalgamation. In October 1906 they proposed that a meeting should be held to discuss a possible merger with Cumann na nGaedheal and the National Council. The leaders of the Dungannon clubs were open to amalgamation because Cumann na nGaedheal were expected to support their policy regarding full independence, which would strengthen both the clubs and the imminent launch of the *Republic*. They were less certain of the reaction of Griffith's National Council.[29]

The first meeting to discuss a possible amalgamation was held in Dundalk on 21 October 1906 with Hobson, McCullough and McCartan representing the Dungannon clubs. Griffith, W.L. Cole and T.J. Sheehan represented the National Council while S. Doyle, P. O'Brien and A. Ingoldsby represented Cumann na nGaedheal.[30] At this meeting the representatives of the Dungannon clubs put forward the suggestion that in case of amalgamation the constitution should read: 'That our object is to secure the independence of Ireland believing that the people of Ireland are a free people and that no law made without their authority or consent is or ever can be binding on their conscience.'[31] After discussion of this suggestion it was agreed 'that the new amalgamation should include men who believe in the Constitution of [17]82 as a final settlement and men who believe in separation and that the demand should be *independence*'. Cumann na nGaedheal were expected to accept this, as was the majority of the National Council's executive – although Cole, 'purely an '82 man', strongly objected.[32] A suggestion was also put forward that 'a council consisting of an equal number of representatives from each executive should be formed to work out the Sinn Féin policy and agree on a common line of action'.[33] In the end Griffith's National Council rejected the proposed amalgamation, so Hobson and McCullough decided to push for 'unity of action with the Cumann na nGaedheal people in Dublin'.[34]

Hobson promised Irish-American nationalists to do his best to bring about a merger upon his return to Ireland. As a result, the executives of the Dungannon clubs and Cumann na nGaedheal, both of which were controlled by IRB men, held a meeting in Dundalk in early April 1907 at which they decided to amalgamate immediately, calling the newly merged organisation the Sinn Féin League.[35] The league's main objective was 'the regaining of the sovereign independence of Ireland'. Although this wording implied a rejection of the 1782 settlement of legislative independence, it did not assert overt republicanism. At a second meeting on 21 April P.T. Daly was elected president, with McCullough and McGarry as joint secretaries. MacDermott retained his position as a paid organiser, only now he worked for the Sinn Féin League rather than the Dungannon clubs. Richard Davis has suggested that Hobson's demotion to a position as a mere member of the executive committee may have been designed to appease Griffith in hopes of coming to a future settlement.[36]

Griffith and his National Council, however, remained aloof. Ironically, the term 'Sinn Féin' has been associated with Griffith even though he did not belong to the first body bearing that name, which was in fact an organisation that he resented.[37] As Michael Laffan points out: 'Almost a year earlier Griffith had appropriated the term "Sinn Féin" by using it as the title for his own newspaper, and a feeling of affronted proprietorship may have been part of the reason for his hostility towards the new party. He virtually ignored it in the columns of *Sinn Féin*.'[38] The isolation of Griffith and the National Council was short lived. The conversion of Irish Parliamentary Party MP Charles J. Dolan of North Leitrim to Griffith's political views in June 1907, combined with the demise of the *Republic* the previous month, strengthened Griffith's hand. This allowed him to dictate favourable terms when his National Council finally amalgamated with the Sinn Féin League at the end of August 1907.[39]

This merger helped to bring unity to Dolan's re-election campaign in North Leitrim on a Sinn Féin platform, which both the National Council and the Sinn Féin League supported. The campaign lasted from June 1907 until the by-election in February 1908. Dolan was ultimately defeated by the Parliamentary Party candidate, F.E. Meehan, by 1,157 votes to 3,103.[40]

In June 1907, when Dolan resigned from the Irish Parliamentary Party and contested his North Leitrim seat on a Sinn Féin platform, Hobson set out to help him. He informed McGarrity that

> If a good fight is made in Leitrim other MPs will resign and once we win a seat the fight will be on and we will rouse the whole country. Four or five others are ready to come over to us and others can be forced presently. Things are moving very fast but not yet as fast as I would like. We are doing all we can to hurry them however.[41]

Hobson had to abandon his plans to help Dolan in North Leitrim after being denounced 'from the altar as a dangerous person' and described in the local press as a Salvation Army preacher from Belfast and an Orangeman.[42] The *Sligo Champion* reported that the UIL had drummed Hobson out of the United States.[43] In light of such bad publicity, Hobson felt his 'presence would do Dolan more harm than good'.[44] MacDermott, armed with his credentials as a County Leitrim-born Catholic, assisted Dolan instead.

The decision to amalgamate the Sinn Féin League and the National Council was finally made after a two-hour discussion at the third annual congress of the National Council in Dublin at the end of August 1907. Hobson, O'Hegarty and Daly put forward the views of the Sinn Féin League in this discussion. The newly amalgamated body initially retained the name of Griffith's organisation. Hobson was elected as a non-resident member of the National Council's executive.[45] A week later he was re-appointed to the National Council's banking and insurance committee, which had been assigned the task of investigating the establishment of a model Sinn Féin bank.[46] Once Hobson moved to Dublin six months later, he was able to participate more fully on the executive of the National Council, which was known as Sinn Féin from September 1908 onwards. At the annual congresses in 1908 and 1909 Hobson and Griffith were elected co-vice-presidents of the organisation. In the election for the latter year, Hobson received only twenty-nine votes to Griffith's fifty,[47] indicating that he remained secondary to Griffith.

Move to Dublin

Hobson moved to Dublin on 11 March 1908, lodging with McCartan at 18 Belvidere Road.[48] He sought employment from several insurance companies but with no success.[49] Crime Special Branch received information that the National Council proposed to employ him as an organiser of cottage industries around the country, a position which, they feared, would give him many opportunities to advance the Sinn Féin doctrine.[50] This job never materialised.

Hobson ended up working as sub-editor for W.P. Ryan at the *Peasant*, which was based at 12 Temple Lane, off Dame Street.[51] In 1908 Hobson also established a short-lived weekly newspaper with a Sinn Féin editorial policy, which was issued from the *Peasant* office. It was called the *County Dublin Observer*, though it circulated elsewhere in Ireland.[52]

Prior to leaving Cushendall, Hobson had approached Casement about donating or advancing £200 to support a planned revamp and expansion of the *Peasant*. The plan, which did not come to fruition until the beginning of 1909, involved the paper changing its name to the *Irish Nation and the Peasant*, in order to appeal to a wider nationalist readership. The name change was designed to signify that the paper had outgrown, but had not repudiated, its roots as an agricultural paper.[53] Casement was unable to provide the requested £200,[54] but promised to give £50 and contacted some friends, including Bigger, about raising a lump sum of about £250 'for putting the paper on its legs for a long spell'.[55] As the paper fought a constant battle to stay afloat, Casement continued to worry about Hobson's employment prospects, wishing that he was 'fixed up' as Lynd was in London. O'Hegarty later came up with a scheme to subsidise the *Irish Nation and the Peasant* with £3 per month in order to keep the paper going.[56]

In yet another bid to help Hobson out financially, Casement proposed in April 1909 that his young friend should become his commission agent in Ireland. Previously Casement had used a London firm. He thought that Hobson could do the job just as well, and ensure that all goods were made in Ireland. Hobson was to receive a commission of 5 per cent on all expenditure. The arrangement began immediately.[57] Hobson sent items to Casement in Rio, care of the Foreign Office, Whitehall, London.[58]

During this time Hobson continued to propagate the Sinn Féin policy through speaking engagements. On 6 September 1908 he represented the Sinn Féin movement in a debate on 'Sinn Féin versus parliamentarianism' held in Glasgow. Hobson's opponent was J.J. O'Neill, a member of the Partick branch of the UIL, who defended the policy of the Irish Parliamentary Party.[59] During this debate Hobson voiced his disapproval of Irish universities being affiliated with different religious creeds, which he regarded as a British ploy to keep the Irish disunited.[60] In his rebuttal O'Neill ignored Hobson's overall criticism of religiously affiliated Irish universities, instead emphasising in particular the implication that Hobson criticised the erection of a Catholic university. He accused Hobson and the Sinn Féin Party of defying the wishes of the Catholic majority in Ireland by advocating secular education.[61] When he pointed out that Hobson was not a Catholic, members of the audience and the chairman of the debate urged O'Neill to withdraw this comment.[62] Hobson considered press coverage of this Glasgow debate 'meagre',[63] so he arranged to have the proceedings published as a pamphlet, entitled *Ireland or Westminster!*

Hobson's views on secular education had generated controversy before. The *Republic* repudiated the suggestion that Hobson had stated that 'the Sinn Féin policy aimed at divorcing religion and education in Ireland' during the course of a speech that he had delivered in Clontarf in December 1906. This suggestion was blamed on an 'entirely false and misleading' report published in the *Irish Independent*. Sinn Féiners were duly advised to get their Sinn Féin news from Sinn Féin newspapers.[64]

While based in Dublin, Hobson continued to develop his insurance scheme for nationalists, which was first announced in the *Republic* in late January 1907. Two years later, in February 1909, Hobson reported to McGarrity that the scheme was finally up and running: 'It has been a good deal altered and made more of a business proposition and now that it has been started it is doing very well.'[65] Hobson himself was insured for thirty shillings per week.[66]

Defensive warfare

The next item on Hobson's agenda was to follow up the insurance scheme with 'a programme of political action based upon it' and the publication of a pamphlet. Hobson asked McGarrity whether the Sinn Féin Club of Philadelphia would help fund the publication of the pamphlet: 'It would cost $75 and as you know (I suppose) I have not a dollar to spare in the world.'[67] The pamphlet in question was *Defensive warfare: a handbook for Irish nationalists*, which was published by the West Belfast branch of Sinn Féin in 1909. It outlined the Sinn Féin gospel according to Hobson. Influenced by the writings of Lalor, Hobson did not offer his readers any historical foreign parallels, but rather just plain common sense. The pamphlet was aimed at 'those who are working in the stress of a national movement'.[68]

Writing seven years before the Easter Rising, Hobson asserted significantly that 'we must not fight to make a display of heroism, but fight to win'.[69] Years later O'Shannon revealed that Hobson had the pamphlet published in Belfast by the successor of the first Dungannon Club because its message 'did not find favour with the IRB in Dublin'.[70] This foreshadows the split between Hobson and such IRB colleagues as future insurrectionists MacDermott and Tom Clarke (1857–1916).

In *Defensive warfare* Hobson did not repudiate the use of arms. Instead, he repudiated the *futile* use of arms:

> For those nations that are not strong enough to resort to arms to obtain and retain their independence, there is yet another means whereby they can assert themselves, and which can be made on occasion even more effective than an appeal to arms because it does not stake its whole fortunes on the chance of a hard fought field.[71]

What he sought to do was to suggest a defensive policy of resistance that would suit countries like Ireland, India and Egypt, which did not have the military might to oust their foreign ruler.

Hobson outlined a middle road between the insurrections of the past, which had failed, and constitutional agitation, which recognised a foreign government's right to rule over Ireland. Instead he recommended that the Irish people stop sending representatives to the Westminster parliament, using British manufactured goods, investing their money in British commerce, and enlisting in the British military, naval and police forces. In addition, they should stop acting as magistrates to administer British law in Ireland and appealing to that law to settle disputes. They should even decrease their consumption of taxed commodities such as whiskey in order to deprive the British government of tax revenue.[72]

Hobson pointed out that 'the intruding government' had only two weapons against such a policy of defensive warfare: conciliation and coercion.[73] Nationalists could defend themselves against conciliation by coming to a 'complete agreement' about their aims and determining 'to stop at nothing short of the fulfilment of those aims'.[74] As to coercion, Hobson argued that in Europe the time was past when artillery could be trained on a non-combatant people.[75] Instead, coercion would take the form of 'imprisonment and plunder', the latter referring to the imposition of fines and the seizure of goods.[76]

To offer people a degree of protection from such tactics of coercion, Hobson recommended the establishment of a community of 'financial solidarity'.[77] This community would take the form of an insurance scheme, which would 'protect Irish nationalists against loss of their employment on account of their activity in the national cause'.[78] The pamphlet's appendix outlined the terms of An Cumann Cosanta, the insurance scheme initiated by Hobson.

Alliance with Markievicz and Molony

Hobson's residence in Dublin provided him with the opportunity to forge a short-lived alliance with two nationalist women, Helena Molony (1883–1967) and Countess Constance Markievicz (1868–1927). Molony, who had joined Inghinidhe na hÉireann in the summer of 1903,[79] was a future Abbey Theatre actress and trade union official. She and her sister-in-law, Mrs M. Molony, shared an active interest in nationalist politics. Mrs Molony was a vice-president of Inghinidhe na hÉireann and in 1908 a member of the Sinn Féin executive.[80]

Hobson and Molony may have been acquainted before he moved to Dublin. The pair certainly would have had opportunities to meet through their active involvement in the advanced nationalist movement. For instance, in August 1903 Inghinidhe na hÉireann invited visiting members of the Belfast branch of Cumann na nGaedheal and the Protestant National Society to a *ceilidh* in Dublin.[81]

Hobson met Markievicz in Dublin in 1908 and served as her first mentor in the Sinn Féin movement. The countess had been converted to nationalism after stumbling across a bundle of back issues of the *Peasant* and *Sinn Féin*. She initially approached Griffith about getting involved in the movement, but her Anglo-Irish credentials roused his suspicions that she was a British spy. She then met Hobson who was, as she later put it, 'leader of the opposition' against Griffith on the Sinn Féin executive. The all-embracing Hobson kindly (or self-interestedly) took her in hand and launched her into the nationalist world. He arranged for her to join the Drumcondra branch of Sinn Féin and introduced her to Molony, who brought her into the fold of Inghinidhe na hÉireann. Years later, after their friendship had soured, due to political differences, the countess insisted that Hobson only patronised her in order to gain another ally in his power struggle with Griffith.[82]

Hobson assisted Molony in the establishment of the nationalist women's newspaper *Bean na hÉireann*. Molony had wanted Inghinidhe na hÉireann to start a monthly paper to counteract the dual-monarchy

3 Countess Markievicz (centre of second row) and Bulmer Hobson (seventh from right in third row) with Na Fianna Éireann

idea propagated by Griffith's paper *Sinn Féin*. She and her colleagues envisioned 'a women's paper, advocating militancy, separatism and feminism', but had no money to start such a venture.[83] Hobson, whom Molony later described as a 'spellbinder', suggested a way of financing the proposed paper. She recalled: 'We circularised a number of people whom we knew to be favourable to an Irish Ireland, asking them to help in the publication of a woman's national paper, by subscribing one shilling per month for six months, by which time we hoped to cover our printing bill by our advertisements.' The plan succeeded. Molony became editor of *Bean na hÉireann*, which featured 'a mixture of guns and chiffon' that appealed to both women and young men.[84] Sydney Czira recalled that the staff of the paper included, apart from herself, Markievicz, Gonne, Madeleine ffrench-Mullen, McCartan, McGarry and Hobson, the latter writing under the pseudonym 'B'.[85] *Bean na hÉireann* lasted from November 1908 until March 1911.[86] By then the need for the paper was not so urgent because a republican paper, *Irish Freedom*, and a women's suffrage paper, *Irish Citizen*, had been started.[87]

In August 1909 Hobson wrote to Devoy to introduce 'his friends' Mr and Mrs Molony. Helena's brother Frank and his wife had decided to emigrate to New York.[88] McCartan warned Devoy that in listening to Mrs Molony's inside story of the current state of the Sinn Féin movement, he was to take into account the fact that she disliked Griffith and favoured Hobson.[89] Markievicz replaced Mrs Molony on the Sinn Féin executive.[90]

Prior to the Molonys' departure for America, their home provided Helena with a base where she often socialised with nationalist friends on Sunday evenings. Many schemes were hatched at these gatherings. For instance, in early August 1909 Hobson and Markievicz decided to establish the second incarnation of Na Fianna Éireann as a militarised, nationalist boy-scout organisation.[91] Markievicz had been trying to set up a similar group for the past several months, but the project did not take off until she solicited Hobson's help.

On 16 August 1909 Hobson chaired a meeting 'to form a national boys' organisation to be managed by the boys themselves on national non-party lines'. The meeting was held in the hall at the rear of 34 Lower Camden Street, which Markievicz had rented.[92] It was the very same hall where Hobson had visited the Irish National Theatre Society in 1902 when he had been engaged in setting up the Ulster Branch of the Irish Literary Theatre.[93] In response to the blessing of a nationalist schoolmaster and announcements in *An Claidheamh Soluis* and *Sinn Féin*,[94] about one hundred boys turned up, 'mostly adventurers from the Coombe and neighbourhood'.[95] Hobson, Markievicz, Molony and a few other adults were also in attendance.[96] In his address Hobson explained that the organisation would be run on a semi-military basis, along the lines of the Boy Scout movement founded in the previous year by Robert Baden-Powell (1857–1941). In fact, it was one of the immediate objectives of this new group to counteract the influence of Baden-Powell's pro-British body.[97] Hobson's own aim was 'to recruit suitable members of the new Fianna into the IRB'.[98]

Michael Lonergan was about fifteen years of age when he attended the inaugural meeting of the Fianna. He later viewed this meeting held in a 'dingy hall' as the beginning – militarily – of the events leading up to Easter Week. '[That hall] should really be designated some kind of a national shrine for it was there that things actually started,' he asserted. 'This first organisation meeting of the Fianna was the beginning of the military history of recent time. Previous to that, nothing whatever was being done by any organisation in a military way.'[99] The Fianna were the first to begin drilling in twentieth-century Ireland. They went on to train members of the IRB and were among the few men, other than ex-British soldiers, to possess the military training necessary to become officers when the Irish Volunteers were formed in 1913.

Almost three months after the Fianna's formation, Hobson had to move home to Belfast for a year. During this period away, he made occasional visits to Dublin and continued his interest in the organisation. In his absence the countess was elected president, a position that she retained even after Hobson moved back to Dublin.[100]

Around the time that Hobson and Markievicz started Na Fianna Éireann, they also hatched a scheme to establish an abortive agricultural commune in Raheny. Hobson had come up with the idea of living on a small farm, possibly in an agricultural colony, so that he could spend half of his time farming and the other half reading and writing.[101] The problem was that he had no money for such a scheme.

The plan had been inspired by E.T. Craig's book *A History of Ralahine*. This book outlined the fortunes of a short-lived co-operative colony started by County Clare landlord John Scott Vandeleur on his Ralahine estate. Vandeleur had been inspired by a series of lectures given by the originator of the co-operative movement, Robert Owen, in Dublin in 1823. He invited Craig, an English follower of Owen, to organise the experiment among the tenants on his estate.[102] The Ralahine project worked for a while, but was later scuttled by a combination of Vandeleur's gambling debts and the fact that there was no legal recognition of the collective ownership of the property.[103]

Hobson lent Craig's book to Markievicz, who was charmed by the idea of an agricultural commune. Not only that, she had the financial means to put his idea into action. Fired with enthusiasm, Markievicz and Hobson, with Molony in tow, decided to resurrect the commune in Raheny. Markievicz rented Belcamp Park, 'a fine, big, roughcast-limestone house about six miles north of Dublin off the Malahide Road'. For a rent of about £100 a year, they got the house, which had about twenty rooms, seven and a half acres of land, stables and a walled garden – all in a state of disrepair.[104] They moved into the house at the end of the summer of 1909. The commune mainly consisted of Hobson, Markievicz, Molony and Donald Hannigan, a graduate of Glasnevin Agricultural College.[105] It was soon inundated by Fianna boys, with the countess and Molony ending up cooking and washing up from eight in the morning to eight at night. Hobson went into Dublin daily to deal with his political commitments. Only Hannigan was free to engage in any gardening.[106]

Hobson's decision to start the commune may have been influenced by his latest employment difficulties. By August 1909 Hobson's position at the *Irish Nation and the Peasant* was tenuous; he was allegedly being treated badly, presumably by the editor and others on the staff. McCartan revealed to Devoy that Hobson 'was considering whether or not he should throw up the whole thing'.[107] Casement considered the negative attitude toward Hobson 'stupid at best, and ungrateful in every way, for without you I doubt if it would be now alive'. He added that the paper was 'deadly dull' and that he subscribed to it 'only from a sense of loyalty to Ireland, as it means well'. The situation was so tense by September 1909 that Casement instructed Hobson to call at the paper's office to 'demand' a letter addressed to Hobson containing a postal order for an ill friend, if he had not already received the letter.[108]

The countess's husband, Casimir, arrived back from Poland to discover that his wife was the laughing stock of Dublin. Even their friend McGarry had branded Hobson, Molony and the countess 'idiots' for starting the commune.[109] Not surprisingly, the project had given rise to a medley of rumours: 'one was that Count Markievicz wanted to fight a duel with Hobson; another, that Hobson's Belfast friend, McCullough, feared that this married aristocratic lady would destroy Hobson as another woman not long before had destroyed Charles Stewart Parnell'.[110] Less whimsical rumours linked Hobson and Molony romantically. In Dublin pubs like Neary's, Count Markievicz was treated to a barrage of winks and jokes about the Raheny commune. Soon he too was exploiting the drama and comedy of the situation, being, as Sean O'Faolain put it, 'a man whose mind at the most slight and tenuous cobweb of a suggestion filled at once with fantastic visions of intrigue, three-cornered situations, assignations, and what-not'.[111]

To try to put an end to the commune, Count Markievicz harassed its members by telling unscrupulous stories about them. When this tactic did not work, he started to turn dinners at Belcamp Park into board meetings. The countess became uncommunicative when asked leading questions about the scheme by her husband. Molony 'leaned back and smiled' at the bohemian count's efforts 'to be business-like'.[112] Showing himself to be a surprisingly astute businessman, the count, armed with figures provided by George Russell, deflated their enthusiasm for the scheme. O'Faolain reported that the Raheny experiment, which lasted for about two months (probably September and October 1909), cost in net loss £250.[113] The countess and Molony remained until they could get out of the five-year lease.[114] Hobson headed back to the North in early November 1909, leaving behind rumours that a romance between him and Molony had failed along with the commune.[115]

Back to Belfast

In December 1909 Casement heard that Hobson had gone to an island in Strangford Lough, which was a refuge of his.[116] After a long silence, Hobson wrote to Casement in late January 1910. The latter replied that he wished he could help his young friend out of his difficulties, financial and otherwise, but could not, due to the distance and his own financial shortfall. Casement could only offer words of hope: 'Please God things will brighten for you ere long – I feel *convinced* of that. You have your days before you and much to do in them for Ireland – and yourself.'[117]

Due to lack of employment in Dublin, Hobson resided in Belfast until early 1911. During this time he joined McCullough in reviving the first Belfast Dungannon Club, reflecting the pair's continuing frustration with Griffith's leadership of Sinn Féin. Hobson was chosen honorary president of the Dungannon Club on 5 November 1909, delivered a lecture to 250 people at the annual Manchester Martyrs commemoration later that month and presided at the weekly Friday night meetings, at which members, such as Blythe and O'Shannon, delivered papers.[118] Based in Smithfield Square, the club held weekly classes in Irish language, history and traditional dancing. The women's division, Cumann na Cailíní, also offered classes in crochet and needlework.[119] Police detectives noted that Hobson, McCullough, McCartan and Richard Bonner met up in a pub in Carrickmore in late December to discuss the potential re-organisation of the Dungannon Club there.[120]

During his time back in Belfast Hobson helped Bigger with a number of publishing projects. These included a series of volumes on United Irishmen from Ulster (only the volume on William Orr ever appeared) and a centenary history of the Royal Belfast Academical Institution (or 'Inst', as it is commonly known), where Bigger had been a student.[121] When the school's Board of Governors read the completed manuscript, they refused to publish it. Hobson explained: 'They had thought, mistakenly, that their grandfathers and great-grandfathers had held the same narrow political views that they did. They were quite shocked at the discovery that they did not.'[122] A later history of the school stated that Bigger, 'with his nationalist sympathies, found it impossible to reconcile his interpretation of the early history of Inst with its subsequent development'. As a result, new authors were commissioned to write a rushed history in time for the school's centenary in 1910.[123]

Despite the failure of the Raheny commune, Hobson still harboured hopes of becoming a part-time farmer. In January 1910, on the suggestion of McCartan, McGarrity offered Hobson his family's farm in Carrickmore. The project came to nothing because it was believed Hobson would be unable to make a success of it. Hobson himself admitted he knew 'nothing about general farming', although his involvement with the Cushendall Poultry Society and the Raheny commune had provided him with some knowledge of 'poultry and vegetables – things that I could make out on if I were near a large town'. Hobson and his acquaintances in the area were also concerned that he would have trouble with the AOH and the local priest. 'If the AOH objected I could not get a man or a horse for a day's work in the district,' remarked Hobson. He kept himself busy with literary work, although he was not sure whether he would be able to stay in Belfast after the winter of 1910. Sometimes he thought he would be forced to emigrate, although he did not want to do that unless it was absolutely necessary. He had been out of work one year in the last three. He told McGarrity: 'Well – there's no use grumbling. I don't think there would be any use my taking up the place at Carrickmore under the circumstances – but I am none the less obliged to you for your offer.'[124]

In August 1910 Casement offered to loan Hobson £150 at the end of the year to buy 'that farm': 'There is no one I should wish to help more than you – for your sake and the sake of Ireland. Look on it as a loan to Ireland if you accept.' Casement urged him to discuss the proposal with his father. If Benjamin Hobson did not favour the farm scheme, Casement suggested that the money could be used to set Hobson up independently elsewhere, perhaps in America for a while. He recommended that 'if the farm is the best and most permanent outlook', then Hobson should 'stay on the old soil and face destiny straight in the eyes in Ireland'.[125] Instead of accepting a loan, Hobson suggested that Casement buy the farm so that he could become his tenant, a scheme which Casement warmly approved.

Casement looked forward to playing 'landlord and tenant' with his young friend. He joked: 'I'll make a hard dour landlord and evict you straight on your attempting to vote for Home Rule or anything connected with Ireland. You may vote for the British Empire, the Chin Tartars or the Yogis or any other number of the great British family but not for the Irish.' Casement also enquired about what sum would be needed to supply and stock the farm, glorying 'in the thought of going to *inspect* you and make damaging remarks on your system of culture'. He preferred to pay for the farm quarterly, rather than in one lump sum, so that they 'might get a better-sized place too with a spare room for the landlord, God help him, to arm and dress in when he called in for the rent'.[126]

Upon becoming better acquainted with Hobson's plans, however, Casement began to question the proposition because he felt Hobson was trying to juggle too many activities. Fearing that none of Hobson's endeavours would prosper if he spread himself too thin, Casement advised his young friend to give up writing in favour of the spade or the plough, so that he would have stable and secure employment. 'What I feel about it is, that you want above all things steady and regular work that must be done every day and each day. It is a tonic to have that kind of work and when a young man is so employed his spare time is much more enjoyable and much more profitable too.' Casement worried that if Hobson did not rethink his plans he would 'merely be saddled with a small white elephant'. He urged Hobson to choose between town and country, between the furrow of his brow and the furrow of the soil.[127] The farm plan was later put off because Casement could not spare the money at that time – and in any case he wanted to see the property before making a decision. 'I feel a brute saying this and putting you off,' admitted Casement, 'but I can't help it for the time.'[128]

Leaving Sinn Féin

Shortly after his move back to Belfast, Hobson returned to Dublin for a controversial secret meeting of the Sinn Féin executive on 20 December 1909. For several months the Hobson faction in Sinn Féin had been concerned about Griffith's willingness to countenance a potential alliance with 'dissident parliamentarian' William O'Brien's All-for-Ireland League, thus jeopardising Sinn Féin's commitment to abstention from Westminster.[129] O'Brien had founded the All-for-Ireland League in the hope of unifying 'all parties against the extreme unionists on one hand and the Parliamentary Party allied with the sectarian [AOH] on the other'. Both Griffith and O'Brien were anti-sectarian, preferred unionists to Irish parliamentarians and criticised 'Lloyd George's budget and the land bill buying out Irish landlords'.[130] Hard-line support for Sinn Féin's abstentionist policy was the main stumbling block to an alliance.

The December 1909 meeting featured a heated discussion of a proposal by O'Brien's Dublin solicitor, James Brady, that he and George Gavan Duffy should stand for election in Dublin constituencies, backed by both Sinn Féin and the parliamentary blocs of O'Brien and T.M. Healy.[131] Although Griffith feigned impartiality on the question, Hobson and Daly pressed him to concede that he supported compromise. Eight members of the executive voted in favour of Brady's proposal, while eleven members, including Hobson, remained adamantly against any sort of compromise with parliamentarians.[132] The extremists had won this battle over the moderates, but ultimately decided to walk out on the war.

Markievicz found it puzzling that Hobson did not take advantage of this victory. After the meeting he acted in what she considered 'an incomprehensible way':

> He had achieved what he had long been scheming for, and had got a definite majority for the extremists and in favour of ideas for which they stood. Mr. Griffith had received a definite set-back, and there was now nothing to prevent him from pushing up into Mr Griffith's position, taking the lead and forcing the pace of the organisation.[133]

Instead, Hobson and most of his supporters quietly dropped out of the Sinn Féin movement after the next annual convention, thereby contributing to the decline of the organisation.

Hobson's enforced move back to Belfast may have made it difficult for him to capitalise on his victory. In addition, he may have concluded that his energies would be used more profitably within the IRB, which was undergoing a revival, than within Sinn Féin, which was going into decline. The outcome of the general election in January 1910 had given the Irish Parliamentary Party the balance of power in Westminster. As a result, the public were more supportive of Redmond than ever. At the same time, a dynamic younger generation, with the support of veteran Fenian Tom Clarke, was gaining ground within the IRB.[134]

In October 1910 the sixth annual congress of Sinn Féin was held in the Mansion House in Dublin. Many usual attenders, such as former presidents John Sweetman and Edward Martyn, sent their regrets. The weekly *Sinn Féin* newspaper had grown thin in content, partially due to the dearth of news from a decreasing number of branches. The daily

Sinn Féin newspaper had closed down in January 1910, having existed for only six months. Hobson and McCullough did not put themselves forward for re-election. Tom Kelly replaced Hobson as Griffith's co-vice-president. Countess Markievicz, although she was part of the Hobson faction, remained a member of Sinn Féin and was elected to the resident executive. She later explained that she had stayed in Sinn Féin because it was one of the few organisations that admitted women as members.[135]

Hobson left Sinn Féin in late 1910. The frustrations that precipitated his decision to leave the organisation were similar to those that spurred him and McCullough to start the Dungannon clubs. Hobson recalled attending Sinn Féin committee meetings night after night. In his view some of these committees were more interested in winning seats in Dublin Corporation than in organising the movement around the country. The seeming futility of endless committee meetings and Hobson's continuing inability to work with Griffith resulted in his decision to drop out of Sinn Féin. O'Hegarty and McCullough left at the same time and for similar reasons.[136] Although Hobson linked the decline of Sinn Féin to their departure, the organisation was already on a downward slope before they left.[137] After leaving Sinn Féin, Hobson focused his energy on the IRB and the Fianna, the establishment of the newspaper *Irish Freedom*, and the formation of the Freedom Clubs, which supported the paper's republican message.[138]

In Hobson's view, political and temperamental differences led to his inability to work in harmony with the senior Sinn Féin leader. Griffith supported dual monarchy while Hobson advocated complete separation from Britain. Hobson viewed Griffith as 'a dogmatic and stubborn man who surrounded himself with people who echoed his opinion', adding that 'with a mind of my own I couldn't stand that'. Hobson later conceded that 'it was a bad thing for the movement that we didn't mix', and expressed his admiration for 'Griffith's single-mindedness and the manner in which he worked away in poverty for his ideals'.[139]

Views differ regarding the root of the rivalry between Hobson and Griffith and its effect on the Sinn Féin movement. Markievicz and McCullough saw the rivalry as more personal than political.[140] McCullough accounted for the tension between the two men in the following way:

> Hobson was a very headstrong and somewhat egotistical person, and being much younger than Griffith, the latter naturally resented Hobson's endeavouring to force his or our opinions on Griffith and his friends. This naturally created a certain amount of friction between two strong personalities, but I must say that I never knew it to interfere with either of them, in any action that would be for the good or forwarding of the movement.[141]

In contrast, Markievicz believed that the rivalry between Hobson and Griffith detracted from the efficacy of the movement, reporting that 'the two men became more and more bitterly opposed, and more concerned in blocking each other's schemes than in getting work done for Ireland'.[142] Michael Laffan has noted that the manoeuvrings of Hobson and Griffith 'took place on a modest, insignificant scale, and most Irish nationalists remained unaware of these sectarian squabbles between rival leaders who had few followers'.[143]

Conclusion

Hobson's chances of successfully challenging Griffith for the leadership of the Sinn Féin movement were slim – even if that had been Hobson's intention. He appears to have been more interested in spurring the Sinn Féin movement forward than in toppling Griffith from his senior position. Although Hobson was a much more dynamic public speaker than Griffith, his youth, extremist views, financial instability and tendency to spread himself too thin worked against him. Age and experience had taught Griffith that his forte was newspaper propaganda and that a degree of compromise was more likely to attract a wider variety of adherents to the ideology of Sinn Féin. This earned Griffith respect, enabled him to propagate his views and make a meagre, but steady living through his various newspapers and contributed to his political longevity (as compared to Hobson's). In addition, he had laid claim to the Sinn Féin 'brand' by bestowing the name on his newspaper in 1906.

Even outside Ulster, Hobson's support for separatism and his unwillingness to compromise made it difficult for him to maintain paid employment and a stable income. This was unlikely to earn him respect, especially from his elders. His establishment of the short-lived Raheny agricultural commune and interest in becoming a part-time farmer may have been attempts to apply Sinn Féin principles of self-reliance to his own life. As Casement noted, however, Hobson had a propensity to engage in too many activities simultaneously, thus lessening the chances for any one endeavour to prosper for long. Due to this tendency, Hobson suffered from exhaustion at key points during his nationalist career, which impacted negatively on his decisions and actions.

Both Hobson and Griffith were political theorists and propagandists with strong personalities who wanted things their own way. Griffith's willingness to compromise in order to attract a wider variety of supporters, or at least antagonise fewer people, frustrated the youthful Hobson. When a more mature Hobson later adopted this tactic himself, it was misunderstood by his IRB colleagues and contributed to his downfall within the nationalist movement. Although both men disapproved of the 1916 Easter Rising, one would benefit politically while the other would be condemned to the sidelines. The accidental and erroneous association of Sinn Féin with the insurrection would enable Griffith, who was 'lucky' enough to receive the benediction of imprisonment, and his party to fill the ensuing political vacuum while, ironically, Hobson, who once played the extremist to Griffith's moderate within the Sinn Féin movement, would later be ousted from the Irish Volunteers by an extremist *coup d'état*.

Notes

1 Robert Lynd, *Irish and English: portraits and impressions* (London, 1908), pp. 119–20.
2 Ibid., p. 120.
3 Ibid., p. 122.
4 Ibid. For Hobson's own account of this event, see *IYT*, pp. 27–8.
5 Davis, *Sinn Féin*, p. 32.
6 Hobson, *IYT*, p. 10. Devoy's invitation to Hobson and the result of the tour are mentioned briefly in the introduction to F.M. Carroll, *American opinion and the Irish question, 1910–23* (Dublin, 1978), p. 9.
7 'Irish Ireland – the National Council – the Resident Executive', *SF*, 2 Feb. 1907, p. 1; *R*, 14 Feb. 1907, p. 3.
8 Shane O'Neill (probably McCartan), 'Sinn Féin steadily gaining strength', *GA*, 2 Feb. 1907, p. 1.
9 'Hobson's American tour', *GA*, 2 Feb. 1907, p. 1; 'Bulmer Hobson's tour', *GA*, 16 Feb. 1907, p. 1. For a more detailed discussion of Hobson's first American tour, see Hay, 'Bulmer Hobson', pp. 83–90.
10 McCullough, 'Bulmer Hobson's work', *GA*, 16 Feb. 1907, p. 1; O'Neill, 'Sinn Féin steadily gaining strength', *GA*, 2 Feb. 1907, p. 1; Lynd, 'Hobson as a speaker', *GA*, 16 Feb. 1907, p. 1.
11 Hobson's itinerary included: 15 Feb. 1907, Grand Central Palace, New York City; 17 Feb 1907, the quarters of the Brooklyn Gaelic Society, Brooklyn, New York; 24 Feb. 1907, Park Theatre, Philadelphia, Pennsylvania; 1 Mar. 1907, Catholic Club Auditorium, Cleveland, Ohio; 3 Mar. 1907, Tomlinson Hall, Indianapolis, Indiana; 4 Mar. 1907, YMCA Hall, Chicago, Illinois; 7 Mar. 1907, Hibernian Hall, St. Louis, Missouri; 10 Mar. 1907, Faneuil Hall, Boston, Massachusetts.
12 'Hobson sails for home', *GA*, 30 Mar. 1907, p. 8.
13 'Indianapolis greets Hobson', *GA*, 9 Mar. 1907, pp. 1, 5.
14 'Sons of Erin honor Emmet', *Chicago Daily Tribune*, 5 Mar. 1907, p. 2; see *Boston Sunday Post* and *Boston Post*, 24 Feb.–12 Mar. 1907.
15 'Bulmer Hobson coming', *GA*, 19 Jan. 1907, p. 5; 'Bulmer Hobson's tour', *GA*, 16 Feb. 1907, p. 1.

16 McGarrity to McCartan, 17 Feb. 1907 (NLI, JMcG, MS 17,458 (2)); 'Bulmer Hobson's tour', *GA*, 9 Feb. 1907, p. 4.
17 'Bulmer Hobson's speech', *GA*, 23 Feb. 1907, pp. 4–5.
18 'Hobson is assailed by Irish leaguers', *Boston Post*, 5 Mar. 1907, p. 2.
19 'Hobson and the croakers', *GA*, 16 Mar. 1907, p. 4.
20 'Hobson sails for home', *GA*, 30 Mar. 1907, p. 8.
21 Qtd. in *R*, 4 Apr. 1907, p. 8.
22 'Bulmer Hobson is defended', *Boston Post*, 6 Mar. 1907, p. 10; Martin Mulroy, 'What the coming of Irish orator Bulmer Hobson to Boston means to cause', *Boston Sunday Post*, 10 Mar. 1907, p. 27.
23 McGarrity to McCartan, 26 Mar. 1907 (NLI, JMcG, MS 17,458 (2)).
24 Ibid.
25 McGarrity to McCartan, 17 Feb. 1907 (NLI, JMcG, MS 17,458 (2)).
26 'Hobson sails for home', *GA*, 30 Mar. 1907, p. 8.
27 *R*, 4 Apr. 1907, p. 7.
28 Davis, *Sinn Féin*, p. 28.
29 McCartan to McGarrity, 2 Oct. 1906 (NLI, JMcG, MS 17,617 (1); Sinn Féin amalgamation meeting minutes, 21 Oct. 1906 (NLI, MS 8198).
30 Sinn Féin amalgamation meeting minutes, 21 Oct. 1906 (NLI, MS 8198).
31 Ibid.
32 McCartan to McGarrity, 23 Oct. 1906 (NLI, JMcG, MS 17,617 (1)).
33 Sinn Féin amalgamation meeting minutes, 21 Oct. 1906 (NLI, MS 8198).
34 McCullough to Richard P. Davis, 14 Oct. 1957 (UCDA, DMcC, P 120/23 (12)).
35 'Sinn Féin League', *R*, 11 Apr. 1907, p. 1; McCullough, witness statement, 8 Dec. 1953 (UCDA, DMcC, P 120/24 (18); NAI, BMH, WS 916); McCullough to Davis, 14 Oct. 1957 (UCDA, DMcC, P 120/23 (12)).
36 *P*, 13 Apr. 1907, 27 Apr. 1907; Davis, *Sinn Féin*, p. 33.
37 Michael Laffan, *The resurrection of Ireland: the Sinn Féin party, 1916–1923*, p. 26.
38 Ibid., p. 25.
39 Ibid., pp. 25–6.
40 Ciarán Ó Duibhir, *Sinn Féin: the first election, 1908* (Manorhamilton, 1993), p. 82.
41 Hobson to McGarrity, 29 June 1907 (NLI, JMcG, MS 17,612).
42 Hobson to McGarrity, 21 July 1907 (NLI, JMcG, MS 17,612).
43 Ó Duibhir, *Sinn Féin*, pp. 26, 39.
44 Hobson to McGarrity, 21 July 1907 (NLI, JMcG, MS 17,612).
45 'The National Council – the third annual congress', *P*, 7 Sept. 1907, p. 5.
46 'An Chomhairle Naisiunta – the resident executive', *P*, 14 Sept. 1907, p. 6; 'An Chomhairle Naisiunta', *P*, 28 Sept. 1907, p. 5.
47 Davis, *Sinn Féin*, p. 174.
48 Précis, CSB, Mar. 1908 (NAL, CO 904/118).
49 Précis, SS, Mar. 1908 (NAL, CO 904/11).
50 Précis, CSB, Mar. 1908 (NAL, CO 904/118).
51 'The Irish Ireland Publishing and Printing Works', *P*, 7 Dec. 1907, p. 5.

52 Virginia E. Glandon, *Arthur Griffith and the advanced nationalist press in Ireland, 1900–1922* (New York, 1985), p. 278; Cathal O'Shannon, 'Bulmer Hobson, key republican figure of the early days of the century', *IT*, 9 Aug. 1969, p. 10. Glandon notes that the *Observer* was established in 1908, while O'Shannon states that it appeared in 1909.
53 Announcement in *P*, 12 Dec. 1908, p. 4.
54 Casement to Hobson, 19 Dec. 1907 (NLI, BH, MS 13,158 (3)).
55 Casement to Hobson, 10 Jan. 1908 (NLI, BH, MS 13,158 (4)).
56 Casement to Hobson, 7 Feb. 1909 (NLI, BH, MS 13,158 (5)).
57 Casement to Hobson, 7 Apr. 1909 (NLI, BH, MS 13,158 (5)). Hobson's work for Casement may have inspired his father to make a career change. In 1913 Benjamin Hobson began to be listed as a commission agent in the *Belfast and Ulster Directory*.
58 Casement to Hobson, 13 Apr. 1909 (NLI, BH, MS 13,158 (5)).
59 *Ireland or Westminster! Sinn Féin v. parliamentarianism: a debate in Glasgow between Mr Bulmer Hobson, Belfast and Mr J.J. O'Neill, Glasgow* (Dublin, 1908), p. 3.
60 Ibid., p. 8.
61 Ibid., p. 14.
62 Ibid., p. 19.
63 Ibid., p. 4.
64 'Secular education', *R*, 20 Dec. 1906, p. 2.
65 Hobson to McGarrity, 23 Feb. 1909 (NLI, JMcG, MS 17,453).
66 Hobson's An Cumann Cosanta acceptance form, 14 Feb. 1909 (NLI, BH, MS 13,165(2)). This form is filed amongst documents related to the Irish Volunteers' insurance scheme.
67 Hobson to McGarrity, 23 Feb. 1909 (NLI, JMcG, MS 17,453).
68 Bulmer Hobson, *Defensive warfare: a handbook for nationalists* (Belfast, 1909), p. 58. For a discussion of how Lalor influenced Hobson's strategy to gain Irish independence, see Chapter 1.
69 Hobson, *Defensive warfare*, p. 55.
70 O'Shannon, 'Bulmer Hobson, key republican figure', *IT*, 9 Aug. 1969, p. 10.
71 Hobson, *Defensive warfare*, p. 19.
72 Ibid., pp. 16–17.
73 Ibid., p. 26.
74 Ibid.
75 Ibid., p. 25.
76 Ibid., p. 27.
77 Ibid., p. 30.
78 Ibid., p. 59.
79 Nell Regan, 'Helena Molony', in Mary Cullen and Maria Luddy (eds.), *Female activists: Irish women and change, 1900–1960* (Dublin, 2001), p. 142.
80 Hobson to Devoy, 10 Aug. 1909, in William O'Brien and Desmond Ryan (eds), *Devoy's Postbag* (2 vols, Dublin, 1979), ii, p. 384. Richard Davis lists Frank Molony's wife as 'Mrs M. Moloney' (*Sinn Féin*, p. 174).

81 'Cumann na nGaedheal', *UI*, 22 Aug. 1903, p. 7.
82 Constance de Markievicz, 'Memories', *Éire*, 18 Aug. 1923, p. 5.
83 R.M. Fox, *Rebel Irishwomen* (Dublin, 1935), p. 121.
84 Helena Molony, witness statement, n.d. [probably 1950] (NAI, BMH, WS 391).
85 Sydney Czira, *The years flew by* (Dublin, 1974), pp. 50, 52.
86 Regan, 'Helena Molony', pp. 143, 146.
87 Molony, witness statement, n.d. (NAI, BMH, WS 391).
88 Hobson to Devoy, 10 Aug. 1909, in O'Brien and Ryan (eds), *Devoy's Postbag*, ii, p. 384.
89 McCartan to Devoy, 9 Aug. 1909, in O'Brien and Ryan (eds), *Devoy's Postbag*, ii, pp. 383-4.
90 Jacqueline Van Voris, *Constance de Markievicz in the cause of Ireland* (Amherst, 1967), p. 72.
91 Molony, witness statement, n.d. (NAI, BMH, WS 391). For more detailed discussions of Hobson's involvement in Na Fianna Éireann, see Marnie Hay, 'The foundation and development of Na Fianna Éireann, 1909-16', *IHS*, xxxvi (2008), pp. 53-71; Marnie Hay, 'This treasured island: Irish nationalist propaganda aimed at children and youth, 1910-16', in Mary Shine Thompson and Celia Keenan (eds), *Treasure islands: studies in children's literature* (Dublin, 2006), pp. 33-42.
92 Hobson, 'IRB and Fianna', pp. 18-19.
93 Ibid.
94 'A National Boys' Brigade', *ACS*, 14 Aug. 1909, p. 10; 'A Boys' Brigade', *SF*, 14 Aug. 1909, p. 4.
95 Michael Lonergan, witness statement, 1 Aug. 1948 (NAI, BMH, WS 140).
96 Despite reports to the contrary, Casement and Patrick Pearse did not attend this first meeting.
97 Eamon Martin, witness statement, n.d. (NAI, BMH, WS 591).
98 Hobson, 'IRB and Fianna', p. 20.
99 Lonergan, witness statement, 1 Aug. 1948 (NAI, BMH, WS 140).
100 Hobson, 'IRB and Fianna', p. 21; Hobson, *IYT*, p. 17.
101 León Ó Broin, *Protestant nationalists in revolutionary Ireland* (Dublin, 1985), p. 37.
102 'A history of Ralahine', *IF*, Oct. 1912, p. 2.
103 Sean O'Faolain, *Constance Markievicz* (2nd edn, London, 1987), pp. 88-9.
104 Ibid., p. 89.
105 Ibid., p. 91; Anne Marreco, *The rebel countess* (London, 1967), p. 133.
106 O'Faolain, *Constance*, p. 91.
107 McCartan to Devoy, 9 Aug. 1908, in O'Brien and Ryan (eds), *Devoy's Postbag*, ii, p. 383.
108 Casement to Hobson, 7 Sept. 1909 (NLI, BH, MS 13,158 (6)).
109 Molony, witness statement, n.d. (NAI, BMH, WS 391).
110 Ó Broin, *Protestant nationalists*, p. 37.

111 O'Faolain, *Constance*, p. 92.
112 Ibid., pp. 93–4.
113 Ibid., p. 94.
114 Ibid.
115 Regan, 'Helena Molony', p. 144. It would appear that Hobson moved back to Belfast in early Nov. 1909, given that he was chosen as the honorary president of the revived Dungannon Club in Belfast on 5 Nov. 1909 and chaired subsequent meetings of this body ('Dungannon Club, Belfast', *INP*, 13 Nov. 1909, p. 8). In addition, from 7 Nov. 1909 onwards Markievicz, rather than Hobson, presided over Fianna meetings in Dublin ('Na Fianna Éireann', *INP*, 13 Nov. 1909, p. 8). In mid Nov. 1909 police detectives noticed that Hobson was absent from Dublin and assumed that he had returned to Belfast. See Précis, SS, Nov. 1909 (NAL, CO 904/12).
116 Casement to Hobson, 23 Dec. 1909 (NLI, BH, MS 13,158 (6)).
117 Casement to Hobson, 16 Feb. 1910 (NLI, BH, MS 13,158 (7)).
118 'Dungannon Club, Belfast', *INP*, 13 Nov. 1909, 20 Nov. 1909, p. 8; 'Manchester Martyrs commemoration in Belfast', *INP*, 27 Nov. 1909, p. 8. Dubbed the Manchester Martyrs, William O'Meara Allen, Michael Larkin and William O'Brien were hanged for their complicity in the attack on a police van transporting two Fenian prisoners from the Manchester courthouse to the county jail in Sept. 1867. The attack resulted in an unarmed policeman being shot to death.
119 'Dungannon Club classes', *INP*, 18 Dec. 1909, p. 8.
120 Précis, CSB, Dec. 1909 (NAL, CO 904/118).
121 O'Shannon, 'Bulmer Hobson, key republican figure', *IT*, 9 Aug. 1969, p. 10.
122 Hobson, *IYT*, p. 36.
123 John Jamieson, *The history of the Royal Belfast Academical Institution, 1810–1960* (Belfast, 1959), p. 146.
124 Sean Cronin, *The McGarrity papers* (Tralee, 1972), p. 27.
125 Casement to Hobson, 8 Aug. 1910 (NLI, BH, MS 13,158 (7)).
126 Casement to Hobson, 28 Jan. 1911 (NLI, BH, MS 13,158 (7)).
127 Casement to Hobson, 11 Feb. 1911 (NLI, BH, MS 13,158 (7)).
128 Casement to Hobson, 30 May 1911 (NLI, BH, MS 13,158 (7)).
129 Richard Davis, *Arthur Griffith* (Dundalk, 1976), p. 15.
130 Davis, *Sinn Féin*, p. 61.
131 Ibid., p. 62.
132 Ibid., p. 63.
133 Markievicz, 'Memories', *Éire*, 1 Sept. 1923, p. 4.
134 See chapter 5.
135 Davis, *Sinn Féin*, pp. 66–8; Laffan, *The resurrection of Ireland*, pp. 30–1.
136 Hobson, *IYT*, p. 12; Hobson, witness statement, 26 Jan. 1948 (NAI, BMH, WS 82).
137 Ó Lúing, 'Talking to Bulmer Hobson', *IT*, 6 May 1961, p. 10; Hobson, *IYT*, p. 12; Laffan, *The resurrection of Ireland*, pp. 30–1.
138 See Chapter 5 and Hay, 'Na Fianna Éireann, 1909–16'.

139 Ó Lúing, 'Talking to Bulmer Hobson', *IT*, 6 May 1961, p. 10.
140 Markievicz, 'Memories', *Éire*, 18 Aug. 1923, p. 6.
141 McCullough, witness statement, 13 Apr. 1948 (NAI, BMH, WS 111).
142 Markievicz, 'Memories', *Éire*, 18 Aug. 1923, p. 6.
143 Laffan, *The resurrection of Ireland*, p. 24.

5

Rising fortunes in the IRB

Until mid 1908, surviving police reports portrayed Hobson as a leader of the Sinn Féin movement and an anti-recruitment activist with a propensity for delivering 'violent speeches' against Ireland's connection with Britain. From June 1908 onwards, a new picture began to emerge: police detectives definitely linked him to the IRB.[1] Even though Hobson had been a member of the IRB since 1904,[2] it is not overly surprising that police detectives did not recognise a direct link between Hobson and the IRB until four years later. It was not until Hobson moved to Dublin in March 1908 that his fortunes within the IRB really began to rise.

Hobson's move south happened to coincide with the return to Ireland of Tom Clarke, who had served fifteen years in English prisons for his part in an 1883 bombing mission. By accident rather than by design, the homecoming of this Fenian hero would be a contributing factor to an admittedly small-scale national revival of the IRB, whose membership figures were down to about one thousand men, mainly based in Dublin. Clarke, despite being old enough to be their father, supported the dynamic, younger rank-and-file members of the IRB, such as Hobson, who were engaged in publishing their own brand of republican propaganda. Lax discipline within the IRB at the time had allowed them to operate with little influence or interference from the organisation's leadership.[3] Clarke and these 'young gun' propagandists advocated a more active policy than the cautious course that had been pursued in recent years. They would eventually triumph over the existing IRB leadership. Whether or not discipline improved under the new regime is, however, open to debate. In any case, Hobson's rising IRB career must be seen in the context of this revival of the organisation during the period 1907–14.

The return of Tom Clarke

Although McCullough, with the help of Hobson, had been revitalising the IRB in Ulster for several years prior to late 1907, the national revival of the organisation is traditionally linked to Clarke's return, though Owen McGee has argued that such a conclusion is too simplistic.[4] Hobson and Clarke first met in early 1907, when Clarke made the arrangements for Hobson's American lecture tour, which began in February of that year. Clarke and his wife, Kathleen, the niece of John Daly, a veteran Fenian who had been one of Clarke's fellow inmates, returned to Ireland in November 1907 after an eight-year stint in New York. In early 1908 Clarke bought a tobacconist's shop on Amiens Street in Dublin and a year later he purchased a second shop at 75a Parnell Street (formerly Great Britain Street), where he operated as both a newsagent and a tobacconist. His Parnell Street shop soon became for IRB men from all around Ireland a meeting place where they could exchange the latest news, formulate plans for the future and share stories from IRB folklore.[5]

It was in Clarke's shop that Hobson, a frequent visitor, heard the tale of a few hundred IRB men who were marched out to Tallaght in 1867 with 'few arms ... no plan, no military objective, no commissariat'. A small group of British soldiers rounded them up, cut off their trouser buttons and marched them back to Dublin with their hands in their pockets: it was the easiest way for such a small guard to maintain control of so many prisoners. Some of the men in Clarke's shop laughed when Captain Harry Filgate of San Francisco told the story. Hobson, however, 'was filled with rage at the thought of decent men being so humiliated because of stupid and inept leadership'. As a result of the Tallaght fiasco, when the IRB was re-organised in 1873 the Supreme Council inserted a provision into the constitution forbidding a war against Britain without the support of the majority of the Irish people.[6]

While Hobson insisted on adhering to this provision in the constitution, Clarke and others would later ignore it. Hobson had received a key message from IRB folklore: the mistakes of the past, such as the staging of a futile insurrection, should be avoided in future. Clarke and others, however, had received a different key message: a blow for Irish freedom should be struck, no matter how futile the attempt.

Clarke's move to Dublin coincided with a shift in Hobson's base from his native Belfast to Dublin in March 1908. He resided in the capital until late 1909, when unemployment forced him to return to Belfast. Thereafter he visited Dublin on a regular basis, finally moving back in early 1911, possibly in April or May.[7]

4 Tom Clarke, a veteran revolutionary and father figure within the IRB

It was through Hobson that Clarke met many of the young republicans from the North, such as MacDermott and McCullough. Despite differences in age, there was a strong mutual attraction between Clarke and the active, enthusiastic, younger men of the IRB, who also included McCartan, O'Hegarty, McGarry and Diarmuid Lynch. Hobson and MacDermott, in particular, developed close relationships with Clarke.

According to Kathleen Clarke, her husband envisioned Hobson as 'another John Mitchel', the Ulster Protestant journalist and revolutionary of the nineteenth century.[8] Kathleen appreciated Hobson's kindness, especially to children. When their eldest son, Daly, was recovering from typhoid fever, Hobson came over to read stories to him on evenings when he was free. As much as she liked Hobson, however,

Kathleen warned Tom on more than one occasion that 'he was idealising the man too much'.[9]

Shortly after his arrival in Ireland, Clarke was co-opted to the Supreme Council as a replacement for P.T. Daly, who was alleged to have expropriated IRB funds contributed by Clan na Gael in America.[10] Prior to his fall from grace, Daly had formed, with Fred Allan and Jack O'Hanlon, a triumvirate that had led the Supreme Council for many years. Clarke had previously been a rank-and-file man, but was given the position of Treasurer on the Council's Executive 'partly because of his popularity and partly because the Clan knew and trusted him best'.[11] Clarke gravitated toward the younger men who were starting to gain positions on the Supreme Council. These included McCullough, who began representing Ulster circa 1908, O'Hegarty, who represented the South of England, and McCartan, a co-opted member. Together, they 'unconsciously' formed a bloc that challenged the leadership of Allan and O'Hanlon, who favoured a cautious, less active policy.[12] As McGee has pointed out, however, the Supreme Council by this point had limited power over the disparate activities of Irish separatists.[13]

The struggle for control of the IRB[14]

With the *Republic* long gone, Hobson and other young IRB men were keen to launch a new paper to give them a voice in the struggle for Irish freedom. Clarke recognised the need for such a paper and supported them in opposition to the conservative old guard of Allan, O'Hanlon and others.[15] According to Hobson, Allan and O'Hanlon finally gave way when Hobson declared that if they did not allow the young men to start a paper, he would establish one himself.[16] This was the genesis of a new monthly paper entitled *Irish Freedom*.

The newspaper was the first venture of the newly formed Dublin Central Wolfe Tone Clubs Committee (DCWTCC), which had been established as a cover for IRB projects. Its ostensible purpose was to provide direction to the Wolfe Tone Clubs, which were founded

> To propagate the principles of the United Irishmen and the men of '98 who strove for the complete independence of Ireland; to encourage the union of Irishmen of all creeds and of all sections for the freedom of their country; to inculcate the spirit of self-sacrifice and self-reliance by which alone true liberty can be obtained.

Among the DCWTCC's members were Hobson, Clarke, MacDermott, Allan and McGarry. The committee met in September 1910 to finalise arrangements for the new paper and to appoint an editorial committee that consisted of Clarke (chairman), MacDermott (secretary and treasurer), Hobson, McCartan, McGarry and Piaras Béaslaí.[17] Forced to agree to the publication of the paper, Allan and O'Hanlon refused to countenance Hobson as editor. Instead McCartan and MacDermott were named editor and business manager respectively.

Irish Freedom, which first appeared in November 1910, was openly separatist and republican. Not only was its key message controversial for the time, but the identity of its true editor was also a source of controversy. If Allan had hoped to edit the paper himself, with McCartan merely serving as nominal editor, he was soon disappointed. In the first issue McCartan ran Allan's editorial as an article and instead used an article by Hobson as the editorial, in which he boldly announced:

> We stand, not for an Irish Party, but for national tradition – the tradition of Wolfe Tone and Robert Emmet, of John Mitchel and John O'Leary. Like them, we believe in and would work for the independence of Ireland – and we use the term with no reservation, stated or implied: we stand for the complete and total separation of Ireland from England and the establishment of an Irish Government, untrammelled and uncontrolled by any other government in the world. Like them, we stand for an Irish Republic – for, as Thomas Devin Reilly said in 1848, 'Freedom can take but one shape amongst us – a republic.'[18]

Although McCartan insisted that he edited the paper from its inception until early 1912,[19] Hobson and O'Hegarty maintained that Hobson undertook most of the editorial work.[20]

Hobson and O'Hegarty wrote about 75 per cent of the paper's content, including most of the editorials as well as numerous articles. Hobson resurrected his pseudonyms from the *Republic*, penning some articles under the names of Fergus MacLeda and Curoi MacDare. P.S. O'Hegarty's *noms de plume*, Sarsfield, Lucan and Landen, related to the seventeenth-century Jacobite military commander after whom he had been named: Patrick Sarsfield, Earl of Lucan, who had been killed at the battle of Landen. Other contributors included Patrick Pearse, Thomas MacSwiney, Béaslaí and Blythe.

Allan and O'Hanlon made their disapproval of *Irish Freedom*'s openly separatist and republican editorial policy clear. Hobson alleged that after McCartan refused to be his editorial puppet, Allan tried to use money as a way of gaining control of the paper. To keep the paper afloat, either all IRB members or selected members were each levied a shilling per month.[21] As a key member of the Supreme Council, Allan held these monthly subscriptions and allegedly delayed making them available to the paper.[22]

During the same month that *Irish Freedom* made its news-stand debut, Hobson was appointed IRB secretary for Ulster instead of Patrick Dempsey, who was not only the last remaining 'old-timer' in the IRB in Ulster, but the Belfast Centre who had sworn Hobson into the IRB.[23] As Ulster secretary, Hobson became the official deputy of McCullough, who was the Ulster representative on the Supreme Council. In this new job Hobson was responsible for collecting monthly reports from county centres on the position and progress of the IRB in their area, forwarding these reports to the secretary of the executive of the Supreme Council and ensuring that officers were elected in each county for a two-year term.[24]

For security reasons, the IRB favoured oral over written communication. One of Hobson's first duties as Ulster secretary was to travel around counties Donegal and Tyrone between 12 and 19 November 1910, meeting with various IRB contacts in places such as Raphoe, Townawilly and Carrickmore.[25] Although police detectives, who trailed Hobson and other IRB suspects, knew when meetings took place, they only found out what was said during meetings if an informant was present.

In this period Hobson was a frequent speaker and organiser on the circuit of nationalist commemoration events, such as the annual remembrance of the execution of the Manchester Martyrs.[26] In November 1910, after his inaugural tour of Donegal and Tyrone as Ulster secretary, Hobson returned to Belfast to speak at a Manchester Martyrs demonstration on 20 November, which was mainly attended by IRB men. Three days later he arranged a similar meeting, which was addressed by Countess Markievicz. She asked the audience, which consisted of about a hundred boys under the age of seventeen, for a show of hands to indicate how many of those present were willing, in the same way that the Manchester Martyrs had been, to die for their country. Receiving an overwhelmingly positive response, she urged the audience to learn from the teachings of Hobson in order to prepare themselves for a future battle against Britain. Hobson then headed down to County Cork to speak at a torchlight procession and public meeting in honour of the Manchester Martyrs on 27 November in Macroom. He informed the assembled audience of five hundred that 'if Ireland was ever to get Home Rule it would be by such movements as the Fenian movement and not by constitutional agitation'.[27] Commemoration of the dead was always combined with a contemporary political message.

Occasionally, Hobson was able to combine nationalist speaking engagements with his work as Ulster secretary. For instance, on 10 June 1911, after giving a lecture at the Sinn Féin Hall in Newry in which he encouraged Sinn Féiners to dissuade fellow Irish people from acknowledging the king during the forthcoming royal visit, Hobson met with three IRB men to ascertain IRB strength in counties Down and Armagh.[28]

Thanks to a County Armagh-based police informant, it is possible to gain some insight into Hobson's ability to carry out his duties as Ulster secretary of the IRB. Trying to ensure the prompt election of officers proved to be a challenge in that county. On 25 March 1911 Hobson chaired a meeting attended by fifteen centres, which was held in Portadown to elect county officers. Thomas Cormackan of Lurgan raised the issue of arming the IRB, noting that money had been sent for arms four or five years previously, but all that they had ever received was a sample rifle. He also complained that every two years a stranger was sent to the county elections, making promises that were never fulfilled. As a result of Cormackan's remarks, the incumbent county centre refused to take office again and no one else volunteered as a candidate. Thus, they were unable to proceed with the elections. Hobson recommended that the old office bearers retain their positions until suitable candidates for office could be found.[29]

It was difficult to find a resolution to the problem. At the quarterly IRB meeting held on 17 April 1911 in Armagh, the county centre told the county secretary and the sixteen centres and members assembled that he had had no further instructions from Hobson since the meeting held on 25 March. New officers for the next two years still had not been elected when the Armagh centres held a meeting in the home of the county centre near Moy on 25 May. The men at this meeting expressed their displeasure that Hobson, who had been invited, was not in attendance and had not replied to any of the communications they had sent him.[30] By August 1911 a new Armagh county centre, John Southwell of Newry, had finally been elected.[31] It is unknown whether Hobson was more effective in Omagh on 2 May 1911, when a meeting was held to elect the centre for County Tyrone. On this latter occasion there was no informant present either to confirm his success or criticise the performance of his duties.[32]

Hobson's ineffectiveness in County Armagh may have been exacerbated by a breakdown in communications resulting from his second move from Belfast to Dublin, as well as by tensions in the IRB between the old guard and Clarke's youthful associates. Hobson explained: 'The conflict was the recurring one between an older generation, who wished to go slowly and quietly, and the younger generation eager to get things done.'[33] It was over the course of 1911 that the main battles for control of the IRB were fought.

Clan na Gael in America chose to back the Clarke faction. From December 1910 onwards it stopped answering Allan's letters.[34] This decision was echoed in the IRB company that McGarrity kept when he returned home for a holiday in July and August 1911: he associated with Clarke, Hobson, McCartan, McCullough and O'Hegarty during his travels through Dublin, Belfast and his native Carrickmore. The younger men joined him for jaunts in his motor car and for late-night chats at his hotel. He also attended meetings at Clarke's shop and at the *Irish Freedom* office. RIC Special Branch considered McGarrity's trip to Ireland significant, especially as the appointment of IRB officers in certain Ulster counties was synchronised with his visit.[35]

Allan and his colleagues may have lost American support, but they did manage to win the battle over the official IRB response to the July 1911 visit of King George V and Queen Mary, which was a source of friction between the two factions. The IRB leadership, in order to avoid anything overtly 'political', had decided that there should be no resolutions relating to the upcoming royal visit proposed during the DCWTCC's second venture, the March 1911 commemoration of the birth of Robert Emmet, the republican martyr of the 1803 rising. The commemoration meeting at the Rotunda featured a rousing oration by the future martyr of the 1916 rising, Patrick Pearse (1879–1916). Emboldened by Pearse's assertion that 'Dublin would have to do some great act to atone for the crime of not producing a man to dash his head against a stone wall in an effort to rescue Robert Emmet', McCartan wrote on the back of an envelope a resolution against a loyal address by Dublin Castle. Dashing his head against the brick wall of IRB discipline, he jumped on stage to propose his resolution. Clarke, although he had warned McCartan against making such a resolution, joined him on stage to second it. Court-martialled by the IRB for their act of indiscipline, the pair were later acquitted.[36]

The IRB leadership, in co-operation with Griffith and Sinn Féin, took measures to keep any potential hotheads among its membership in check during the royal visit itself. The women of Inghinidhe na hÉireann, who planned a protest for the day of the royal procession through Dublin, were angry and disgusted to find that their sympathetic young male friends in the IRB had been 'ordered' to boycott the procession (and, by extension, their anti-British demonstration) by undertaking a pilgrimage to Wolfe Tone's grave in Bodenstown, County Kildare.[37] How seriously IRB members took such orders is open to question. In any case, Markievicz and Molony persuaded themselves that they had convinced Hobson to disobey orders and join them on the streets of Dublin, and so felt doubly betrayed when he too travelled to Bodenstown on 8 July

1911. He even addressed the crowd at the graveside – although he was not on this occasion a headline speaker, that task being entrusted to John MacBride, the hero of the Irish Brigade that fought in the Boer War. Three days later Hobson went to visit Markievicz at her cottage at Ballally in Dundrum, County Dublin, where the Fianna scouts were holding a camp.[38] No doubt she treated him to a colourful expression of her disapproval. In 1923, Markievicz, by then contemptuous of Hobson because of his rejection of the 1916 rising, scathingly remarked that 'he was one of those who preferred the limelight and laurels to be won by a fierce speech at a rebel's graveside to the possibility of getting a hammering from the police or being arrested'.[39] In the future Hobson would have fewer scruples about disobeying IRB orders, but this would do nothing to alter the countess's increasing disillusionment with him. The orders that Hobson disobeyed were orders that she would have followed.

The IRB old guard eventually lost the war for control over the IRB on the battlefield of *Irish Freedom*. The conflict shifted into open ground in December 1911, when Allan and O'Hanlon seized that month's issue of *Irish Freedom*, half of which had been printed, and substituted their own version. As McCartan had possession of the galley sheets of the original version, he, along with Hobson and Clarke, decided to retaliate by publishing a rival edition. Although Hobson suggested making a fresh start with a new title, McCartan and Clarke insisted on retaining the name *Irish Freedom*. To distinguish their version, they printed on the cover the caption 'edited by Dr P. McCartan'. In response to the publication of two versions of the paper, the Supreme Council met to debate the issue, with Hobson, by special invitation, in attendance. O'Hegarty recalled that this meeting featured 'brilliant dialective by Hobson, and some very clever leading questions by Tom Clarke, and some very clever answers by MacDermott'.[40] The meeting led to the resignations of Allan and O'Hanlon not only from the Supreme Council but also from the IRB.[41] Clarke and the younger generation had finally trounced the old guard.

Getting ahead in the IRB

Hobson soon reaped the rewards of victory. Upon his return to Dublin in early 1911, he had transferred to the Teeling circle of the IRB. The Teeling circle, which operated under the pseudonym of the Bartholomew Teeling Literary and Debating Society, was, in Hobson's opinion, 'the largest and about the intellectually toughest circle in Dublin' and included many members of the Gaelic League.[42] As a result of the departure of

Allan and O'Hanlon, Michael Cowley chose to resign as centre of the Teeling circle. After Cowley's resignation, Hobson 'was surprised to find [him]self elected centre without there being anyone else proposed'. As centre of the Teeling circle, Hobson became a member of the Dublin Centres Board and soon succeeded Seamus O'Connor as chairman of that board in 1912. After Hobson's election as chairman he formed a special Fianna circle of the IRB that consisted of members of the Fianna.[43] As Dublin Centre Hobson became a member of the Leinster Executive. He was subsequently elected chairman of that body as well as Leinster representative on the Supreme Council. At that time (1912) about 1,500 men belonged to the IRB and about half of those members were based in Dublin.[44] Thus, Hobson came to represent a majority of IRB members.

Hobson also benefited when McCartan resigned the editorship (nominal or otherwise) of *Irish Freedom* in early 1912 because he was moving to his native County Tyrone to go into private medical practice. Hobson assumed the full editorship of the paper. He had the delicate task of wielding the editor's 'blue pencil' over his mentor's series of articles entitled 'Glimpses of the life of an Irish felon'. When Clarke received the proofs he was disappointed to find that Hobson had edited out a paragraph containing a heartfelt tribute to John Daly because it was too 'gushy'. Clarke abided by Hobson's decision because, as he explained to Daly, 'I trust in his literary judgement much more than I dared in my own'.[45] In reference to another instalment in the series, Clarke was less willing to accept Hobson's viewpoint, because he did not feel that Hobson possessed the life experience to judge the passage in question. In reflecting on his prison days, Clarke had found it particularly difficult to write a description of the 'silent system', which confined inmates to perpetual silence. The resulting description received the Hobson seal of approval, but Clarke was more interested in Daly's opinion because 'you have experienced what it is; he has not'.[46] Clarke appreciated Hobson's energy, enthusiasm and skill as a propagandist and organiser, but never forgot that his young friend had not suffered for the cause as he had.

In addition to his editorial work Hobson continued to ride on the republican bandwagon of speakers, which followed a regular schedule outlined by the nationalist calendar of commemoration. He had the distinction of being one of the headline speakers at the annual pilgrimage to Wolfe Tone's grave in Bodenstown on 23 June 1912. The Wolfe Tone and United Irishmen Memorial Association organised the event. The main function of this association, which was an IRB front that pre-dated the DCWTCC, was to raise money for a stone or bronze monument to be erected in Dublin in memory of the United Irishmen. Hobson served on a sub-committee of this association that was responsible for producing designs and plans for a monument and compiling information for fundraisers. Participants in the pilgrimage took the train to Sallins and then marched to Bodenstown, accompanied by a pipe band and Fianna boys dressed in uniform. Clarke presided over a short meeting at the graveside, at which Hobson and Cathal Brugha gave addresses in English and Irish respectively.[47] As is evident from this event, despite his participation in the Gaelic League and holidays spent in the Gaeltacht, Hobson mainly forged his name as a propagandist in the English rather than the Irish language.

In 1912 Hobson, having dropped out of Sinn Féin the previous year, began encouraging readers of *Irish Freedom* to start Freedom Clubs to propagate the principles for which the paper stood and to provide a sense of unity and cohesion for the scattered nationalist men and women 'who are not yet ready to bow the knee to the successful Empire'.[48] The Freedom Clubs were a republican propagandist organisation controlled by the IRB. The first club was inaugurated on 7 June 1912 in the Fianna Hall at 117 Victoria Street in Belfast. It is doubtful whether Hobson was in attendance, as his name does not appear in the *Irish Freedom* report of the inaugural meeting, at which McCullough, Blythe, Lester and O'Shannon assumed leading roles.[49] Later that year, on 15 October, Hobson gave the first weekly lecture to the newly established Dublin Freedom Club, which met on Tuesdays at 41 Rutland Square. This address, the base of the DCWTCC, underlines the IRB connection. *Irish Freedom* reported that other clubs were formed in Sligo, Galway and Maryborough (Port Laoise).[50] Áine Ceannt, the wife of future insurrectionist Éamonn Ceannt (1881–1916), recalled attending a meeting of a Freedom Club in the Dolphin's Barn area of Dublin, at which Hobson delivered a paper entitled 'Ireland a Nation'. She was critical of Hobson's judgement as a speaker, commenting that 'this was a very learned paper undoubtedly, but not suitable for the audience'.[51]

In addition to holding lectures, the Belfast Freedom Club also published leaflets, the first of which was entitled *The Flowing Tide*. It was a reprint of an article by Hobson that had been published in *Irish Freedom*. It may have been to reinforce the message of the Freedom Clubs that the Supreme Council financed the 1913 publication of *The Voice of Freedom*, a collection of articles from *Irish Freedom* selected by Hobson and O'Hegarty. Like so many of Hobson's nationalist projects, the Freedom Clubs started with much fanfare (at least in the pages of *Irish Freedom*) and then seem to have faded away.

By October 1913 the younger members of the Belfast Freedom Club deemed it 'not sufficiently active'.[52] In response, they joined with young members of the Gaelic League, the Fianna and Belfast working-class organisations to form the Young Republican Party in order to propagate nationalism and republicanism among young people. The Young Republican Party held indoor and outdoor meetings that featured lectures from invited speakers. Hobson addressed a meeting on 28 December 1913 while he was home to spend Christmas with his parents, who then resided in Marino, County Down.[53] Among the party's leading members were O'Shannon, who gave the inaugural address on 25 October 1913, and Nora Connolly, daughter of labour leader and future 1916 insurrectionist James Connolly (1868–1916).[54] The Young Republican Party was steeped in the tradition of the nationalist youth organisations that Hobson had established in his early days as a Belfast-based propagandist.

The emergence of potential threats

Not everyone agreed that Hobson merited his heightened position in the IRB. His rising fortunes resulted in harsh criticism from a fellow Protestant member of the Teeling circle and future famous playwright. In sketching a pen portrait of Hobson, Sean O'Casey (1880–1964) described him as

> Protestant secretary of the IRB, editor of *Irish Freedom*, and head bottle-washer of all Nationalist activities, with his moony face, bulbous nose, long hair covered by a mutton-pie hat, a wrapped [sic] look on his face, moving about mysterious, surrounded by the ghostly guns of Dungannon: Ireland awoke when Hobson spoke – with fear was England shaken.[55]

The portrait is an unflattering one. O'Casey hated Hobson, who he believed exploited his Protestantism in the national movement.[56] He was dismissive of Hobson's literary ability[57] and resented Clarke's adoration of this 'white-haired boy', who held such a high and seemingly unquestionable position in the IRB.[58]

By 1912–13 Hobson was arguably the most powerful person in the republican movement in Ireland, and, as such, likely to engender such hostility from individuals who believed they could do the job better than he. As F.X. Martin has pointed out, Clarke may have been the 'father-figure' who was revered for the traumatic years he spent in English prisons, but Hobson, with his seemingly endless energy, was the key organiser. In 1913 Hobson was at the apex of his IRB career.

O'Casey was unimpressed with Hobson's contributions to *Irish Freedom* as editor and writer. When O'Casey claimed that IRB members only read the paper out of duty and criticised Hobson's articles for being dull, Clarke threatened to throw him out of his shop and declared that he loved Hobson as he loved his own son.[59] If O'Casey had been angling for the editor's job for himself, he chose the wrong way to make his case to Clarke. This disagreement over Hobson was O'Casey's 'first difference' with Clarke. He later declared that 'it was pathetic to see Clarke's devotion to this Protestant shit'. As a Protestant active in the nationalist movement, O'Casey was probably resentful that Clarke viewed Hobson, and not himself, as 'another Tone or McCracken', two prominent Protestant United Irishmen.[60]

Other differences emerged as a result of O'Casey's increasing devotion to the labour cause. Jim Larkin's speeches and George Bernard Shaw's writings had had a strong attraction for O'Casey, the product of a working-class background. At O'Casey's instigation, an IRB committee was formed to explore how the IRB and the labour movement might help one another. O'Casey and MacDermott were delegated to meet with Larkin in order to get the labour newspaper, the *Irish Worker*, to cover IRB-influenced activities. Larkin agreed and in turn requested that *Irish Freedom* do the same for the labour movement. O'Casey was bitterly disappointed when only he and Clarke turned up for the committee meeting designated for discussion of this request. Hobson, Seamus O'Connor, Seamus Deakin and Peadar Kearney were absent. O'Casey suspected that Clarke had known all along that the others would not turn up.[61]

Although Clarke was sympathetic to the working class and the labour movement, he ranked the nationalist movement as the first priority.[62] The same prioritisation was reflected in the official position of the IRB and the personal position of Hobson, much to O'Casey's disgust. Hobson's 'friendly but neutral attitude' to the 1913 workers' Lockout, which he put forward in the pages of *Irish Freedom*, may also have alienated Connolly, who is reputed to have once encouraged Hobson to abandon Sinn Féin in favour of the labour movement.[63]

O'Casey eventually chose socialism (and ultimately communism) over nationalism, leaving the IRB during the 1913 Lockout. The catalyst for his departure was a general meeting of the IRB at which Hobson convinced the audience that, as a democratic organisation supportive of all Irish citizens regardless of class, the IRB should not intervene on the side of the workers. In response to Hobson's persuasive speech, O'Casey complained that the IRB 'was making no progress, and appealed only to clerks and artisans – the great body of the workers were set aside'. O'Casey's words were met with a surge of protest and a modicum of support. In the ensuing pandemonium Hobson, on the platform, allegedly drew a gun.[64]

Much of O'Casey's hatred of Hobson appears to have been class based. O'Casey may have assumed that Hobson's middle-class background played a beneficial part in his rise in the nationalist movement, and the IRB in particular. O'Casey also believed that, unlike himself, Hobson was among those whom the IRB had paid for their nationalist work.[65] The issue of whether or not Hobson was paid for some of his work in the nationalist movement dogged him for many years after the 1916 rising. According to O'Hegarty, however, Hobson was not paid for his work as editor of *Irish Freedom*, which was in contrast to MacDermott, who was paid for his work as business manager.[66] In any case, to O'Casey it appeared that while the IRB extended sympathy to a middle-class Belfast Protestant who had lost jobs because of his devotion to the nationalist movement, no such sympathy was extended to a working-class Dublin Protestant who devoted a great deal of time to the nationalist movement while trying to eke out a meagre living as a labourer.

Once the old guard had been cleared out of the Supreme Council and the way was finally open for new leaders to forge ahead, it was perhaps inevitable that competition between the contenders would ensue. Hobson was not the only one who had risen through the ranks of the IRB under the fatherly gaze of Clarke. The star of MacDermott, whom Hobson and McCullough had recruited into the IRB in 1906, was also in the ascendant.

Outgoing, athletic and handsome, MacDermott possessed, like Hobson, 'enormous self-confidence, single-minded drive and organisational ability'.[67] His biographer, Gerard MacAtasney, portrayed him as an ambitious young man whose desire to become a teacher was thwarted by his poor performance in mathematics in the King's Scholarship examination.[68] MacDermott worked as a gardener and a tram conductor before finding his true calling as a full-time, paid organiser within the nationalist movement.[69] Future detractors, who resented MacDermott for his role in the deceptions prior to the Easter Rising, questioned the depth of his intelligence and his past allegiance to the AOH. For instance, McCartan dismissed MacDermott as 'bright and energetic but mentally superficial': 'He had not an idea in his head when Hobson took him up and directed his "education" by telling him what to read and giving him books ... He was cunning rather than clever.' McCartan and Hobson both viewed MacDermott's talent for intrigue as a hangover from his AOH days.[70] Clarke's opinion, however, was ultimately the one that mattered. Although he once rebuked MacDermott for descending to tricks to gain votes during the North Leitrim by-election,[71] Clarke found in the young man a talented and seemingly loyal partner-in-revolution who shared his goals, his methods for attaining these goals and his propensity for string pulling.[72]

Despite his electioneering tricks, MacDermott had impressed Clarke

5 Sean MacDermott, Hobson's one-time protégé turned rival within the IRB

with his campaigning work during the 1907 County Leitrim by-election. Waged on his home turf, this campaign had allowed MacDermott to emerge from the shadow of Hobson and McCullough.[73] As a result, Clarke convinced him to become national organiser of the IRB at the end of 1908.[74] It was a job that gave MacDermott the opportunity to travel and meet nationalists around the country, building on the organisational work that he had previously done for the Dungannon clubs and Sinn Féin. In time MacDermott became business manager of *Irish Freedom* and succeeded John MacBride as Connacht representative on the Supreme Council. After Clarke and his supporters gained full control of the IRB, the Supreme Council sent MacDermott, whom Clarke described as 'one of the finest young fellows of the young school', as their delegate to the Clan na Gael convention in Atlantic City, New Jersey in September 1912.[75] Armed with ambition, a nationalist network throughout Ireland and Clarke's patronage, MacDermott was Hobson's most serious rival among the young men of the IRB.

In the autumn of 1911 MacDermott experienced a personal setback when he was nearly killed by an attack of polio.[76] After his recovery he stayed with the Daly family in Limerick before returning to work in Dublin, where he spent much time at the Clarke home under Kathleen's care.[77] Once physically dynamic, MacDermott was now crippled, forced to walk slowly with the aid of a walking stick.[78] In light of MacDermott's increasing closeness to the Clarke family in the aftermath of his illness, C. Desmond Greaves has surmised that 'Hobson may have suspected danger to his position as Tom Clarke's chief confidant'.[79]

O'Hegarty later claimed that from about 1912 onwards Hobson's relations with both Clarke and MacDermott began to deteriorate.[80] This deterioration was more perceptible and more rapid in relation to MacDermott. Louis Le Roux, the Breton journalist and biographer of Clarke and Pearse, revealed that from 1912 onwards MacDermott 'often had differences of opinion with Hobson, and professed no great love for his colleague'.[81] Although Hobson was unlikely to admit it, a rivalry for Clarke's affection, esteem and confidence appears to have sprung up between himself and MacDermott. The pair had been friendly during their Dungannon Club days in Belfast, but, according to Hobson, they began to drift apart after they moved to Dublin – even though police reports suggest that they stayed in the same cottage at 15 Russell Place between 1911 and 1913.[82]

The year 1912 is significant for two reasons. It was the first year in which Clarke and the younger men finally had full control of the IRB's destiny. It was inevitable that differences in opinion over future policy and tactics would emerge among the new leaders. It was also the year in which MacDermott began coping with life after polio.

Hobson blamed his drift apart from MacDermott partly on differences in background, education and values. While he never doubted MacDermott's deep sincerity as a nationalist, he did question his narrow partisanship, his judgement and his methods.[83] Hobson also suspected that after his illness MacDermott harboured an unconscious resentment of Hobson's able-bodied capacity for activity.[84] His suspicion may bear some credence in light of Le Roux's assertion that MacDermott's attitude toward Hobson changed in 1912.

In addition to the closer ties resulting from the time that MacDermott spent with the Daly/Clarke family, Clarke's shift in confidence from Hobson to MacDermott may also have been a response to Hobson's connection to people beyond the circles of the IRB. Hobson had a propensity for mixing with people from a variety of social classes and creeds, ranging from Catholic, working-class Fianna boys to titled Protestants such as Countess Markievicz and Sir Roger Casement.[85] While Clarke welcomed Hobson's involvement with the former group, he questioned his links to the latter group, even suspecting Casement of being a British spy.[86] Hobson's friendship with Casement certainly opened him up to a social and political world far beyond the circles of the IRB.

The formation of the Irish Volunteers

The year 1912 was not just that in which the entwined relationships of Hobson, MacDermott and Clarke began to fray. More significantly, it was the year in which the Liberal Party, dependent on the support of John Redmond's Irish Parliamentary Party, was induced to introduce the third Home Rule bill. Due to the abolition of the veto power of the House of Lords, the bill actually had a chance of passing this time. In response, unionists in Ireland and Britain mobilised against it. Among the unionist initiatives was the foundation in January 1913 of the Ulster Volunteer Force to defend Ulster against Home Rule by force of arms, if necessary.

Like many others both inside and outside the IRB, Hobson saw the formation of the Ulster Volunteers as an opportunity to start a similar Irish Volunteer movement. Hobson recognised that

> Here was a development of the first importance, for if the North could arm against Home Rule, and get away with it, the rest of Ireland would soon be shaken out of its foolish belief in constitutional agitation and would be compelled to arm also; and if on the other hand the Ulstermen were suppressed by English forces the wayward loyalty of the Northern province would probably take some new orientation which would enable North and South to come together on a basis of common antagonism to English interference in the affairs of Ireland.[87]

Realising that Ulster Unionist leader Edward Carson (1854–1935) 'had opened a door that could not easily be closed again', Hobson and his IRB colleagues decided to bide their time while getting 'ready to take advantage of the new situation that was rapidly emerging'.[88]

In his capacity as chairman of the Dublin Centres Board of the IRB, Hobson asserted at a meeting of this body in July 1913 that the time would soon be ripe to start an Irish Volunteer movement in Dublin. He suggested that members should start drilling immediately to ensure that they would have the skills necessary to take a leading role in the new movement. Drilling subsequently began at 41 Parnell Square, which was the house of the Irish National Foresters where Fianna leader Pádraig Ó Riain's father served as caretaker. Ó Riain, Michael Lonergan, Con Colbert and Eamon Martin, all of whom belonged to the Fianna circle of the IRB, drew on their Fianna training to provide instruction to members of the IRB.[89]

During that same month Hobson wrote to Devoy, urging him to support Pearse's plans to undertake an American lecture tour to raise funds to keep his school, St Enda's, open. Pearse, like Hobson, recognised the importance of providing youngsters with an education sympathetic to Irish nationalism. In preparation for this tour Hobson swore Pearse into the IRB in December 1913.[90] In the letter which he had shown Clarke and MacDermott Hobson confirmed that Pearse was 'all right and in line with us here'. He went on to praise the school's contribution to the nationalist movement:

> St Enda's in the only college preparing boys for the universities that is really and intensely national in tone, and although it is only a few years started already some of its ex-pupils have become active workers in the national movement, and if the school can continue I think we can look to it as the training ground of the one class in the community whose help the national movement most needs, and of whom it has fewest at the present time.[91]

The quotation underlines Hobson's belief that people from all social classes were valuable – even essential – to the nationalist movement and helps to explain his reluctance to provide active support to one class – the workers – during the 1913 Lockout.

Hearing nothing back from Devoy, Hobson wrote again in October 1913. Not only was Pearse proposing to undertake his American tour that winter, but he wanted Hobson to accompany him. 'This I am not inclined to do,' confessed Hobson, adding that in any case he would not consent to join Pearse on tour unless he knew that his presence 'on such a mission' had Devoy's approval.[92] Hobson was probably reluctant to go over to America at that point because he was busy helping to establish the Irish Volunteers.

In October 1913, according to Hobson, the Dublin Centres Board decided that the IRB should take the initiative in starting a Volunteer movement before someone else did. Hobson not only gained the Supreme Council's agreement to the scheme, but was deputed to act on the IRB's behalf.[93] The first challenge was to find a respected, but politically non-controversial, individual who could serve as the focal point for an Irish Volunteer movement. The IRB hit upon Eoin MacNeill (1867–1945), Gaelic League founder and professor of Early and Medieval Irish History at UCD, after his article entitled 'The North Began' appeared in *An Claidheamh Soluis* on 1 November 1913.[94] This article advocated the formation of an Irish Volunteer force.

Hobson did not want to contact MacNeill directly because he was concerned that his own known extremist views might prejudice MacNeill against the scheme.[95] Instead he met with the manager of *An Claidheamh Soluis*, Michael O'Rahilly (1875–1916; known as 'The O'Rahilly'), to discuss the formation of such a force. Hobson recalled: 'O'Rahilly said that if we could get fifty reliable men he would join them. I said I could find five hundred.'[96] Although O'Rahilly was not a member of the IRB, Hobson believed he understood the allusion to that organisation. O'Rahilly agreed to approach MacNeill about taking the chair at a meeting to discuss the formation of an Irish Volunteer force. When O'Rahilly and Hobson visited him, MacNeill sensed the hidden hand of the IRB and recognised that he was being recruited to play the part of the moderate frontman.[97] Although MacNeill was willing to play this part, he was determined to write his own script. With MacNeill on board, Hobson and O'Rahilly issued invitations to eleven or twelve selected men, five of whom were IRB members, to attend a meeting on 11 November 1913 at Wynn's Hotel on Lower Abbey Street in Dublin.[98] Although Hobson did not attend this first meeting, choosing to leave Dublin on business that night because he was concerned that his reputation as an extreme nationalist might prove problematic, he did attend subsequent meetings.[99]

In his book about his father's contribution to the Easter Rising, O'Rahilly's son, Aodogán, alleged that Hobson and the IRB did not play an important part in the formation of the Irish Volunteers. He based his argument on Éamonn Ceannt's account of the formation of the Irish Volunteers that appeared in the *Irish Volunteer* newspaper on 20 June 1914. Aodogán O'Rahilly argued that, as this article, which 'would have been read by all those who were involved', made no mention of the IRB's involvement, Hobson and the IRB could not have been responsible for the establishment of the Volunteer movement.[100] The reality is that the IRB was a secret republican organisation and any mention of its involvement in June 1914 would have jeopardised the concealment of the IRB connection, provided Redmond with more justification for his bid to control the new movement and alienated the moderate nationalists who were essential for swelling the numbers and maintaining the movement's all-party complexion. Showing a misunderstanding of the inner workings of the IRB, an organisation which he dismissed as 'largely imaginary', Aodogán O'Rahilly also suggested that Hobson did not attend the first meeting at Wynn's Hotel because he had to gain permission for his involvement in the Volunteer movement from Devoy.[101]

A second meeting with a broader base of invitees was held at Wynn's Hotel on 14 November 1913. It was at this meeting that a Provisional Committee, which eventually expanded to a membership of thirty, was formed.[102] The purpose of the Provisional Committee of the Irish Volunteers was to direct the Volunteer movement until a representative body could be elected. MacNeill and Laurence J. Kettle, the brother of Irish Parliamentary Party MP Tom Kettle, were appointed to the nominal position of joint honorary secretary of the committee. They were chosen for their moderate political views and public standing, which were likely to attract a wide constituency of supporters to the new movement. Behind the scenes Hobson served as the committee's unpaid secretary.[103]

Hobson maintained that the IRB had no formal control in selecting or appointing the men who were invited to the first meeting in Wynn's Hotel and those who were subsequently appointed to the Provisional Committee: 'The IRB were satisfied to see the Volunteer movement started and run on a practical basis, and they left the selection of the Provisional Committee to me.'[104] The men who attended these initial meetings represented a broad range of nationalist opinion. They included members of the IRB, the UIL, the Irish Parliamentary Party, the AOH and individuals who, at that time, had no official affiliation with any of these organisations.[105] They paid subscriptions to cover the cost of the room rental; Hobson and solicitor Seamus O'Connor each paid £1, which was supplied from the coffers of the IRB.[106]

By design, the Provisional Committee included nationalists of various hues. Due to the work of Hobson, the IRB in particular had a strong presence on the committee. What the Provisional Committee did not include was any official representation from the Irish Parliamentary Party, the UIL and the AOH. From the beginning the Provisional Committee had been willing to co-operate with Redmond and the Irish Parliamentary Party. Convinced, however, 'that Parliament was capable of solving every problem', Redmond, the leader of the most popular political party in Ireland, refused to countenance a physical force movement.[107] Any supporters of his party or members of the UIL or AOH who joined the Provisional Committee or the Volunteers did so in a private capacity.

Ironically, Hobson's involvement in the Irish Volunteers signalled the beginning of the end of his IRB career. Although the active role that he played in the formation of the Volunteers benefited the IRB, it was also a cause for concern. Early on, Hobson took an independent line in relation to the Volunteers that brought him into conflict with key members of the IRB. O'Hegarty later claimed that the Supreme Council of the IRB

> issued an order that members of the organisation while they were free to join the Volunteers were not to take a prominent part in starting them, or to be prominent in office amongst them, unless there was no alternative, that is unless there were not enough men in the particular district to start and to guide the local company. We attached importance to this, because we felt that there was great danger that the British might suppress the movement at its start, if it looked to be a physical force separatist movement rather than an all-party movement.[108]

Although Hobson in particular was publicly associated with 'physical force separatism', he was reluctant to abandon a project in which he had been such a key force. His decision, against what he probably viewed as IRB instructions rather than orders, to accept an official position on the Provisional Committee induced anxiety in members of the Supreme Council such as Clarke.[109] According to Clarke's wife, Kathleen, 'It shook the complete faith he had in Hobson.' Clarke and MacDermott decided to make the best of it, however, agreeing that 'perhaps the secretaryship was too important a position to leave in other hands than those of a member of the IRB'.[110]

In Hobson's view, by taking a leading role within the Volunteers he was helping to steer a broad-based movement that had an important part to play in working towards the IRB goal of an independent Ireland. His IRB colleagues, however, feared that Hobson's position on the Provisional Committee might jeopardise the secrecy of the IRB connection and, by extension, the continuance of the movement. In addition, Clarke and MacDermott may have begun to suspect that, with Hobson at the steering wheel, they might not be able to control the direction of the Volunteer movement.

Ireland and a potential war between Britain and Germany

Hobson's involvement in forming the Irish Volunteers did not divert his thoughts from the issue of Ireland's position in a potential war between Britain and Germany. As early as 1910, Hobson and Casement had begun discussing the developing political situation between Britain and Germany. They agreed that the two countries would go to war sooner or later and feared that Germany might mistake Ireland for a loyal part of the British Empire. Hobson engaged in similar discussions with Seamus O'Connor from August 1911 onwards, when he became a frequent visitor to O'Connor's new marital home in Drumcondra. O'Connor recalled: 'To show that the separation of Ireland from England was essential to the destruction of the Empire, and incidentally to ensure German aid in the event of such a war breaking out, we decided that it was necessary that the whole Irish situation should be placed before the German Government.'[111] As a result of these discussions, in late 1911 Hobson wrote two *Irish Freedom* articles that were designed to open the minds of Irish nationalists to possible outcomes for Ireland.[112] In these articles, Hobson predicted that if Ireland supported Britain in the war, the Irish would share Britain's ruin if Britain lost, but not the advantage if Britain won. If Ireland helped Germany to win the war, however, the Irish could secure their independence.[113]

Two years later, in 1913, Hobson asked Casement to write a memorandum on the issue. After Pádraig Ó Riain typed it up in Hobson's office, Hobson and Ó Riain destroyed the original, incriminatingly written in Casement's hand. On one of his visits to the O'Connor home, Hobson showed his IRB colleague the 'lengthy' memorandum. Deciding that it should be given to the Germans, Hobson and O'Connor induced the latter's wife to carry the memorandum on her person so that it would not fall into the wrong hands in the mean time.

In late 1913 Hobson approached the Supreme Council of the IRB to gain its sanction for a trip to America to give the memorandum to Count Von Bernstorff, the German Ambassador in Washington. The council not only agreed, though only by a small majority,[114] but also paid Hobson's expenses. Hobson duly sailed from Cobh to New York (probably via Southampton, because the Cunard line had recently and controversially stopped picking up passengers in Cobh) on 12 February 1914,[115] joining Pearse, who was on his lecture tour to raise money for St Enda's.

Upon arrival in New York, Hobson met with Devoy. Although Hobson later claimed that Devoy and other Clan na Gael leaders were 'sceptical about the probability of a European War', Desmond Ryan reported that as early as 1911 Devoy 'had advocated an Irish-German understanding, and prophesied a European war'.[116] In any case, Devoy was adamant that, if Hobson was going to return to Ireland, he should not meet with Von Bernstorff personally because such a meeting might leave a trail for the British Secret Service to follow. Hobson gave the memorandum to Devoy, who showed it to the German Ambassador.[117] Casement's memorandum was later published as a series of articles in the *Gaelic*

American under the title 'Ireland, England, Germany and the freedom of the seas'.[118] Casement followed up his memorandum in July 1914 with a trip to America, from where he subsequently journeyed to Germany.

Hobson's second trip to America was a significantly lower-key affair than his first visit. In addition to delivering the memorandum and renewing old acquaintance, he spoke at meetings sponsored by Clan na Gael.[119] Only two of his speaking engagements were covered by the *Gaelic American*. The success of his 1907 lecture tour was not forgotten, however. In promoting Hobson's forthcoming address at the Emmet Commemoration on 8 March 1914 in New York, the *Gaelic American* noted: 'Those who heard Mr Hobson on a previous visit, at a time when he was a mere boy, expect a telling speech from this sturdy Northern nationalist.'[120] Later that month Hobson and Pearse also addressed a Clan na Gael meeting in Philadelphia.[121] Their lectures were designed to serve three main purposes: to raise awareness about the need for an education system that served Ireland rather than Britain; to promote the Irish Volunteer movement; and to reassure Irish Americans that, contrary to unionist newspaper reports, Ireland was not on the verge of civil war.[122]

Hobson's absence from Ireland between 12 February and 24 April 1914[123] was badly timed, however. It diminished the IRB's influence on the Irish Volunteers during a key developmental period in which certain members of the Provisional Committee, without the sanction of their colleagues, began negotiating with Redmond. The ensuing battle for control of the Volunteers would lead to Hobson's downfall within the IRB.

Conclusion

Hobson's rising fortunes in the IRB coincided with the admittedly small-scale national revival of the organisation in the period 1907–14. A number of factors facilitated Hobson's rise in the IRB. His moves to Dublin in March 1908 and again in early 1911 brought him to the physical centre of the IRB's power base. On arrival he was a known quantity who had proven his worth through his able assistance to McCullough in reviving the IRB in Ulster and his prominent Sinn Féin activism. The return of Clarke to Ireland and his support for the dynamic young men of the IRB, including Hobson in particular, was instrumental in his rise. Clarke's age and prison record lent weight to the energy and enthusiasm of the young men, ensuring their success against the conservative old guard in the ensuing tug of war for control of the IRB. The most public manifestation of this conflict was fought on the field of the republican newspaper *Irish Freedom*, which Hobson not only helped to establish but also edited. Once the old guard had been trounced, Hobson rose quickly through the ranks of the IRB until he became a member of the Supreme Council. His heightened position enabled him to take several initiatives, such as the foundation of the Freedom Clubs, the formation of a Fianna circle of the IRB, the drilling of Dublin IRB members, the establishment of the Irish Volunteers and the delivery of a memorandum to the German Ambassador in Washington.

Yet, even while Hobson's star was in the ascendant, there were indications that it could just as easily descend. Firstly, he began to garner harsh criticism from certain resentful members of the IRB, such as O'Casey, who alleged that his high position in the nationalist movement was unmerited. Secondly, once the old guard had been cleared out of the Supreme Council, it was inevitable that the younger men would jockey for position within the new leadership and differences over future policy and tactics would emerge. Hobson was not the only one who had benefited from Clarke's support. MacDermott, Hobson's one-time protégé, had not only reaped the rewards of Clarke's patronage but had grown increasingly close to Clarke and his family after his recovery from polio. In addition, Hobson's connections to people, such as Casement, who moved in a social and political world beyond the circles of the IRB began to cause the narrowly focused Clarke some concern. Ultimately, however, it was Hobson's natural propensity to follow, rather than suppress, his own counsel when it conflicted with that of his IRB colleagues that ensured the inevitability of his downfall within the organisation. Hobson's decision to take an official position on the Provisional Committee of the Irish Volunteers, in defiance of Clarke and MacDermott, was to foreshadow key future events.

Notes

1 Précis, SS, June 1908 (NAL, CO 904/11).
2 See Chapter 3.
3 Owen McGee, *The IRB* (Dublin, 2005), pp. 349–50.
4 Ibid., p. 349.
5 Le Roux, *Tom Clarke*, pp. 80–1.
6 Hobson, *IYT*, pp. 32–3; Ó Lúing, 'Talking to Bulmer Hobson', *IT*, 6 May 1961, p. 10. See IRB constitution, 1873 (NLI, BH, MS 13,163).
7 As police reports indicate that Hobson spent extended periods of time in Dublin during April and May 1911, he may have moved back to Dublin at that time. It is difficult, if not impossible, to pinpoint the exact date because he was travelling back and forth between Dublin and Belfast so frequently that even the police who trailed him did not report that he was based in

Dublin until Nov. 1911 (Précis, SS, NAL, CO 904/13).
8 Kathleen Clarke, *Revolutionary woman: Kathleen Clarke, 1878–1972: an autobiography*, ed. Helen Litton (Dublin, 1991), p. 40.
9 Ibid., p. 46.
10 To what purpose Daly used this money appears to be in dispute. McGee notes that it was used to fund Sinn Féin city councillors' electoral campaigns (*IRB*, p. 350), while Leon Ó Broin indicates that the money was to cover family expenses (*Revolutionary underground: the story of the IRB, 1884–1924* (Dublin, 1976), p. 134).
11 McGee, *IRB*, p. 350.
12 McCullough, statement, 14 Oct. 1957 (UCDA, DMcC, P 120/29).
13 McGee, *IRB*, p. 351.
14 For a brief outline of this struggle, see Kevin B. Nowlan, 'Tom Clarke, MacDermott and the IRB', in Martin (ed.), *Leaders and men of the Easter Rising*, pp. 112–13.
15 Le Roux, *Tom Clarke*, p. 88.
16 Hobson, *IYT*, p. 38.
17 Le Roux, *Tom Clarke*, pp. 89–90. See 'The Wolfe Tone Clubs', *IF*, Dec. 1910, p. 3.
18 *IF*, Nov. 1910, p. 4.
19 McCartan, BMH witness statement, 11 Dec. 1947 (UCDA, DMcC, P 120/24/4); McCartan, witness statement, 5 Apr. 1948 (NAI, BMH, WS 100); McCartan, witness statement, 15 Dec. 1952 (NAI, BMH, WS 766).
20 In his witness statement, dated 19 Sept. 1947, O'Hegarty claimed that he and McCartan were both named nominal editors of *Irish Freedom*, but Hobson was the real editor (NAI, BMH, WS 26).
21 Accounts of how the newspaper was financed differ. The assertion of Le Roux that McCartan and John Daly provided £40 each for the initial capital to start the paper was not confirmed by McCartan. There was also a difference of opinion in regard to whether all or some IRB members were levied a monthly shilling to keep the paper going. See Le Roux, *Tom Clarke*, pp. 89, 91; McCartan, witness statement, 5 Apr. 1948 (NAI, BMH, WS 100); Hobson, *IYT*, p. 38; McCullough, witness statement, 13 Apr. 1948 (NAI, BMH, WS 111).
22 Hobson, *IYT*, p. 39.
23 Précis, SS, Nov. 1910 (NAL, CO 904/12); McCullough, witness statement, 13 Apr. 1948 (NAI, BMH, WS 111); Hobson, witness statement, 17 Oct. 1947 (NAI, BMH, WS 30).
24 At a local level in the IRB, members elected a centre to govern each circle of the IRB, which usually corresponded to a town or parish. In Ireland all of the centres in a given county elected a county centre. County centres, in turn, elected a provincial centre which would represent the province on the Supreme Council. A similar system was used to elect representatives for Scotland and the North and South of England. See IRB constitution, 1873 (NLI, BH, MS 13,163).
25 Précis, SS, Nov. 1910 (NAL, CO 904/12).

26 See Chapter 4.
27 Précis, SS, Nov. 1910 (NAL, CO 904/12).
28 Précis, CSB, June 1911 (NAL, CO 904/119).
29 Précis, SS, Mar. 1911 (NAL, CO 904/13).
30 Précis, SS, May 1911 (NAL, CO 904/14 Part 1).
31 Précis, CSB, Aug. 1911 (NAL, CO 904/119).
32 Précis, SS, May 1911 (NAL, CO 904/14 Part 1).
33 Hobson, *IYT*, p. 39.
34 León Ó Broin, *Revolutionary underground*, p. 135.
35 Précis, CSB, Aug. 1911 (NAL, CO 904/119); Précis, SS, July 1911 (NAL, CO 904/13).
36 McCartan, BMH witness statement, 11 Dec. 1947 (UCDA, DMcC, P 120/24/4).
37 Molony, witness statement, n.d. (NAI, BMH, WS 391).
38 Marreco, *Rebel countess*, p. 142; Précis, SS, July 1911 (NAL, CO 904/13). According to this police report there were 300 people at the graveside. Le Roux, in contrast, claimed that 5,000 people attended (*Tom Clarke*, p. 97).
39 Qtd. in Marreco, *Rebel countess*, p. 142.
40 O'Hegarty, witness statement, 19 Sept. 1947 (NAI, BMH, WS 26).
41 Hobson, *IYT*, p. 39; Ó Broin, *Revolutionary underground*, pp. 144–5; McCartan, BMH witness statement, 11 Dec. 1947 (UCDA, DMcC, P 120/24/4); McCartan, witness statement, 15 Dec. 1952 (NAI, BMH, WS 766).
42 Hobson, TV interview, 5 Dec. 1963 (RTÉ Libraries and Archives).
43 Hobson, *IYT*, p. 17.
44 Ibid., p. 36.
45 Tom Clarke to John Daly, 24 May 1912, qtd. in Le Roux, *Tom Clarke*, p. 110.
46 Clarke to Daly, 26 Dec. 1912, qtd. in Le Roux, *Tom Clarke*, p. 111.
47 'The Wolfe Tone memorial', *IF*, July 1912, p. 1; 'Wolfe Tone and United Irishmen Memorial Committee', *IF*, June 1912, p. 1.
48 'To our Belfast readers', *IF*, June 1912, p. 1; 'Freedom Clubs', *IF*, Sept. 1912; 'The scope and objects of the Freedom Clubs', *IF*, Nov. 1912, p. 4.
49 'Freedom Club established in Belfast', *IF*, July 1912, p. 1.
50 'Freedom Clubs', *IF*, Oct. 1912, p. 4; 'Freedom Clubs', *IF*, Nov. 1912, p. 1.
51 Áine Ceannt, witness statement, n.d. (NAI, BMH, WS 264).
52 Archie Heron, witness statement, n.d. (NAI, BMH, WS 577).
53 Précis, SS, Dec. 1913 (NAL, CO 904/14, Part 1).
54 'Republican meetings in Belfast', *IF*, Nov. 1913, p. 8; Cathal Ua Seanain (Cathal O'Shannon), 'The Young Republican Party', *IF*, Nov. 1913, p. 8.
55 Sean O'Casey, *Drums under the windows* (London, 1945), pp. 186–7.
56 Sean O'Casey to Shaemas O'Sheel, 26 May 1951, in David Krause (ed.), *The letters of Sean O'Casey, 1942–54* (4 vols, New York, 1980), ii, p. 800.
57 O'Casey, *Drums*, p. 273.
58 O'Casey to O'Sheel, 26 May 1951 (Krause, *O'Casey letters*, ii, p. 800).

59 O'Casey, *Drums*, p. 187; O'Casey to Horace Reynolds, 6 Feb. 1938, in David Krause (ed.), *The letters of Sean O'Casey, 1910–41* (4 vols, London, 1975), i, p. 697.
60 O'Casey to O'Sheel, 26 May 1951 (Krause, *O'Casey letters*, ii, p. 800).
61 O'Casey, *Drums*, pp. 191–2.
62 Le Roux, *Tom Clarke*, p. 122.
63 Desmond Ryan, *The rising* (Dublin, 1949), p. 26.
64 O'Casey to Reynolds, 6 Feb. 1938 (Krause, *O'Casey letters*, i, p. 697); Ó Broin, *Revolutionary underground*, p. 157.
65 O'Casey, *Drums*, p. 273.
66 O'Hegarty, witness statement, 19 Sept. 1947 (NAI, BMH, WS 26).
67 Michael Foy and Brian Barton, *The Easter Rising* (2nd edn, Gloucestershire, 2004), p. 6.
68 MacAtasney, *Seán Mac Diarmada*, p. 9.
69 Ibid., pp. 9, 19, 24.
70 McCartan to William Maloney, 18 Jan. 1924 (NLI, PMcC, MS 17,675/5); Hobson qtd. in McCullough, BBC interview transcript, 1964 (UCDA, DMcC, P 120/36). McCartan's and Hobson's assessment of their former IRB colleague is, of course, coloured by the role played by MacDermott in the deceptions leading up to the Easter Rising.
71 MacAtasney, *Seán Mac Diarmada*, p. 40.
72 Foy and Barton, *Easter Rising*, p. 6.
73 MacAtasney, *Seán Mac Diarmada*, p. 39.
74 Le Roux, *Tom Clarke*, p. 83.
75 Ó Broin, *Revolutionary underground*, p. 145.
76 C. Desmond Greaves, *Liam Mellows and the Irish Revolution* (London, 1971; reprinted 1988), p. 42.
77 Ibid., p. 45.
78 Foy and Barton, *Easter Rising*, p. 6.
79 Greaves, *Liam Mellows*, p. 60.
80 In his witness statement, dated 19 Sept. 1947, O'Hegarty indicates that relations between the trio began to deteriorate in the two years prior to their June 1914 showdown over the acceptance of Redmond's nominees to the Provisional Committee of the Irish Volunteers (NAI, BMH, WS 26).
81 Louis Le Roux, *Patrick H. Pearse* (Dublin, 1932), p. 287.
82 Précis, SS, Feb.–Apr. 1911 (NAL, CO 904/13); Précis, SS, Jan. 1913 (NAL, CO 904/14 Part 1).
83 Hobson, *IYT*, pp. 52, 71.
84 Ibid., p. 71.
85 Casement was baptised a Catholic, brought up a Protestant and died a Catholic, thus having a foot in both religious camps. Markievicz later converted to Catholicism.
86 Hobson, *IYT*, p. 52.
87 Bulmer Hobson, MS of 'The origin of Óglaigh na hÉireann', an article published in *An t-Óglách* (Mar. 1931), pp. 1–8 (NLI, BH, MS 13,169).
88 Ibid.

89 Hobson, 'IRB and Fianna', pp. 21–2.
90 Hobson indicated that he swore Pearse into the IRB in Dec. 1913 while Le Roux claimed that Pearse became a member in Nov. 1913. See Hobson, BMH witness statement, 26 Jan. 1948 (NLI, BH, MS 13,170). Twice before Nov.–Dec. 1913, Pearse had been nominated and rejected for membership in the Teeling circle of the IRB because of his past support for devolution and because certain members suspected him of political ambition. Due to these previous rejections the Supreme Council took the unusual step of co-opting him to the IRB (Le Roux, *Tom Clarke*, pp. 120, 126–7).
91 Hobson to Devoy, 4 July 1913 (O'Brien and Ryan (eds), *Devoy's Postbag*, ii, p. 413).
92 Hobson to Devoy, 11 Oct. 1913 (O'Brien and Ryan (eds), *Devoy's Postbag*, ii, p. 415).
93 Hobson, MS of 'The Origin of Óglaigh na hÉireann' (NLI, BH, MS 13,169).
94 Hobson, *IYT*, p. 43.
95 Eibhlín Tierney, Hobson interview notes, 4 Oct. 1954 (UCDA, EMacN, LA1/G/119).
96 Hobson, *IYT*, p. 43.
97 Eoin MacNeill, memoir, 1932 (UCDA, EMacN, LA1/G/371), qtd. in Tierney, *Eoin MacNeill*, p. 112. In his recollections Hobson does not mention being present during the initial approach to MacNeill. See Hobson, *IYT*, pp. 43–4; Hobson, 'Ireland's hour of destiny', in Martin (ed.), *Irish Volunteers*, p. 24; Eibhlín Tierney, Hobson interview notes, 4 Oct. 1954 (UCDA, EMacN, LA1/G/119).
98 The IRB members were: Bulmer Hobson, Sean MacDermott, Seamus Deakin, Piaras Béaslaí and Éamonn Ceannt. The non-IRB men were: Eoin MacNeill, The O'Rahilly, Patrick Pearse, W.J. Ryan, Sean Fitzgibbon, Joseph Campbell and D.P. Moran. Although Hobson did not remember inviting Moran, O'Rahilly maintained that he was on the invitation list (Hobson, 'Ireland's hour of destiny', pp. 25, 30).
99 Ibid., p. 25.
100 Aodogán O'Rahilly, *Winding the clock: O'Rahilly and the 1916 Rising* (Dublin, 1991), p. 98.
101 Ibid.
102 Ryan, Campbell and Deakin dropped out (Martin (ed.), *Irish Volunteers*, p. 96).
103 Hobson, *IYT*, p. 46.
104 Hobson, witness statement, 11 Nov. 1947 (NAI, BMH, WS 51).
105 Bulmer Hobson, 'Drilling moves on apace', *IT*, 21 Nov. 1963 (UCDA, DMcC, P120/40); Hobson, witness statement, 11 Nov. 1947 (NAI, BMH, WS 51); Hobson, 'Ireland's hour of destiny', pp. 30–1. In these sources Hobson listed the affiliations of the members of the Provisional Committee as follows: IRB members – Bulmer Hobson, Sean MacDermott, Piaras Béaslaí, Seamus O'Connor, Eamon Martin, Pádraig Ó Riain, Robert Page, Con Colbert, Michael Lonergan, Peadar Macken, Liam Mellows; Members

Rising fortunes in the IRB

of the UIL / Irish Parliamentary Party – John Gore, Laurence Kettle, Col. Maurice Moore, T.M. Kettle; Members of the AOH – Peter O'Reilly, Michael J. Judge, James Lenahan, George Walsh; Members not formally affiliated with any party – Patrick Pearse, The O'Rahilly, Thomas MacDonagh, Joseph Plunkett, Roger Casement, Éamonn Ceannt, Eoin MacNeill, Sean Fitzgibbon, Peadar White, Liam Gogan, Colm Ó Lochlainn. Pearse, MacDonagh and Plunkett later joined the IRB. In his various accounts regarding the Irish Volunteers, Hobson sometimes lists Éamonn Ceannt as an IRB member and sometimes as unaffiliated. This discrepancy may have arisen because Hobson was uncertain whether Ceannt, who is generally accepted to have joined the IRB in 1913, was sworn into the organisation before or after the formation of the Volunteers. In contrast, the witness statement of Ceannt's wife Áine recorded her suspicion that he joined the IRB on 12 Dec. 1912 (NAI, BMH, WS 264). The year listed in her statement may reflect a typographical error or a lapse of memory.

106 Hobson, *IYT*, pp. 43–4; Hobson, 'Ireland's hour of destiny', p. 26.
107 Denis Gwynn, *The life of John Redmond* (London, 1932), p. 19.
108 O'Hegarty, witness statement, 19 Sept. 1947 (NAI, BMH, WS 26).
109 Ibid.
110 Clarke, *Revolutionary woman*, p. 44.
111 Seamus O'Connor, BMH witness statement, 14 June 1948 (UCDA, EMacN, LA1/G/117).
112 Hobson, MS of 'The Origin of Óglaigh na hÉireann' (NLI, BH, MS 13,169).
113 Fergus MacLeda (Bulmer Hobson), 'When Germany fights England', *IF*, Nov. 1911, p. 5.
114 O'Connor, BMH witness statement, 14 June 1948 (UCDA, EMacN, LAI/G/117).
115 Précis, SS, Feb. 1914 (NAL, CO 904/14 Part 2); Précis, CSB, Feb. 1914 (NAL, CO 904/120/2).
116 Ryan, *Rising*, p. 24.
117 Hobson, BMH witness statement, 26 Jan. 1948 (NLI, BH, MS 13,170); Ryan, *Rising*, pp. 21, 25.
118 The first instalment appeared in the *Gaelic American* on 22 Aug. 1914 (pp. 7–8). The first part of the series was written in Aug. 1911 while subsequent parts were written between the end of 1912 and Nov. 1913.
119 Carroll, *American opinion*, p. 30.
120 'Ready for New York Emmet celebration', *GA*, 7 Mar. 1914, p. 5. For more coverage of Hobson's 1914 New York speaking engagement, see also 'Three notable speeches', *GA*, 28 Feb. 1914, p. 5; 'Hear hopeful messages from Ireland', *GA*, 14 Mar. 1914, p. 1.
121 'Pearse in Philadelphia', *GA*, 21 Mar. 1914, p. 8; 'Irish visitors in USA', *IF*, April 1914, p. 7.
122 See transcripts of Philadelphia speeches by Pearse and Hobson, Mar. 1914 (NLI, JMcG, MS 17,634). Parts of Hobson's speech appear garbled.
123 Précis, CSB, Feb. 1914 (NAL, CO 904/120/2), Apr. 1914 (NAL, CO 904/120/3).

6

The struggle for control of the Irish Volunteers

O'Hegarty, speaking as a member of the IRB's Supreme Council, once remarked that 'from the start of the Volunteers, we had had trouble with him'. He was referring to Hobson. In defiance of instructions from the Supreme Council, Hobson not only took a prominent role on the Provisional Committee of the Irish Volunteers, but later employed an IRB member as assistant secretary at Volunteer headquarters. In O'Hegarty's opinion:

> [Hobson] was, and is, a man of very great ability, earnestness, single-mindedness, and patriotism, who made very heavy sacrifices for the cause, but he was never able, or at any rate he has never been known to, subordinate his own judgement to the considered judgement of his associates. He had to boss everything and get his own way in everything. He was not co-operative unless when he was laying down policy and giving instructions.[1]

Hobson's innate confidence in his own judgement and refusal to follow orders with which he did not agree ensured that he would come into conflict with the IRB leadership at some time. His involvement with the Irish Volunteers provoked such a conflict.

Over the course of 1914 a public struggle emerged over who would control the Irish Volunteers: the original members of the Provisional Committee, many of whom secretly represented the IRB, or John Redmond, the leader of the Irish Parliamentary Party. This public struggle brought to the surface a private conflict over who would dictate IRB policy, particularly with regard to the Irish Volunteers. This second struggle was waged between Hobson on the one hand and Clarke and MacDermott on the other.

Michael Foy and Brian Barton have suggested that 'the story of Irish republicanism up to the Easter Rising was largely shaped by the fluctuating relationships between [the] triumvirate' of Clarke, MacDermott and Hobson: 'Their association began harmoniously but ultimately imploded spectacularly into mutual loathing and enmity which knew no cease.'[2] The underlying issue that divided the trio was their differing visions of the IRB's future path at a time when the IRB was finally in a position to influence political developments in Ireland through the conduit of the Irish Volunteers.

The Irish Volunteers and the IRB

The Provisional Committee of the Irish Volunteers decided to hold a public meeting on 25 November 1913 to enrol recruits in an Irish Volunteer corps. Although Hobson claimed that he had made all of the arrangements for this meeting, Seamus O'Connor, one of the IRB representatives on the Provisional Committee, reported that a deputation from the committee had booked the venue. Hobson was probably a member of this group.[3]

The deputation initially approached the Lord Mayor of Dublin, Lorcan Sherlock, about using the Mansion House, but, as a supporter of Redmond, Sherlock refused to give the committee permission. In Hobson's opinion, the Lord Mayor's response exemplified the official attitude of the Irish Parliamentary Party to the Volunteer venture.[4] In the end, the committee hired the Rotunda's Small and Large Concert Halls, the latter of which held about five hundred people, and the Rotunda Rink, a temporary building in the grounds of the Rotunda Gardens with a capacity of about four thousand.[5] As it turned out, even this, the largest venue at the time in Dublin, turned out to be too small for the event.

IRB men and Fianna boys, armed with pads of enrolment forms, served as stewards at the meeting, which attracted a full house in all three venues plus a crowd of three thousand, who packed the Cavendish Row area. Hobson and Piaras Béaslaí estimated that the number of enrolment forms filled out that night ranged from three to four thousand.[6] The main speakers were MacNeill, Laurence J. Kettle and Pearse.

Due to his extremist reputation, Hobson initially decided not to speak at the event,[7] but ended up addressing the overflow meeting in the Rotunda Gardens.[8] In contrast to his earlier nationalist career,[9] Hobson undertook few speaking engagements promoting the Irish Volunteers. This was particularly important in the early days of the movement's development, given that his extremist reputation would have been more of a hindrance than a help in attracting Irishmen of all political shades of nationalism.

At the Rotunda meeting the Provisional Committee issued a manifesto to the Irish people. The manifesto, written by MacNeill, outlined the object of the Irish Volunteers, which was 'to secure and maintain the rights and liberties common to all the people of Ireland'. Open to 'all able-bodied Irishmen without distinction of creed, politics, or social grade', the force was to be 'defensive and protective' and would not 'contemplate either aggression or domination'.[10]

The purpose (ostensible or otherwise) of the Irish Volunteers was the creation of a military force that would serve broad Irish national interests, as opposed to narrow party interests. There does not seem to have been any agreement, however, on what Ireland's broad national interests actually were. Members of the Provisional Committee as well as individual Volunteers appear to have fallen into two main categories, as identified by Colonel Maurice Moore, the brother of the writer George Moore. Some Volunteers, such as Moore, favoured the Irish Parliamentary Party's alliance with the Liberal Party and saw the Irish Volunteers as a mere 'political counterblast' to the Ulster Volunteers. The only fighting expected by members of this category was against Orangemen who refused to submit to Home Rule. Other Volunteers, such as Hobson and MacDermott, had long awaited the opportunity to raise a military force that could be used to recover Irish freedom. For them, England was the real enemy and they 'looked with horror on any appearance of an alliance with an English Party however temporary'.[11] Ultimately, it would prove impossible to keep members of these two categories together.

The self-elected Provisional Committee consisted of thirty members who held disparate nationalist views and, with the exception of Moore, had no military background.[12] Twelve were members of the IRB, four were members of the UIL or the Irish Parliamentary Party, four were members of the AOH, and ten were unaffiliated at that time.[13] Thus, the IRB formed over one-third of the Provisional Committee.

Hobson insisted that the IRB members who sat on the Provisional Committee did not form a secret caucus: 'They were free to differ and did differ on many questions.' According to Hobson, 'although the IRB had taken steps to secure and keep control at points that were considered vital, we made a genuine effort to get men from every party to work together in a non-party movement'.[14] Moore concurred with Hobson:

> Politics were never mentioned and party considerations did not influence the discussions. Indeed, it would have been difficult to discover the opinions of members; only in private conversations outside committee, the various groups to which the members inclined were disclosed. All were cordially interested in the Volunteers, and ready to sacrifice personal opinions in their interests.[15]

In response to the various challenges that faced the movement, this unified spirit dissipated over time.

Hobson praised MacNeill for his role as chairman in holding all of the disparate elements on the committee together: 'His charm of manner, his friendliness with men of all parties, his gift for conciliation and his absolute impartiality enabled him to hold together a Committee composed of very discordant elements. I knew of no other chairman who could have done this.'[16] It was not until after the first Volunteer convention of October 1914 that the Irish Volunteers gained a formal executive. Hobson claimed that, up until that convention, he met with MacNeill and Sean Fitzgibbon 'almost daily'. Moore, Casement and O'Rahilly often joined them for these meetings, which were frequently held in MacNeill's house in Herbert Park.[17] These individuals appear to have served as an informal executive.

Until the Provisional Committee of the Irish Volunteers rented an office of its own, meetings continued to be held at Wynn's Hotel. Hobson's private office at 12 D'Olier Street, where he worked as a freelance journalist, initially served as the organisation's address.[18] In early 1914, while Hobson was in America on IRB business, the Provisional Committee acquired its own independent base by renting two rooms on the first floor of 206 Great Brunswick Street (now Pearse Street).[19]

Although Hobson was committed to 'a genuine and frank co-operation between men of all parties', he used his position on the Provisional Committee to manipulate people and events on behalf of the IRB.[20] He secured a measure of IRB control by becoming secretary of the committee and ensuring that an IRB man was appointed to the position of paid assistant secretary at Volunteer Headquarters.[21] He explained that this measure of control 'was intended only to prevent the Volunteers from being captured by any other party and diverted from its publicly declared aims and used for partisan ends by other parties'. In his view, the conflict that developed between himself and Clarke and MacDermott resulted from their desire for IRB members on the committee to function as a caucus. Hobson feared that if the IRB formed a caucus, other elements would do the same and it would be impossible to keep the committee and the movement united.[22]

Hobson claimed that 'the control of the IRB was not apparent or suspected, but it operated very efficiently in practice'.[23] A shrill exposé of the Irish Volunteers written by Michael J. Judge, one of the few members of the AOH who joined the Provisional Committee, belies the first part of Hobson's claim. Judge certainly suspected a link to a secret circle, but, at least in print, did not name the IRB:

> It soon became evident that there were at least two cliques in the committee. One of these was dominated by Hobson, and always acted mysteriously. Peculiarly drafted resolutions would be sprung upon the

committee from time to time, and efforts would be made to get them adopted without discussion. Certain members of the committee would be prepared to vote for those resolutions, and, when possible, would cloture [*sic*] discussion.[24]

This alleged Hobson-dominated clique could not have been a mere IRB faction, as Moore, who was not an IRB member, often supported the resolutions in question. In his memoirs Moore praised the so-called extremists Hobson and MacDermott for being reasonable and easy to work with, but alluded to Judge as 'the noisiest and most obstructive' member of the Provisional Committee.[25]

Hobson's machinations helped to foster hatred in Judge, who openly admitted: 'Hobson in particular inspired me with feelings of dislike, almost repulsion, and from the moment of our first meeting that distrust and dislike grew stronger, despite my efforts to overcome it, until in a very short period it developed into active antagonism.'[26] Throughout his exposé, Judge attacked Hobson repeatedly. In his view, Hobson was a politician rather than a military man. Judge abhorred politicians, who he believed were all 'intriguers'.[27] He asserted that he had 'never met a man who possessed such a passion for intrigue as Hobson' and that 'even in the most trifling matters this spirit was manifested'.[28]

Judge had a penchant for attacking people in print. His involvement in the Volunteers was a source of derision frequently mined by Francis Sheehy Skeffington, the editor of the pro-suffrage newspaper the *Irish Citizen*. The newspaper criticised Judge for writing to Dublin's *Evening Telegraph* in July 1912 in order to make a suggestion for dealing with suffragettes: 'Why not use whips on the shoulders of those unsexed viragoes? Slender, springy, stinging riding-whips would serve the purpose admirably, and if freely used would teach them a lesson they are very badly in need of.' Sheehy Skeffington expressed concern that Judge might represent the general view of the Volunteer movement towards women – a view that he feared would be eclipsed only when they were needed to raise money.[29]

Judge accused Hobson of engaging in intrigue in order to influence the appointment of a paid assistant secretary for Volunteer Headquarters. It was one of the first divisive issues to face the Provisional Committee. Hobson proposed an unidentified young Belfast man who, in Moore's opinion, had the best qualifications on paper. Due to the Hobson connection, however, it was feared that he might be an extremist.[30] Judge felt that a Dublin candidate would be more appropriate because the Dublin-based Volunteer companies formed the largest part of the membership and thus provided the most funding to the organisation. Judge credited himself with countering Hobson's influence on this occasion through his success in rescinding Hobson's resolution to appoint his Belfast friend.[31] In the end, Liam Gogan, a student of MacNeill's at UCD, was appointed as paid assistant secretary. The appointment was made while Hobson was absent in America.

Judge's success was short-lived. Upon his return to Ireland, Hobson found that Gogan 'was not equal to the task', and pointed this out to MacNeill. As an outcome of their conversation, the Fianna organiser, Liam Mellows, replaced Gogan as paid assistant secretary, with, according to Hobson, 'satisfactory results'.[32] No doubt, in Hobson's (admittedly prejudiced) view, Mellows' IRB connection made him a more suitable candidate. Moore considered Mellows well qualified for the position, but no less an extremist than the rejected Belfast candidate.[33] Hobson later ensured that two other IRB members, Eimar O'Duffy and Barney Mellows, a brother of Liam, joined the office staff.[34]

Due to Hobson's efforts in mid 1913 to initiate drill instruction for IRB men, members of the Volunteers who were also members of the IRB tended to be better trained in drill than most of their fellow Volunteers. Hobson, at his own request, became chairman of the weekly meetings of the drill instructors, who were ex-British Army men. He asked them to train the most promising men as officers, insisting that 'in their selection they were to have regard only to efficiency and to choose the best material irrespective of party affiliations'. Thus, a preponderance of IRB men became officers in the Volunteers.[35]

Growth of the Irish Volunteers

By December 1913 ten thousand men had joined the various Irish Volunteer companies that were forming all over the country,[36] and the numbers continued to increase in the new year. The popularity of the movement created a plethora of organisational challenges for the insufficiently prepared and militarily inexperienced Provisional Committee. These challenges included developing policies and procedures, keeping track of affiliated companies, collecting subscriptions, recruiting experienced drill instructors, renting drill halls, and procuring the all-important arms. For without arms the Volunteers would be nothing more than a paper tiger. Arms procurement was particularly problematic, due to lack of funds and the British government's proclamation against the importation of arms into Ireland, which was announced shortly after the establishment of the Irish Volunteers.

Moore reported that discussions at Provisional Committee meetings tended to be 'diffuse', due to the size of the committee and MacNeill's policy of letting everyone have their say in order to ensure that all parties were treated equally. In Moore's view, it was impossible for such a large committee to provide efficient and effective military leadership. At his instigation, the Provisional Committee formed sub-committees responsible for specific organisational issues. He also advocated the creation of a three-member executive which, in his opinion, would be better able than a large committee to make military decisions.[37]

One of the basic tenets of the Irish Volunteer movement was that Irishmen would serve together 'without distinction of creed, politics, or social grade'. Thus, companies were to be established on a territorial rather than a party basis. Moore revealed that, although bringing together men of different religions, parties and classes pleased popular opinion, secret attempts were made by various political organisations to form companies made up solely of their own members.[38] The Provisional Committee refused to allow these companies to affiliate with the organisation. Not only would these companies be in contravention of Volunteer regulations, but they might try to band together to capture the movement for one political party. O'Rahilly alleged that the AOH, at the behest of Redmond and his associates John Dillon and Joseph Devlin, had been secretly instructed to form companies, affiliate with Volunteer headquarters, gain control of their local district and outnumber the original Volunteers at a future national convention in order to dominate the movement.[39] Even Judge, an AOH member, deplored this attempt to contravene the Volunteers' commitment to an all-party organisation.

Volunteer numbers increased significantly in response to the Curragh Incident on 20 March 1914 and the Ulster Volunteer Force's gunrunning at Larne in April 1914. When military officers stationed at the Curragh were given the option of resigning rather than coercing Ulster on the Home Rule issue, this sent a message to nationalist Ireland that the British government could not be relied upon to tackle the Ulster Volunteers.[40] The viewpoint was reinforced when the authorities took no action after the Ulster Volunteers ran guns into Larne, County Antrim, in defiance of the recent proclamation against arms importation into Ireland. Charles Hannon explains:

> The suspicion that the government was in cahoots with the Carsonites was to many 'proved' by the Larne gun-running. The distrust of the nationalist supporters of the British government was complete. The Volunteers now had to look to themselves for protection against unionist threats. This realisation proved to be a landmark in the development of the Irish Volunteers and led to a massive influx of recruits.

Between 24 April and the end of May 1914 at least 192 new Volunteer companies were formed, with another 64 companies established in early June.[41] Membership numbers were now nearing a hundred thousand.

Hobson, as the IRB's prime mover on the Provisional Committee, missed part of this developmental period while he was away from Ireland between 12 February and 24 April 1914.[42] Upon his return from the United States, he became aware that, in his absence, MacNeill, Casement and Moore had begun negotiating with Redmond regarding the governance of the Irish Volunteers. The trio's decision to approach Redmond – a decision that was made without consulting the Provisional Committee – was symptomatic of the crosscurrents on the committee and the lack of concurrence on the Irish Volunteers' underlying purpose.

Moore, in consultation with MacNeill and Casement, instigated negotiations. As the only military officer on the Provisional Committee, he was more conscious than anyone else of the deficiencies of the Irish Volunteer movement. The Ulster Volunteers, whom he feared the Irish Volunteers would be forced to fight, had the benefit of money, legal advisors, retired army officers and the backing of the Conservative Party. In contrast, the Irish Volunteers had no money, no arms and the hostility of a 'jealous political party' that was 'more powerful than ever', due to the imminent passage of the third Home Rule bill.[43] He recognised that 'only Redmond was in such a position of authority that a call to arms would be obeyed by the whole country ... a countermand from him would paralyse our actions'.[44] Thus, Moore came to the conclusion that 'if the great Ulster Tory alliance were to be countered, all National Ireland must be bound in a solid phalanx, and this could not be effected without the co-operation of the Irish Party'.[45] For the Irish Volunteers, 'co-operation' was the operative word.

The pressures that accompanied the expansion of the Volunteer movement also convinced MacNeill and Casement that it was necessary to secure Redmond's support. Their overtures were well timed. As Charles Hannon has noted, 'the prospect of an armed Irish Volunteer Force controlled by an independent body of men free from any discernible political allegiance backed and supported by the population at large could not but be a major anxiety for Redmond'.[46] Alarmed by events in Ulster and the resulting growth of the Irish Volunteers, Redmond was now keen to gain control of the movement that he had previously spurned, so that he could bolster up his influence in both Ireland and London.[47] For Redmond, 'control' was the operative word.

Although initial contact was made by Moore in March 1914, negotiations with Redmond began in earnest the following month and continued throughout May and into June.[48] Unbeknown to Redmond, these negotiations had no official sanction from the Provisional Committee: MacNeill, Casement and Moore were not authorised by the committee to negotiate on its behalf and they did not report back to it.[49]

Although Moore conceded that the negotiations were never discussed at committee meetings, he maintained that members knew what was going on and recognised the need to secure Redmond's co-operation.[50] In Hobson's view, the committee was not 'bound by anything unless it was formally reported to, and accepted by, us, and that if, in the meantime, MacNeill could maintain contacts or create understanding at least no harm was being done and much good might result'.[51] Had Hobson been aware of the exact proposals under discussion, he might have felt differently. Judge, ever suspicious of Hobson, unjustly accused him of being 'concerned in the intrigue' and influencing MacNeill in the negotiations.[52] Hobson's position on the informal executive probably fed Judge's suspicions.

During the negotiations two main plans were discussed: the formation of a joint executive consisting of three to nine members; and the possibility of Ireland's two Volunteer movements coming together as a territorial army – even though the negotiators were uncertain whether British legislation relating to such an army extended to Ireland.[53] IRB representatives on the committee would not have agreed to either of these plans. The plan for a joint executive would have weakened the IRB's position within the Volunteer movement because none of the proposed members was an IRB man.[54] The territorial army proposal was put forward in the hope of securing officers, arms and money. MacNeill, Casement and Moore eventually realised, however, that this proposal could not be reconciled with the patriotism of individual Volunteers, who most certainly had not joined the movement just to become a part of the British Army in Ireland.[55] Aside from that major obstacle, neither the Ulster Volunteers nor the British War Office was likely to agree to it. As Casement wrote to Moore:

> I think the best idea now is to drop the idea altogether, and simply stick to our full national programme here. Get the movement fully supported in Ireland; get as many men drilled and trained as we can; encourage the national feeling, and try to bring back pride, manly pride, to a discouraged and depressed people. Let that alone be our task – and leave the future of such an 'Irish Army' to the future.[56]

The self-appointed negotiators appear to have finally comprehended that they had overstepped the bounds of their authority.

In Hobson's retrospective account of the negotiations, he reported that Redmond was only interested in gaining the 'homage and obedience' of the Irish Volunteers.[57] It was due to Redmond's insistence on domination rather than co-operation that the private negotiations ultimately came to nothing. While these negotiations were under way, the struggle for control of the Irish Volunteers was also evident in the public press.

Initially, the Irish Parliamentary Party insinuated that the Volunteer movement was a spontaneous manifestation of the will of the people rather than the brainchild of the Provisional Committee. As negotiations started to break down the party began to raise questions regarding the 'direction of the Volunteer movement and its real purpose'.[58] Redmond's party machine proved more successful than the Provisional Committee in putting forward its viewpoint, particularly in the provincial press.[59]

The self-appointed nature of the Provisional Committee made it vulnerable to Redmond's attempts to gain control. Recognising this, the committee decided on 9 May 1914 to organise a representative conference of the Irish Volunteers at which elections could be held. The Provisional Committee 'had no desire to retain office, and would have held a convention at an earlier date had the state of the Volunteer organisation allowed', explained Hobson, adding that the movement was still 'disorganised and fluid' with new recruits flowing in. In light of the 'political storms ahead', however, the committee 'decided that the sooner a convention was held and an elected governing body put into the saddle the better'.[60]

The co-option of Redmond's nominees onto the Provisional Committee

Hobson believed that plans to hold a Volunteer convention forced Redmond's hand. The Irish Party leader shocked the Provisional Committee with an ultimatum published in the Irish press on 10 June 1914. He demanded that twenty-five of his own nominees from different parts of the country be allowed onto the Provisional Committee to ensure not only more balanced geographic representation, but increased representation in support of his party, which, unlike the current Provisional Committee, had been elected by the majority of Irishmen. If the committee did not accede to his demands, he threatened to start rival Volunteer county boards among his own supporters around the country.[61]

This threat held considerable weight in reference to areas outside Dublin where effective organisation of the Volunteers had proved problematic. As Charles Hannon has pointed out, 'due to the presence of the Provisional Committee and the ease of travel, in Dublin City the Volunteers were highly organised at an early stage'.[62] Organisational progress was much slower elsewhere in the country because of a lack of trained military officers and the obvious travel barriers. Redmond possessed the party machinery and popular support necessary to seize local leadership around the country. Hobson later described Redmond's threat as 'an attempt to force an immediate show-down, quite in keeping with Redmond's dictatorial attitude when he was in Ireland', adding that if Redmond had been 'half as tough in his dealings with the British government he might have cut a much better figure in history'.[63]

The Provisional Committee needed to respond to Redmond's ultimatum immediately and met on the day that it was published in order to formulate a reply. Hobson reported that committee members 'were quite willing to welcome the addition of representative men to their body, but they held that such men should be really representative of the Volunteers, and not merely of a political machine that had since their foundation been hostile to the Volunteers'.[64] By adding twenty-five of his own supporters to the Provisional Committee, Redmond would upset the balance of the all-party composition of the Committee in order to shift control into the hands of one party – his own. Committee members feared that this would turn the Volunteers into a servant of party interests, rather than a servant of the national interests of the Irish people. In response to Redmond's letter, the committee ordered the election of a representative from each of the thirty-two counties to sit on the Provisional Committee.[65]

Redmond chose to see this plan to make the Provisional Committee more representative as a rejection of his offer to co-operate with the Volunteers. Hobson found it ironic that Redmond, who attacked the Provisional Committee for being self-elected and unrepresentative, 'was bitterly opposed to the only method by which that defect in their constitution could be remedied'.[66] In a second letter of ultimatum, published on 13 June 1914, Redmond insisted that it was too early in the Volunteer movement's development both to hold debates regarding control of the organisation and to elect delegates who were capable of providing 'a fair and full representation of the Volunteer body' – even though, by his own admission, at least 95 per cent of the rank and file of the Volunteers were supporters of his party and its policy. He insisted that what the governing body of the Volunteers needed was 'men of proved judgement and steadiness'. If the Provisional Committee did not agree to his demands, he again threatened to set up a rival Volunteer organisation.[67] It would appear that Redmond did not trust democratically elected representatives (even if they supported his party) to serve the party's interests on the governing body of the Volunteers.

The Provisional Committee took more time to deliberate over its response to Redmond's second ultimatum. Behind the scenes, the Supreme Council of the IRB had decided that although any reasonable suggestion that could avoid a split in the Volunteer movement should be accepted, it should only be a suggestion that could 'maintain inviolate the Volunteer constitution and organisation'. As Redmond's 'co-option proposal was deemed not to be such a proposal', the Supreme Council issued an order that all members of the IRB should oppose it.[68]

Hobson did not take this order seriously. During his early years in the IRB, discipline had been lax. The change in the organisation's leadership may not have resulted in a universal change in attitude toward the issue of control. Hobson certainly continued to operate as he always had by going his own way.

On 15 June 1914 Hobson and Moore spent the morning visiting Casement, who was ill in bed at Buswell's Hotel. The previous night Casement and MacNeill had thought that the 'only dignified course' open to them was probably resignation. According to Casement, Hobson and Moore were inclined to agree. While the trio were deliberating over the various options, all of which 'threatened calamity', Clarke and MacDermott arrived. They urged Casement to fight Redmond, but Casement refused.[69]

Between the hard-line position of the IRB and the various positions of non-IRB committee members, a conflict of opinions raged. The three main options were: refuse to accept Redmond's nominees; accept his nominees; or resign from the committee. Despite the IRB order, Hobson characteristically preferred to think for himself. Later that day he left the office and went for a long walk to unravel the tangle of his thoughts. He recalled:

> I saw that the Redmondite members of the committee would follow their leader, others would retire from the movement, and our men would refuse to yield, and the Provisional Committee, and with it the Volunteer movement would be hopelessly split. If this happened all we had succeeded in doing since we had started the Volunteers would have been lost, in a conflict between rival Volunteer factions. To me the one vitally important thing was to keep the Volunteer movement intact.

Hobson recognised that he and his current colleagues on the Provisional Committee would not be able to work with Redmond's nominees for long because, fearing that the Volunteers would become armed and independent of him, Redmond 'would nominate men whose only object would be to control or stifle the movement as he directed'. In Hobson's opinion, the current members of the committee could work around the nominees because among them were 'the abler men' who already held the key positions: MacNeill was chairman, O'Rahilly was treasurer, Mellows was paid assistant secretary, Ceannt kept the books and the most active officers in Dublin and Cork were IRB members. Aside from that, the most important Volunteer work went on outside the committee. Essentially, what they needed to do, concluded Hobson, was to put the future of the Volunteer movement before their own personal feelings and political interests. He returned from his walk determined to persuade the Provisional Committee 'to accept Redmond's nominees as a lesser evil than a split in the Volunteer movement'. Although he realised his action 'would probably be misunderstood and be misrepresented', especially by his IRB colleagues, he could see no alternative way of saving the Volunteers from a split.[70]

Hobson's role in formulating a response to Redmond's second ultimatum led to his fall from grace within the highest IRB circles. Against the orders of his colleagues on the Supreme Council, he not only supported the co-option of Redmond's nominees on the Provisional Committee of the Irish Volunteers, but also influenced Casement and others to support the co-option. This led to a permanent breach between Hobson on the one hand and Clarke and MacDermott on the other.

On the morning of 16 June 1914 Hobson first visited Casement, still ill in bed at Buswell's Hotel, and then went to see MacNeill at his home. At these meetings Hobson sought to dissuade Casement and MacNeill from resigning from the Volunteers and abandoning Irish politics altogether, fearing that other non-aligned members of the committee would follow suit. 'If we failed to hold an all-party committee together we should be left with the IRB and the Fianna, and the Volunteers would be a small and ineffective body,' realised Hobson. 'All we had achieved in the last six months would be lost and little further hope of achieving anything would remain.'[71] As Casement later explained to Devoy, 'the only thought influencing Hobson was that [thought] that swayed me – to save the Volunteers from disruption and Ireland from a disgraceful faction fight in which all original issues would have gone by the board.'[72] Hobson returned to Buswell's Hotel with MacNeill in tow. After much discussion, MacNeill, Casement and Hobson agreed that the best way to prevent the disruption of the Volunteers was to accept Redmond's ultimatum. Moore later joined them and they brought him around to their way of thinking.[73]

In contrast to Casement and Moore, MacNeill did not give Hobson any credit for influencing his decision to accept the Redmond's nominees, possibly because he resented the common assumption that Hobson heavily influenced him in Volunteer matters.[74] Believing that Liberal Prime Minister H.H. Asquith had pressured Redmond into trying to capture the Volunteers, MacNeill 'calculated that an open breach with Redmond was the very thing that would give most satisfaction to the Liberal back sliders and would enable them to throw on Irish nationalism the responsibility of not fulfilling their Home Rule pledges'. According to MacNeill, both he and Casement held the view that refusing Redmond would have led to a political crisis in Ireland and a clear victory for Ulster Unionist leader Edward Carson. In addition, Casement had suggested to him that individual Volunteers, eager for arms, were more likely to adhere to Redmond than to the original members of the committee because they would believe that Redmond might be able to get Asquith to supply the Volunteers with arms.[75] These were the main factors that influenced his decision to co-opt the nominees.

At the time that the decision to accept Redmond's nominees was made, Hobson, Casement and MacNeill were among the select few who were aware of the plan that culminated in the Howth and Kilcoole gunrunning in July and August 1914. As O'Rahilly later noted, a split in the Volunteers probably would have led to the miscarriage of this plan and the loss of their arms.[76] Hobson, in particular, was concerned that a split in the Volunteers between the parliamentarians and the advanced nationalists at this point would hinder not only their ability to run guns into Ireland, but the IRB's chances of controlling these guns.[77] In striking contrast to his generally passive IRB colleagues, Hobson was taking an active role in organising the importation of arms into Ireland. The gunrunning plan was to serve the dual purpose of arming selected groups of Volunteers and awakening the minds of the Irish public.[78]

Still ensconced in Buswell's Hotel, Hobson and Casement helped MacNeill to draft a document to be submitted to the Provisional Committee later that evening, 16 June 1914. Moore, who was suffering from a liver complaint, was too ill to do anything except make criticisms or suggestions. The document stated explicitly that they 'accepted Redmond's dictation only as a lesser evil and to avoid having our organisation split into two rival factions'.[79]

When the Provisional Committee met that evening in the Volunteer office, MacNeill proposed the adoption of this draft document. Knowing that MacNeill usually asked each member in turn to express his opinion on important questions, Hobson chose a seat that would ensure that he was the last person to speak.[80] He recalled:

> I said that, while I completely sympathised with the point of view of the people who had spoken against the acceptance of Redmond's terms, I thought that our first duty was to preserve the Volunteers and to maintain as great a measure of control as we could, in order to guide the movement to fulfil the purpose for which we had started it … I appealed to the members and to those who had spoken against it to suppress their natural indignation at the course Redmond had taken and to stand together to save the Volunteer movement from disruption or from being destroyed by a Redmondite majority.[81]

To those who were not privy to the discussions in Buswell's Hotel, Hobson's viewpoint must have come as a veritable bombshell. Moore reported that, aside from a mutter from the least creditable person in the room, none of the speakers were interrupted. Judge, to whom Moore probably alluded, stated that Hobson was the only speaker that night whose remarks were interrupted.[82] In any case, Hobson was such 'a very eloquent and persuasive speaker' that his speech carried the motion by eighteen votes to nine, 'swaying four other members of the committee who would normally have voted against it'.[83] According to McGarry, 'some of those present (who should have known better) because of Hobson's position in the IRB seemed to regard his attitude as official' and voted with him.[84] In addition to Hobson, at least two other IRB members, Ó Riain and O'Connor, voted in favour of the co-option of Redmond's nominees. Both were close associates of Hobson.

One person whom Hobson's speech did not convince was, not surprisingly, Judge. He revealed: 'I refused Hobson's hand that night, and said I would never take it while I lived. I blamed him even more than I blamed any of the others for the sudden *volte face*.'[85] Key leaders of the IRB shared Judge's opinion.

Nobody misunderstood and reviled Hobson's action more than Clarke. McGarry recalled:

> I was with Tom when the news came and to say he was astounded is understating it. I never saw him so moved. He regarded it from the beginning as cold-blooded and contemplated treachery likely to bring about the destruction of the only movement in a century which brought promise of the fulfilment of all his hopes. During his life he had had many, very many grievous disappointments but this was the worst and the bitterness of it was increased by the fact that it was brought about by a trusted friend.[86]

Between the all-day conference in Buswell's and the 'extreme pressure' of Redmond's ultimatum, Hobson had not taken time to defend his decision to the IRB executive before the meeting. In any case Hobson believed that Clarke and MacDermott were suspicious of his co-operation with individuals like Casement and MacNeill, who represented viewpoints with a wider popular appeal than those of the IRB, and, as such, were unlikely to be helpful.[87] They would have hindered his plan to save the Volunteers from a split.

Hobson saw this co-operation as the most effective way to work towards Irish independence: 'If the IRB was ever going to become a power and was not to remain forever a small organisation of little clubs meeting in back rooms, this could only come about by our linking-up with and permeating much larger organisations which had a wider national appeal.'[88] Despite the view to the contrary held by other IRB leaders, Hobson believed he was acting in the best interest of both the Volunteer movement and the IRB.

It was not so much Hobson's personal decision to support the co-option of Redmond's nominees, but his influence on others to which Clarke and MacDermott objected. This influence challenged their authority within the IRB leadership. According to O'Hegarty:

> Clarke and MacDermott both told me that if [Hobson] had told them in good time that he had changed his mind, and if he had argued it out with them, and if he had contented himself with voting and not attempting to influence others, they would not have thought so much of it. But it was the fact that he not alone voted for the co-options but took practically charge of the motion and so arranged the seating that he was the last speaker that they felt was unforgivable.[89]

Hobson later conceded that Clarke and MacDermott 'may have had some justification' for feeling that they were not 'consulted sufficiently'.[90]

Shortly after the Provisional Committee agreed to the co-option of Redmond's nominees, Hobson was summoned to a meeting of the IRB executive held in Clarke's home. There he found himself in a showdown facing Clarke, the treasurer, MacDermott, the secretary, possibly Seamus Deakin, the president and O'Hegarty, a Supreme Council member, who happened to be in Dublin.[91] Clarke and MacDermott bombarded Hobson with accusations of having betrayed the movement and being in the pay of Redmond, while O'Hegarty remained neutral, neither accusing nor moderating. Hobson had expected disapproval of his action, but not this 'storm of hysterical abuse'. He felt it was impossible to argue his side of the story in such 'an overcharged atmosphere', and when he 'made a little attempt to do so, this seemed to increase their fury'.[92]

In recalling the showdown, O'Hegarty took the view that Hobson 'resented being questioned about his action', adding that it was 'characteristic of [Hobson's] temperament that the fact that he had, in cold fact, played the organisation false, without explanation, and had actually defeated it, troubled him not at all'. Hobson's defence that he acted as he did 'because he thought the country could not afford a split at that juncture' was not explanation enough for O'Hegarty. Despite his disagreement with Hobson's action, O'Hegarty did concede that the co-option of Redmond's nominees was generally supported outside Dublin, citing the opinion of his brother, who told him 'it was all very well for Dublin but that a split would have killed them in Cork'.[93]

Hobson's initial instinct was 'to fight out the question' of his actions at a meeting of the Supreme Council. As he himself noted, 'my combined offices of Leinster Centre, chairman of the Dublin Centres Board and editor of *Irish Freedom* placed me in an exceptionally powerful position in the brotherhood'. In light of that position, he was convinced that he could sway a majority on the Supreme Council to support him.[94] Upon reflection, however, Hobson, who was taken aback by the depth of his colleagues' hostility, feared that his success in averting a split within the Irish Volunteers might lead to a split within the IRB that would render the latter organisation impotent. Disgusted and weary, he resigned from the Supreme Council and as editor of *Irish Freedom*, the two positions that brought him into contact with Clarke and MacDermott. He retained the chairmanship of the Dublin Centres Board as well as a position on the Leinster Executive. He was aware that his resignation from the Supreme Council was exactly what Clarke and MacDermott wanted.[95]

In his biography of Clarke, Louis N. Le Roux stated that Hobson was court-martialled by the Supreme Council for disregarding its instructions and that, even though 'Hobson made a good defence', the court decided that he must resign from all of his IRB offices, including his position as chairman of the Dublin Centres Board.[96] Neither Hobson nor O'Hegarty, however, mentioned a formal court martial in their accounts of the episode. A police report reveals that Hobson, O'Hegarty, Clarke, MacDermott, McCullough and Deakin attended an IRB meeting held at the old Town Hall in Clontarf from 8.30 a.m. to 4.15 p.m. on 5 July 1914.[97] The date, three weeks after the acceptance of Redmond's nominees, and the fact that the attendees were all members of the Supreme Council, suggest that this may have been the meeting at which Hobson had initially planned to fight out the question of his actions, but instead decided to resign the positions that brought him into contact with Clarke and MacDermott.

According to Hobson, his role in the controversial acceptance of Redmond's nominees was debated in a 'frank and friendly' manner at the next meetings of the Teeling circle, the Dublin Centres Board and the Leinster Council. As a result, Hobson retained his positions as Teeling Centre, chairman of the Dublin Centres Board and Dublin representative on the Leinster Council.[98] Hobson always denied allegations, made after the 1916 rising, that the Supreme Council had deprived him of all his offices.[99] McCullough, who was a member of the Supreme Council at the time in question, backed up Hobson's denials and dispelled further rumours that his colleague had been expelled from the IRB.[100]

In resigning from the Supreme Council, Hobson left it to what he considered the misguided leadership of Clarke and MacDermott: 'I felt that policies of which I might not approve could hardly be as disastrous as a conflict which might well leave the movement incapable of pursuing any policy at all.'[101] Yet there was already a split in the IRB leadership, one that had been developing since the establishment of the Volunteers.

The fact that Hobson was able to convince fellow IRB members to support the acceptance of Redmond's nominees is proof of that. Michael Tierney commented in his study of MacNeill: 'It does not seem to have occurred to Hobson, then or subsequently, that the IRB was obviously already "split" and that his withdrawal was conceding victory to the opposing faction. Neither does he seem to have reflected on the danger to which he was exposing the Volunteers.'[102]

Although he never acknowledged it in public, Hobson later realised this. In 1934 he admitted to McGarrity that his resignation had been 'a blunder', resulting from overwork and a 'distaste for fighting old friends': 'I ought to have stayed and fought them to a finish as I easily could have done.' Hobson revealed that, had O'Hegarty, who had shared his views in the past, supported him at the executive showdown, he might not have resigned from the Supreme Council.[103]

O'Hegarty later lamented that the rift between Hobson on the one hand and Clarke and MacDermott on the other ultimately deprived the nationalist movement 'of the services of Hobson, whose work for the cause was second only to [Clarke and Griffith's], and whose political sagacity was second only to that of Griffith'.[104] Ironically, O'Hegarty, had he supported Hobson at this juncture, might have been able to secure his friend's services for the future of the movement.

Hobson's action to save the Volunteers from a split impacted on some of his personal relationships, most significantly on his once-close connection with Clarke. Although O'Hegarty and Hobson remained friends, MacDermott and Hobson were never again on good terms.[105] Clarke, who had once idealised Hobson, dropped all association with him.[106]

As a member of the Supreme Council and a long-time associate of Hobson's, McCullough was in a unique position to provide insight into the characters of both Clarke and Hobson. In his opinion:

> Clarke, who was a man of a very simple mind, loved and admired Hobson immensely. Consequently, when Hobson was guilty of what Tom considered a betrayal, the rift was very bitter and Tom would not forgive him or trust him again. Bulmer Hobson was the most single-minded nationalist I knew in my time. He found it hard, however, to work under orders, as he had the supremest confidence (and still has) in his own judgement. A person of this temperament was bound to get at loggerheads, sooner or later, with those who were controlling the activities of the IRB by methods which he did not understand and did not approve.[107]

McCullough's estimation of Hobson matches O'Hegarty's view noted above.

Hobson's decision to support the co-option of Redmond's nominees to the Provisional Committee of the Irish Volunteers had financial repercussions as well. Hobson had been dividing his time between voluntary work for the Irish Volunteers and paid employment as a freelance journalist – hence, his admission that he had been suffering from overwork. At that time, one of his few sources of regular income was the ten dollars per month that he received for his contributions as the Irish correspondent for the *Gaelic American*, the Clan na Gael organ. Clarke wrote to Devoy, the newspaper's editor, blaming Hobson for the surrender to Redmond.[108] Devoy, in turn, not only rejected an article that Hobson had written in defence of the acceptance of Redmond's nominees, but dismissed Hobson from his position as correspondent. Devoy also intimated that, 'under present circumstances and in view of the very general irritation here over what has just occurred', Casement should abandon his plan to come to America to follow up the memorandum that had been shown to the German Ambassador earlier that year.[109] Casement, however, was already en route by the time Hobson received word from Devoy.

Upon receiving Devoy's communication, Hobson responded with a 'tart' letter that not only explained his actions but 'expressed surprise that the author of the New Departure should condemn me unheard for taking a far more easily defended course than he had done'. The New Departure was the project championed in the late 1870s by Devoy and Michael Davitt (1846–1905) to convince the Fenians to work with Parnell, thus fusing the land and national questions. According to Hobson, his retort resulted in his reinstatement, which Devoy failed to mention in his memoirs. In two of his accounts, Hobson stated that he had had enough and did not write for Devoy again; in one account he explained that he may have written one more article, but postal censorship due to the war made it impossible to contribute further articles.[110]

Under the Defence of the Realm Act (DORA) the British authorities could seize and censor post that was considered 'seditious'. Advanced nationalists in Ireland were affected by this policy.[111] For instance, a warrant for the seizure and censorship of Hobson's post was in effect between 23 November and 31 December 1914. His mail, probably due to self-censorship, proved so unthreatening that on 29 December the under-secretary at Dublin Castle, Matthew Nathan, advised the secretary in the General Post Office in Dublin to temporarily cease detaining Hobson's post for examination by the military intelligence officer, Major Ivor Price.[112]

Pearse felt that Hobson had been dealt with too harshly and feared that, having no income due to the loss of his jobs as editor of *Irish Freedom*[113] and correspondent for the *Gaelic American*, Hobson might have to leave Dublin, 'which would be an incalculable loss'.[114] How

Hobson managed to afford to stay in Dublin at this time remains a mystery, as he insisted that, despite suggestions to the contrary, he was not paid for his Volunteer work. One of Markievicz's biographers, Anne Marreco, noted that he had a small private income, but did not cite her source for this information.[115] If he did have such an income, either it had not been large enough to maintain him in Dublin in late 1909 or he did not receive it until a later date. Perhaps he inherited this alleged income from his maternal grandmother, Ann Bulmer, who died in June 1913.[116] Financial mysteries aside, Hobson did not value the words of support that came from Pearse, of whose rapid conversion to advanced nationalism he was suspicious. Instead, Hobson revelled in the irony that, at the inception of the Volunteers, Pearse had warned MacNeill 'of the danger of allowing extreme nationalists like me to gain control',[117] but that six months after Hobson had sworn Pearse into the IRB, 'I wasn't nearly revolutionary enough for him'.[118] He complained that Pearse wrote to 'people in America, to whom I had introduced him, telling them that I was not sufficiently reliable, from a revolutionary point of view, to be entrusted with funds or given support'.[119] In addition, he may have resented Pearse's growing prominence as a speaker, writer and activist within the advanced nationalist movement because it challenged his own position.

Working with Redmond's nominees

The composition of Redmond's list of twenty-five nominees belied his claims that his aim was to ensure that the membership of the Provisional Committee was geographically representative and better known to the public. The list consisted of eleven nominees from Dublin and representatives from the following cities and counties: Belfast, Carlow, Cork, Derry, Donegal, Down, Mayo, Sligo, Tipperary and Waterford. This geographic spread certainly was not as representative of all thirty-two counties as the Provisional Committee's election plan would have been. Of the nominees, who included five clergymen, four justices of the peace, three members of parliament and two mayors, only William Redmond, the brother of John Redmond, and Joseph Devlin were well known to the public.[120] As O'Rahilly later pointed out, nominees with a military background were noticeably absent.[121] Ironically, Lorcan Sherlock, who had denied the Provisional Committee the use of the Mansion House for the first public meeting of the Volunteers, was among those who accepted a nomination to the governing body of the Irish Volunteers.[122] The composition of the list suggests that Redmond was, indeed, only interested in party control.

The first meeting of the newly expanded Provisional Committee was held on 14 July 1914, twelve days before the Irish Volunteers succeeded in running guns and ammunition into Howth, County Dublin on 26 July 1914.[123] MacNeill, who had been elected by the old committee to act as chairman until a Volunteer convention could take place, presided over the meeting which twenty-three of Redmond's twenty-five nominees attended. It was decided that the new fifty-two-member Provisional Committee would meet monthly, while a seventeen-member Standing Committee, to which Hobson and later MacDermott were appointed, would meet weekly. The organisational sub-committees were re-appointed in order to give representation to the new nominees.[124]

The Standing Committee and the enlarged Provisional Committee only worked together for nine weeks. From the beginning, meetings reflected the division between the original Provisional Committee members and the new nominees. Hobson, as well as O'Rahilly, reported that the nominees, with the exceptions of William Redmond and James Creed Meredith, 'made almost every question a party question, and thus drove the majority of the old committee to act together as an opposing party'.[125] As a result of this partisan wrangling, the most important work, the arming and training of the Volunteers, occurred outside the committee.[126] In his study of the Volunteers, Charles Hannon concluded that ordinary Volunteer recruits were unaware of 'this internal faction fighting' unless they were 'included in the machinations of the inner circles of a faction'.[127]

The main battles were fought over who would receive money and arms. One of the key issues was whether money raised to cover the cost of arming was channelled through Redmond or O'Rahilly, the incumbent treasurer.[128] In addition to alleging that American funds were diverted to Redmond and his party, O'Rahilly suspected that certain nominees were trying to discredit the Volunteer movement by influencing the Standing Committee to authorise a spending spree on the rental of multiple offices that could have bankrupted the organisation over time.[129] Due to Redmond's interference, the committee members who were serious about arming the Volunteers found it difficult to secure funding to buy rifles and ammunition.[130] This was particularly provoking at a time when the British government had withdrawn the prohibition on importing arms into Ireland.[131]

During this period Hobson suffered a fit of pique that helped to fuel his life-long resentment of Pearse. This was in response to a July 1914 letter written by Pearse. In it, Pearse asked McGarrity, to whom Hobson had introduced him, to secure arms for the Volunteers but, in doing so, to bypass the Provisional Committee, setting aside any previous requests from 'MacNeill or anyone else', and to deal directly with himself, MacDermott, Ceannt and Fitzgibbon, who was not a member of the IRB. Hobson took the 'anyone else' to mean himself and chose to ignore Pearse's compliment that, of the members of the new Standing Committee of the Volunteers, 'only Hobson and Fitzgibbon can be absolutely relied on'.[132] (MacDermott had yet to be appointed to the committee.)

Redmond's nominees pushed for the arms that the Volunteers did manage to procure in this period to be sent to northern Catholics. As a result, Pearse feared that Volunteers would 'be used to force Home Rule on Ulster, and possibly to enforce the *dismemberment of Ireland*'.[133] That Redmond's nominees failed to request ammunition to be sent north suggests that the threat was not serious.[134]

In supporting the co-option of Redmond's nominees, Hobson had been confident that 'Redmond's control would prove to be more apparent than real'[135] because 'an able and united minority can run most committees'.[136] He later boasted to McCartan that

> Redmond's crowd were never in control – they were given a barren victory to save the movement from shipwreck but we never lost grip. I even appointed the office staff at headquarters while there was a Redmondite majority on the committee and they don't know yet how it happened. Ninety per cent of the officers were our men because I had taken the precaution to drill them well before starting the Volunteers ... Redmond's men balked a lot and were very tiresome but we ran the movement. We controlled the office staff – the best of the officers and the money.[137]

The IRB contingent and their allies on the Provisional Committee may have controlled the office staff and the 'best' officers, but Redmond succeeded in thwarting them over money.

Members of the original Provisional Committee of the Irish Volunteers were not just irritated by Redmond's interference in the areas of money and arms. Even more provoking was his propensity to dictate Volunteer policy by making public announcements without seeking the prior consent of the Provisional Committee. For instance, on 3 August 1914 Redmond, in a spontaneous speech to the House of Commons, pledged that the Irish Volunteers were willing to join together with the Ulster Volunteers in order to defend Ireland's shores so that the British military could concentrate its efforts on the war in Europe, which broke out the following day. In Redmond's opinion the war was an opportunity for Ireland to prove its loyalty. In contrast, the IRB saw the war as a chance to strike a blow for Irish freedom: in mid August 1914, the Supreme Council of the IRB decided to stage a rising before the end of the war. Ironically, both Redmond and the IRB viewed the Irish Volunteers as instrumental to their differing wartime plans. It was Redmond's propensity to dictate policy without prior consultation, however, that would ultimately lead to the split within the Irish Volunteers that Hobson had hoped to delay with his support for the co-option of Redmond's nominees.

The split within the Irish Volunteers

The split was precipitated by an address made by Redmond on 20 September 1914 to a Volunteer parade at Woodenbridge, County Wicklow, in which he announced that it was the duty of the Irish Volunteers to enlist in the British Army in order to fight in the European War. The Irish Volunteers had been founded to provide Ireland with a national defence force, not as a recruiting ground for British troops. In response to Redmond's announcement, twenty out of the twenty-seven original members of the Provisional Committee, including Hobson, signed a manifesto on 24 September 1914 ousting Redmond's nominees.[138] Under the leadership of MacNeill they took control of the Volunteer headquarters, which had recently moved to 41 Kildare Street, and called a convention of the Irish Volunteers. Redmond, his nominees and his few supporters from the original Provisional Committee started a rival organisation, the National Volunteers, which the majority of Volunteers supported. Its numbers dwindled away, however, as its members headed off to fight in the war and the prospect of Home Rule drifted further into the future.

Within days of the split Hobson wrote to a Miss MacNeill – probably Ada MacNeill, a friend of his mother, Mary, and of Casement – providing a contemporary glimpse of his ambivalent feelings about the ejection of Redmond's nominees:

> I am afraid that the whole Volunteer movement is in confusion over Redmond's recruiting campaign and our reply to it – and though we could not consistently take any other course I doubt if we have done any good by breaking away. I am by no means satisfied with the situation – it is very puzzling.

Hobson wished that Casement, who was in America, 'were back to help us with the situation here'. He concluded: 'I suppose we will pull through somehow.'[139] Hobson's mixed feelings were still evident a month later when he wrote to Molly Childers, the wife of Erskine Childers, about the need to heal the split within the Volunteer movement.[140] This ambivalence may have stemmed from Hobson's belief that, aside from the partisan wrangling at the Provisional Committee level, the Volunteers had made real gains in terms of organisation, training and vitality after Redmond endorsed the movement.

Hobson's support for the ejection of Redmond's nominees failed to rehabilitate him with Clarke and MacDermott – although Louis N. Le Roux, the biographer of Clarke and Pearse, reported a brief reconciliation between Clarke and Hobson on the outbreak of the war.[141] Despite this, Hobson never felt the need to apologise for his role in the acceptance of the nominees. In 1924 he even informed McCartan that he regarded his involvement in the co-option of Redmond's nominees 'as one of the wisest and most misunderstood of my actions'.[142] He was adamant that the 'intervening months' between the acceptance of Redmond's nominees and their ejection made all the difference to the Volunteers by consolidating the work that had been done to organise the force. From his viewpoint, the Volunteers, particularly after the successful gunrunning operations at Howth and Kilcoole, 'were rapidly integrating into a very vital organisation'.[143] In the opinion of MacNeill's son-in-law, Michael Tierney, 'probably the most disastrous consequence' of the decision to accept Redmond's nominees was the rift between Hobson and the IRB leadership.[144]

Although he had voted against the acceptance of the nominees, Eamon Martin, a Fianna officer who joined the IRB and the Volunteers, later came to the conclusion that through his actions Hobson had succeeded in postponing the inevitable split until the fledgling Volunteer organisation was strong enough to withstand it. He did not share the view, often put forward by Hobson detractors, that the split only came 'after irreparable harm had been done by the acceptance of Redmond's ultimatum'.[145]

F.X. Martin concurred that Hobson, MacNeill and Casement had 'acted wisely' in accepting Redmond's nominees: 'To have withstood Redmond at the height of his popularity in June 1914 would have been to court disaster for the Volunteers.' Due to the maintenance of outward unity within the Volunteer organisation at this critical time, the Howth and Kilcoole gunrunning plans, which provided essential arms for the 1916 rising, were a success.[146] When the split in the Volunteer movement finally came in September 1914, it was over a more fundamental issue: whether the Volunteers would fight for Britain in the war. Splitting over this issue actually served, over the course of the war, to strengthen the Irish Volunteers.[147] It purged the moderate nationalists, about 150,000 of whom joined Redmond's National Volunteers, leaving a concentration of between 3,000 and 10,000 advanced nationalists.[148]

Although Hobson had initial reservations about the split in the Volunteers, he later concluded that it 'left in the ranks a small minority, but one which was firm of purpose and knew its own mind, which had a policy and had the courage and determination to put that policy to the test'.[149] Within this minority, however, a difference of opinion arose. Some asserted that the Irish Volunteers should remain, as their constitution stated, purely defensive while others believed that they should become an instrument for insurrection, the IRB Supreme Council having decided to stage a rising before the end of the war. Hobson and MacNeill advocated the former view while Clarke and MacDermott were determined that the latter view would prevail.

Conclusion

The Provisional Committee of the Irish Volunteers was hampered by its large size, its self-elected nature, its inexperience in military affairs and its lack of agreement on the underlying purpose of the Irish Volunteer movement. All of these factors made it vulnerable to Redmond's attempts to capture the movement. After the failure of private negotiations, which were not authorised by the Provisional Committee, Redmond publicly threatened to split the Volunteer movement if twenty-five of his nominees were not co-opted to the committee. Hobson, in defiance of IRB orders, was instrumental in ensuring the acceptance of these nominees in order to avoid a split in the movement that, in his opinion, would have been disastrous at that time. His actions to save the Irish Volunteers incurred the wrath of Clarke and MacDermott, leading to his fall from grace within the highest level of the IRB leadership.

Although Hobson's clash with Clarke and MacDermott led to his resignation from the Supreme Council and a decline in his position within the IRB, he remained a power to be reckoned with. Not only did he hold an influential position within the Volunteer leadership, but he retained the chairmanship of the Dublin Centres Board of the IRB. After the split in the Volunteer movement, the secret battle to decide how the Irish Volunteers would be used in the struggle for Irish independence shifted from the Supreme Council of the IRB to the governing body of the Irish Volunteers.

Notes

1. O'Hegarty, witness statement, 19 Sept. 1947 (NAI, BMH, WS 26).
2. Foy and Barton, *Easter Rising*, p. 3.
3. See Hobson, *IYT*, p. 45; O'Connor, BMH witness statement, 14 June 1948 (UCDA, EMacN, LA1/G/117).
4. Bulmer Hobson, *A short history of the Irish Volunteers* (Dublin, 1918), p. 18.
5. Hobson, *IYT*, p. 45; Hobson, 'Ireland's hour of destiny', p. 27; The O'Rahilly, 'The Irish prepare to arm', in Martin (ed.), *Irish Volunteers*, p. 77.

6 Hobson, *A short history*, p. 28; Hobson, *IYT*, p. 45; Hobson, 'Ireland's hour of destiny', p. 28; Piaras Béaslaí, 'The National Army is founded', *II*, 5 Jan. 1953, p. 3, reprinted in Martin (ed.), *Irish Volunteers*, p. 82.
7 Hobson, 'Ireland's hour of destiny', p. 28.
8 'Irish Volunteer Movement', *II*, 26 Nov. 1913, reprinted in Martin (ed.), *Irish Volunteers*, pp. 106–10.
9 See Chapters 3–4, which discuss Hobson's speeches to promote the Sinn Féin movement.
10 'Manifesto of Irish Volunteers', in Martin (ed.), *Irish Volunteers*, p. 100.
11 Moore actually divided Volunteers into three categories, but two of his categories appear to be indistinguishable. See Col Maurice Moore, 'Trouble in Cork', *IP*, 5 Jan. 1938, in Col Maurice Moore, 'History of the Irish Volunteers' (NLI, ILB 94,109). An Irish-language version of this material was published as Maurice Moore, *Tús agus Fás, óglách na hÉireann, 1913–1917* (Dublin, 1936).
12 Hobson, 'Drilling moves on apace', *IT*, 21 Nov. 1963 (UCDA, DMcC, P120/40); Hobson, witness statement, 11 Nov. 1947 (NAI, BMH, WS 51).
13 For a list of members and their affiliations, see Chapter 5; Martin, *Irish Volunteers*, pp. 30–1; Charles Hannon, 'The Irish Volunteers and the concept of military service and defence, 1913–1924' (PhD thesis, UCD, 1989), pp. 11–12.
14 Hobson, *IYT*, p. 46.
15 Moore, 'Pen-pictures of the leaders', *IP*, 6 Jan. 1938.
16 Hobson, *IYT*, p. 47.
17 Ibid., pp. 46–7.
18 Ibid., p. 46; Hobson, 'Drilling moves on apace,' *IT*, 21 Nov. 1963 (UCDA, DMcC, P120/40); Hobson, witness statement, 11 Nov. 1947 (NAI, BMH, WS 51). MacDermott later took over Hobson's D'Olier Street office.
19 Hobson, BMH witness statement, 17 Dec 1947 (NLI, BH, MS 13,170).
20 Hobson, *IYT*, p. 46.
21 See Chapter 5.
22 Hobson, *IYT*, p. 46.
23 Ibid.
24 M.J. Judge, 'The inner history of the Irish Volunteers', *IN*, 9 Sept. 1916, p. 6. See also Judge, 'Inner history', *IN*, 19 May 1917, p. 7.
25 Moore, 'Pen-pictures of the leaders', *IP*, 6 Jan. 1938, 'Two great leaders: The O'Rahilly and Sean MacDermott', *IP*, 7 Jan. 1938. In the first article noted, Moore mentioned that the 'noisiest and most obstructive' member of the Provisional Committee was appointed to all of the sub-committees formed in Feb. 1914. As Judge was the only individual appointed to all of these sub-committees, he must be the man to whom Moore alluded. For the sub-committee membership lists, see Hobson, *A short history*, p. 51.
26 Judge, 'Inner history', *IN*, 29 July 1916, p. 6.
27 Judge, 'The Volunteers', *IN*, 10 Nov. 1917, pp. 1–2.
28 Judge, 'Inner history', *IN*, 19 Aug. 1916, p. 6.
29 *Irish Citizen*, 14 Feb. 1914, p. 305.

30 Moore, 'Pen-pictures of the leaders', *IP*, 6 Jan. 1938.
31 Judge, 'Inner history', *IN*, 19 Aug. 1916, p. 6.
32 Hobson, BMH witness statement, 26 Jan. 1948 (NLI, BH, MS 13,170).
33 Moore, 'Pen-pictures of the leaders', *IN*, 6 Jan. 1938.
34 Hobson, 'Drilling moves on apace', *IT*, 21 Nov. 1963 (UCDA, DMcC, P 120/40); Hobson, witness statement, 11 Nov. 1947 (NAI, BMH, WS 51).
35 Hobson, *A short history*, p. 35; Hobson, *IYT*, p. 46; Judge, 'Inner history', *IN*, 12 Aug. 1916, p. 6.
36 Hobson, *A short history*, p. 53.
37 Moore, 'Pen-pictures of the leaders', *IP*, 6 Jan. 1938. For more information about the sub-committees, see Chapter 7.
38 Moore, 'The importance of Derry City', *IP*, 18 Jan. 1938.
39 The O'Rahilly, *The secret history of the Irish Volunteers* (Dublin, 1915), p. 6.
40 Hannon, 'Irish Volunteers', p. 23.
41 Ibid., p. 26.
42 See Chapter 5.
43 Moore, 'Two great leaders', *IP*, 7 Jan. 1938.
44 Moore, 'Interviewing the "Party"', *IP*, 8 Jan.1938.
45 Moore, 'Two great leaders', *IP*, 7 Jan. 1938.
46 Hannon, 'Irish Volunteers', p. 34.
47 Gwynn, *John Redmond*, p. 307.
48 The negotiations between MacNeill and Redmond are outlined in Tierney, *Eoin MacNeill*, pp. 129–38, Gwynn, *John Redmond*, pp. 311–17, and Moore, 'History of the Irish Volunteers' (NLI, ILB 94,109).
49 Hobson, *IYT*, p. 49; Judge, 'Inner history', *IN*, 12 Aug. 1916, p. 6.
50 Moore, 'Interviewing the "Party"', *IP*, 8 Jan. 1938.
51 Hobson, *IYT*, p. 49.
52 Judge, 'Inner history', *IN*, 19 Aug. 1916, p. 6.
53 Moore, 'Interviewing the "Party"', *IP*, 8 Jan. 1938; 'Devlin and the Volunteers', *IP*, 10 Jan. 1938.
54 Hobson, witness statement, 5 Nov. 1947 (NAI, BMH, WS 50; NLI, BH, MS 13,170). Possible members of the proposed joint executive included Eoin MacNeill, John Gore, Laurence J. Kettle, The O'Rahilly, William Redmond, Roger Casement, Joseph Devlin, Col Maurice Moore and Michael Davitt [not the Michael Davitt of Land League fame] (Gwynn, *John Redmond*, p. 314). Negotiations broke down over Davitt's name because at the public meeting to start enrolling Volunteers on 25 Nov. 1913 Davitt had given a speech that offered only lukewarm support to the movement.
55 Moore, 'The money problem', *IP*, 17 Jan. 1938.
56 Casement to Moore, 5 Apr. 1914, qtd. in Moore, 'After the Mutiny', *IP*, 13 Jan. 1938.
57 Hobson, *A short history*, p. 95.
58 Hannon, 'Irish Volunteers', p. 35.
59 Ibid., pp. 43–4.
60 Hobson, *A short history*, p. 99.

The struggle for control of the Irish Volunteers 149

61 J.E. Redmond, letter to the editor, *Freeman's Journal*, 10 June 1914, p. 7; Hobson, *A short history*, pp. 110–11.
62 Hannon, 'Irish Volunteers', p. 19.
63 Hobson, *IYT*, p. 49.
64 Hobson, *A short history*, p. 113.
65 Ibid., p. 114.
66 Hobson, *A short history*, p. 102.
67 J.E. Redmond, letter to the editor, *Freeman's Journal*, 13 June 1914, p. 7; Hobson, *A short history*, pp. 117–19.
68 O'Hegarty, witness statement, 19 Sept. 1947 (NAI, BMH, WS 26).
69 Casement to Devoy, 21 July 1914 (O'Brien and Ryan (eds), *Devoy's Postbag*, ii, pp. 461–2). This letter by Casement, Hobson's various accounts (which are noted below), and Moore, 'Redmond gains his point', *IP*, 26 Jan. 1938 have been used to reconstruct the steps leading to the decision to co-opt Redmond's nominees.
70 Hobson, statement to McGarrity, 1934 (NLI, BH, MS 13,171).
71 Hobson, *IYT*, p. 50.
72 Casement to Devoy, 21 July 1914 (O'Brien and Ryan (eds), *Devoy's Postbag*, ii, p. 463).
73 Hobson, *IYT*, p. 51; Moore, 'Redmond gains his point', *IP*, 26 Jan. 1938.
74 Helena Molony refers to this common assumption in her witness statement (NAI, BMH, WS 391). Hobson's alleged influence on MacNeill was one of the reasons why the IRB kidnapped him before the Easter Rising. See Áine Ceannt, witness statement, n.d. (NAI, BMH, WS 264).
75 Eoin MacNeill, 1932 memoir, pp. 83–4 (UCDA, EMacN, LA1/G/371).
76 O'Rahilly, *Secret history*, p. 8.
77 Martin, 'McCullough, Hobson and republican Ulster', p. 103.
78 Hobson's involvement in the gunrunning at Howth will be examined in Chapter 7.
79 Hobson, *IYT*, p. 51; Moore, 'Redmond gains his point', *IP*, 26 Jan. 1938.
80 Hobson, 'John Redmond and the Volunteers', in Martin (ed.), *Irish Volunteers*, pp. 48–9.
81 Ibid.
82 Moore, 'Redmond drops a bombshell', *IP*, 27 Jan. 1938; Judge, 'Inner history', *IN*, 7 Oct. 1916, p. 6.
83 O'Hegarty, witness statement, 19 Sept. 1947 (NAI, BMH, WS 26). The following eighteen men voted for the co-option of Redmond's nominees: Eoin MacNeill, Roger Casement, The O'Rahilly, Bulmer Hobson, Col Maurice Moore, John Gore, Thomas Kettle, Laurence J. Kettle, Joseph Plunkett, Seamus O'Connor, Pádraig Ó Riain, Liam Gogan, Colm Ó Lochlainn, Peadar Macken, Peter O'Reilly, James Lenahan, George Walsh and Robert Page. The following nine men voted against the co-option: Patrick Pearse, Sean MacDermott, Éamonn Ceannt, Piaras Béaslaí, Sean Fitzgibbon, Liam Mellows, Eamon Martin, Con Colbert and Michael J. Judge (NLI, BH, MS 13,174 (10)).
84 Sean McGarry, witness statement, 15 Apr. 1950 (NAI, BMH, WS 368).

85 Judge, 'Inner history', *IN*, 7 Oct. 1916, p. 6.
86 McGarry, witness statement, 15 Apr. 1950 (NAI, BMH, WS 368).
87 Hobson, 'John Redmond and the Volunteers', p. 49; Hobson, *IYT*, p. 52.
88 Hobson, *IYT*, p. 52.
89 O'Hegarty, witness statement, 19 Sept. 1947 (NAI, BMH, WS 26).
90 Hobson, *IYT*, p. 52.
91 In one of his accounts of the proceedings, Hobson indicated that Deakin may have been present. See Hobson's statement to McGarrity, 1934 (NLI, BH, MS 13,171). Deakin, a chemist, was often absent from IRB meetings due to his business commitments. In *IYT*, Hobson says McCullough, as president, should have been at the meeting, but wasn't summoned (p. 52). McCullough, however, did not become president of the executive of the Supreme Council until 1915.
92 Hobson, *IYT*, pp. 52–3.
93 O'Hegarty, witness statement, 19 Sept. 1947 (NAI, BMH, WS 26).
94 Hobson, 'John Redmond and the Volunteers', p. 50.
95 Hobson, *IYT*, p. 53; Hobson, statement to McGarrity, 1934 (NLI, BH, MS 13,171).
96 Le Roux, *Tom Clarke*, p. 135; Le Roux, *Patrick Pearse*, p. 287. Le Roux does not divulge the identity of his informant.
97 Précis, SS, July 1914 (NAL, CO 904/14 Part 2).
98 Hobson, *IYT*, pp. 53–4.
99 Ibid., p. 37.
100 McCullough, BMH witness statement, 8 Dec. 1953 (UCDA, DMcC, P 120/24/18).
101 Hobson, *IYT*, p. 71.
102 Tierney, *Eoin MacNeill*, p. 167.
103 Hobson, statement to McGarrity, 1934 (NLI, BH, MS 13,171).
104 P.S. O'Hegarty, *A history of Ireland under the Union, 1801–1922* (London, 1952), p. 679.
105 Hobson, statement to McGarrity, 1934 (NLI, BH, MS 13,171).
106 Kathleen Clarke, *Revolutionary woman*, p. 46.
107 McCullough, BMH witness statement, 25 Sept. 1952 (UCDA, DMcC, P120/24/9).
108 John Devoy, *Recollections of an Irish rebel* (New York, 1929), p. 409.
109 Devoy to Hobson, 3 July 1914 (O'Brien and Ryan (eds), *Devoy's Postbag*, ii, p. 458).
110 Hobson, *IYT*, p. 53; Hobson, statement to McGarrity, 1934 (NLI, BH, MS 13,171). In this statement to McGarrity, Hobson noted: 'In his book, written many years afterwards when he was very old, Devoy refers to my dismissal. I think he had forgotten my letter and his second cable and only remembered that I never wrote for him again'. The last article that appeared in the *Gaelic American* with Hobson's by-line explained why Redmond's nominees were accepted: see Bulmer Hobson, 'Redmond wins by traitorous threats', *GA*, 4 July 1914, p. 1.

111 See Ben Novick, 'Postal censorship in Ireland, 1914–16', *IHS*, xxxi (1999), pp. 343–56.
112 Warrant, 23 Nov. 1914; Matthew Nathan to secretary, GPO, Dublin, 29 Dec. 1914 (NAL, CO 904/164).
113 According to O'Hegarty's witness statement, dated 19 Sept. 1947, Hobson was never paid for his work for *Irish Freedom* (NAI, BMH, WS 26).
114 Pearse to McGarrity, 17 July 1914, qtd. in Cronin, *The McGarrity Papers*, p. 43.
115 Marreco, *Rebel countess*, p. 104.
116 Mary Hobson, 'Bulmer family chronicle', p. 191 (NLI, MS 5220).
117 Hobson, *IYT*, p. 45; Hobson, 'Early days', *IT*, 20 Nov. 1963 (UCDA, DMcC, P120/40).
118 Transcript, *Old Ireland free* (BBC Written Archive, Reading). Hobson's interview was recorded on 14 Oct. 1964, while the resulting radio documentary was broadcast on 24 April 1966.
119 Hobson, BMH witness statement, 26 Jan. 1948 (NLI, BH, MS 13,170).
120 Hannon, 'Irish Volunteers', p. 55.
121 O'Rahilly, *Secret history*, p. 7.
122 Hobson, *A short history*, p. 18.
123 For a discussion of the Howth gunrunning, see Chapter 7.
124 The members of this Standing Committee were: Eoin MacNeill, The O'Rahilly, Bulmer Hobson, Sean Fitzgibbon, J.D. Nugent, Martin Burke, Rev. Fr. O'Hare, Michael J. Judge, John Gore, L.J. Kettle, George Walsh, James Creed Meredith, J.T. Donovan, William Redmond, MP, Col Maurice Moore, Sean MacDermott and J.J. Scannell (Hobson, *A short history*, pp. 138–9).
125 Ibid., p. 169.
126 Ibid., pp. 170–1.
127 Hannon, 'Irish Volunteers', p. 63.
128 Ibid., p. 55.
129 O'Rahilly, *Secret history*, p. 11.
130 Ibid.
131 The British government withdrew this prohibition in response to public outcry after the military fired on a crowd of civilians at Bachelor's Walk on 26 July 1914, the day of the Howth gunrunning. The military had been marching back to their barracks after an unsuccessful attempt to disarm the Irish Volunteers when they met with the jeering crowd. See Chapter 7.
132 Pearse to McGarrity, 17 July 1914, qtd. in Cronin, *The McGarrity Papers*, pp. 43, 45.
133 Pearse to McGarrity, 17 July 1914 (NLI, BH, MS 13,162); emphasis in the original.
134 Hobson, *IYT*, p. 52.
135 Ibid., p. 50.
136 Hobson, statement to McGarrity, 1934 (NLI, BH, MS 13,171).

137 Hobson to McCartan, 13 Feb. 1924 (NLI, PMcC, MS 17,675 (5)).
138 The following men signed the manifesto ejecting Redmond's nominees: Eoin MacNeill, The O'Rahilly, Thomas MacDonagh, Joseph Plunkett, Piaras Béaslaí, Michael J. Judge, Peadar Macken, Sean Fitzgibbon, Patrick Pearse, Pádraig Ó Riain, Bulmer Hobson, Eamon Martin, Con Colbert, Éamonn Ceannt, Sean MacDermott, Seamus O'Connor, Liam Mellows, Colm Ó Lochlainn, Liam Gogan and Peter White (Hobson, *A secret history*, p. 202).
139 Hobson to Miss MacNeill, 28 Sept. 1914 (NLI, BH, MS 17,453).
140 Hobson to Molly Childers, 18 Oct. 1914 (TCD, Childers Papers, 7848/509); cited in Hannon, 'Irish Volunteers', p. 123.
141 Le Roux, *Patrick Pearse*, p. 288.
142 Hobson to McCartan, 13 Feb. 1924 (NLI, PMcC, MS 17,675 (5)).
143 Hobson, MS of 'The origin of Óglaigh na hÉireann – II', an article published in *An t-Óglách* (June 1931), pp. 5–13 (NLI, BH, MS 13,169).
144 Tierney, *Eoin MacNeill*, p. 142.
145 Martin, witness statement, n.d. (NAI, BMH, WS 591). For other criticisms of the acceptance of Redmond's nominees, see Judge, 'Inner history', *IN*, 7 Oct. 1916, p. 6; Le Roux, *Patrick Pearse*, p. 285.
146 Martin, 'McCullough, Hobson, and republican Ulster', p. 103.
147 Martin, witness statement, n.d. (NAI, BMH, WS 591).
148 R.F. Foster, *Modern Ireland 1600–1972* (London, 1989), p. 473.
149 Hobson, MS of 'The origin of Óglaigh na hÉireann – II' (NLI, BH, MS 13,169).

7

A Quaker and an Irish Volunteer

As a member of the Provisional Committee of the Irish Volunteers, Moore was surprised to discover that Hobson, despite his association with extremism,

> repudiated the view that Irishmen should rebel in or out of season; he maintained, on the other hand that ineffective attempts did harm to the national cause, and rendered preparation more difficult. He thought that every opportunity ought to be taken to organise and train our people, so that when a favourable international situation arose, they might be found ready to take advantage of it, to secure the liberty of their country.

Where in future years some people would see (or choose to see) cowardice, Moore saw bravery: Hobson 'always had the courage of his opinions, and the courage to face unpopularity; a moral courage which few possess'.[1] This courage probably derived in part from Hobson's Quaker upbringing.

Hobson's opposition to rebellion without any hope of military success and his efforts to ensure that the policy of the Irish Volunteers was one of defensive, rather than offensive, warfare led to tension between himself and IRB men and others who supported a policy of unconditional insurrection. Hobson was in favour of a rising only if Germany provided enough assistance to ensure military success. Instead, he advocated the implementation of a policy of guerrilla warfare if Britain tried to suppress or disarm the Irish Volunteers or impose conscription. These views help to explain his opposition to the Easter Rising of 1916.[2]

Commentators such as the Casement biographer Roger Sawyer and the Hobson enthusiast Des Gunning have referred to Hobson as a pacifist, implying that his opposition to the Easter Rising stemmed from his Quaker background.[3] Yet Hobson's involvement with the Irish Volunteers, which led to his resignation from the Society of Friends, belies such an interpretation. Hobson himself explained in 1963: 'I have about 300 years of Quakerism behind me and I had a certain horror of war, but I had a stronger desire to get Irish independence and there didn't seem to be any escape from it.'[4] Finding a way to fight for Irish independence with some chance of military success was more important to Hobson than adhering to the pacifist principles of the Quaker faith – or following the orders of the IRB executive.

As a founding member and secretary of the Irish Volunteers, Hobson created a high-level niche for himself that facilitated his involvement in the governance of the Volunteer organisation until the Easter Rising in April 1916. This chapter will examine Hobson's contributions to the Irish Volunteer movement in the areas of office administration, production of propaganda, gunrunning, military organisation and policy making in light of his Quaker background and the controversy over his alleged pacifism.

November 1913 to June 1914

From the beginning the Irish Volunteers were billed as a defensive military force, with stated aims that were vague enough to attract a broad spectrum of nationalists. Privately, however, various members harboured differing views of the ultimate purpose of the organisation. The IRB in particular saw the movement as a tool for staging an insurrection. Desmond FitzGerald, a Volunteer organiser in County Kerry, recalled that in December 1913 Hobson assured him that 'the movement would be clearly directed towards a rising'.[5] MacNeill also alluded to discussion of the Volunteers' potential to organise a rebellion. Such discussion appears to have taken place at the time of the movement's inception.[6]

Hobson, Casement and MacNeill were of the opinion that the precondition for a successful rising in Ireland was the assistance of at least fifty thousand German troops or 'equal forces to the British'.[7] At the time of his conversation with FitzGerald, Hobson was about to take Casement's memorandum delineating the state of Irish-German relations in the event of a European war to the United States so that it could be delivered to the German Ambassador, Count von Bernstorff. By communicating with Germany, Casement and Hobson 'hoped to force the question of Irish independence onto the international agenda'.[8]

Facilitating international intrigue was only part of Hobson's involvement in the Irish Volunteers. The leaders of the movement could not expect to be taken seriously by Germany, Britain or even their fellow Irishmen and women if they did not undertake the quotidian work of committee meetings and administration, military organisation and training, promotion and fundraising, and the procurement of arms and equipment. Hobson threw himself into such work with energy and enthusiasm, dividing his time between his Volunteer commitments and eking out a living as a freelance journalist.

In drawing a pen-portrait of his fellow committee member, Moore characterised Hobson as 'a man more of action than of words'. Despite this, he 'was a good speaker, moderate and measured in his language, and impressive in his manner', even though he lacked Pearse's 'fine literary style'. Moore described Hobson's mind as 'clear and direct, unclouded by unpractical ideals and willing to weigh arguments for and against'. In committee meetings Moore found him 'sound and sensible', adding that 'his advice was always worthy of consideration, because he went straight to the root of the matter under discussion'.[9] Such qualities made Hobson an influential committee member.

As unofficial secretary of the Irish Volunteers, Hobson was a denizen of the Volunteer office. The organisation's first address was his private office at 12 D'Olier Street.[10] In early 1914, while Hobson was in America, the office moved to 206 Great Brunswick Street. In August or September 1914 these rooms proved inadequate, so Hobson rented a house at 41 Kildare Street. After Dublin Corporation condemned the house, Volunteer headquarters moved to 2 Dawson Street, where it remained from April 1915 until the rising.[11]

Drawing on his previous experience as a Sinn Féin propagandist, Hobson encouraged the production of newspaper propaganda to promote the Irish Volunteers. The Provisional Committee recognised that the new force needed a propagandist vehicle to communicate with recruits and to provide a sense of unity. In December 1913 the proprietors of the *Enniscorthy Echo* contacted the committee in order to propose that they should start a weekly paper called the *Irish Volunteer*, which would be recognised as the official organ of the new movement.

In discussions regarding this proposal, Judge insisted that the Volunteers should receive a percentage of any profits made on the paper. He reported:

> Hobson and others, who were credited with possessing considerable journalistic experience, pooh-poohed the idea of any newspaper being a profit making concern. Indeed, from their arguments one might be induced to believe that the proprietors of newspapers ran them for purely philanthropic motives. Being a business man, I did not quite swallow the philanthropic potion.

At Judge's behest the future editor of the proposed paper, Laurence de Lacey, who was a Volunteer and an IRB man, 'quite readily agreed, on behalf of the proprietors, to pay to the Volunteer treasurers ten per cent of the profits made on the paper'.[12] Due to his previous experiences working on cash-strapped nationalist publications with a more limited potential audience, it might not have occurred to Hobson that the Volunteer organ could turn a profit.

The *Irish Volunteer* first appeared on 7 February 1914 and remained under external management until November of the same year. It was designed to be 'a record of the progress of the movement and an invaluable handbook for every recruit', providing 'simple lessons in the various branches of training', such as drill, rifles and rifle practice, semaphore signalling and ambulance work.[13] Although the paper had 'a large circulation amongst the Volunteers', it was not 'an ideal official organ' because it was not edited and printed in Dublin under the close eye of headquarters staff. As Hobson pointed out, 'the committee had no control over the paper beyond that the proprietors were bound by an agreement to print anything in the paper to which the committee desired to give publicity'.[14]

Hobson was involved in the military organisation of the Irish Volunteers from the body's inception until the 1916 rising. Although he himself had no military experience, his involvement with the Fianna, which was run on a semi-military basis, provided him with some background knowledge regarding military training and organisation. This knowledge, combined with his prestigious position as a founding member of the military force and his ability to get along with colonels Maurice Moore and Edmond Cotter, two of the few Volunteer leaders who had previous military experience in the British Army, helped him to take a leading role in the military organisation of the Volunteers.

On 3 February 1914 the Provisional Committee of the Irish Volunteers was divided into four sub-committees to undertake specific aspects of organisation under the categories of: finance; country; Dublin city and county; and uniform and equipment. Hobson, Moore, Judge, MacDermott, Ó Riain and Peadar Macken were appointed to the country sub-committee, which dealt with organisation outside of Dublin city and county.[15] It sent out speakers to meetings around Ireland and, until the force's organisational structure expanded, made sure that companies outside the Dublin area received military instruction.[16] It was probably under the auspices of this sub-committee that Hobson undertook two speaking engagements to promote the Volunteers in Bagenalstown, County Carlow and Bree, County Wexford which were reported in the *Irish Volunteer* in June 1914.[17]

Sub-committees in charge of military inspection and arms were added later. Hobson, Moore, Cotter and Fitzgibbon were appointed to the military inspection sub-committee on 23 June 1914. Initially, this sub-committee was responsible for the periodic inspection of the companies throughout Ireland. Later it 'took over the whole military organisation of the movement and supervised the military training' until the split in the Irish Volunteers in September 1914.[18] Hobson was probably engaged in work relating to this committee in August 1914 when police detectives spotted him touring the country in a motor car on Volunteer business.[19] MacNeill and O'Rahilly led the arms sub-committee, which was responsible for the purchase of arms and their subsequent sale to Volunteers. It was at the request of this sub-committee that Hobson co-ordinated the landing of guns and ammunition at Howth in July 1914, which will be discussed in detail below.[20]

Questions regarding military organisation provoked much discussion, often ill-informed, among the mainly civilian Provisional Committee members. The size of companies was an issue, with Hobson advocating seventy-nine officers and men per company while some other members, such as Judge, plumped for a total of a hundred. What Judge dubbed Hobson's 'pet scheme' for the formation of seventy-nine-member companies won out.[21] Committee members also advocated different types of drill from continental Europe and America. In the end, the 1911 British Army drill was deemed the most practicable because all of the corps in Ireland at this time had access to local ex-army men and reservists who knew this drill and could serve as instructors.[22] In December 1914 companies were expanded to include a hundred members and the 1914 system of drill was adopted.[23]

Controversy emerged over the selection of officers for the various corps around the country. Two options were considered: Volunteer headquarters could appoint officers who had passed a qualifying examination or the corps could elect their own officers, who would then take a qualifying examination after a few months. Although Hobson conceded that the first option was preferable, he viewed the second as more practicable at the time: 'The creation of a competent examining authority capable of conducting examinations immediately in 32 counties was quite beyond our resources, and the new corps that were springing up everywhere had to be officered at once.'[24] Judge reported that the Provisional Committee initially supported the first option. The men whom instructors had selected for officer training (most of whom were IRB members) were already studying for their forthcoming examinations when, at the last minute, Hobson and Moore succeeded in substituting the election option.[25] Judge objected to how Hobson and his supporters went about getting their way on this issue.

In May 1914 Hobson, Moore, O'Rahilly, O'Connor and Ó Riain held a meeting of the country sub-committee during a meeting of the Provisional Committee in order to vote in favour of the election of officers. When Judge came into the inner room to call them into the general meeting, he discovered what they were planning to do and pointed out that they did not have a quorum. They said that his presence provided a quorum. When the quintet joined the general meeting, over which Judge was presiding, Hobson went around the table whispering to certain members of the Provisional Committee. Moore proposed the adoption of a resolution in favour of officer elections, which he said had been passed by the country sub-committee. While he and Judge bickered about whether or not the sub-committee had had a quorum, Hobson kept repeating 'Put the question, Mr Chairman'. Judge recalled:

> In the end I put the question to the meeting, and the voting was six for and five against (two members did not vote), and the resolution was carried. In order to delay the matter until it was fully discussed, I entered a notice of motion to rescind, but this was counteracted by Moore and Hobson, who went straight from the meeting to the newspaper offices (they had everything pre-arranged), and the whole elective scheme was published in the morning papers over the name of Colonel Moore, Inspector-General of Irish Volunteers.

In Judge's opinion, their actions were 'obviously an attempt to rush those elections before matters reached a crisis' between the Provisional Committee and Redmond, who, alarmed by the growth of the Irish Volunteers, was trying to gain control of the organisation.[26] As noted previously, the Provisional Committee was forced in June 1914 to accept twenty-five of Redmond's nominees to the governing body in order to avoid splitting the Irish Volunteer movement.[27]

July 1914 to September 1914

Redmond's affirmation of the Irish Volunteers attracted new blood to the organisation. Many ex-British Army officers joined the Inspection Staff of the Volunteers that was instituted in June 1914.[28] For instance, Colonel Edmond Cotter, an Irishman formerly of the Royal Engineers, was among the retired British Army officers who volunteered their services in this period. He came over from England at his own expense to work for the Volunteers between July and September 1914.[29] He and Hobson became friendly and maintained contact after Cotter returned home.

In mid 1914 Moore, as Inspector-General, organised an impromptu staff to co-ordinate the military side of the Volunteer movement. In addition to Moore himself, the military staff consisted of Cotter, who was appointed Chief of Staff, Hobson and Fitzgibbon. Hobson was asked to assist Cotter, who had limited knowledge of conditions in Ireland.[30] Hobson also found himself taking 'on the delicate task of keeping the peace' between Moore and Cotter, as the two old colonels (and their egos) tended to clash.[31]

Redmond's benediction of the Volunteers also boosted financial support for the movement. After the co-option of Redmond's nominees to the Provisional Committee, Henry Harrison organised the Volunteer Aid Association to collect subscriptions for the Irish Volunteers. Hobson supported a resolution in favour of the object of this new organisation at a public meeting in July 1914, declaring: 'Ireland had long occupied the degraded position of being an unarmed and, therefore, an abject nation. [The Irish Volunteers] stood for a disciplined and permanently-armed Ireland.'[32] This declaration implies that some of the money collected by the Aid Association was to be used to pay for arms. The Aid Association, which was aimed at 'many citizens of Dublin who were of such ultra-respectability and loyalty that they could not be recruited into the Irish Volunteers', opened an office at 44 Dawson Street.[33]

Claire Gregan (1887–1958), Hobson's future wife, worked there as a secretary. They met when he dropped by on business one day when the office was bustling with people paying subscriptions. Hobson's sister Florence later told his son that Gregan 'was the first woman in whom she was aware of [her brother] taking a serious romantic interest'.[34] It would appear that Hobson's alleged romance with Molony was either unknown to his sister or not considered 'serious'. Upon closure of the Volunteer Aid Association, Hobson offered Gregan a job as his personal typist at Volunteer headquarters down the road at 2 Dawson Street. They both had offices on the third floor of the building. She recalled working there for about six months before the rising.[35]

In an episode that could be described as 'propaganda of deed', Hobson co-ordinated the landing of the shipment of guns and ammunition at Howth on 26 July 1914.[36] Casement had taken the initiative in organising a London committee whose members subscribed £1,500 to purchase arms and ammunition that, in turn, would be sold to the Irish Volunteers. Darrell Figgis and Erskine Childers were dispatched to the Continent to buy 1,500 Mauser rifles and 45,000 rounds of ammunition, with Childers and Conor O'Brien volunteering to transport these purchases back to Ireland in their yachts. After consulting MacNeill and O'Rahilly, who, according to Hobson, had 'produced no practicable plan', Casement turned to his old friend in June 1914.[37] As Hobson pointed out in 1915, 'it was not the sort of invitation that an Irish Volunteer would be likely to refuse, so I set to work without delay'.[38] Eager as he was to formulate a plan, Hobson had one proviso: that he would not be 'hampered by any committee'.[39]

The thinking behind Hobson's plan reveals his talents as a PR man: 'I decided that 1,500 rifles would not go very far ... but that if we could bring them in in a sufficiently spectacular manner, we should probably solve our financial problem and the problem of arming the Volunteers as well.'[40] He cycled from Greystones to Balbriggan, examining every harbour along the way, and finally settled on Howth. His idea was 'to march a large number of Volunteers to meet the yacht, to arm them on the spot and march them back to Dublin'. He explained:

> I felt that this could be done, provided the movement was executed with sufficient rapidity to enable us to get back past the narrow neck of land at Sutton before [Dublin] Castle had time to intervene. I felt that the task of seizing so many guns from so many individual Volunteers, who would be scattered over a wide area, would be beyond the powers of either police or soldiery.[41]

Hobson successfully proposed this plan to Casement and Childers at a Sunday meeting in Buswell's Hotel in June 1914. The following day Hobson and Childers headed out to Howth to decide where and when the yacht would come in. They settled on 26 July at noon.

At Hobson's request MacNeill proposed at the next meeting of the Provisional Committee that the Dublin Volunteer companies begin holding joint route marches on Sunday mornings. The police took great interest in the first Sunday morning route march. Their interest lessened with each subsequent Sunday march until 26 July, when they took no interest at all.[42] Other tactics were also used to divert the attention of the authorities, such as Hobson telling a loquacious solicitor that they were planning to run guns into Waterford.[43]

Despite his falling-out with Clarke and MacDermott, Hobson's status within the IRB was still such that he could turn to some of his IRB colleagues for assistance in preparation for the gunrunning. He asked members of the IRB who were carpenters to make two hundred oak batons, which were to be used in case of an attack by the police.[44] IRB members also played a part on the day of the event. Some were instructed to go to Howth early in the morning to act like tourists and help to moor the *Asgard*, Childers's yacht. Others were instructed to invite lady friends out for the day, take them in taxis to Howth and order lunch in the hotel. When the yacht hove into sight, they were to ditch their ladies and lunch and bring their taxis up to the harbour. Then the taxis were to be loaded up with ammunition and sent off to various destinations.[45]

About eight hundred Volunteers, few of whom knew what was in store, met at Father Mathew Park in Fairview on that bright, sunny morning. According to Judge, it was the first time that Hobson and MacNeill had turned up for a Sunday morning route march.[46] The Volunteers arrived at Howth just as the *Asgard* sailed into the harbour. It took half an hour to unload the guns and ammunition, most of the latter being transported by taxi. Once the Fianna, under the command of Ó Riain, had distributed the oak batons from their trek cart, they then loaded it up with the remaining two thousand rounds of ammunition.[47]

The gunrunning at Howth was a highly successful publicity stunt that led to a stream of donations flowing into the Volunteer coffers. While the event reflects well on Hobson's PR acumen, the return journey to Dublin gave rise to some questions about his military judgement (or rather lack of it). Both MacNeill and Judge criticised Hobson for allowing the men to rest in Raheny, because this gave the authorities more time to move against the Volunteers. MacNeill asked Hobson to order the men back on the march, later reflecting that the halt in Raheny enabled Assistant-Commissioner William Vesey Harrel of the Dublin Metropolitan Police 'to intercept the Volunteers outside of the city. Once among the houses he would hardly have dared to do anything to them.'[48] Although he agreed with Hobson that refreshment was needed, Judge deemed it was 'not absolutely necessary and could have been postponed'.[49]

O'Rahilly's son Aodogán, who was a child at the time of the gunrunning, accused Hobson of more than poor military judgement. He alleged that Hobson stopped the men at Raheny because he was too cowardly to continue and only moved on at MacNeill's request.[50] Aodogán O'Rahilly's allegation probably owes more to pride in his father's fateful decision to join the Easter Rising and scorn at Hobson's equally fateful decision not to participate, than to cowardice on Hobson's part on the day of the gunrunning.

Aware of the opposition forces gathering ahead, Hobson concluded at Raheny that 'it was quite impracticable' to ask the exhausted Volunteers 'to approach Dublin by longer and indirect routes', and that they should continue on and deal with the police and soldiers when they met them.[51] The showdown came in Clontarf, where Harrel confronted Bodkin, the drill instructor chosen to lead the march, and Hobson, who had joined him at the head of the column. When Harrel ordered the assembled members of the Dublin Metropolitan Police and the King's Own Scottish Borderers to seize the arms, some of them ignored the order while others rushed at the Volunteers. Harrel and Hobson looked on as a brief fight ensued in which nineteen rifles were seized and Judge received a bayonet wound.[52] The police and soldiers, acting without orders, soon withdrew from the mêlée. Future insurrectionist Thomas MacDonagh (1878–1916) and Darrell Figgis joined Hobson at the front of the column and began arguing with Harrel. Knowing that the pair had the ability to 'talk him blind', Hobson took the opportunity to run to the back of the column and order the men to disperse. A dazed Harrel was still listening to the pair when Hobson returned, having watched all but one company vanish through the hedges.[53]

Judge later criticised Hobson for ordering that ammunition not be handed out to the Volunteers,[54] who, in Hobson's estimation, 'were far too raw and undisciplined' to be trusted with it. Instead they were armed with oak batons.[55] Handing out ammunition probably would have led to greater bloodshed on that day, possibly resulting in the suppression of the Volunteers.

While marching back to their barracks after the fracas at Clontarf, the King's Own Scottish Borderers fired on a crowd at Bachelor's Walk who were jeering at them. Three members of the crowd were killed and another thirty-eight wounded, causing a public outcry. The events of 26 July 1914 led to a Royal Commission of Inquiry, which ruled that military intervention had been unwarranted.[56]

The day after the gunrunning Moore went to Dublin Castle to demand the return of the nineteen rifles that had been seized. According to Hobson, 'the authorities were in such a state of panic they gave them to him'.[57] As a result of the gunrunning at Howth and the shootings at Bachelor's Walk, Moore estimated that the ranks of the Irish Volunteers increased by 25 per cent.[58] The sensational events of 26 July attracted clergy, local councillors, minor politicians and ex-British Army officers to the movement, as well as offers of facilities for training, rifle practice and parading.[59]

Of the 1,500 guns purchased, 900 came into Howth on the *Asgard*. The remaining 600 guns and some ammunition, which were on Conor O'Brien's yacht, the *Kelpie*, were transferred to Sir Thomas Myles's yacht, the *Chotah*, off the coast of Wales and then landed at Kilcoole, County Wicklow. According to Hobson, MacNeill offered him the chance to organise a second landing, but he 'was much too busy with the arrangements for Howth, and with other work, to take on this additional responsibility'. There was also the chance that both yachts might arrive at the same time. Instead Fitzgibbon was put in charge of co-ordinating the Kilcoole landing, which, so soon after the Howth publicity stunt, was conducted under the cover of night on 1 August 1914.[60] Fitzgibbon, who was not a member of the IRB, invited Hobson to come along for the late-night gunrunning because he was concerned that some of the IRB members might not accept his orders.[61] Garry Holohan, a Fianna member, recalled seeing Hobson 'very happy and satisfied looking',[62] heading back to Dublin in style on the back of a large motor charabanc. Unfortunately, it 'was so overloaded with men, guns and ammunition that it broke a back axle' in the middle of Bray at about five o'clock in the morning. A motorcyclist had to be dispatched to Dublin to order some taxis and trucks to finish the journey. There was no sign of the Bray policemen.[63] Despite attempts by Redmond's supporters to commandeer the cargo brought in at Howth and Kilcoole, the guns and ammunition remained hidden in the hands of individual Volunteers and IRB men. They resurfaced for use during Easter Week 1916.

The outbreak of the war in Europe in August 1914 impacted on the Irish Volunteers in a number of ways. It served as a catalyst for the planning of an insurrection, disrupted plans for further military organisation of the Volunteers and contributed to a split in the movement. The split served to strengthen the IRB's grip on the Irish Volunteers. Whether Hobson or Clarke and MacDermott would wield the most influence remained to be seen.

Shortly after the war broke out, the Supreme Council of the IRB decided to organise a rebellion in Ireland before the end of hostilities. Meanwhile in New York, a deputation from Clan na Gael met with the German ambassador, Count von Bernstorff, to discuss the possibility of Germany providing arms and officers to assist the Irish in the staging of an insurrection.[64] This approach to the German government was a follow-up to Casement's memorandum which Hobson had delivered to Devoy earlier in the year. Clarke and MacDermott envisaged that the Irish Volunteers would play a key role in the rebellion.

They kept the decision to stage a rising a secret from Hobson, whom they no longer trusted. In any case Hobson was only in favour of an insurrection under certain limited circumstances. Instead, he advocated a guerrilla warfare campaign, which, he believed, would have more chance of success. Having learned the lessons of history derived from previous futile attempts at rebellion, Hobson remained loyal to the 1873 IRB constitution, which forbade insurrection without the support of the majority of the Irish people. Clarke and MacDermott, however, believed that they were in a better position than the Irish people to judge what was in Ireland's best interest. Fearing that Ireland would be lulled into permanent West Britonism through the tranquilliser of Home Rule, the pair refused 'to be constitutionalised out of insurrection'.[65]

The war impacted on plans to improve the organisation of the Irish Volunteers. Over the course of the summer of 1914, Cotter had been engaged in devising and instituting what Charles Hannon has called 'the first effective organisational scheme for the Volunteers as a national body'. Cotter also 'devised and introduced a scheme for organisational development and administrative procedures for the Volunteer Headquarters military staff'.[66] On 14 August 1914 his proposed reorganisation scheme was passed unanimously by the military sub-committee, of which Hobson was a member.[67] As Hannon pointed out, 'given the experience of the inspection staff and the intentions of the military staff by mid August 1914 the Volunteers were about to be militarised formally for the first time since their foundation'.[68] Implementation of Cotter's scheme was first delayed because the European war effort robbed the Volunteers of many men and instructors[69] and then abandoned due to the split in the Volunteer movement in September 1914.[70] A week before the split, Cotter resigned and returned home to England because he had run out of money and did not wish to be a drain on the Volunteers' purse.[71]

The split occurred after Redmond made a speech urging the Irish Volunteers to join the British Army and fight in the war in Europe. As a result, over two-thirds of the original members of the Provisional Committee, including Hobson and MacNeill, signed a manifesto on 24 September 1914 ejecting Redmond's nominees from the governing body of the Volunteers.[72] MacNeill's contingent retained the name Irish Volunteers and Redmond's supporters, who comprised about 93 per cent of the Volunteer membership, formed the National Volunteers.[73] MacNeill lost the military know-how of ex-British Army men like Moore, but kept the advanced nationalists, many of whom were IRB members. The nominal loyalty of Redmond's National Volunteers ensured that the British authorities treated them with more tolerance than the Irish Volunteers, especially in relation to arms importation.[74]

October 1914 to April 1916

In October 1914 Hobson was appointed honorary general secretary at Volunteer headquarters, replacing Liam Mellows, who had served as paid assistant secretary until he was sent on the road as the Irish Volunteers' first organising instructor. In this administrative role Hobson was responsible for organising the first convention of the Irish Volunteers,[75] which was held on 25 October 1914 at the Abbey Theatre. This convention marked a new phase in the history of the Irish Volunteers.

About 160 delegates attended the convention and elected an Executive Committee to run the re-constituted Irish Volunteer movement under the direction of a General Council, the new governing body. The General Council consisted of the Executive Committee as well as elected representatives from each of the thirty-two counties and nine principal towns. Hobson and the other members of the original Provisional Committee who had signed the manifesto ousting Redmond's nominees were unanimously elected to the new Executive Committee.[76]

Despite official reports of unanimity, there was one person who was unhappy to see members of the old Provisional Committee returned to power. Judge later claimed that immediately after the convention he sent his letter of resignation from the Executive Committee to MacNeill because he felt that members of the old committee were not the best men to run the organisation efficiently. He also objected to certain clauses that were included in the constitution, as well as to the exclusion of certain other details.[77] MacNeill, however, convinced Judge to withdraw his resignation.[78] Judge duly attended the first meeting of the new General Council on 6 December 1914 and was one of the members of the Executive Committee assigned a portfolio after the convention.[79]

MacNeill and O'Rahilly were re-elected as president and treasurer respectively at the first convention. Judge recalled that an unidentified delegate proposed, to much applause, that he [Judge] should be elected honorary secretary 'as a token of appreciation of [his] services to the movement'. MacDonagh and Hobson, who was already serving in this position, countered this suggestion, declaring that it was out of order to elect officers at the convention and that the new General Council or Executive Committee should elect the remaining officers. Hobson, no doubt, was motivated by a combination of self-interest and the need to keep an IRB man in this key position. Judge's reputation within the Volunteer governing body as a troublemaker may have motivated MacDonagh to support Hobson. Judge's conviction that he would have won by a large majority had the election of the honorary secretary been held at the convention further fuelled his hatred of Hobson.[80]

The Executive Committee met after the convention to divide up portfolios of work among members who would meet as a Central Executive on a weekly basis. The following appointments were made:

General Secretary: Bulmer Hobson
Financial Secretary: Éamonn Ceannt
Press Secretary: Patrick Pearse
Publication Secretary: Pádraig Ó Riain
Affiliation and Record Secretary: Sean Fitzgibbon
Musketry Training: Seamus O'Connor
Organisation: Michael J. Judge
Purchase of Arms: Eoin MacNeill and The O'Rahilly

Joseph Plunkett was later appointed by the Executive Committee as co-treasurer with O'Rahilly.[81] Of the ten members of the Central Executive, six belonged to the IRB: Hobson, Ceannt, Pearse, Ó Riain, O'Connor and Plunkett.

The first convention of the Irish Volunteers was not the only significant event that occurred in October 1914. During that month – unbeknown to Hobson and MacNeill – the Supreme Council of the IRB set up an Advisory Committee consisting of IRB members who were commandants and vice-commandants in the Irish Volunteers to develop a plan for a rising. The committee came up with a plan for a Dublin insurrection but Clarke, concerned about the security implications of so large a committee, rejected its report. After the committee lapsed, Clarke and MacDermott established in early 1915 what became known as the Military Council. This consisted of Pearse and two aspiring military strategists, Éamonn Ceannt and Joseph Plunkett.[82] Others were later co-opted to this council: Clarke and MacDermott in September 1915, James Connolly in January 1916 and MacDonagh in April 1916.

October 1914 also saw the beginning of Casement's mission to Germany. He had three aims: 'to secure a diplomatic dialogue with Germany; to educate the German government and people about Ireland; and to organise Irish prisoners of war into a competent military unit to fight for the independence of Ireland'.[83] Aware of his friend's mission, Hobson continued to allude to the possibility of a German-supported rebellion. In describing a meeting with Hobson in late 1914, FitzGerald reported:

> One gathered that [Hobson] knew all that was to be known about the war and how it was going to develop. And with that vast knowledge he looked to the immediate future with an absolutely equable mind ... His whole tone and manner also definitely assured me that there would be no fear that the war would end suddenly and unexpectedly before we had struck a blow. I could not question him on such matters, as apparently he was deep in the confidence of the German leaders, and it would look as though I doubted that or were asking him to betray their confidence.[84]

Hobson, of course, was not in the confidence of the Germans. The pretentious performance that he put on for FitzGerald was derived from his knowledge of Casement's plans and activities.

Casement experienced some initial success: the Germans affirmed their support for Irish independence in November 1914 and agreed to the formation of an Irish Brigade in December 1914. His fortunes then began to flag. He recruited few men to the Irish Brigade because most of the Irish prisoners of war were Home Rulers who viewed him as a traitor, trying to help a Protestant state that had invaded Catholic Belgium. As a result, Casement's currency with Germany diminished in value.

The Military Council sent Plunkett to negotiate with Germany. Ostensibly recuperating from ill-heath, Plunkett spent April to July 1915 on the Continent. While in Germany he and Casement collaborated on the production of a document called the Ireland Report, which outlined 'the contemporary Irish situation, the various Irish nationalist organisations, the structure and activities of the Irish Volunteers, political attitudes in Ireland and the strength of the British military and police forces'. The pair hoped that the document would convince the German government to send a sizeable force to Ireland to support a rising.[85] The Germans were sceptical, but did not reject the IRB's entreaties outright. Instead they made a commitment to help the Military Council on the condition that the Irish offered proof of serious intent, such as setting a date for an insurrection and developing a concrete plan of action.[86]

Upon his return from Germany, Plunkett put a pessimistic spin on German intentions in order to cover up the plans of the Military Council. Fitzgibbon received a second-hand report from Hobson that Plunkett had met with German army staff who showed little interest in Ireland and said that if they did decide to invade the island, the Irish Volunteers would only be in their way.[87] Hobson apparently took Plunkett's words at face value because his advocacy (albeit limited) of rebellion appears to have dissipated as the hope of receiving any significant support from the Germans diminished. Although Hobson continued to believe – perhaps to hope – that Germany would win the war, he began over the course of 1915 to advise a 'wait and see' attitude.[88] Influenced by Casement, Hobson predicted that, if Germany won the war, Ireland would be recognised as a republic, but if Britain won, the best Ireland could achieve (as it indeed transpired) would be dominion status.[89]

In his capacity as general secretary of the Irish Volunteers, Hobson served as office administrator at Volunteer headquarters. He was responsible for a variety of tasks. For instance, he co-ordinated the printing and distribution of stationery, such as enrolment forms, membership cards and roll books; processed applications for the Volunteer training camps held in the summer of 1915; collected affiliation fees from the various Volunteer corps and subscriptions for the Defence of Ireland Fund and the Irish Volunteers Prisoners Defence Fund; and hired office employees. In carrying out the latter duty he showed a flair for nationalistic nepotism, favouring IRB men, such as Liam Mellows, and individuals who, like himself, had been victimised in some way for their nationalist viewpoint. For instance, he gave jobs to future playwright and novelist Eimar O'Duffy, who had had a falling-out with his father over the war, and Mabel FitzGerald, after her husband Desmond was jailed as a result of his work on behalf of the Volunteers.[90]

Hobson garnered some criticism for the way in which he undertook his duties as general secretary of the Irish Volunteers. Desmond FitzGerald viewed Hobson's reception of visitors to his office at

Volunteer headquarters as pompous and rude. On one occasion, when he and fellow Volunteer organiser Ernest Blythe went to visit Hobson, FitzGerald was surprised by the coolness of Hobson's welcome, considering that Blythe was 'an old and loyal friend' and he himself 'was suffering for the cause'. He recalled that Hobson 'looked up from what he was writing and nodded, and then continued writing as though we were not there'. FitzGerald regarded the length of time that Hobson ignored them as 'offensive and ill-mannered'. He was about to leave when Hobson finally put down his pen and began talking to them 'genially'.[91] After this meeting, FitzGerald complained to Blythe about his friend's initial reception of them. Blythe laughed and said 'that was just to impress you … That is his way.' Although the pair laughed off Hobson's behaviour as 'an amiable foible', FitzGerald 'still maintained that it was damn bad manners, and told Blythe that he should make an opportunity to point out to his friend that it might not always have the effect that he expected'.[92] The historian Alice Stopford Green, who helped to produce Volunteer propaganda, proffered further criticism, questioning Hobson's efficiency as an office administrator. She informed Casement that 'his lack of training shows itself. His Volunteer office is wholly unorganised.'[93]

Delegates to the first Volunteer convention indicated that there was a need to develop a fund 'to assist men who were victimised by the government or by employers on account of their connection with the Irish Volunteers'. Hobson, who from his Sinn Féin days had previous experience of the need to insure nationalists, suggested to the Executive Committee that a mutual insurance society might serve this purpose. The General Council, at its first meeting after the convention, agreed to put such a scheme in place. This led to the formation of An Cumann Cosanta.[94] Volunteers could insure themselves for the amount of their ordinary income upon payment of a small fee. If a member lost his job, due to his involvement in the Volunteer movement, he was paid the full amount of his ordinary income (up to £2 per week) for up to three months or until he found new employment.[95] Michael O'Hanrahan, one of the men later executed for his role in the Easter Rising, became the secretary of this new venture, under the direction of Hobson.[96]

Such an insurance scheme was necessary. After the split in the Irish Volunteer movement, the British authorities used DORA legislation to clamp down on Irish Volunteer organisers who were seen to be inciting sedition and curtailing army recruitment at a time when Britain was at war. For instance, FitzGerald's organisational work for the Volunteers in County Kerry led to his expulsion to County Wicklow in late 1914. Although Hobson helped to instigate An Cumann Cosanta to aid men who fell foul of the authorities, he 'did not pour out sympathy' for the way the British had treated FitzGerald. Instead, he viewed British repression as good propaganda for the Volunteer cause.[97]

After the proprietors of the *Enniscorthy Echo* announced their plans to discontinue publication of the *Irish Volunteer* at the end of November 1914,[98] responsibility for the organ shifted to Volunteer headquarters, where Hobson managed the production of the newspaper and served as unofficial editor. The paper received an initial subsidy from Volunteer funds and then soon paid for itself. In Hobson's opinion, J.J. 'Ginger' O'Connell, who later became a colonel in the Irish army, and Eimar O'Duffy contributed the most valuable articles to the paper.[99] They wrote about military topics, covering everything from guerrilla-style fighting to strategic points in Irish counties, from important historic Irish battles to victories of non-governmental forces. To help prepare the Irish Volunteers for a potential guerrilla warfare campaign, they adapted their military instruction to the peculiarities of Irish terrain and the limitations of the Volunteer force. According to Hobson, O'Connell's series of notes on the European War 'were so ably written and displayed such knowledge of what was going on in France and Russia that the Military Authorities became alarmed and we had to discontinue them to avoid having the paper suppressed'. In addition, MacNeill, Pearse and Ó Riain contributed political notes, the Headquarters Bulletin and Fianna news respectively.[100]

After the Volunteer convention the Executive Committee's first task was to develop a new scheme of military organisation and training. It recommended to the General Council that a military headquarters staff be appointed to oversee the military organisation and training of the Irish Volunteers. At its first meeting on 6 December 1914 the council agreed to the appointment of this body, which 'relieved the Executive Committee of a large part of the work'. The following officers were initially appointed to the military headquarters staff:

Chief of Staff: Eoin MacNeill
Director of Arms: The O'Rahilly
Director of Training: Thomas MacDonagh
Director of Military Organisation: Patrick Pearse
Director of Military Operations: Joseph Plunkett
Quartermaster: Bulmer Hobson

In 1915 the staff was expanded to include:

Director of Communications: Éamonn Ceannt
Chief Inspecting Officer: J.J. O'Connell[101]

This line-up, which contained five IRB members, remained in place until the Easter Rising.[102] Four staff members, Pearse, Plunkett, Ceannt and MacDonagh, became members of the IRB Military Council that planned the rising.

Characteristically, Judge was unhappy with the way in which the military headquarters staff had been appointed and the powers it claimed. In a letter to the editor published in the *Irish Independent* on 19 December 1914, Judge announced his resignation from the governing body of the Irish Volunteers. He complained that the rights and liberties that the organisation had been established to protect were being assailed by a 'small section' within the Volunteer leadership that 'seeks to obtain complete control of the movement and strives after arbitrary powers before which the militarism of the Kaiser's government would fade into insignificance'.[103] The small section to which he referred was Hobson and his IRB colleagues. He was unaware that by this time the IRB contingent was split between advocates of conditional and unconditional insurrection. Although Judge later insisted that 'this protest was made in the best interests of my comrades',[104] they did not agree. As a result of his letter, Company C, 1st Dublin Battalion, of which Judge was commander, requested that the Executive Committee dismiss Capt. Judge as commander. The request was granted.[105] Judge, who, upon his unanimous election as commander, had been hailed as 'an indefatigable worker … more energetic in working for the Volunteer movement than perhaps any other man in Ireland', left the Irish Volunteers a bitter man. He blamed Hobson more than anyone for what he saw as the failure of the Volunteer movement to uphold its original aims.[106]

In Hobson's new capacity as quartermaster of the Irish Volunteers, one of his responsibilities was to procure tents and other equipment. Such items were expensive and in short supply in 1915 because the regular manufacturers had large contracts with the British War Office. To overcome this difficulty, a factory was set up at Volunteer headquarters. Under Hobson's management, it manufactured tents, haversacks, belts and bayonet frogs at a competitive price.[107]

The split in the Volunteer movement deprived MacNeill's followers of military instructors who had previous experience in the British Army. Such instructors had focused mainly on drill, neglecting training in the use of firearms and scouting. In developing a new training programme, the Irish Volunteers recognised that these two neglected areas and guerrilla warfare needed to be addressed.[108]

Within the Irish Volunteer movement the concept of guerrilla warfare was first introduced in November 1914, the same month that the organisation put its new scheme of military organisation and training into place. Charles Hannon suggests that 'this new concept was as much an effort to restore the morale of those Volunteers who stayed with MacNeill as it was a plan of action given the much reduced numbers of the Irish Volunteers'.[109] As Hobson pointed out, the Irish Volunteers, initially left with an estimated three thousand to eleven thousand men, could not hope to put a regular army in the field.[110] Guerrilla warfare, the tactics of which were outlined in the *Irish Volunteer* newspaper, offered 'the only method by which resistance could be maintained over any length of time or with any prospect of success'.[111]

In late 1914 and early 1915 the Irish Volunteers hired a number of organising instructors to organise and train the various corps around the country that were still affiliated with the MacNeill branch of the movement.[112] During the summer of 1915 further training was provided at camps, for which Hobson was responsible for providing equipment.[113] Most of the instructors had a connection to Hobson. Ernest Blythe, Alf Monaghan and Alf Cotton had been members of the Belfast Freedom Club,[114] while Liam Mellows was a Fianna member. Hobson had recruited O'Connell to the Volunteers after they met in New York in early 1914.[115] Due to the grass-roots nature of their work, the organising instructors were vulnerable to expulsion, deportation, or arrest under DORA legislation. For instance, Blythe was deported to England and Cotton expelled from Kerry.

O'Connell, who was hired as a military instructor in January 1915 and later became chief inspecting officer, criticised the military headquarters staff for not undertaking the military management of the Volunteers seriously. Weekly staff meetings to discuss such matters were often neglected. O'Connell remembered 'one occasion on which Hobson sent to Pearse and MacDonagh the following message: "MacNeill is lecturing in the Mansion House, I am going to listen to the lecture, O'Rahilly is dining out, and O'Connell is going to a dance – there will be no meeting of the staff to-night."'[116] Meetings that did take place tended to degenerate into 'rambling discussion' unless the 'business-like' Ceannt was presiding.[117]

Most members of the headquarters staff lacked practical military experience. 'The higher command of the Volunteers consisted of men who could not "slope arms" properly – having never drilled in the ranks, men who moreover thought themselves above sloping arms,' revealed O'Connell. Instead of drilling they read about the campaigns of Ulm, Austerlitz and Jena.[118] Hobson's recollection of a visit from MacDonagh illustrates O'Connell's point:

He pulled out a book and he put it down on my desk; he said, 'Hobson, did you ever read that?' And I picked it up; it was Caesar's *Gallic Wars*. I said I had read it a good many years ago, what about it? 'But,' he said, 'don't you carry it about in your pocket?' 'No,' I said, 'why should I?' 'Well,' he said, 'you can't understand strategy without it.'[119]

Even Hobson himself serves as an example. In his various accounts of his time with the Volunteers, Hobson never mentioned his own participation in drilling or revealed the name of the company to which he belonged. In O'Connell's opinion, 'the Volunteer higher command had put the cart before the horse when they set out to learn their business'.[120]

Although the higher command 'was ... deficient in technical grip', O'Connell deemed the subordinate officers quite knowledgeable, 'anxious to learn more and not in the least ignorant of their own limitations'. As their efficiency increased through systematic training, 'so did their capacity to see the limitations of their superiors'.[121] He mentioned Pearse, MacDonagh and Plunkett by name, but his criticism probably extended to Hobson. O'Connell, however, recognised that Hobson at least was fully cognisant of the Volunteers' limitations.[122]

O'Connell and Judge justly criticised both Hobson and MacNeill for rarely attending military functions.[123] They were seen as 'acting the part of politicians' rather than taking 'the military side of the organisation seriously'. They were more likely to be spotted speaking from the platform at an anti-conscription rally, such as the one held in the Mansion House on 14 December 1915,[124] than participating in route marches. Their attendance at the review of the Irish Volunteers at College Green on St Patrick's Day in 1916 was seen as a welcome divergence from their usual habit.[125] A trawl of the *Irish Volunteer* newspaper bears out the suggestion that Hobson was rarely associated with military manoeuvres. One exception occurred on 16 August 1914, when Hobson assisted Ó Riain in commanding the Red Force against Darrell Figgis's White Force in field operations in County Tyrone. The Reds won.[126] The most spectacular exception to Hobson's neglect of military functions was his involvement in the Howth gunrunning.

Both the Volunteers and the IRB expected to profit from the circumstances arising from the war. While extremists like Clarke, MacDermott and Pearse saw it as the perfect opportunity to stage an insurrection, moderates such as Hobson, MacNeill, O'Connell and Fitzgibbon took a longer-term view. According to the historian F.X. Martin,

> The policy of the MacNeill group was to arm and organise so that by the end of the European war there would be a resolute and widespread body of Volunteers, who would be joined, it was hoped, by thousands

of disillusioned Irish ex-soldiers who had fought for 'the rights of small nations' on the battlefields.[127]

This would place the Irish Volunteers in a position of strength to demand Irish independence. The MacNeill group was intent on developing a system of training for guerrilla warfare to prepare for the three possible events that, in its opinion, would justify military action (as opposed to military preparation) during the war: the landing of a German force; the attempted suppression or disarmament of the Irish Volunteers; or the imposition of conscription within Ireland.[128]

As the war raged on, fears of conscription in Ireland heightened. According to Hobson, the governing body of the Irish Volunteers, through much discussion, developed a plan that could be implemented if conscription were imposed. He recalled:

> it was intended that men drafted for the army should join small flying columns in various parts of the country, defend themselves from being captured, with whatever arms we could obtain, and conduct a guerrilla war against the forces sent to draft them into the British armies ... We, on the Volunteer executive, knew that if it was attempted to impose conscription almost the entire population would actively support our resistance to it ... We believed that not only could we make conscription unworkable, but that, in the ensuing struggle, we could make a continuance of the British government of Ireland impossible also.

This second goal was to be achieved through Sinn Féin's policy of passive resistance, which would involve non-co-operation with the Dublin Castle administration.[129]

Hobson's role in the formation and ongoing organisation of a military force like the Irish Volunteers was extraordinary in light of his Quaker background. The Quakers themselves found it particularly surprising. In 1915 the Lisburn Monthly Meeting of the Society of Friends dispatched a letter to Hobson asking whether he wanted to retain his membership in the Meeting.[130] The Society of Friends had long been conscious of how the actions of one member could create a negative impression of the entire Quaker community, and it was not unusual for Meetings to take members to task for actions that contravened their internal code. This letter may have been the first step towards the imposition upon him of a penalty called 'disownment'.[131]

Hobson wrote back that he was no longer an adherent of the principles of the Society. The Meeting accepted this letter as his resignation.[132] In memoirs and media interviews Hobson asserted that he resigned from the Religious Society of Friends in 1914, recognising that his participation in such an openly military organisation as the Irish Volunteers was inconsistent with the pacifist principles of the Quaker faith.[133] The records of the Society of Friends list his resignation date as 14 October 1915.[134] There are a number of possible reasons for this discrepancy in the year of his resignation. For example, Hobson may have got his dates mixed up or he may have resigned orally in 1914 but the Lisburn Monthly Meeting required written confirmation. William Glynn, an Irish Quaker who delivered a graveside tribute to Hobson, interpreted his resignation as a way of 'in fact holding to a more fundamental principle in Quaker teaching: he was acting according to his understanding of the truth and as a man of his word'.[135] Hobson, however, had long deviated from the Quaker norm, having joined a secret society (the IRB) and taken an oath in 1904.

The second convention of the Irish Volunteers was held in the Abbey Theatre on 31 October 1915. MacNeill, O'Rahilly and Hobson were re-elected to their respective positions as president, honorary treasurer and honorary secretary. MacDonagh, Fitzgibbon, Plunkett, Pearse, MacDermott, Mellows, O'Connell, Ceannt and O'Connor formed the rest of the Central Executive.[136] Eight members of the IRB were now on the Central Executive: Hobson, MacDonagh, Plunkett, Pearse, MacDermott, Mellows, Ceannt and O'Connor.

By late 1915 the Military Council's plans for a rising were starting to come together. With four members on the Volunteer Central Executive, the council was in a position to commandeer the manpower of the Irish Volunteers. In September 1915 Pearse dispatched Diarmuid Lynch, an IRB Supreme Council member, to the south-west to research possible landing places for a German arms shipment.[137] The year 1915 had seen the development of the Military Council's plans for a rising and the diminishment of Hobson's limited support for rebellion. Not surprisingly, Seamus O'Connor began to notice within the Volunteer leadership a growing enmity between Hobson on one side and the future insurrectionists on the other. 'They never suspected his honesty, but they didn't like his ideas as they feared that he was more of a politician than a revolutionist,' claimed O'Connor.[138]

In late 1915 and early 1916 labour leader James Connolly delivered speeches and published articles in the *Workers' Republic* that ridiculed the cautious policy of Hobson and MacNeill and threatened imminent insurrection by the Irish Citizen Army, which had been established during the 1913 Dublin Lockout to protect striking workers from the police. In appealing to rank-and-file Volunteers, Connolly hoped to incite them into pressuring the leadership into military action.[139] Connolly's articles and speeches sparked much talk among Volunteers and IRB men about the perceived need for rebellion.

Hobson recalled having a discussion with Pearse on this topic at a Dublin restaurant. Getting up from the table, Pearse said, 'I cannot answer your arguments, but I *feel* that we must have an insurrection.'[140] The same topic came up at a vegetarian restaurant where Connolly came in and joined Hobson and Sean Lester, who were having tea. They were arguing about 'the necessity or non-necessity of an insurrection' when Connolly declared: 'The working class is always revolutionary – somebody's just got to strike a match – it goes up like powder.' Hobson countered, 'Connolly, if you must talk in metaphors, the working-class [is] not a powder magazine. It's a wet bog.'[141]

The one place where a policy of insurrection was not proposed was at meetings of the headquarters staff and the Central Executive of the Irish Volunteers.[142] A defensive military policy, as advocated by MacNeill and Hobson, remained the official line within the Irish Volunteer movement.

In light of the atmosphere created by Connolly's articles and speeches, Hobson persuaded MacNeill to meet with Connolly at Volunteer headquarters on 16 January 1916. Connolly was candid about his determination to use the Irish Citizen Army to stage a rebellion. MacNeill was equally candid about the Irish Volunteers' opposition to the scheme and its poor prospects for success. An alarmed Pearse, who was also present, listened quietly.[143] After Connolly left, Pearse assured MacNeill that he would persuade Connolly to abandon his project. A few days later Pearse reported that he had succeeded in his object.[144]

After Pearse had alerted his IRB colleagues to the danger of a premature action by Connolly, which could precipitate British repression and scuttle the Military Council's advancing plan, Connolly disappeared for three days between 19 and 22 January 1916 during which he was in negotiation with Pearse, MacDermott and Plunkett. They persuaded him to abandon his plans and form an alliance with them.[145] It was not at all what MacNeill had in mind when he agreed to let Pearse use his powers of persuasion on Connolly. Although MacNeill and Hobson prevailed in Volunteer committee meetings, Pearse and his associates were determined to undermine the official Volunteer policy outside the committee room.

It has been suggested that Hobson's advocacy of a defensive military policy and his opposition to the Easter Rising were the result of latent Quakerism.[146] However, Hobson, by his own admission, placed more importance on achieving Irish independence than on adhering to Quaker principles. Even Catholic MacNeill shared Hobson's support for a defensive military policy. MacNeill deemed military action without 'a reasonably calculated or estimated prospect of success, in the military sense' as morally wrong, incurring 'the guilt not only of that action itself but of all its direct consequences', such as murder.[147] Their concern with military success, as opposed to heroic futility, may have been a way of trying to reconcile the military use of violence in a just war with a regard for human life.

In *History Ireland* Roger Sawyer and Des Gunning have referred to Hobson as a pacifist, ignoring ample evidence to the contrary.[148] In military terms, Hobson's role within the Irish Volunteer leadership was to provide logistical support to front-line units. Serving as general secretary and quartermaster, his role was an integral and essential part of any military force, and, as such, was not a role that a pacifist could embrace.

Neither Hobson himself nor his contemporaries labelled him a pacifist. When the most notable Irish pacifist of the time, Francis Sheehy Skeffington, wrote an open letter to a leading member of the Irish Volunteers in May 1915 to warn him of the danger that the movement would be used for aggressive rather than defensive purposes, he wrote to MacDonagh, not Hobson.[149] To Quakers, Hobson was not a pacifist.[150] As a member of the Irish Volunteers, Hobson not only owned a rifle, but organised the unloading and distribution of guns and ammunition during the gunrunning at Howth and participated in the subsequent Kilcoole episode. According to the *Oxford English Dictionary*, a pacifist is someone 'who totally opposes war, believing that disputes should be settled by peaceful means'.[151] A rifle owner, gunrunner and advocate of guerrilla warfare did not fit this definition.

Conclusion

Whether in politics or religion, Hobson was a man who went his own way, acting in response to his own understanding of the truth. He defied IRB orders when they ran counter to what he believed were the best interests of the Irish Volunteers in particular and the nationalist movement in general. His commitment to the struggle for Irish freedom could not be reconciled with the pacifist principles of his ancestral faith. Thus his involvement in the Irish Volunteers led to his resignation from the Supreme Council of the IRB and from the Society of Friends.

During the period 1913–16 Hobson contributed to the Irish Volunteers in the areas of governance, office administration, production of propaganda, gunrunning, military organisation and policy making. His track record in these areas was mixed. Through his genuine collaboration with men of differing backgrounds and political views Hobson garnered warm admirers, like colonels Moore and Cotter, and harsh critics, like Clarke and Judge. As a leading member of the governing body of the Irish Volunteers, he facilitated the placement of IRB members in strategic positions (which subsequently backfired on him) and succeeded in postponing a potentially disastrous split in the Volunteer movement. The postponement of the split ensured the successful importation of arms and ammunition later used in the Easter Rising and provided members with more time to train with men who had military experience.

As an office administrator, he was accused of being slipshod, self-important and nepotistic. Ensconced in his office at Volunteer headquarters, Hobson, like MacNeill, was not engaged in the type of grass-roots organisational work that led to FitzGerald's expulsion and later imprisonment or Blythe's deportation to England. Hobson's years of experience in avoiding arrest and the nature of his role within the Irish Volunteers ensured that he did not suffer for the cause as some other Volunteers did. This, coupled with his pompous attempts to impress, probably lessened any future sympathy for him.

Hobson's organisation of the landing of guns and ammunition at Howth was a propagandist coup, but it raised questions about his military judgement. Although he faced criticism for halting at Raheny, his decision not to hand out ammunition when the Volunteers were challenged by the authorities limited bloodshed and allowed the Irish Volunteers to capture the moral high ground. Hobson recognised the shortcomings and limitations of the Irish Volunteers in terms of manpower, training, equipment and weapons and co-operated with men of military experience to try to address these issues. Despite this, he was lax about attending route marches and other military functions, giving the impression that he did not take the military side of the Volunteers seriously enough.

Hobson helped to develop a defensive military policy for the Irish Volunteers that not only adhered to the constitutions of both the Volunteers and the IRB, but was designed to maximise the chance of military success. Although he influenced the adoption of this policy by the Volunteers, he was unable to ensure that the policy was implemented, because the machinations of the IRB Military Council eventually overrode the organisation's official commitment to a defensive military policy.

Hobson was more of a strategist than a soldier. His guerrilla-warfare strategy, which was characteristically prosaic rather than poetic, offered a better chance of military success than did insurrection. Such a pragmatic plan, however, did not appeal to men determined to strike some kind of blow before the end of the war.

Notes

1. Moore, 'Pen-pictures of the leaders', *IP*, 6 Jan. 1938.
2. See Chapter 8.
3. Roger Sawyer, letter to the editor, *History Ireland*, Summer 2002, p. 10; Gunning, 'Bulmer Hobson', *History Ireland*, Spring 2002, p. 5.
4. Hobson, TV interview, 5 Dec. 1963 (RTÉ Libraries and Archives).
5. Desmond FitzGerald, *Memoirs of Desmond FitzGerald*, ed. Fergus FitzGerald (London, 1968), p. 29.
6. F.X. Martin (ed.), 'Eoin MacNeill on the 1916 rising', *IHS*, xii (1961), p. 245.
7. Ryan, *Rising*, p. 43.
8. Angus Mitchell, *Casement* (London, 2003), pp. 81–2.
9. Moore, 'Pen-pictures of the leaders', *IP*, 6 Jan. 1938.
10. Hobson, *IYT*, p. 46; Hobson, 'Drilling moves on apace,' *IT*, 21 Nov. 1963 (UCDA, DMcC, P 120/40); Hobson, witness statement, 11 Nov. 1947 (NAI, BMH, WS 51).
11. Hobson, BMH witness statement, 17 Dec 1947 (NLI, BH, MS 13,170).
12. Judge, 'Inner history', *IN*, 26 Aug. 1916, p. 6.
13. 'Future issues', *IV*, 7 Feb. 1914, p. 1.
14. Hobson, *A short history*, p. 50.
15. Ibid., p. 51.
16. Ibid., p. 53.
17. 'County regiments – Carlow', *IV*, 6 June 1914, p. 4; 'The firing line', *IV*, 20 June 1914, p. 9.
18. Hobson, *A short history*, p. 52.
19. Précis, SS, Aug. 1914 (NAL, CO 904/14 Part 2).
20. Hobson, *A short history*, p. 52.
21. Judge, 'Inner history', *IN*, 19 Aug. 1916, p. 6. A description of the formation of companies is included in Hobson, *A short history*, pp. 36–9.
22. Hobson, *A short history*, pp. 53–4.
23. Judge, 'Inner history', *IN*, 19 Aug. 1916, p. 6.
24. Hobson, *A short history*, p. 54.
25. Judge, 'Inner history', *IN*, 19 Aug. 1916, 23 Sept. 1916, p. 6.
26. Judge, 'Inner history', *IN*, 23 Sept. 1916, p. 6.
27. See Chapter 6.
28. Hannon, 'Irish Volunteers', p. 69.
29. Ibid., p. 53.
30. Hobson, *A short history*, p. 173.
31. Hobson, *IYT*, p. 55.
32. 'National Volunteers – meeting of Aid Association', *IT*, 24 July 1914 (NLI, BH, MS 13,173 (5)).
33. Hobson, witness statement, 5 Nov. 1947 (NLI, BH, MS 13,170; NAI, BMH, WS 52).
34. Declan Hobson to Jeff Dudgeon, Mar. 1999, qtd. in Jeffrey Dudgeon, *Roger Casement: the Black Diaries with a study of his background, sexuality, and Irish political life* (Belfast, 2002), p. 541.

35 Claire Hobson (née Gregan), witness statement, n.d. (NAI, BMH, WS 685).
36 Aodogán O'Rahilly alleges that his father, rather than Hobson, organised the landing of the rifles and ammunition at Howth, noting that 'Eoin MacNeill and Bulmer Hobson were aware of the plans, but did not play an active part' (*Winding the clock*, p. 134). Yet The O'Rahilly does not appear to have challenged Hobson's contemporary version of events, which appeared in the *Irish Volunteer* newspaper ('The gun-running at Howth by the organiser thereof', *IV*, 24 July 1915, pp. 5–6). Although this article was unsigned, Judge confirmed that it was written by Hobson ('Inner history', *IN*, 18 Nov. 1916, p. 7). For more discussion in reference to the Howth gunrunning, see Chapter 6.
37 Hobson, *IYT*, p. 59.
38 'The gun-running at Howth by the organiser thereof', *IV*, 24 July 1915, p. 5.
39 Hobson, *IYT*, p. 59. In addition to the account of the Howth gunrunning that appears in Hobson's memoir (*IYT*), an almost identical account by Hobson also appears in Martin (ed.), *Irish Volunteers*, pp. 32–43 and F.X. Martin (ed.), *The Howth gun-running and the Kilcoole gun-running, 1914* (Dublin, 1964), pp. 128–38.
40 Hobson, *IYT*, p. 60.
41 Ibid.
42 Ibid.
43 Ibid., p. 61.
44 Ibid., pp. 60–1.
45 Ibid., p. 61.
46 Judge, 'Inner history', *IN*, 25 Nov. 1916, p. 2.
47 Hobson, *IYT*, p. 62.
48 Eoin MacNeill to Roger Casement (draft letter), 15 Aug. 1914 (NLI, BH, MS 13,174 (3)).
49 Judge, 'Inner history', *IN*, 25 Nov. 1916, p. 2.
50 O'Rahilly, *Winding the clock*, p. 126.
51 Hobson, *IYT*, p. 62.
52 Ibid., p. 63. In Aodogán O'Rahilly's account of the Clontarf incident, he refers to the man who was bayoneted as 'Judd (or Judge)' (*Winding the clock*, p. 126).
53 Hobson, *IYT*, pp. 63–4.
54 Judge, 'Inner history', *IN*, 25 Nov. 1916, p. 2.
55 Hobson, *IYT*, pp. 60–1.
56 See Royal Commission of Inquiry into the circumstances connected with the landing of arms at Howth on July 26th, 1914, *Report of commission and minutes of evidence* (London, 1914).
57 Hobson, TV interview, 'The gun runners – The Howth gun running', 26 July 1964 (RTÉ Libraries and Archives).
58 Moore, 'Death at Bachelor's Walk', *IP*, 1 Feb. 1938.
59 Hannon, 'Irish Volunteers', pp. 58–9.
60 Hobson, *IYT*, p. 66.
61 Ibid., p. 67.

62 Garry Holohan, witness statement, n.d. (NAI, BMH, WS 328).
63 Hobson, *IYT*, p. 67.
64 Ó Broin, *Revolutionary underground*, pp. 158–9.
65 Foy and Barton, *Easter Rising*, pp. 10–11.
66 Hannon, 'Irish Volunteers', p. 58.
67 Ibid., p. 69.
68 Ibid., p. 72.
69 Ibid., pp. 65, 73.
70 See Chapter 6.
71 Hobson, *IYT*, p. 55.
72 The following men signed the manifesto ejecting Redmond's nominees: Eoin MacNeill, The O'Rahilly, Thomas MacDonagh, Joseph Plunkett, Piaras Béaslaí, Michael J. Judge, Peadar Macken, Sean Fitzgibbon, Patrick Pearse, Pádraig Ó Riain, Bulmer Hobson, Eamon Martin, Con Colbert, Éamonn Ceannt, Sean MacDermott, Seamus O'Connor, Liam Mellows, Colm Ó Lochlainn, Liam Gogan and Peter White (Hobson, *A secret history*, p. 202).
73 Hannon, 'Irish Volunteers', p. 103.
74 Ben Novick, 'The arming of Ireland: gun-running and the Great War, 1914–16', in Adrian Gregory and Senia Pašeta (eds.), *Ireland and the Great War* (Manchester, 2002), p. 95.
75 Hobson, MS of *A short history of the Irish Volunteers*, ii, pp. 2–3 (NLI, BH, MS 12,178).
76 *IV*, 31 Oct. 1914, p. 12.
77 'Editor's Note', *IN*, 21 Oct. 1916, p. 8.
78 Judge, 'Inner history', *IN*, 19 May 1917, p. 7.
79 *IV*, 12 Dec. 1914, p. 4.
80 Judge, 'Inner history', *IN*, 12 May 1917, p. 6.
81 Hobson, MS of *A short history*, ii, p. 14 (NLI, BH, MS 12,178); 'Meeting of the Central Executive', *IV*, 14 Nov. 1914, p. 3.
82 Foy and Barton, *Easter Rising*, p. 16. According to the BMH 1913–21 Chronology, Part 1, the Military Council was formed in early February 1915 (UCDA, DMcC, P 120/24 (13)).
83 Mitchell, *Casement*, p. 97.
84 FitzGerald, *Memoirs*, pp. 70–1.
85 Foy and Barton, *Easter Rising*, pp. 19–22.
86 Ibid., p. 31.
87 Sean Fitzgibbon, 'The Easter Rising from the inside – I', ed. Michael J. Lennon, *IT*, 18 Apr. 1949, p. 4. In letters to the newspaper's editor, Seamus O'Connor and Colm Ó Lochlainn raised questions about the accuracy of Lennon's transcript of conversations with Fitzgibbon because the narrative displayed a rancour that they felt was not in keeping with the character of their late friend (O'Connor to editor, *IT*, 20 Apr. 1949, p. 5; Ó Lochlainn to editor, *IT*, 22 Apr. 1949, p. 5). Plunkett's sister Geraldine Dillon also wrote to the editor. She declared that Fitzgibbon 'was as gutless as a jellyfish and could not be relied upon', ironically adding that she deplored 'all this mud-slinging' (Dillon to editor, *IT*, 23 Apr. 1949, p. 8).

88 FitzGerald, *Memoirs*, p. 113.
89 Ryan, *Rising*, pp. 21–2.
90 Claire Hobson, witness statement, n.d. (NAI, BMH, WS 685).
91 FitzGerald, *Memoirs*, p. 70.
92 Ibid., p. 71.
93 NLI, MS 14,100, qtd. in Dudgeon, *Roger Casement*, p. 173.
94 Hobson, MS of *A short history*, ii, pp. 44–5 (NLI, BH, MS 12,178); 'Meeting of the General Council', *IV*, 12 Dec. 1914, p. 4.
95 An Cumann Cosanta forms and brochures (NLI, BH, MS 13,165 (1)).
96 Hobson, MS of *A short history*, ii, p. 45 (NLI, BH, MS 12,178).
97 FitzGerald, *Memoirs*, p. 70.
98 Hobson, MS of *A short history*, ii, p. 27 (NLI, BH, MS 12,178).
99 Hobson, *IYT*, pp. 68–9.
100 Hobson, MS of *A short history*, ii, pp. 36–8 (NLI, BH, MS 12,178).
101 Hobson, MS of *A short history*, ii, pp. 19–20 (NLI, BH, MS 12,178); 'Meeting of the General Council', *IV*, 12 Dec. 1914, p. 4; 'Headquarters Bulletin', *IV*, 12 Dec. 1914, p. 5; 'Headquarters Bulletin', *IV*, 19 Dec. 1914, p. 4; *IV*, 21 Aug. 1915, p. 4; *IV*, 20 Nov. 1915, p. 4.
102 Hobson, Pearse, Plunkett, Ceannt and MacDonagh were members of the IRB.
103 Michael J. Judge to editor, *II*, 19 Dec. 1914, p. 3.
104 Judge, 'Inner history', *IN*, 27 Jan. 1917, p. 7.
105 'Headquarters Bulletin', *IV*, 2 Jan. 1915, p. 4.
106 *IV*, 4 July 1914, p. 8.
107 Hobson, MS of *A short history*, ii, pp. 41–2 (NLI, BH, MS 12,178); *IV*, 19 June 1915, p. 4. A bayonet frog was a cloth sheath for a bayonet, which had a loop so that it could hang from a belt.
108 Hobson, MS of *A short history*, ii, p. 16 (NLI, BH, MS 12,178).
109 Hannon, 'Irish Volunteers', pp. 110–11.
110 Hobson, *IYT*, pp. 58, 70. Figures for MacNeill's supporters differ depending on the source.
111 Ibid., p. 70.
112 Ibid., p. 40; McCullough, witness statement, 11 Dec. 1953 (NAI, BMH, WS 915); FitzGerald, *Memoirs*, p. 50.
113 Hobson, MS of *A short history*, ii, p. 41 (NLI, BH, MS 12,178).
114 Harry Osborne, witness statement, n.d. (NAI, BMH, WS 240).
115 Hobson, MS of 'The origin of Óglaigh na hÉireann – II', *An t-Óglách* (June 1931), pp. 5–13 (NLI, BH, MS 13,169).
116 Colonel J.J. O'Connell, MS of 'History of the Irish Volunteers', Chap. 6, p. 5 (NLI, BH, MS 13,168).
117 O'Connell, 'Irish Volunteers', Chap. 8, p. 7.
118 O'Connell, 'Irish Volunteers', Chap. 6, pp. 3–4.
119 Transcript, *Old Ireland Free*, 24 Apr. 1966 (BBC Written Archives, Reading).
120 O'Connell, 'Irish Volunteers', Chap. 6, pp. 3–4.
121 Ibid.

122 O'Connell, 'Irish Volunteers', Chap. 14, p. 2.
123 Ibid., p. 3; Judge, 'Inner history', *IN*, 25 Nov. 1916, p. 2.
124 'Dublin protest – conscription issue – meeting in Mansion House', *II*, [15 Dec. 1915] (NLI, BH, MS 13,173; Hobson, MS of *A short history*, ii, p. 87 (NLI, BH, MS 12,178).
125 O'Connell, 'Irish Volunteers', Chap. 14, p. 3.
126 'Field operations in Co. Tyrone', *IV*, 29 Aug. 1914, p. 2.
127 Martin (ed.), 'MacNeill on the rising', pp. 228–9.
128 Hobson, MS of 'The origin of Óglaigh na hÉireann – II', *An t-Óglách* (June 1931), pp. 5–13 (NLI, BH, MS 13,169); Martin (ed.), 'MacNeill on the rising', pp. 228, 234.
129 Hobson, *IYT*, pp. 70–1.
130 Chapman to Hay, 6 May 2003.
131 Harrison, *Dictionary*, p. 17.
132 Chapman to Hay, 6 May 2003.
133 Hobson, *IYT*, p. 1.
134 FHLD, Gen. File 69/2.
135 William Glynn to the editor of *IP* (draft letter), 12 Aug. 1969 (FHLD, MSS Box 3A, No. 85).
136 Hobson, *IYT*, p. 69.
137 Foy and Barton, *Easter Rising*, p. 32.
138 O'Connor, BMH witness statement, 14 June 1948 (UCDA, EMacN, LAI/G/117).
139 Foy and Barton, *Easter Rising*, p. 38.
140 Hobson, *IYT*, p. 74.
141 Transcript, *Old Ireland Free*, 24 April 1966 (BBC Written Archives, Reading; UCDA, DMcC, P 120/36). Hobson also described this conversation in *IYT*, p. 74.
142 Hobson, MS of *A short history*, ii, p. 153 (NLI, BH, MS 12,178); Martin (ed.), 'MacNeill on the rising', p. 248.
143 Foy and Barton, *Easter Rising*, p. 38.
144 Martin (ed.), 'MacNeill on the rising', p. 246.
145 Foy and Barton, *Easter Rising*, pp. 38–9.
146 This suggestion has often been made at seminars at which I have presented papers on Hobson.
147 Martin (ed.), 'MacNeill on the rising', p. 234.
148 Roger Sawyer to editor, *History Ireland*, Summer 2002, p. 10; Gunning, 'Bulmer Hobson', *History Ireland*, Spring 2002, p. 5.
149 Francis Sheehy Skeffington, 'An open letter to Thomas MacDonagh', *Irish Citizen*, 22 May 1915, p. 4. This letter was reprinted in Owen Dudley Edwards and Fergus Pyle (eds), *1916: The Easter Rising* (Dublin, 1967), pp. 149–52.
150 Liam (William) Glynn, 'The Quaker in Bulmer Hobson – Part 1', *Irish Young Friend*, [Apr. or May] 1972 (clipping, Cork Archives Institute); Chapman to Hay, 6 May 2003.
151 *Oxford Paperback Dictionary* (Oxford, 1994), p. 576.

8

The Easter Rising and its aftermath

By mid-January 1916 at the latest, Hobson was aware that the IRB was planning an insurrection.[1] The Supreme Council of that body had held a meeting on 16 January in Clontarf Town Hall, at which MacDermott had proposed the reaffirmation of the council's August 1914 decision to stage a rising before the end of the war. Although McCartan had protested that they did not have a mandate from the majority of the Irish people, the proposal was passed.[2] The Military Council had already set a date for the event – Easter 1916 – but did not share this information with its colleagues. McCullough, the president of the Supreme Council, met with Hobson the next day.

Hobson, as chairman of the Dublin Centres Board and quartermaster of the Irish Volunteers, was in an influential position. He had been telling some of the younger men that despite Britain's preoccupation with the war, the time was not yet ripe for Ireland to provoke a military confrontation. McCullough hoped that he might be able to use his influence resulting from their long nationalist association to bring his friend into line. With the council's consent, McCullough informed Hobson that a rising was inevitable and warned him to 'adjust his attitude and actions accordingly'.[3]

McCullough pointed out that 'divided counsels would only weaken any action taken, and as a responsible member of the organisation, [Hobson] was bound to obedience'. According to McCullough, Hobson assured him that, in light of the Supreme Council's decision, he would not 'proceed further on the lines he had been following'.[4] Despite these assurances, however, Hobson ignored McCullough's warning, which he later dismissed as 'quite vague' and not 'conveyed to [him] in any regular manner'.[5] Instead, he took every action possible, within the constraints of his IRB oath of secrecy, to avert an insurrection.

January to April 1916

Once Hobson was aware that plans for a rising were afoot, he 'tried to ginger [Eoin] MacNeill up to taking a definite line' that would bind the leadership of the Irish Volunteers to a policy of guerrilla warfare rather than insurrection.[6] Hobson, however, found that MacNeill, whom he esteemed as 'a fine scholar, a first-rate mind, and a very charming person', 'would do anything to avoid a showdown or fight'.[7] MacNeill downplayed evidence that a rising was being planned beneath his nose. While in Limerick in September 1915, he learned that Pearse had been issuing orders without his authority. Pearse had directed Limerick commandant Michael Colivet to 'hold the line of the Shannon in the event of actual hostilities'. After receiving a letter on 6 April from an American correspondent warning him of a planned insurrection, MacNeill merely mentioned this news to MacDermott. MacNeill also repudiated alleged plans for a rising in his editorial notes published in the 22 April edition of the *Irish Volunteer*, hoping that this would scuttle any proposed endeavour.[8] He later defended his position: 'I had great reluctance to show distrust and preferred to rely on the assurances I had received.' Frustrated by MacNeill's gullibility, Hobson raised the policy question several times in staff meetings, but his colleagues were reluctant to discuss the matter.[9]

In the aftermath of his meeting with Connolly in mid-January 1916, MacNeill had received assurances from Pearse, Plunkett and MacDonagh that no plans for an insurrection had been adopted. Despite this, Pearse's promulgation of his belief in the need for a blood sacrifice continued to concern MacNeill. In an attempt to allay these concerns MacNeill wrote a letter to Pearse in early February 1916 in which he outlined the aims and policy of the Irish Volunteers. Although the letter was meant to be a personal communication, Pearse read it out at the next meeting of the Central Executive.[10] As MacNeill had been unable to attend the meeting, the letter was taken as his contribution to the discussion. Yet no real discussion ensued, ostensibly because the others needed time to develop position papers that were as polished as MacNeill's letter to Pearse. In J.J. O'Connell's opinion, 'it was quite plain that discussion was the last thing desired by some of the executive and that no stone would be left unturned to postpone and prevent it'.[11]

Shortly after this meeting, O'Connell, at Hobson's request, prepared a memorandum on the current state of the Irish Volunteers' capacity to engage in warfare. Hobson, whose position within the Volunteers afforded him 'the greatest number of opportunities of meeting men from different parts of the country', commissioned this memorandum 'for the guidance of men through the country, who might not be in a position to take a comprehensive view of our situation as a whole. He was of the opinion that some such memorandum as this might be of service in dispelling illusions and checking any exaggerated views of our capacity for action.'

O'Connell concluded that the Volunteers should not 'enter into a state of war' unless the British government forced them into it through conscription, disarmament or seizure of Ireland's food supply. Neither O'Connell nor Hobson indicated how widely the document was circulated, but O'Connell noted that 'some of our colleagues were of the opinion that we would not be allowed to follow this policy to its logical conclusion'.[12]

As the war in Europe continued, the Irish Volunteers became increasingly uneasy that the British authorities would suppress them. This fear was heightened by an incident on 20 March 1916 in Tullamore, County Offaly in which violence broke out between pro- and anti-war nationalists. The Irish Volunteer Hall in Tullamore was stormed by supporters of 'separation women', the wives of Irish soldiers in the British army who survived on 'separation money' while their husbands fought in Europe. A Volunteer named Peadar Bracken fired above the crowd. Upon the arrival of the police, he fired at a police inspector and wounded a sergeant before managing to escape. As a result, the police arrested thirteen Volunteers and charged them with attempted murder. The charges were later dropped on a technicality.[13]

The *Irish Volunteer* portrayed the incident as a police attack on the Volunteers.[14] Even moderate members of the Volunteer leadership preached resistance at all costs. At a protest meeting against deportation under DORA legislation, which was held at the Mansion House on 30 March, MacNeill accused the government of trying to provoke the Volunteers into rebellion.[15]

Hobson, O'Connell and Fitzgibbon remained sceptical about their colleagues' intentions. They urged MacNeill to hold a special day-long meeting of the headquarters staff of the Irish Volunteers in an attempt to gain adherence to the official policy of the organisation. They also asked MacNeill to prepare a policy statement and proposed that staff members should be asked to either assent to or dissent from it. The meeting was held on 5 April 1916 at Woodtown Park in Rathfarnham, where MacNeill and his family were then living with his brother James. MacNeill, Hobson, Pearse, O'Rahilly, Ceannt, MacDonagh and O'Connell were in attendance. Plunkett was absent due to illness. At this meeting Pearse explicitly denied any intention to draw the Volunteers into an insurrection and chided his colleagues for harbouring such suspicions. In light of Pearse's protestations, MacNeill did not request a subscription to his memorandum on policy and slipped the document into a drawer. Instead, MacNeill drew up an order, to which everyone present assented, that no non-routine order would be issued without his countersignature.[16]

MacNeill's memorandum covered the same ground as his letter to Pearse. In it he asserted that the decision to take military action should be based on actualities, not on feelings or instincts, and that military action taken without 'a reasonably calculated or estimated prospect' of military success was morally wrong.[17] He argued that 'the only possible basis for successful revolutionary action is deep and widespread popular discontent', a condition which did not currently exist in Ireland. He was confident, however, that such a condition would develop over time.[18]

In the 8 April 1916 edition of the *Irish Volunteer* Pearse, as director of organisation, published an order calling for field manoeuvres that would begin on Easter Sunday.[19] It sounded innocent enough – the Volunteers had participated in Easter manoeuvres the previous year. This time, however, it was a pretext for an insurrection.

Holy Week: 16 to 22 April 1916

On Palm Sunday, 16 April 1916 Hobson, while attending a concert at 41 Parnell Square organised by Cumann na mBan, was asked to make an impromptu speech to fill in for some performers who had not turned up. He took the opportunity to offer a coded warning 'of the extreme danger of being drawn into precipitate action', asserting that 'no man had a right to risk the fortunes of a country in order to create for himself a niche in history'.[20] FitzGerald, who was in the audience, recalled the reaction to this speech:

> One could feel he was treading on dangerous ground. There was a certain breathlessness in the hall. One could see glances passing between those who were probably aware of what decisions had already been taken. When it was all over there were groups talking earnestly together, some denouncing him and others praising his speech. On the following days that speech was a general subject of conversation. Opinions differed from those who thought that it was a timely word of caution, to those who thought that it was black treachery. It was quite clear that those who knew most about the plans regarded it as disastrous.[21]

McCullough was also in the audience. He was aware that a rising was imminent, but had not yet received definite information. Frustrated that his warning had done nothing to stop Hobson's antagonism of IRB colleagues who supported a rising, McCullough left the hall and promptly ran across MacDermott. In response to McCullough's declaration that Hobson was spouting 'outrageous stuff', MacDermott replied, 'We'll soon stop this bloody fellow'.[22]

The Military Council of the IRB met the next day, Monday 17 April 1916. In light of Hobson's performance the previous evening, the decision to kidnap him later in the week was probably made at this meeting. The Military Council also approved the draft of the Proclamation of the Irish Republic and the circulation of the 'Castle Document'.[23] This document, whose contents originated from Dublin Castle, outlined drastic measures that the British authorities were planning to take against the Irish Volunteers, Redmond's National Volunteers, Sinn Féin, the Gaelic League and even prominent clerics such as the Archbishop of Dublin, William Walsh. Charles Townshend has revealed that the document, although considered by many to be a forgery, was a 'sexed up' version of 'a despatch from General [L.W.] Friend to the Irish Office in London, detailing precautionary measures in the event of conscription being imposed'. Plunkett had received information outlined in the document from Eugene Smith, a sympathetic civil servant.[24]

On 13 April 1916 Plunkett had asked his brother George and Colm Ó Lochlainn, a young UCD postgraduate whom MacNeill had brought into the Volunteer movement, to set up and print the document on a small hand press at his family's estate in Kimmage. Ó Lochlainn noted a mistake in the document: the Archbishop's house in Drumcondra was referred to as *Ara Coeli*, which was actually the name of Cardinal Logue's house in Armagh. Plunkett told them to leave out the name of the house.[25] By circulating the Castle Document, the members of the Military Council hoped to generate a situation in which even moderates like MacNeill would be reconciled to their plans for insurrection. Not only would the Irish Volunteers believe that the British were about to crack down on them, but Hobson's kidnapping would ensure the removal of his influence on MacNeill.

At Plunkett's request, Rory O'Connor showed the document to Patrick J. Little, the editor of *New Ireland*, Dr Séamus Ó Ceallaigh, Francis Sheehy Skeffington and L.P. Byrne, who had been briefed beforehand about intelligence being leaked from Dublin Castle. O'Connor told them that in Plunkett's opinion the contents of the document should be shared with the bishops and the newspapers. During the weekend of 15 April 1916 Ó Ceallaigh was given the task of passing the text along to MacNeill, as well as to Archbishop Walsh, Bishop of Down and Connor Joseph MacRory and Dr MacCaffrey of Maynooth.[26] Little tried to publish the document in *New Ireland*, but the military censors blocked its publication.[27]

The contents of the document galvanised MacNeill into action. Receiving the document from Ó Ceallaigh, a trusted friend, probably convinced him of its authenticity. On Tuesday 18 April 1916 MacNeill showed the document to Hobson and asked him to circulate copies around the country. Hobson was sceptical about the Castle Document's contents and origin, but MacNeill assured him that it was genuine.[28] MacNeill convened an emergency meeting of the executive on Tuesday at O'Rahilly's house in order to avoid being arrested en masse at Volunteer headquarters. According to MacNeill, MacDermott informed them at this meeting that a secret session of the British parliament was being held to discuss peace with Germany.[29] He appears to have been trying to increase the pressure exerted by the Castle Document to take military action, in hopes of nudging his moderate colleagues into insurrection before the end of the war. Although MacNeill drafted an order in response to the Castle Document, it was not agreed upon until a further meeting held the next day.

On Wednesday, 19 April 1916, the atmosphere was tense at Volunteer headquarters, where members of Cumann na mBan were urgently making field dressings.[30] Hobson, despite his increasing doubts, carried out MacNeill's order to circulate copies of the Castle Document and a covering letter to selected people throughout the country, including Catholic bishops.[31] He sent his fiancée, Claire Gregan, to deliver an envelope containing a copy of it to Peter de Loughrey in Kilkenny.[32] De Loughrey, an ironfounder and general merchant, was a prominent member of both the IRB and Sinn Féin.[33] To dodge the censor, Little had passed the document along to Alderman Tom Kelly, who read it out at a Dublin Corporation meeting that day, generating widespread media coverage. Dublin Castle maintained that the document was a 'fabrication'.[34]

A second emergency meeting of the Volunteer executive and headquarters staff was also held on Wednesday at the Henry Street restaurant of nationalist activist Jenny Wyse Power.[35] At this meeting MacNeill finalised and issued an order in response to the Castle Document. In light of 'a plan on the part of the Government for the suppression and disarmament of the Irish Volunteers', members were to take measures 'to preserve the arms and organisation of the Irish Volunteers' and 'to defend themselves and each other in small groups'.[36] The order was in line with the guerrilla warfare plan advocated by Hobson and O'Connell.

That same evening the Military Council of the IRB finally informed Volunteer commandants who were in on the conspiracy that the insurrection would begin on Easter Sunday, 23 April 1916, at 6.30 p.m. in Dublin and 7 p.m. elsewhere in the country.[37] The Military Council envisioned that the Irish Volunteers would seize a defensive ring of strategic buildings in Dublin, inspiring support elsewhere in the country. The Provisional Government of the Irish Republic would occupy the General Post Office (GPO) in O'Connell Street. The arrival of a large shipment of German arms would spark a rising in the west. To avoid a sectarian bloodbath, no shots were to be fired in Ulster; instead, Irish Volunteers in Ulster were to join Liam Mellows and the Galway Volunteers in the west.[38]

The Military Council had already started giving individual Volunteers specific instructions regarding forthcoming manoeuvres. The nature of these instructions was such that individual Volunteers might not realise that they were being drawn into an insurrection. Two moderate members of the Central Executive of the Irish Volunteers, Fitzgibbon and O'Connell, were among the Volunteers given specific instructions. Bringing the pair – even partially – into their confidence was a serious risk on the part of the Military Council. Fitzgibbon and O'Connell, however, could offer valuable expertise. Fitzgibbon had successfully organised the Kilcoole gunrunning in August 1914 and O'Connell was reputed to possess 'the best military mind in the Volunteers'.[39] As Michael Foy and Brian Barton have pointed out, sending the pair on assignments outside Dublin prior to the rising suited the Military Council because it would 'increase MacNeill's isolation and remove Fitzgibbon from his post as vice-commandant of de Valera's 3rd Battalion'.[40]

On Saturday 15 April 1916 Ceannt had ordered Fitzgibbon to land a shipment of German guns in Tralee and send them on to Cork, Limerick and Galway. When Fitzgibbon asked whether MacNeill was aware of the plan, Ceannt told him that Pearse was going to inform him. The next day, Pearse assured Fitzgibbon that MacNeill was fully on board. Fitzgibbon duly headed west. On Holy Thursday he ran across Tom Clarke's wife, Kathleen, in Limerick and received further assurances that Hobson was enthusiastic about the gunrunning plan.[41]

There are differing accounts of when and how Hobson found out that an insurrection was planned for Easter Sunday. In his biography of Tom Clarke, Louis Le Roux stated that Hobson overheard a conversation between IRB members at a meeting of the Volunteer Executive held at O'Rahilly's house on Herbert Park on Wednesday,[42] though the meeting of the executive at the O'Rahilly home was actually held on Tuesday. Diarmuid Lynch accepted this mistake as truth in his account of Holy Week.[43] Desmond Ryan got the date right (Holy Thursday), but the circumstances wrong, saying that Hobson and O'Connell learned about the rising when they overheard a conversation at Volunteer headquarters or at a Volunteer executive meeting.[44] All of these accounts differ from those proffered by eye-witnesses Hobson and Eamon Martin.

Martin told two different stories about how Hobson first found out about the rising, one to the Bureau of Military History (BMH) circa 1950 and one in a letter to the editor of the *Sunday Press* in 1960. Only his second account tallies with Hobson's recollections. The conversation outlined in Martin's first account may have taken place on an earlier date during Holy Week.

In his BMH witness statement Martin recorded that on Holy Thursday he and Garry Holohan, who were both members of the Fianna circle of the IRB, were on their way home from a meeting about plans for the rising when they stopped off at the home of Ó Riain. They found Hobson there too. Ó Riain informed them that he had been ordered to proceed to County Tyrone with Eimar O'Duffy, who was in charge of operations in that area. Although Hobson 'made no secret of his [negative] attitude to the project', Martin got the impression that Hobson 'was resigned to being "dragged" into it since the plans had gone so far'. Considering the hostile attitude of Clarke and MacDermott toward Hobson, it is surprising that Ó Riain, possibly Hobson's closest friend at the time, was included in the secret plans for an insurrection. Martin suspected that Connolly, who 'had a great regard for Pádraig and a high respect for his ability', had insisted that Ó Riain should be given the opportunity to participate in the rising.[45] In his various memoirs Hobson did not mention this alleged meeting at the Ryan home. If such a meeting occurred earlier during Holy Week, Hobson may not have mentioned it because he wished to protect the reputations of his Fianna/IRB colleagues, who may have inadvertently let him in on the secret.

In his later *Sunday Press* account Martin reported that on Holy Thursday he, Con Colbert and Paddy Daly held a last-minute meeting in a room at 41 Parnell Square, 'the usual IRB venue', to discuss plans for the attack on the Magazine Fort, which was to signal the start of the rising. Near the end of their conference Hobson poked his head around the door to ask whether they were almost finished because he was waiting to hold a meeting of the Dublin Centres Board. Holohan, though not an IRB centre, attended Hobson's meeting at which members produced orders from Pearse. Hobson made a mental connection between Pearse's orders and a telegram that he had received earlier that day from O'Connell asking to meet him 'on an urgent and important matter'. Hobson ended the meeting abruptly and headed over to Volunteer headquarters to meet with O'Connell.[46]

Hobson recorded that he received 'the first direct and reliable information' about the rising at 10 p.m. on Holy Thursday, when O'Connell and O'Duffy came to his office.[47] O'Connell had been ordered to take charge of the Volunteers in south-east Leinster, apparently with

MacNeill's authority. The ever-dubious O'Connell, however, decided to verify his orders with Hobson.[48] O'Connell's orders confirmed Hobson's suspicions that an insurrection was imminent. If Hobson had heard about plans for the rising at the Ryan home earlier in the week, he would have been silenced by his IRB oath and unable to act upon this information. O'Connell's orders would have enabled Hobson to take action by shifting his knowledge of the plans from the secret sphere of the IRB to the open domain of the Irish Volunteers.

Hobson, O'Connell and possibly O'Duffy immediately went to MacNeill's home, rousing him from his bed to inform him of the planned rising. MacNeill accompanied them to St Enda's, where they arrived at about 2 a.m. to awaken Pearse. MacNeill, Hobson and O'Connell confronted Pearse, who finally admitted to the plans for the rising. Although Pearse informed Hobson that his IRB oath bound him to join the rebellion, Hobson, ever the rationalist, countered that in actual fact Pearse and his fellow conspirators had taken an oath to the IRB constitution that banned them from undertaking an insurrection until the majority of the Irish people gave them an express mandate to do so.[49]

Hobson, MacNeill and O'Connell then returned to Woodtown Park, where MacNeill wrote up a series of orders. He reaffirmed his earlier order which instructed 'Irish Volunteers to act on the defensive in case of attack or attempted disarmament'. He cancelled 'all orders of a special character issued by Commandant Pearse or by any other person heretofore, with regard to military movements of a definite kind' and declared that in future all special orders would be issued by himself or his successor as Chief of Staff. He empowered 'Commandant Hobson' to issue orders in pursuance of his own (MacNeill's) orders, and commanded 'every officer and man of the Irish Volunteers' to act on Hobson's orders. MacNeill sent O'Connell to Cork and put him in charge of the Volunteers in Munster.[50]

Hobson arrived at the Volunteer office early on the morning of Good Friday. He started preparing copies of MacNeill's orders for circulation around the country. He planned to send them out on Friday night so that they would reach their destinations on Saturday. He did not want to dispatch MacNeill's orders any earlier because that might give Pearse and his associates time to countermand them. Hobson also hoped (in vain) that over the course of the day MacNeill would be able to induce Pearse to abandon his plans.[51] Hobson instructed the office staff to burn letters and lists of names in order to prevent the authorities from finding out the identity of Volunteers around the country. Hobson received a note from MacNeill asking him to take no more action until he arrived.[52] As a result of this note and Hobson's subsequent kidnapping by the IRB,

MacNeill's orders, drafted in the early hours of Good Friday, were never dispatched around the country.

The note was written in response to a breakfast-time meeting between MacNeill and MacDermott. Pearse and MacDonagh later joined them. At this meeting MacDermott told him about the shipment of arms that was due to arrive from Germany. MacNeill recognised that the landing of German arms was a direct challenge to the British government.[53] He recalled: 'I was convinced that all was over with our movement and nothing left for us except to sell our lives as dearly as possible.'[54] Persuaded that the rising was inevitable, MacNeill agreed to join in. 'It was often easier to convince MacNeill that nothing could be done than it was to spur him into positive action,' Hobson would later comment acidly.[55]

At this breakfast meeting MacDermott also convinced MacNeill that the orders he had sent out with Hobson and O'Connell would be ignored. As a result, MacNeill drafted a new order, dated 21 April 1916. It stated:

> Government action for the suppression of the Volunteers is now inevitable and may begin at any moment; preparations are going on for that purpose. We are compelled to be on our guard until our safety is assured. All government statements through the press or otherwise are in the circumstances worthless.

The last line referred to Dublin Castle's (unsurprising) assertion that the Castle Document was fake.[56]

That same morning Casement and two members of the Irish Brigade, Robert Monteith and Daniel Bailey, washed up on Banna Strand in Country Kerry. After disembarking from the German submarine U-19, they had spent nearly two hours battling the waves in a rowboat that eventually capsized. Not only had they failed to rendezvous with the *Aud* and its arms shipment, but there were no Volunteers on shore to greet them. Although the *Aud* had turned up at the appropriate time, its captain had weighed anchor beyond the sight of the submarine. In addition, the Volunteers were not expecting the shipment until 23 April and had not devised contingency plans for an earlier arrival.[57]

The authorities intercepted both the *Aud* and Casement. As a result of a tip-off from the British Admiralty's naval intelligence division that an arms ship had left Germany bound for Ireland, the Royal Navy captured the *Aud* off the coast of Kerry.[58] Responding to reports of strangers on the beach, the RIC arrested Casement shortly after 1 p.m. and held him overnight in Tralee, where he was allowed to speak with a priest with whom he sent a message to MacNeill urging the Volunteer leader to call off the rising.[59] The message never reached MacNeill. Casement was immediately conveyed to London for questioning. Captain Reginald Hall, head of the naval intelligence division, 'refused his request that news of his arrest be published in Ireland together with his appeal that no rising be attempted'.[60] Eunan O'Halpin has surmised that Hall, who opposed the Liberals' conciliatory approach to Ireland, wanted the insurrection to take place in order to force the government into pursuing a policy of repression.[61]

As general secretary of the Irish Volunteers and chairman of the Dublin Centres Board of the IRB, Hobson was, as he himself pointed out, in 'a position that could put a spanner in the business' of insurrection.[62] On Good Friday the IRB put him out of commission. While Hobson was waiting for MacNeill to come into the Volunteer office, Sean Tobin, who had succeeded Hobson as the chair of the Leinster Executive of the IRB, invited him to a meeting of that body. Hobson later claimed that he was reluctant to attend because he could not see what possible purpose it would serve, unless it was a ruse to obstruct his actions.[63]

When Hobson arrived at the alleged meeting at Martin Conlon's house at 76 Cabra Park in Phibsboro, four or five 'minor officers' of the IRB produced guns and told him he was under arrest.[64] He later recalled: 'I laughed and said, "You are a lot of damn fools." There was nothing I could do, so I sat back and accepted the situation. I felt I had done my best to stop the rising, there was nothing more I could do, and I felt almost a sense of relief that the matter was off my hands.'[65] As a member of the IRB, Hobson was the one man among the moderates on the Volunteer executive who had been most conscious of the potential danger of the Irish Volunteers' being drawn into insurrection. He was completely exhausted, having worked under pressure for an extended period without strong enough support from MacNeill.[66] It was no wonder he felt an initial sense of relief.

Neither Hobson nor Seán T. O'Kelly, who later arrived with the order for his release, knew who had ordered his arrest. Hobson assumed that MacDermott and Clarke were behind it. Charles Townshend states that MacDermott and the Military Council issued the order.[67] Although Hobson later claimed that he could not remember the names of the men who arrested him,[68] he reported that his jailers were 'very nice' to him, and that he spent his time in custody reading, as he did not think his guards would want to converse about his opposition to the rebellion that they supported.[69] He asked them no questions and they volunteered no information about what was happening in Dublin or elsewhere in the country.[70]

In contrast to Hobson's account, his jailers described his behaviour during his incarceration as less than peaceful. Conlon recalled:

> On and off in the course of his confinement in my premises, Mr Hobson was inclined to be obstreperous, protesting against his arrest and so on, all of which was quite natural in the circumstances. I did what I could to calm him down, making clear to him my position in the matter as being that of merely carrying out orders.[71]

On Sunday night Hobson gave the guards so much trouble by having 'fainting fits' and wanting to escape that they had to send Mrs Conlon, a member of Cumann na mBan, to the Keating Branch of the Gaelic League to get reinforcements.[72] Maurice Collins and Michael Lynch were sent to guard Hobson. They found him 'in a rather distressed state of mind and had to warn him several times to remain calm and quiet'. They confirmed that he 'did not discuss the situation with us; neither did he show any animosity towards us personally'.[73]

Meanwhile Gregan was rushing around Dublin trying to ascertain her fiancé's whereabouts and secure his release. When FitzGerald met up with Gregan and Lester on Saturday 22 April she 'was in a state of great excitement, constantly asserting' that his kidnappers would shoot him.[74] The IRB, however, had no such plans. As Ceannt explained to Seamus O'Connor during the weekend prior to the rising, 'Hobson has been an obstacle in our path. He is opposed to an insurrection. He is perfectly honest, he is not a traitor, but it would be better that he were as then we could shoot him.'[75] Gregan later heard that Connolly had recommended taking Hobson to the Plunkett estate in Kimmage and chloroforming him there, but 'Pearse or MacDermott or both ... said "No" to that and made the suggestion of arresting him and guarding him in a house'.[76]

Fitzgibbon arrived back in Dublin on Saturday. After hearing about Casement's capture and the sinking of the *Aud*, he had abandoned his assignment. On his way home he met up with Ó Lochlainn in Limerick Junction. Plunkett had instructed Ó Lochlainn to seize a wireless set in Cahirciveen and bring it back to Dublin. Ó Lochlainn's mission had not only failed, but led to the drowning of three of his companions. On their train journey back to Dublin Ó Lochlainn told Fitzgibbon about printing the Castle Document and how his suspicions had been raised by the mix-up over the name of the Archbishop's house. Upon arrival, Fitzgibbon and Ó Lochlainn went first to Volunteer headquarters, where MacDonagh was burning papers, then to Hobson's empty flat and finally to the nearby Herbert Park home of O'Rahilly, who told them about the impending rising and Hobson's kidnapping.[77]

Accompanied by O'Rahilly, they went to Woodtown Park to talk to MacNeill shortly after six o'clock in the evening.[78] It emerged that Fitzgibbon's orders had been given without MacNeill's sanction. Fitzgibbon also convinced MacNeill that the Castle Document was bogus and that

Dublin Castle had never had any plans to suppress the Volunteers. They concluded that the document had been a ruse to justify an insurrection. Appalled by such subterfuge, MacNeill agreed with O'Rahilly and Fitzgibbon that it was still possible to prevent the rising, especially in light of the sinking of the arms shipment.[79]

MacNeill organised a crisis meeting of available members of the Central Executive and headquarters staff and others who might be of help, such as Arthur Griffith. It was held at the home of MacNeill's friend Dr Ó Ceallaigh at 53 Rathgar Road at nine o'clock on Saturday evening.[80] MacDonagh and possibly Plunkett attended, the former stating that he could not agreed to MacNeill's demands without consulting others. MacDonagh headed off to consult with his colleagues. In the mean time MacNeill sent messengers around the country with the countermanding order, which he also arranged to be published in the *Sunday Independent* on 23 April 1916.[81] The order, which was dated 22 April 1916, stated: 'Volunteers completely deceived. All orders for special action are hereby cancelled, and on no account will action be taken.'[82] MacNeill, after cycling to the *Sunday Independent* office and back, left Ó Ceallaigh's house at about three in the morning. MacDonagh and Plunkett turned up at daybreak, looking for MacNeill.[83]

Easter Week: 23–29 April 1916

Incensed by MacNeill's countermanding order, the Military Council held an emergency meeting on the morning of Easter Sunday, 23 April 1916. They decided to postpone the start of the rising until noon the next day. The only dissenter was Clarke, who argued that they should keep to their original schedule because in all likelihood individual Volunteers would disregard MacNeill's order once they saw that the insurrection was under way.[84]

That same morning Gregan went to Liberty Hall to confront the insurrectionists. Although she feared that she might not leave the building alive, she was determined to find out what effect the countermanding order had had on their plans and to demand information about Hobson's whereabouts. She spoke with Connolly, Pearse and MacDermott in turn. They explained that Hobson had been arrested to stop him from interfering with their plans and influencing anyone, such as MacNeill.[85] According to Áine Ceannt, MacDonagh had told her husband that Hobson was 'the evil genius of the Volunteers' and that if they 'could separate MacNeill from his influence all would be well'.[86] Having been assured that her fiancé was safe, Gregan pressed Connolly, Pearse and MacDermott to agree (which they apparently did) that Hobson was 'a man of integrity and sincerity'. In recalling the episode, Gregan described Connolly as surly, Pearse as nice and polite and MacDermott as reassuring and sympathetic – although she thought him 'deadly sly'.[87]

Having remembered that Hobson had mentioned a meeting at the Conlon home, Gregan went to the red brick house on Cabra Park where Maurice Collins and Michael Lynch were guarding Hobson. When she demanded to see her fiancé, the guard who answered the door repeatedly denied Hobson's presence. When he heard her voice, Hobson made a move to come to the door but his guard pointed a gun at him. Gregan finally gave up and left, still convinced that her fiancé was confined inside the house.[88]

On Sunday afternoon MacNeill received a written message from Pearse that he had confirmed MacNeill's countermanding order 'as the leading men would not have obeyed it without my [Pearse's] confirmation'.[89] According to Diarmuid Lynch, this note was designed to lull MacNeill into a false sense of security so that he would take no further action.[90] MacDonagh arrived later to confirm the cancellation of the rising in person.[91] The conversation shifted to Hobson's kidnapping. Fitzgibbon, who was also present, recalled that MacDonagh justified the action taken by referring to Hobson's IRB oath.[92]

On the morning of Easter Monday FitzGerald journeyed out to Woodtown Park to tell MacNeill that the Volunteers had been ordered to mobilise at 10 a.m. MacNeill was convinced that the mobilisation was for nothing more than a route march to spite his countermanding order. He cycled into Dublin with his eldest son, Niall, and Fitzgibbon. By the time they got to Ó Ceallaigh's house, fighting had begun at Portobello Bridge.[93] Volunteer Liam Ó Briain, who ran across the trio on Rathgar Road, recalled that MacNeill initially raged against the insurrectionists, but then decided to go home to put on his Volunteer uniform and return to the city to join his comrades. In the end, having marshalled his emotions, he did not come back to participate in the rising.[94]

Once the insurrection was under way, Hobson's captors were frustrated that their assignment was keeping them on the sidelines. According to Conlon, the guards even considered executing Hobson and dumping his body on the railway line that ran behind the house. Conlon conceded, however, that he was not sure whether this suggestion was in earnest. In any case, after he informed his IRB colleagues that he would not 'countenance any unauthorised action' and that he was prepared to use his revolver if necessary, he succeeded in convincing them to await their orders in reference to the prisoner's fate.[95]

On the evening of Easter Monday O'Rahilly and Piaras Béaslaí urged MacDermott to release Hobson, pointing out that he could do nothing to stop the rising now that it was under way.[96] MacDermott dispatched Seán T. O'Kelly with an order addressed to Maurice Collins. It read: 'Report to Ned Daly at Richmond Hospital and release Hobson. Everything splendid.'[97] O'Kelly found Hobson in the sitting room, ensconced in an armchair with a book in his hands. In contrast, his guard, Collins, sat nearer to the door with a gun in his hand. Conlon and Collins were visibly relieved by the release order, while Hobson said nothing.[98]

On the way into the city centre O'Kelly repeatedly urged Hobson to come to the GPO with him. Hobson refused, insisting that he had to go home to Ranelagh first. O'Kelly was suspicious that Hobson had no real intention of coming back into town to join the rising and told him so. Hobson maintained that he was in earnest. The pair shook hands and each went his own way.[99] Hobson later admitted that he gave O'Kelly evasive answers on purpose because his main objective was to shake off O'Kelly and find MacNeill.[100]

As he walked home on Easter Monday, Hobson saw the Dublin mob looting the shops in O'Connell Street instead of joining Connolly in the GPO. Hobson, who recalled the labour leader telling him that 'the working class was always revolutionary', was struck by the irony of the situation.[101] He continued across the Liffey, heading for home and, as it turned out, relative obscurity.

Hobson chose not to participate in the insurrection. Years later, when McGarrity asked whether this was because his IRB colleagues had kidnapped him and appeared to mistrust him, Hobson said no. He explained that he did not join the rising because he 'was convinced that the thing was wrong, that it was a blunder which I had honestly attempted to prevent, and to join up and add to the victims I felt would be a mistake'.[102] Perhaps he thought that he would be in a position to pick up the pieces after the insurrection had failed. Hobson refused 'to be driven against [his] judgement by being faced with a *fait accompli*'.[103] He was determined that his erstwhile associates Clarke, MacDermott and Pearse would not force him into doing something with which he so vehemently disagreed.

Hobson's sister Florence offered a similar explanation for his refusal to join the rising. When they were children, she could never divert her younger brother from his set course and channel him into hers: 'It was because he had this moral fibre in an unusual degree that he would not agree to go into something he believed to be untimely and therefore wrong.' She maintained that this aspect of her brother's character fuelled his opposition to the Easter Rising,[104] countering Blythe's suggestion that 'the influence of the Quaker pacifist tradition' had 'rendered [Hobson] unfit to take grave national decisions in such troubled times'.[105]

FitzGerald's wife, Mabel, proffered an alternative view. According to Blythe, she blamed Hobson's decision not to participate in the rising on the influence of Gregan, with whom she was friendly.[106] The explanations provided by Hobson and his sister are more convincing.

In Mabel FitzGerald's opinion, Hobson would have been held in the highest esteem of the Irish people if he had decided in the end to participate in the rising. Blythe, however, contended that had Hobson participated, the British probably would have executed him even though he had been so strongly against the rising.[107] There is some merit in Blythe's view, as Dublin Castle's military intelligence officer Major Ivor Price, who had been following Hobson's nationalist activities through Special Branch reports for years, allegedly described Hobson as the 'most dangerous man in Ireland' to the Royal Commission on the rebellion in Ireland in May 1916.[108] Admittedly, Price's intelligence was out of date.

Hobson spent the first night of the rising at his flat, which was located on a terrace off Marlborough Road in Ranelagh. Gregan met him there the next day and they walked out to the MacNeill home at Woodtown Park in Rathfarnham. MacNeill was not there when they arrived. He was hiding out at Orlagh, the Augustinian Priory below Killakee mountain, but returned home after word of their arrival was sent to him.[109] On Tuesday night Hobson and MacNeill had a long talk and decided that there was nothing they could do for the time being. On Wednesday 26 April 1916 Griffith cycled out to the house to discuss the situation with them.[110]

Earlier that day Hobson had come down to breakfast to find MacNeill getting ready to join the insurrection with his sons. Hobson took him aside and pointed out 'the sheer folly of his going in at this stage, and that the fact of his so acting would place all the men who had obeyed his orders in an impossible and false position'. MacNeill soon abandoned his plan.[111]

During Easter Week Woodtown Park hosted a number of refugees from the rising, including Alderman Tom Kelly, Fitzgibbon and Lester, as well as Hobson and Gregan.[112] The artist Cesca Chenevix Trench visited the house during Easter Week and found that the circle gathered there were 'furious' with the insurrectionists and harboured 'the most gloomy views' of the situation. In her diary she quoted Hobson at his begrudging and egotistical best: 'If by a miracle they succeeded, of course, I suppose they'd be justified; but if we'd shot a few of them, I'd have saved the country.'[113] Gregan recalled that they all 'had a horrible feeling listening to the big guns shelling the city'. MacNeill looked grave and said little, while Hobson was 'upset and depressed'. At the end of the week, when they were told how O'Rahilly had lain dying in street, Gregan suffered a breakdown and they had to call for a doctor to sedate her.[114]

FitzGerald turned up at the house, where he found MacNeill, Hobson, Gregan and Lester. He was on the run from the authorities after the evacuation of the GPO. 'They were all horrified at my going there,' he reported. 'They thought I must be mad, as they were waiting to hear the cars bringing the military along.'[115] FitzGerald resented Hobson and MacNeill. In his perception they had stood back while Pearse and his associates planned a rising and then 'asserted themselves only when it was in fact too late'.[116] He was also annoyed with Lester and Gregan for spending the Easter weekend obsessing about Hobson's fate rather than worrying about the impending insurrection.[117] So he took pleasure in taunting them by insisting on giving them a long account of the week.[118]

May 1916 to June 1917

At the beginning of May, a few days after the surrender of 29 April 1916, Gregan was dispatched to Hobson's flat to remove any incriminating evidence before the inevitable military search. After sifting through his things, she made a parcel of his Volunteer cap and some other items – possibly even a revolver – and pinned a copy of the IRB constitution to the inside of her dress. She considered burning the document, but was not sure whether there was another copy in existence. In the end Eoin MacNeill's wife, Margaret, insisted that it be burned because she refused to countenance 'anything of that kind in the house which belonged to James MacNeill'. The military raided Hobson's flat the next day, but did not find anything of importance.

One item that the military did confiscate was a letter addressed to Gregan from a priest in her native Carlow. Gregan had asked him to get a dispensation from the Pope to enable her to marry Hobson. Her current parish priest in Sandymount had put such obstacles in her way that she also appealed to the Archbishop of Dublin through the conduit of his secretary. She threatened to marry Hobson in the registry office if she did not get a dispensation. In his letter the priest asked whether her fiancé had ever been baptised, a question that betrayed his ignorance of Quaker practices. The Society of Friends reject the need for sacraments. Gregan assumed that the military thought the question was a code.[119]

On 2 May 1916, three days after the insurrectionists had surrendered, MacNeill drafted a letter to General John Maxwell suggesting a meeting aimed at stopping any more violence. He asked Hobson to sign it, but his house guest refused on the grounds that it would reveal their whereabouts to Maxwell, who would have them arrested. MacNeill pointed out that they would have no political future if they were not arrested.

Hobson, who had enjoyed playing a cat-and-mouse game with the authorities for years, 'replied that while I probably would be arrested, I was not going to ask for it'.[120]

C. Desmond Greaves, the biographer of Liam Mellows, has said of Hobson that his 'one crippling weakness' was 'a subtly rationalised *amour propre* which paralysed him at moments when he should stoop to conquer'.[121] This was only one of a number of turning points when Hobson might have been able to save his nationalist career by following the advice of someone else and thus stooping to conquer. MacNeill's son-in-law Michael Tierney offered a different interpretation of Hobson's decision not to sign the letter. He saw it as an indication of a tacit intention to retire from public life.[122]

William Glynn, a member of the Society of Friends, viewed Hobson's refusals to participate in the rising and court arrest in order to 'retain his political influence' as examples of a Quaker-influenced 'moral courage to act in accordance with his convictions'. Glynn mused: 'Had [Hobson] been less inflexible he might well have become a minister in the subsequent Irish Free State.' Like Blythe, Glynn also wondered whether there was 'too much of the Quaker' in Hobson 'to make a successful politician'.[123]

The letter to Maxwell did lead to MacNeill's arrest, court-martial and imprisonment, thus facilitating the continuance of his political career (at least until the public outcry against the Boundary Commission proposals of 1925). The officer who came out to Woodtown Park to arrest MacNeill was a Belfast man named McCammond, with whom Hobson had been well acquainted previously, but on this occasion he showed no sign of recognising Hobson.[124] It is unclear whether he genuinely did not recognise Hobson or whether he was protecting an old acquaintance. Maxwell and his associates were still in the first flush of 'executionary' zeal – arrest might have been fatal for Hobson at this point.

After the surrender Hobson arranged for a solicitor to pay all of the debts of the Volunteer organisation out of the Volunteer funds in his possession, to hire a firm of furniture removers to take away the furniture and papers remaining in the Volunteer office after the police and military raids, and to return the office premises to its owner. The surviving papers remained in storage for about eighteen months before Hobson finally had a chance to sort through them and recover 'many documents of value for the history of the Volunteers'.[125]

Hobson remained in Dublin for several months, taking precautions to avoid arrest. The Dublin Metropolitan Police, who sought his apprehension, circulated the following unflattering description of him:

> 5 ft. 8 ins., slight make, brown hair, worn long; grey eyes, long nose, clean shaven, long visage, fresh complexion, theatrical appearance; blinks

with both eyes when speaking; bad teeth; slightly bow legged; wears dark clothes and black trilby hat.[126]

Hobson may have changed his hair and clothing style and grown a moustache or beard to disguise his appearance while on the run. During this time he may have worked as a cook at the Jesuit retreat house in Rathfarnham Castle – at least that is what he told his future neighbours in Roundstone, Connemara, where he spent most of his retirement.[127]

He and Gregan stayed at Woodtown Park until, having finally received a dispensation, they were 'secretly' married on 19 June 1916 in the sacristy at St Mary's Roman Catholic Church in Rathfarnham. Eoin MacNeill's brother James served as one of the witnesses and held a wedding breakfast for the newlyweds.[128] Later that day Hobson, perhaps fearing that their nuptials might betray his whereabouts, went to stay with Mary Hutton, translator of the *Táin Bó Cúailnge*, at Palmerston Lodge on Dartry Road.[129] Her home was considered safe because she was not connected with politics. James MacNeill brought Hobson's bride to see him a few times under cover of night. After a few weeks a priest, who was safeguarding Hobson's papers, drove him on a motorbike to the Hobson family home in Marino, a small lough-side community close to Belfast.[130] Hobson and his wife stayed with his parents in Marino for a year until after the amnesty in June 1917. To evade arrest during this time he did not go into Belfast.

McCartan, like Hobson, was also on the run from the authorities at this time. While he was in hiding, a policeman told a friend of his that the RIC had been ordered not to arrest McCartan and Hobson, but they and their associates were to be watched. Fearing this was a trap to flush him out, McCartan asked a unionist friend to investigate. The friend approached the head constable in Newtownstewart, a fellow Protestant, who confirmed that McCartan was not to be arrested. The veracity of this confirmation is doubtful. In February 1917, three weeks after McCartan returned to practising medicine in his native district, he was arrested and sent to Arbour Hill prison in Dublin before being deported to England.[131]

As McCartan's father's house had been under police surveillance,[132] it is likely that the Hobson family home in Marino was being watched as well. Thus, it is surprising that the authorities were not aware that Hobson was staying with his parents. Police reports for the period April 1916 to October 1917 make no mention of him.[133] In any case, Hobson was not arrested until after the amnesty.[134]

By late May 1916 Hobson's disappearance had fuelled suggestions that he had betrayed the cause.[135] In August 1916 General Maxwell even reported to Prime Minister Asquith 'an unconfirmed rumour' that the IRB had shot Hobson as a traitor during Easter Week.[136] In that same month McCartan congratulated Hobson on being alive and well – and with Claire – and promised to maintain the 'alleged secret' of their marriage although it was 'public property' in the North because 'your dear sister informed Mrs McCullough [probably Denis McCullough's mother] and Mrs McC told someone else and so on'.[137] McCartan also mentioned his efforts to dispel the rumour originating during Easter Week that Hobson had been shot as a spy, asserting that 'I do not think that you can afford to ignore these things. When the time comes they must be faced, if you are to be put right with the people.'[138]

Scurrilous tales about Hobson's alleged treachery and cowardice abounded in the aftermath of the Easter Rising. In a 1934 statement to McGarrity, Hobson revealed: 'Apparently because I was not in jail and had opposed the insurrection the most scandalous stories were circulated about me and a violent personal hostility was organised which after eighteen years has not yet wholly died out.'[139] Presumably an element within the IRB was responsible for the organisation of this alleged hate campaign against Hobson.[140] In quoting MacDermott's comments to comrades in Richmond Barracks, Pearse's biographer Louis Le Roux referred to MacDermott fighting Hobson 'to the end', while, at the same time, making a plea 'that no dishonour should rest on MacNeill's name'.[141] Admittedly, Le Roux's reliability is often questionable. According to O'Shannon, McGarry, who became president of the IRB Supreme Council and general secretary of the Irish Volunteers, was so incensed by Hobson's actions between 1914 and 1916 that he wanted to deny Hobson any credit for his contributions to the nationalist movement.[142]

Such antipathy towards Hobson was not shared by all of the insurrectionists or by all members of the IRB. Pearse's attitude towards Hobson was relatively positive. He apparently told Volunteers at St Enda's that although 'he did not share Hobson's policy or approve his attitude', 'Hobson was not lacking in physical courage', but in 'the imagination and decision of a revolutionary leader'.[143] Some IRB men, such as McCartan, McCullough, O'Hegarty, Blythe and Martin, remained supportive of Hobson.

Further negative reports about Hobson began circulating in the latter half of 1916, when Judge attacked him with a bayonet-sharp pen in 'The Inner History of the Irish Volunteers', a series of articles that were published in the *Irish Nation*.[144] This weekly paper, which Judge also edited, was both anti-Irish Parliamentary Party and anti-Sinn Féin. It promoted a new organisation called the Repeal League, which supported the repeal of the Union with Great Britain.[145] Asserting that he had disliked Hobson from their first encounter at an organisational meeting held at Wynn's Hotel, Judge described Hobson as having a remarkable 'passion for intrigue', questioned his ethics and honesty, and alleged that he made money from the national movement.[146] (Ironically, all of these accusations could just as equally have been aimed at MacDermott, one of the heroes of the Easter Rising.) Although some readers wrote in to complain about the personal nature of these articles and to cast aspersions on the author's motives,[147] Judge's words may have added to the rumours of Hobson's alleged treason that had circulated since Easter Week.

After the amnesty

Blythe and Martin believed that Hobson's political career would have soared had it been saved by a term of imprisonment.[148] Even Hobson himself later recognised that 'not having been in jail, as MacNeill had said, I had no political future'.[149] Ironically, Hobson had been imprisoned – albeit briefly and at the wrong time. His wife, Claire, recalled that shortly after the amnesty of June 1917 she, Hobson, his sister Florence and his mother, Mary, had to travel through Belfast to get to Lisburn, where they planned to attend a garden party at the Friends' School. Hobson was arrested at the railway station in Belfast and taken to the barracks, where he and his companions spent the day, the women only abandoning him long enough to go out for lunch. When the police finally managed to contact Dublin Castle, they were reminded of the amnesty and told to release their prisoner.[150] Hobson did not mention this episode in his memoirs, perhaps because it was not the sort of jail story that was likely to impress anyone who had done time in places like Frongoch.

After he came out of hiding Hobson found that many of his old friends and colleagues in the nationalist movement 'would not notice or come near him'.[151] This ostracism resulted from a misinterpretation of his actions and a determination to punish him. His Quaker background may have given some people the impression that he had been a crypto-pacifist who had misled his associates in the IRB and the Irish Volunteers about his true intentions. In addition, some may have feared that Hobson, with his sixteen distinguished years of nationalist experience, would usurp their newly won power and positions within the nationalist movement. In the estimation of Greaves, Hobson was 'essentially a politician', who 'deserved success more than many who achieved it'.[152] Frozen out, Hobson refused to force himself upon his former associates. This situation left him with no immediate opportunity to explain his actions or the choices that he had made.[153] As a result, Hobson, through either exclusion or choice, did not participate in the nationalist organisations to which he had belonged prior to the Easter Rising.[154]

After the insurrection the new Supreme Council of the IRB had to decide what to do about IRB men who had opposed the rising. When Hobson's case was being discussed in the Dublin circles, Michael Collins contended that 'Hobson could only be tried by his peers who were now all dead'. Valentine Jackson countered that in his view Hobson 'was already being judged and condemned without trial by many of his former colleagues and that surely there were still enough people left who could examine into and prove or disprove these charges'. Collins, changing tack, pointed out that the IRB had far more important things to do than try Hobson and told Jackson to stop talking nonsense. Jackson let the issue drop.[155] In the view of Peter Hart, Collins' most recent biographer, his harsh reaction was motivated by a desire 'to avoid an acrimonious show trial which would do nothing to further the cause', rather than a vendetta, which he was 'rarely interested in pursuing'.[156] In any case Hobson 'had no further connection' with IRB.[157]

In his memoirs Hobson did not mention the circumstances surrounding the end of his involvement in the Fianna. His decision not to participate in the rising, his successful evasion of arrest and Countess Markievicz's undisguised antipathy towards him appear to have ended his connection with the youth organisation. Many officers and older members of the Fianna participated in the insurrection. Some served as commanders and fighters while others engaged in despatch carrying, scouting and reconnoitring. Seven current and former members of the Fianna were killed in action during Easter Week.[158] Among the fifteen leaders executed for their part in the rising were two young men who were or had been officers of the Fianna: Sean Heuston and Con Colbert.[159] Markievicz, who served as one of the commanders at Stephen's Green and the College of Surgeons, was saved from their fate by her gender.

Some members of the Fianna, including Eoin MacNeill's son Niall, were court-martialled by the Fianna for not taking part in the rising. Markievicz, Barney Mellows and a third (unnamed) Fianna officer exonerated Niall MacNeill on the grounds that he had been under his father's influence. MacNeill saw such court martials as a 'face-saving' device to keep certain useful people in the Fianna movement,[160] which after its post-rising re-organisation attracted an all-time high of over thirty thousand members by June 1917.[161] Even if key Fianna officers had viewed Hobson as useful enough to court-martial, it is doubtful that he would have submitted to such a proceeding.

It is also unlikely that Markievicz would have agreed to Hobson's continuance in the movement. After the rising she did not conceal her dislike for Hobson, melodramatically threatening to shoot him the first time she saw him. The next time they met, however, she failed to recognise him. When later apprised of his identity, she expressed her disappointment at this missed opportunity: '"If I had known it," she cried, "I'd have shot him."'[162]

Due to friction between himself and Griffith, Hobson had severed his connection with the Sinn Féin party in late 1910. He does not appear to have tried to renew his membership in the revitalised organisation. When the Sinn Féin convention was held on 25–26 October 1917, at least 1,700 delegates representing over a thousand branches of Sinn Féin were in attendance. Individuals who did not belong to affiliated clubs were denied admittance.[163] Police reports and newspaper accounts of the convention make no mention of Hobson.[164] At this convention Markievicz, Kathleen Clarke and Helena Molony attacked MacNeill for his endeavours to prevent the insurrection, but the women were overridden by Griffith, Éamon de Valera and Seán Milroy, who spoke forcefully in his favour. As a result, MacNeill topped the list of twenty-four members elected to the new executive with a total of 888 votes.[165]

Hobson's hopes for salvaging his nationalist career rested with the Irish Volunteers. On 22 October 1917, MacNeill had written to de Valera about the need to notify the surviving members of the 1915–16 General Council and Executive Committee of the Irish Volunteers about the forthcoming convention to re-organise the movement.[166] De Valera, however, refused to allow MacNeill and the other members of the old Volunteer executive, Hobson, Fitzgibbon and O'Connell, to attend the convention, which was held on 27 October 1917. De Valera's refusal was the last straw: Hobson withdrew from the nationalist movement.[167]

In a crossed-out sentence in a 1934 statement to McGarrity, Hobson noted that he withdrew from the movement because he was 'unwilling to cause dissension by leading a personal following', but failed to mention who might have constituted this fan club.[168] It was not the first time that Hobson withdrew rather than cause further dissension within nationalist ranks. He had followed the same strategy when he severed his ties with Sinn Féin in late 1910 and resigned from the Supreme Council of the IRB in 1914.

Perhaps the effectiveness of a unified nationalist movement did mean more to him than his own position within that movement. Perhaps his ego would not allow him to eat humble pie by, for example, submitting to court martial. Perhaps he was deeply wounded by the fickleness of former friends. Perhaps he was merely exhausted and disillusioned by public life. All of these reasons combined probably contributed to his decision to retire from the nationalist movement. In his draft memoirs he even intimated that having no political future had been 'rather a relief'.[169]

F.X. Martin has noted the contrast between Hobson and his other Volunteer colleagues, MacNeill, Fitzgibbon and O'Connell, who were allowed (or allowed themselves) to continue playing a part in the nationalist movement.[170] Unlike Hobson, however, the trio had not been members of the IRB. A further comparison can be drawn to Lester. Like Hobson, he was an IRB member who did not participate in the rising, but his arrest shortly after the insurrection ensured his continuance in the movement.[171]

Hobson's enemies, both inside and outside the IRB, cast him as a traitor and a coward. Yet it could be argued that he betrayed fellow IRB men, like Clarke and MacDermott, no more – maybe even less – than they betrayed him. All were guilty of violating their oath to the IRB constitution. Clarke, MacDermott, Pearse, Ceannt, Plunkett and MacDonagh staged a rebellion without the support of the majority of the Irish people, while Hobson disregarded the orders of his superior officers. Hobson displayed enormous moral courage in choosing not to join a rising that he believed was morally wrong and militarily doomed to failure. In light of his unrelenting commitment to guerrilla warfare over insurrection, the Easter Rising can not be viewed as a fair test of his physical courage. Had he been arrested and imprisoned at the right time, he might have overcome the allegations against him.

In February 1918 McGarry, who had succeeded Hobson as secretary of the re-organised Irish Volunteers, sent Hobson a letter, inviting him to submit himself for court martial in relation to his Easter Week stance and requesting Volunteer money, property or special information that might be in his possession. When Hobson did not respond, McGarry sent him a second copy of the letter care of MacNeill a month later.[172] Hobson appears to have ignored both letters. He did not submit to a court martial, probably because, in his opinion, it was the insurrectionists, not himself, who had done wrong by violating the constitution of the Irish Volunteers and disregarding MacNeill's countermanding order.

MacNeill tried to stop the rumours that were circulating about Hobson and others who had opposed the insurrection when he gave the Volunteer funds in his possession to de Valera and William Cosgrave in October 1918. In handing over the money, he made two demands, 'one in the interest of the national cause, the other in the interest of justice':

> The first is that resistance to conscription shall be directed genuinely to defeating conscription and therefore shall not take the form of a military demonstration which would have the opposite effect. The second is, that, so far as the influence of the recipients of these funds can go, every attempt to create or maintain an attitude of hostility and obloquy towards those

of all ranks and positions in the Irish Volunteers who opposed the rising of 1916 shall be discountenanced and discouraged.[173]

His second demand appears to have made no difference to Hobson's situation.

Hobson played no part in the subsequent events that preceded the formation of what he referred to in the 1930s as 'the so-called Free State', his choice of adjective revealing his increasingly ambivalent attitude toward the independent Ireland that was created.[174] He watched the events of the War of Independence from the sidelines. For instance, when he was travelling to Cork on 13 May 1919, he happened to get a front-row view of Seán Hogan, one of the Irish Republican Army (IRA) men captured after the ambush of the RIC on 21 January 1919 at Soloheadbeg in County Tipperary, being rescued from the train at Knocklong in County Limerick.[175]

Hobson proved more perceptive about how Irish independence would be achieved than about how his nationalist career could be saved. As Richard Davis has noted, 'It was ironical that Griffith, for a considerable part of the Anglo-Irish War, found himself nominally presiding over the application of Hobson's policy, while the latter was excluded from all influence in the movement.'[176] Although neither man had supported the insurrection, Griffith, unlike Hobson, had received the benediction of arrest and imprisonment after the event. If Hobson had not succeeded in evading arrest prior to the amnesty, he, like MacNeill, might have been able to overcome the hostility that some people felt towards him.

Despite his retirement from the nationalist movement, Hobson may have expected some harassment during the War of Independence or the Civil War. Tom MacDonagh, one of Hobson's neighbours in Roundstone, recalled that, during a visit to Hobson's home in Rathfarnham in the late 1940s, his host showed him the escape route from his garden.[177] The escape route may have been genuine or a trick conjured up by an old political activist to tantalise a young guest. Hobson himself reported that one of the reasons why his collection of Irish Volunteer documents survived was because he was lucky enough not to have been raided by the Black and Tans.[178]

Conclusion

In the years after 1916, Hobson was, for some of his former nationalist colleagues, 'a national leader *manqué*'.[179] For others, he was a republican 'has-been' who failed to make the grade when the fight for Irish independence stopped being a war of words. In the eyes of the general public, he was a once-prominent nationalist who disappeared from view as if he had been executed along with the insurrectionists of 1916, but without the benefit of their subsequent spin doctors.[180]

Hobson's opposition to the rising alone does not explain his fall from public grace. MacNeill opposed the rising but, thanks to his arrest, his political career survived until the Boundary Commission. Thus, Hobson's failure to be arrested after the rising is one explanation. His refusal to follow the orders of the IRB Military Council, despite those orders being contrary to the IRB constitution, may be another explanation. Although Hobson's actions were not intended to be a betrayal of his IRB brothers, they were perceived as such by individuals who interpreted his actions as those of a traitor or a coward. His Quaker background may have given people the impression that he had been a crypto-pacifist who had misled his associates in the IRB and the Irish Volunteers about his true intentions. In addition, Hobson's distaste for fighting the 'freezing-out' to which some nationalists subjected him may help to explain his 'disappearance' from public life.

Notes

1 It is unclear exactly how and when Hobson first found out that plans were being made for a rising. He told a BBC Radio interviewer on 14 Oct. 1964 that he was aware of plans for a rising 'probably early in [19]15'. See transcript, *Old Ireland Free* (BBC Written Archives, Reading). In a 1934 statement to McGarrity, Hobson said that McCullough warned him in Dec. 1915 (NLI, BH, MS 13,171). McCullough, however, told Pádraig Ó Maidín in an undated letter that he informed Hobson of the Supreme Council's decision to stage a rising the day after the meeting when this decision was made (UCDA, DMcC, P 120/23 (20)). The meeting to which McCullough appears to refer was held on 16 Jan. 1916.
2 Ó Broin, *Revolutionary underground*, pp. 166–7.
3 McCullough to Ó Maidín, n.d. (UCDA, DMcC, P 120/23 (20)); McCullough, witness statement, 13 Apr. 1948 (NAI, BMH, WS 111).
4 McCullough, witness statement, 13 Apr. 1948 (NAI, BMH, WS 111).
5 Hobson, statement to McGarrity, 1934 (NLI, BH, MS 13,171). According to McCullough, Hobson ignored his warning both 'then and later' (McCullough to Ó Maidín, n.d. (UCDA, DMcC, P 120/23 (20)).
6 Transcript, *Old Ireland Free*, 24 Apr. 1966 (BBC Written Archives, Reading).
7 Ibid.
8 Martin (ed.), 'MacNeill on the rising', pp. 255–6; Foy and Barton, *Easter Rising*, pp. 45–6; Tierney, *Eoin MacNeill*, p. 193.
9 Martin (ed.), 'MacNeill on the rising', p. 247.
10 Ibid., pp. 246–7; Tierney, *Eoin MacNeill*, p. 187.
11 O'Connell, 'Irish Volunteers', Chap. 14, p. 1.
12 Ibid., pp. 1–2.

13 Foy and Barton, *Easter Rising*, p. 49.
14 'Police attack on Tullamore Volunteers', *IV*, 25 Mar. 1916, p. 3.
15 'Banishment of Irishmen', *IV*, 8 Apr. 1916, p. 3; Tierney, *Eoin MacNeill*, p. 194.
16 Hobson, *IYT*, p. 73; Martin (ed.), 'MacNeill on the rising', p. 247; Tierney, *Eoin MacNeill*, pp. 187–9; Transcript, *Old Ireland Free*, 24 Apr. 1966 (BBC Written Archives, Reading).
17 Martin (ed.), 'MacNeill on the 1916 rising', pp. 234–5.
18 Ibid., p. 240.
19 'Headquarters' Bulletin', *IV*, 8 Apr. 1916, p. 2; Tierney, *Eoin MacNeill*, p. 194, 203.
20 Hobson, *IYT*, pp. 74–5.
21 FitzGerald, *Memoirs*, p. 116.
22 McCullough, statement about the rising (UCDA, DMcC, P 120/31). For a less candid account of McCullough's and MacDermott's reactions to Hobson's speech, see Denis McCullough, 'The events in Belfast', *Capuchin Annual* (1966), p. 382.
23 Foy and Barton, *Easter Rising*, p. 53.
24 Townshend, *Easter 1916*, p. 133.
25 Ryan, *Rising*, pp. 64, 67, 70, 73.
26 Séamus Ó Ceallaigh, *Gleanings from Ulster history* (Draperstown, 1994), pp. 142–3. Dr Ó Ceallaigh's memoir, dated 10 Feb. 1952 and translated by Nollaig Ó Muraíle, covers his involvement in the circulation of the 'bogus document' and the meeting at his home on Holy Saturday 1916 (*Gleanings*, pp. 141–52).
27 Martin (ed.), 'MacNeill on the rising', p. 248.
28 Hobson, *IYT*, p. 74.
29 Le Roux, *Pearse*, p. 347; Martin (ed.), 'MacNeill on the rising', p. 248.
30 FitzGerald, *Memoirs*, p. 118.
31 Martin (ed.), 'MacNeill on the rising', p. 257. It is unclear whether a covering letter and a copy of the document was sent to all of the Catholic bishops in Ireland or just to those who had not been contacted the previous weekend by Ó Ceallaigh.
32 Claire Hobson, witness statement, n.d. (NAI, BMH, WS 685).
33 Greaves, *Liam Mellows*, p. 51.
34 Ryan, *Rising*, pp. 64, 74; Foy and Barton, *Easter Rising*, pp. 53–4; The Royal Commission on the Rebellion in Ireland, *Minutes of evidence and appendix of documents* (London, 1916), p. 7. Ó Ceallaigh offered a slightly different version in his memoirs, stating that he and Little showed the document to the editors of the *Evening Herald*, *Evening Mail* and *Evening Telegraph* on Spy Wednesday, but only the *Mail* took a chance and ran the story (*Gleanings*, pp. 144–5).
35 Martin (ed.), 'MacNeill on the rising', p. 248; Le Roux, *Pearse*, p. 348.
36 Order issued by Eoin MacNeill, Chief of Staff, 19 Apr. 1916 (NLI, BH, MS 13,174 (16)).
37 Foy and Barton, *Easter Rising*, pp. 53–4.

38 Ibid., pp. 39–44. In Dublin Ned Daly's 1st Battalion was assigned to the Four Courts, MacDonagh's 2nd Battalion to Jacob's biscuit factory, de Valera's 3rd Battalion to Boland's bakery and Ceannt's 4th Battalion to the South Dublin Union.
39 Foy and Barton, *Easter Rising*, p. 58.
40 Ibid.
41 Sean Fitzgibbon, 'The Easter Rising from the inside – II', ed. Michael J. Lennon, *IT*, 19 Apr. 1949, p. 4.
42 Le Roux, *Tom Clarke*, p. 192.
43 Diarmuid Lynch, *The IRB and the 1916 insurrection*, ed. Florence O'Donoghue (Cork, 1957), pp. 49–50.
44 Ryan, *Rising*, p. 90.
45 Martin, witness statement, n.d. (NAI, BMH, WS 591).
46 Eamon Martin, 'Bulmer Hobson and Redmondites – "This is a bitter pill – but one we must swallow"', *SP*, 15 May 1960, p. 10.
47 Hobson, statement to McGarrity, 1934 (NLI, BH, MS 13,171). See also Hobson to F.X. Martin, 23 May 1960, qtd. in Martin (ed.), 'MacNeill on the rising', p. 258.
48 Foy and Barton, *Easter Rising*, p. 59.
49 F.X. Martin, '1916 – myth, fact, and mystery', *Studia Hibernica*, no. 7 (1967), p. 88; Eoin MacNeill, memoir, 1932, pp. 119–20 (UCDA, EMacN, LAI/G/371).
50 Orders issued by Eoin MacNeill, Chief of Staff, 21 Apr. 1916 (NLI, BH, MS 13,174 (16)).
51 Hobson, statement prepared for MacNeill's court martial defence, 1 May 1916; qtd. in Martin (ed.), 'MacNeill on the rising', pp. 260–1.
52 Hobson, *IYT*, p. 76; Claire Hobson, witness statement, n.d. (NAI, BMH, WS 685).
53 Tierney, *Eoin MacNeill*, p. 199; MacNeill, memoir, 1932, p. 120 (UCDA, EMacN, LAI/G/371).
54 Martin (ed.), 'MacNeill on the rising', p. 251.
55 Hobson, *IYT*, p. 76.
56 Tierney, *Eoin MacNeill*, p. 201.
57 Mitchell, *Casement*, pp. 112–13; Foy and Barton, *Easter Rising*, p. 65.
58 Eunan O'Halpin, 'British intelligence in Ireland, 1914–1921', in Christopher Andrew and David Dilks (eds), *The missing dimension: governments and intelligence communities in the twentieth century* (London, 1984), p. 59.
59 Mitchell, *Casement*, pp. 112–13; Foy and Barton, *Easter Rising*, p. 65.
60 O'Halpin, 'British intelligence', p. 60.
61 Ibid., pp. 57–8, 60.
62 Transcript, *Old Ireland Free*, 24 Apr. 1966 (BBC Written Archives, Reading).
63 Hobson, *IYT*, p. 76. In contrast, Charles Townshend states that Hobson was arrested at Volunteer Headquarters by some of his colleagues on the Leinster Executive of the IRB and conveyed to the home of IRB member Martin Conlon. See Townshend, *Easter 1916*, p. 137.

64 Ted Nealon, 'Hobson throws new light on IRB caucus', *SP*, 1 May 1960, p. 4. Among his jailers were Seamus O'Doherty and Mortimer O'Connell. See Michael Kevin O'Doherty, *My parents and other rebels* (Dublin, 1999), p. 10; Mortimer O'Connell, witness statement, 16 Feb. 1953 (NAI, BMH, WS 804).
65 Ó Lúing, 'Talking to Bulmer Hobson,' *IT*, 6 May 1961, p. 10.
66 Hobson, *IYT*, p. 77.
67 Townshend, *Easter 1916*, p. 137.
68 Nealon, 'Hobson throws new light on IRB caucus', *SP*, 1 May 1960, p. 4.
69 Ó Luing, 'Talking to Bulmer Hobson,' *IT*, 6 May 1961, p. 10.
70 Nealon, 'Hobson throws new light on IRB caucus', *SP*, 1 May 1960, p. 4.
71 Martin Conlon, witness statement, 9 Feb. 1953 (NAI, BMH, WS 798).
72 Mrs Martin Conlon, witness statement, n.d. (NAI, BMH, WS 419).
73 Maurice Collins, witness statement, n.d. (NAI, BMH, WS 550).
74 FitzGerald, *Memoirs*, p. 121.
75 O'Connor, BMH witness statement, 14 June 1948 (UCDA, EMacN, LAI/G/117).
76 Claire Hobson, witness statement, n.d. (NAI, BMH, WS 685).
77 Sean Fitzgibbon, 'The Easter Rising from the inside – II', ed. Michael J. Lennon, *IT*, 19 Apr. 1949, p. 4; Tierney, *Eoin MacNeill*, p. 206.
78 Tierney, *Eoin MacNeill*, p. 205.
79 According to Ó Ceallaigh, MacNeill only learned about a boat landing on the Kerry coast and the arrest of one of its occupants when he went to the *Sunday Independent* office to drop off the countermanding order for publication (*Gleanings*, p. 149).
80 In addition to Griffith, Sean Fitzgibbon, O'Rahilly, Sean T. O'Kelly, Seamus O'Connor, Eimar O'Duffy, Colm Ó Lochlainn and Pádraig O'Keeffe were in attendance (Tierney, *Eoin MacNeill*, p. 208). Ó Ceallaigh recalled that Liam Ó Briain, Máire (Min) Ryan, her sister Phyllis, her brother James, Joseph Connolly, Fr. Paul Walsh, who all arrived later, were among those who served as messengers around the country (*Gleanings*, p. 148). Min and Phyllis Ryan later married Richard Mulcahy and Sean T. O'Kelly respectively. Their sister Agnes Ryan married Denis McCullough in Aug. 1916.
81 Martin (ed.), 'MacNeill on the rising', pp. 249–50.
82 Facsimile of countermanding order issued by Eoin MacNeill, Chief of Staff, 22 Apr. 1916 (NLI, BH, MS 13,174 (16)).
83 Ó Ceallaigh, *Gleanings*, pp. 150–1.
84 Foy and Barton, *Easter Rising*, p. 74.
85 Claire Hobson, witness statement, n.d. (NAI, BMH, WS 685).
86 Áine Ceannt, witness statement, n.d. (NAI, BMH, WS 264).
87 Claire Hobson, witness statement, n.d. (NAI, BMH, WS 685).
88 Ibid.; Maurice Collins, witness statement, n.d. (NAI, BMH, WS 550).
89 Qtd. in Tierney, *Eoin MacNeill*, p. 215.
90 Tierney, *Eoin MacNeill*, pp. 215–6.
91 Martin (ed.), 'MacNeill on the rising', p. 250.

92 Sean Fitzgibbon, 'The Easter Rising from the inside – II', ed. Michael J. Lennon, *IT*, 19 Apr. 1949, p. 4.
93 Martin (ed.), 'MacNeill on the rising', p. 250; Tierney, *Eoin MacNeill*, p. 218; Ó Ceallaigh, *Gleanings*, p. 152.
94 Foy and Barton, *Easter Rising*, p. 198.
95 Conlon, witness statement, 9 Feb. 1953 (NAI, BMH, WS 798).
96 Piaras Béaslaí, 'Moods and memories', *II*, 24 Apr. 1963, p. 7 (UCDA, DMcC, P 120/40 (14)); O'Rahilly, *Winding the clock*, pp. 212–13. O'Rahilly erroneously stated that Hobson was released on Tuesday evening. He was also mistaken when he recorded that Hobson was kidnapped by so-called 'ultras' during the middle of Holy Week (pp. 195–7). See also Foy and Barton, *Easter Rising*, p. 201; Thomas M. Coffey, *Agony at Easter* (London, 1970), pp. 71–3.
97 Sean MacDermott to Maurice Collins, 24 Apr. 1916 (BMH, Rev. Bro. Allen Collection, CD 75/1/2).
98 Seán T. O'Kelly, *Seán T.*, ed. Proinsias Ó Conluain (Dublin, 1963), p. 177; Seán T. O'Kelly's account of his Easter Week experiences, *IP*, 6–9 Aug. 1961, qtd. in Foy and Barton, *Easter Rising*, pp. 201–2.
99 O'Kelly, *Sean T.*, p. 178.
100 Nealon, 'Hobson throws new light on IRB caucus', *SP*, 1 May 1960, p. 4; Hobson, statement to McGarrity, 1934 (NLI, BH, MS 13,171).
101 Hobson, *IYT*, p. 74; Hobson, witness statement, 17 Dec. 1947 (NLI, BH, 13,170; NAI, BMH, WS 81).
102 Hobson, statement to McGarrity, Apr. 1933 (NLI, JMcG, MS 17,453).
103 Hobson, statement to McGarrity, 1934 (NLI, BH, MS 13,171).
104 Patterson to Glynn, 21 May 1972 (FHLD, Box 3A, No. 85).
105 Blythe, cited in Glynn, 'The Quaker in Bulmer Hobson – Part 1', *Irish Young Friend*, [Apr. or May] 1972 (clipping, Cork Archives Institute).
106 Earnán de Blaghd, *Gaeil á Múscailt* (Dublin, 1973), p. 108.
107 Ibid.
108 Major Ivor Price is quoted on the back cover of Hobson, *IYT*. This quotation is not included in Price's public evidence, which was published in The Royal Commission on the Rebellion in Ireland, *Minutes of evidence and appendix of documents* (Dublin, 1916), pp. 56–60, 64. Price may have described Hobson as 'the most dangerous man in Ireland' when he was giving private evidence to the commission.
109 Claire Hobson, witness statement, n.d. (NAI, BMH, WS 685); Tierney, *Eoin MacNeill*, p. 219.
110 Hobson, *IYT*, p. 77.
111 Hobson, witness statement, 17 Dec. 1947 (NLI, BH, MS 13,170; NAI, BMH, WS 81).
112 Tierney, *Eoin MacNeill*, p. 219; Gageby, *Sean Lester*, p. 13.
113 Hilary Pyle (ed.), *Cesca's diary, 1913–1916* (Dublin, 2005), p. 205.
114 Claire Hobson, witness statement, n.d. (NAI, BMH, WS 685).
115 FitzGerald, *Memoirs*, pp. 174–5.
116 Ibid., p. 126.

117 Ibid., pp. 120–1, 123–5.
118 Ibid., pp. 174–5.
119 Claire Hobson, witness statement, n.d. (NAI, BMH, WS 685).
120 Hobson, *IYT*, p. 77.
121 Greaves, *Liam Mellows*, p. 46.
122 Tierney, *Eoin MacNeill*, p. 222.
123 Glynn, 'The Quaker in Bulmer Hobson – Part 1', *Irish Young Friend*, [Apr. or May] 1972 (clipping, Cork Archives Institute).
124 Hobson, *IYT*, pp. 77–8.
125 Hobson, witness statement, 17 Dec. 1947 (NLI MS 13,170; NAI, BMH, WS 81).
126 *The Police Gazette or Hue-and-Cry*, 7 Nov. 1916, p. 3.
127 Hobson's Roundstone neighbours Joe Rafferty, Tom MacDonagh and Joe MacDonagh provided this information during interviews with the author on 9 Jan. 2003.
128 Mary Hobson, 'Bulmer Family Chronicle' (NLI, MS 5220); Parish marriage register, Rathfarnham (NLI, microfilm no. P 8972).
129 See entry on Mary A. Hutton (née Drummond) in Kate Newmann, *Dictionary of Ulster biography* (Belfast, 1993), p. 116. According to the 1916 *Thom's Directory*, Mrs Mary Anne Hutton was resident at Palmerston Lodge, Dartry Road, Upper Rathmines.
130 Claire Hobson, witness statement, n.d. (NAI, BMH, WS 685).
131 Patrick McCartan, 'Extracts from the papers of the late Dr Patrick McCartan – Part Two', *Clogher Record* (1964), p. 203.
132 Ibid., p. 202.
133 Inspector General's and County Inspectors' monthly confidential reports, Apr. 1916–Oct. 1917 (NAL, CO 904/99–104).
134 Claire Hobson, witness statement, n.d. (NAI, BMH, WS 685).
135 Cesca Chenevix Trench reported these rumours in her diary entry of 21 May 1916. See Pyle (ed.), *Cesca's diary*, p. 228.
136 Maxwell to Asquith, 3 Aug. 1916, qtd. in Laffan, *The resurrection of Ireland*, p. 46.
137 Padraic [McCartan] to Hobson, 18 Aug. 1916 (NLI, BH, MS 13,161 (2)).
138 Ibid.
139 Hobson, statement to McGarrity, 1934 (NLI, BH, MS 13,171).
140 For instance, Michael Tierney postulated that Hobson's 'great abilities were doomed to be wasted, apparently because of the undying animosity of the IRB' (*Eoin MacNeill*, p. 222).
141 Le Roux, *Patrick Pearse*, p. 336.
142 O'Shannon to McCullough, 25 Mar. 1958 (UCDA, DMcC, P 120/15 (3)).
143 Le Roux, *Patrick Pearse*, p. 337.
144 Clippings of many of these articles are available among NLI, BH, MS 13,173 (6).
145 Glandon, *Arthur Griffith and the advanced nationalist press*, p. 272; Inspector General's monthly confidential report, Aug. 1916 (NAL, CO 904/100).

146 Judge, 'Inner history', *IN*, 19 Aug. 1916, 26 Aug. 1916, p. 6.
147 Judge, 'Inner history', *IN*, 26 Aug. 1916, p. 6.
148 Martin, witness statement, n.d. (NAI, BMH, WS 591); de Blaghd, *Gaeil á Múscailt*, p. 108.
149 Hobson, *IYT*, p. 78.
150 Claire Hobson, witness statement, n.d. (NAI, BMH, WS 685).
151 Hobson, statement to McGarrity, Apr. 1933 (NLI, JMcG, MS 17,453).
152 Greaves, *Liam Mellows*, p. 46.
153 Hobson, statement to McGarrity, Apr. 1933 (NLI, JMcG, MS 17,453).
154 C. Desmond Greaves suggests that Hobson was involved in the Irish Volunteers' Dependants Aid Committee, which later amalgamated with the Irish National Aid Association, but this is doubtful. Not only was Hobson on the run when it was established, but it is unlikely that its president Kathleen Clarke would have accepted his assistance. Greaves does not cite the source of his information regarding Hobson's involvement with the Volunteers' Dependants Aid Committee. See Greaves, *Liam Mellows*, p. 112; Margaret Ward, *Unmanageable revolutionaries: women and Irish nationalism* (London, 1995), p. 119.
155 Valentine Jackson, witness statement, n.d. (NAI, BMH, WS 409).
156 Peter Hart, *Mick: the real Michael Collins* (London, 2005), p. 143.
157 Ó Broin, *Revolutionary underground*, p. 179.
158 Robert Holland, *A short history of Fianna Éireann* (Dublin, n.d.), p. 26 (NLI, MS 35,455/3/12A).
159 Joseph Reynolds, witness statement, n.d. (NAI, BMH, WS 191). In his statement Reynolds outlined the participation of leading members of the Fianna in the rising.
160 Col Niall MacNeill, witness statement, 6–7 Jan. 1948 (NAI, BMH, WS 69).
161 Pádraig Mac Fhloinn, 'The history and tradition of Fianna Éireann', in *Fianna Éireann Handbook* (Dublin, 1988), p. 14.
162 O'Faolain, *Constance*, p. 177.
163 Laffan, *The resurrection of Ireland*, pp. 118–19.
164 Inspector General's confidential report, Oct. 1917 (NAL, CO 904/104); 'Sinn Féin convention', *II*, 26 Oct. 1917, pp. 3–4; 'Sinn Féin convention', *II*, 27 Oct. 1917, pp. 3–4.
165 Laffan, *The resurrection of Ireland*, pp. 119–20; Davis, *Sinn Féin*, p. 176.
166 Eoin MacNeill to Éamon de Valera, 22 Oct. 1917 (NLI, BH, MS 13,161 (3)).
167 Hobson, BMH witness statement, 17 Dec. 1947 (NLI, BH, MS 13,170).
168 Hobson, statement to McGarrity, 1934 (NLI, BH, MS 13,171).
169 Hobson, draft memoirs (NLI, BH, MS 18,283 (1)).
170 Martin, 'Myth, fact and mystery', p. 89.
171 Gageby, *Sean Lester*, pp. 13–14.
172 McGarry to Hobson, 12 Feb. 1918, 21 Mar. 1918 (NLI, BH, MS 13,161 (4)).
173 Unsigned note, [10?] Oct. 1918 (NLI, BH, MS 13,161 (4)).

174 Hobson, statement to McGarrity, Apr. 1933 (NLI, JMcG, MS 17,453).
175 Hobson reported that Dan Breen's published account of the event 'coincided exactly' with what he had seen (Ó Lúing, 'Talking to Bulmer Hobson', *IT*, 6 May 1961, p. 10).
176 Davis, *Sinn Féin*, p. 159.
177 Interview with Tom MacDonagh of Roundstone, Connemara, 9 Jan. 2003.
178 Ó Luing, 'Talking to Bulmer Hobson', *IT*, 6 May 1961, p. 10.
179 O'Shannon, 'Bulmer Hobson, key republican figure', *IT*, 9 Aug. 1969, p. 10.
180 Martin, 'Myth, fact and mystery', p. 89.

9

Building a new life

In January 1924 McCartan portrayed Hobson as a busy civil servant, husband and father, who faced an hour-long commute between his home in Rathfarnham and his office in the city centre. McCartan recalled that, back in his friend's Belfast days, he could always be relied upon: if he promised to do something for you, he did it. 'But Dublin and a wife and a wean [child] seems to have changed him', lamented McCartan.[1]

After Hobson emerged from hiding, he and his wife, Claire, moved back to Dublin, where he started to rebuild his life. He found work first in book publishing, and then in the civil service. The couple bought a house on the outskirts of the city and began to raise a family. In their spare time they supported the foundation of a new theatre. His penchant for writing propaganda remained irrepressible until his eyesight gave out. Hobson's life after the 1916 rising featured both continuities and changes. This chapter traces them.

Publisher, 1918 to 1923

By the summer of 1918 Hobson was employed as one of the directors of the Candle Press, which Colm Ó Lochlainn and Seán Mac Giollarna, editor of *An Claidheamh Soluis*, had established in the winter of 1916. Its output included books of Irish interest, prints and cards. By the time Hobson joined the business it was located at 44 Dawson Street.[2] Shortly afterwards he participated in the launch of a new venture called Martin Lester Ltd.[3] Hobson, Ó Lochlainn and James MacNeill (presumably the brother of Eoin) were the directors of this new company, which published books of Irish and general interest and served as the wholesale agent for publications of the Candle Press. Initially located at 44 Dawson Street, it later moved to 78 Harcourt Street.[4]

As a director Hobson was involved in the commissioning, editing, production, promotion and distribution of books published by Martin Lester Ltd. and the Candle Press. He liased with authors and agents, keeping them informed about print runs and sales, and forwarded copies of the finished product and royalties.[5] Through Martin Lester Ltd. he also had the chance to re-issue works that had inspired him, such the writings of Wolfe Tone and an extract of E.T. Craig's history of Ralahine entitled *An Irish Commune*. Ironically, the latter volume included an introduction by George Russell, who had provided Count Casimir Markievicz with the facts and figures to poke fun at the short-lived, Ralahine-inspired commune that Hobson and Countess Markievicz had established in Raheny in 1909.

Martin Lester Ltd. published two books edited by Hobson: *The Life of Wolfe Tone*, which included Wolfe Tone's autobiographical writings and extracts of his political works,[6] and *The Letters of Wolfe Tone*, a selection of letters by Wolfe Tone, his widow and his son that Hobson had found 'scattered among several collections of old papers'.[7] A reviewer for the *Irish Book Lover* praised him for having 'done his work well' because the letters revealed 'the true man, with all his charm, vigour and force of character'.[8]

As part of his publishing work Hobson launched the *Irish review of politics, economics, art and literature* in October 1922. This 12-page periodical was initially envisaged as a fortnightly affair. Early editions provide insight into Hobson's views on the Anglo-Irish Treaty, the ensuing Irish Civil War and the Boundary Commission. For instance, he praised the Irish provisional government's progress in restoring order and blamed de Valera for the outbreak of the civil war. In Hobson's view,

> had [de Valera] acted otherwise the Treaty was a wonderful national triumph – because of him it was accompanied by a bitter national tragedy. He is responsible for the ruin at home, the loss of prestige abroad, the deaths of hundreds of people, and the partition that is about to overtake our country ... Upon such little things as the turn of a vacillating mind do the fortunes of a people rest.

His criticism of de Valera is hardly surprising: the anti-Treaty leader had blocked Hobson's attendance at the 1917 conference to re-organise the Volunteer movement.

In reference to Northern Ireland, Hobson opined that 'economic facts and common sense' would sooner or later encourage the Prime Minister of Northern Ireland, Sir James Craig, to align his government with Dublin rather than London. Like other Irish nationalists, Hobson naively believed that the real obstacle to a settlement between north and south was 'English interference', not steadfast Ulster Unionist resistance.[9] He was dismissive of the Boundary Commission as a policy because it would fail to satisfy anyone caught on the wrong side of the border and such failure had the potential to spark another civil war. 'We do not want a border to divide Ireland, but an understanding that will unite Ireland,' he asserted, adding that the governments of the Free State and Northern Ireland should confer on a regular basis and over an extended period of time until they reached agreement.[10] Instead of partition, he favoured both north and south having 'as much local autonomy as they require' within a united Ireland.[11]

As Alice Milligan noted in a letter to Hobson, the political situation in the early 1920s made it a challenging time to establish a new business.[12] A novel by Milligan and her brother William, entitled *The dynamite drummer*, garnered meagre sales: Hobson had to impart the bad news that only four hundred copies had been sold.[13] In December 1920, possibly while he was in prison, Eoin MacNeill wrote to his wife that some of Hobson's clients 'need pushing and exaggerate their own difficulties and forget their duties'.[14]

Between 1921 and 1922 Hobson and Eimar O'Duffy, whose early books were published by Martin Lester Ltd., kept up a regular correspondence in which the latter offered words of sympathy on more than one occasion because business was so bad.[15] O'Duffy's letters intimate that he was keen to abandon his job as a teacher at Mount St Benedict in Gorey, County Wexford in order to return to the bright lights of Dublin. Hobson suggested some possible contacts to help his friend secure employment.[16] He too may have been casting about for a new job.

Like O'Duffy, Hobson had a wife and a young son to support. By 1920 he and Claire had set up home in the Mill House, a three-storey Georgian property on Whitechurch Road in Rathfarnham.[17] Their children, Declan Bulmer and Camilla Claire, were born in 1921 and 1928 respectively. The Hobson children later attended a Quaker boarding school: Newtown School in Waterford.[18]

Civil servant and economic propagandist, 1923 to 1948

Martin Lester Ltd. proved a short-lived venture. Its demise circa 1923 probably resulted from financial failure and/or Hobson's decision to join the civil service of the new Irish Free State government, which was established on 6 December 1922.[19] In August 1923 he was hired as Temporary Technical Clerk in the Stationery Office at a salary of £250 per annum. He moved up to a permanent, pensionable position in October 1924 after he successfully interviewed for the post of Deputy Director of Stamping in the Office of the Revenue Commissioners. The creation of this new position may have been a result of the Minister and Secretaries Act of 1924, which led to the increased formalisation of staffing of the civil service and of the titles of individual civil servants. The job initially came with a salary scale of £350–£500 per annum plus bonus, but this was later raised first to £500–£600 in 1939 and then, after much debate, in 1944 to £640, with the possibility of further increments.[20]

Ironically, Hobson was based in Dublin Castle, the former bastion of British authority. He was responsible for managing the printing section of the Stamping Department in the Office of the Revenue Commissioners. In those early years the Revenue was responsible for all of the government's 'secure' printing needs, such as postage stamps, pension books, licenses and various government forms.[21] By the late 1940s he had about sixty people working under his supervision.[22]

The Revenue fell under the remit of the Department of Finance, but was an independent entity. As Hobson, for obvious reasons, had no previous experience in the British civil service, it is not overly surprising that he joined an office associated with Finance. Like External Affairs, it was a newly created department, there having been no need for such functions in Ireland under the Union.[23] The newness of Finance may have provided more scope for bringing in new blood. According to a former employee of the Stamping Department, some people who were recruited at its inception had been 'politically involved'.[24] Perhaps Hobson's old friend Blythe, who served as Minister for Finance from September 1923 until March 1932, helped him to secure employment.

As a civil servant, Hobson built on his past employment experience in printing and publishing, but occasionally could indulge his interest in economic matters. For instance, he had the opportunity to serve as secretary to an interdepartmental committee on the sugar beet industry, compiling the committee's May 1933 report.[25] Deputy Director of Stamping was not, however, the position in a new Ireland that one would have predicted, based on his earlier political career. He held this position until his retirement in January 1948, even though his increasingly poor eyesight eventually made it difficult for him to supervise the output of the printing presses. Opportunities for further advancement were limited because he had been hired at the highest level within the technical (or industrial) grades of the civil service. At that time it would have been very difficult for him to move over to the more prestigious, non-technical grades.[26]

While Hobson's work at Dublin Castle filled his days, he was free to participate in cultural activities in the evening, much as he had done in his Belfast days as a founding member of the ULT. In the late 1920s Hobson and his wife, Claire, supported the establishment of the Gate Theatre. The actor Hilton Edwards pitched his plan for the foundation of a new theatre for the production of both international and Irish plays to a group of Dublin residents one spring night in 1928. This meeting took place in 'The Little Theatre', one of the few nightclubs in Dublin at the time. Run by Madame Daisy Bannard Cogley – known as 'Toto' – and her partner, Gearóid Ó Lochlainn, it could be found 'in an obscure thoroughfare at the back of Grafton Street'.[27] Cogley, a petite French woman who had married an Irish republican, held a cabaret there every Saturday night.[28] The writer Mervyn Wall recalled that Claire Hobson 'was one of a bohemian group who frequented' this nightclub during the Emergency (as the Second World War was known in Éire),[29] possibly after the break-up of her marriage.

In late 1928 Cogley and Ó Lochlainn joined Edwards and Micheál Mac Liammóir as the founding directors of what was to become the Gate Theatre. To fund the theatre's first season of plays, Edwards asked interested people to pay a one-guinea subscription.[30] The Hobsons, along with McCartan and McCullough, joined a committee to organise the business side of the burgeoning theatre company. Out of a series of meetings held in 'private rooms in big hotels' emerged a shareholding scheme, a limited company, a board of directors and a list of possible premises.[31] The Hobsons also helped Mac Liammóir to research famous episodes in Dublin history for a pageant in honour of the city's annual civic week in September 1929. *The ford of the hurdles* was a historical epic covering the period from the Viking invasion to the Easter Rising.[32] The Gate later revived the play. In 1934 Hobson edited a beautifully illustrated book, entitled *The Gate Theatre*, which summarised the theatre company's first six years of existence and served as a fundraiser for future productions.[33]

During this period Hobson took on two other major editing projects, both of which shared a similar design in terms of typeface, layout and illustration. Dublin Corporation commissioned him to edit *A book of Dublin*, which first appeared in May 1929 and was then reprinted in June 1930.[34] Billed as an 'official handbook', this illustrated volume presents the city of Dublin as historically and culturally significant and economically thriving. Potential tourists and investors appear to have been the target audience. The book did not find favour with one reviewer in particular: Fr Timothy Corcoran, SJ, the editor of the *Catholic Bulletin*. He objected to the content of the volume, describing its two editions as 'manuals for the Ascendancy mind' that 'exuded in every page the drippings of deliquescent Protestantism'.[35]

Under the direction of a committee appointed by the Minister for Industry and Commerce, Hobson also edited the *Saorstát Éireann Official Handbook*, which 'aimed to give an account of the Irish Free State as it is to-day', as well as the historical background necessary for understanding modern Ireland.[36] The book was also a report on the achievements of the Cumann na nGaedheal government during the first decade of Irish independence. Unfortunately, the publication of the handbook was badly timed: it appeared in 1932, just as the electorate rejected Cosgrave and Cumann na nGaedheal in favour of de Valera and Fianna Fáil.

Corcoran again lambasted Hobson in gleeful purple prose in a review of the *Handbook*. Edited by a Protestant and designed to provide an account of the first ten years of the Free State, the book was unlikely to find favour in the *Catholic Bulletin*, which reflected an extremist Catholic and an anti-Treaty ethos. Corcoran objected to the book's cover as well as its contents. He referred to the cover design as 'Bulmer's blurb' and described it as 'an attempt to make Celtic traceries prance about as if they were cubist figures performing motley mummery to jazz music'. He found 'the Bulmer within' even 'more objectionable' than the gaudy cover: he dismissed Hobson's introduction as a 'crude chunk of party propaganda' and gave mixed reviews to articles by individual contributors.[37]

Hobson and Corcoran may not have shared a taste in cover art or agreed on what aspects of Ireland to promote in government-funded publications, but they had one thing in common. Independent (or partially independent) Ireland wasn't turning out quite the way either of them wanted it to.

For Hobson, Irish independence had proved a disappointment. When the Irish Free State was founded in 1922, he had anticipated 'a period of economic reconstruction' that would undo the effects of the Union between Britain and Ireland. Instead, he witnessed what were, in his opinion, 'protracted and barren conflicts over verbal differences of politics which only the contestants, and not many of them, could understand, and these conflicts developed a fanatical bitterness which found its outlet in civil war'. He saw 'the high hopes, born of a national victory' get sucked into a quagmire of 'violence and folly'.[38]

Hobson was frustrated that the Irish government did not institute 'a bold national policy of reconstruction' to tackle poverty, unemployment and emigration.[39] In the 1930s Hobson resuscitated his propagandist career by turning his pen to these issues. In light of the economic conditions of the time, his employment in the Revenue, and his early writings on economic nationalism in newspapers like the *Republic* and the *Peasant*, Hobson's interest and energy in raising awareness about ways to combat poverty, unemployment and emigration are not surprising. Due to his position as a civil servant, Hobson had to publish some of his writings on economic issues anonymously or under a pseudonym.

Hobson praised the 1929 Shannon hydro-electric scheme, which harnessed the waters of the River Shannon to generate electricity, and pushed for it to be followed up by further bold steps to encourage Irish industry.[40] He advocated a policy of re-afforestation in order to provide Ireland with a native source of wood for the manufacturing industry, to generate much-needed employment in rural areas, and to preserve the Gaeltacht. In 1931 he privately published a 23-page pamphlet entitled *A national forestry policy*. In this pamphlet he proposed 'the establishment of 525,000 acres of plantations within fifteen years', criticising the government's aim to plant 200,000 acres as too modest because it would not benefit the current generation socially and industrially.[41] He recommended the creation of a forestry authority, the development of 'a programme of land acquisition and planting on an adequate scale and for a definite and extended period', and a financial policy that 'would enable the work to proceed as planned and without interruption'.[42]

A critic in the *Dublin Magazine* lauded Hobson's 'far-reaching suggestions' as 'worthy of earnest consideration', but criticised him for ignoring the existence of forestry expertise within the Department of Agriculture. Instead Hobson had suggested 'the importation of trained technicians from abroad to advise on the utilisation of ... non-agricultural land'. The critic pointed out that when a 'distinguished German arboriculturist' who was unfamiliar with Irish conditions had served as an advisor on a plantation in Knockboy, Connemara the results were disastrous.[43]

Hobson's advocacy of re-afforestation in the Gaeltacht stemmed from both cultural and economic concerns. In 1936 Hobson declared that 'the failure of successive Governments to attempt the economic reconstruction of the Gaeltacht [was] the most profoundly disappointing feature of the first fourteen years of Irish self-government'. In his view the economic renewal of the poverty-stricken Gaeltacht, 'which all our enthusiastic city Gaels have told us [was] essential for the survival of Irish language and culture', would do more to maintain the native language than 'superimposing Fr O'Growney on the educational system of Archbishop Whately'.[44] (Fr Eugene O'Growney was the author of the standard Irish-language textbooks used in the early twentieth century, while Church of Ireland Archbishop Richard Whately played a leading role in the establishment of the Irish national school system in the nineteenth century.) Hobson argued that employment created through re-afforestation of the Gaeltacht would enable 'the people of the western counties ... to enjoy a good and an improving standard of life as the result of their own labours in the places where they live', instead of having to migrate to another country as casual labourers or draw the dole 'to save them from destitution'.[45]

In the autumn of 1932 Hobson presented de Valera, the new President of the Executive Council, with a draft 'plan to break the economic depression in Saorstát Éireann and to relieve the government of the cost of maintaining the unemployed'. Hobson, like many others, probably hoped that the new Fianna Fáil government would jumpstart the Irish economy. In addition, he may have wished to ingratiate himself with his new taskmasters. Hobson's plan involved the establishment of an Economic Recovery Commission, which would supervise and co-ordinate the work of two sub-commissions, one on Land Reclamation, Drainage and Forestry and the other on Housing and Town Planning. According to Hobson, de Valera said 'he entirely agreed with [the economic plan] and that it was just what he wanted to do – but he did nothing'.[46]

In September 1933 Hobson again wrote to de Valera about these economic proposals, asserting without modesty that 'after another year's close study I am still more completely satisfied that they are the best, if not the only real solution of the problem of unemployment here'.[47] Hobson offered to meet with de Valera to answer any objections to his proposals that might have deterred the president from adopting them. Hobson had obviously circulated his memorandum to others, because he explained in the letter that he had been asked to publish it, but he wanted to get de Valera's permission first. In conclusion, Hobson wrote: 'I hope you will believe that I only return to the subject from a desire to help in the solution of the most urgent problem which confronts the country.'[48] De Valera appears to have given Hobson permission to publish the memorandum anonymously. Hobson privately published a revised version, entitled *National Economic Recovery: an outline plan*, in 1934, which was reprinted by the Talbot Press the following year.[49]

This outline plan was not Hobson's first anonymous publication on economic issues. In 1933 he published a pamphlet entitled *The new querist*, which drew on the tradition of Church of Ireland Bishop George Berkeley's eighteenth-century pamphlet *The querist* by posing a series of nearly two hundred economic queries for 'the consideration of the public'.[50] *The new querist* reflects Hobson's belief that a change in monetary policy and government investment in projects like re-afforestation and housing could combat poverty, unemployment and emigration.

Berkeley was an advocate of self-sufficiency as one way of tackling Ireland's economic problems. In looking to Berkeley, Hobson was tapping into a tradition that was also being mined by Fianna Fáil. In an article tracing the direct and indirect influence of Berkeley's ideas on Fianna Fáil economic policy, William Murphy points out that Hobson drew on some of Berkeley's ideas, but for the most part used the bishop's 'structure and reputation' to convey some of Hobson's own ideas.[51] In particular, *The new querist* reflects his interest in the social credit movement.

The founder of this movement was Major C.H. Douglas, who published his theories of society in numerous articles, pamphlets and books. He came to public attention shortly after the First World War, when some of his articles were published in a popular British avant-garde periodical called *New Age*. Douglas had 'a unique interpretation of the role of banks in issuing credit and creating money', believing 'that banks [could] create money for their own use or for loan simply by forming an account and crediting it with whatever amount they desire'. Douglas himself wrote that 'deposits are created, to a major extent, by purely book-keeping transactions on the part of the banking institutions': if banks could create money (or, to be more precise, increase the money supply), then governments could tap into this money supply for the public good.[52]

Hobson was intrigued with Douglas's ideas regarding the creation of money. In *The new querist* he asked 'whether anything is scarce in this country except money?'[53] He suggested that the state should create money and spend it on wages to employ people to build much-needed houses, schools and roads, and to work on land drainage and re-afforestation projects. This in turn would provide people with an income that they could spend on goods, thus creating a demand for various commodities produced in Ireland. In his view, following such a plan would enable the Irish government to increase consumption and production in the home market, the only market over which it had any control.[54]

Hobson's interpretation of social credit was only one strand of his economic thinking: another strand was similar to Keynesianism. He himself noted that critics dismissed his economic writings as 'merely an adaptation' of the ideas contained in John Maynard Keynes's 1936 book *The general theory of employment, interest and money*.[55] As a result of this influential book, government control of expenditure began to be seen as the way to provide full employment. What his critics failed to note was that Hobson's *New querist* and *National economic recovery* actually pre-dated Keynes's book. In 1937 Hobson commented that 'the new trend in English economic thinking which has recently appeared is tremendously important. I am very pleased that I had published my proposals before Keynes' recantation'.[56]

Hobson's ideas were ahead of their time in a country where Department of Finance officials would not start to 'absorb and come to terms with Keynesian economics in an Irish context' until the later years of the Emergency.[57] Thus, Hobson's economic pamphlets made little if any impact. In 1934 he admitted: 'I cannot say that my efforts have made any impression on our politicians, who seem to see all the facts except the relevant ones and have time to do everything except think.'[58] Despite being faced with such indifference, he kept writing and publishing his views.

In 1935 he established a small monthly paper called *Prosperity* to raise awareness about economic issues. The paper was published by the League against Poverty, which aimed to unite 'people of all parties, or of none, who wished to see the standards of economic life raised in Saorstát Éireann'.[59] Hobson served as editor of the paper, while Fred Johnson, the son of Tom Johnson, the former leader of the Labour party in the Dáil, worked as manager. Lord Monteagle Foynes, Frank Hugh O'Donnell and McCartan provided funding for the publication.[60] The paper, which had an initial circulation of three hundred, published schemes for the economic reconstruction of Ireland and tapped into the Catholic social action movement by providing interpretations of the papal encyclicals on social issues, such as *Quadragesimo Anno* of 1931. Hobson wrote most of the articles under a variety of pseudonyms.[61]

Minister for Finance Sean MacEntee was so 'perturbed by the criticisms that were being levelled against his party's financial policy by the League against Poverty' that 'he requested that the Department of Justice identify the group behind it'. Garda (police) special branch, which maintained dossiers on a number of organisations in the 1930s, delivered its report on the group on 23 April 1936.[62] Hobson is not mentioned in this report, suggesting that the investigation by the Gardaí found no solid evidence to link him with the organisation, which proved purely nominal.[63] Hobson had gained considerable experience dodging police detectives back in his days as an advanced nationalist propagandist and member of the IRB.

In August 1936 the League against Poverty became the League for Social Justice, which was 'composed of people of all parties, or none, who wish to see the social and economic teaching of the papal encyclicals, given practical effect in Saorstát Éireann'.[64] Its twenty-six-member council included Lord Monteagle, Fred Johnson, three clergymen, one Fianna Fáil TD (Sean Brady) and City Librarian of Dublin Roisín Walsh, among others.[65] Hobson's name does not appear on the list of council members. The League for Social Justice organised meetings to discuss Catholic social principles and published a series of pamphlets entitled *Towards a new Ireland*.[66]

In September 1936 *Prosperity* changed its name to *Social Justice*. The paper, however, folded in June 1937 after only twenty monthly issues.[67] As Hobson later noted, 'less than 100 people were sufficiently interested in the ideas it stood for to purchase it at the modest price of 2d a copy'.[68]

Hobson's editorship of *Prosperity* brought him in touch with Mrs

B. Berthon Waters, a writer on economic affairs, and the Rev. Edward Cahill, SJ, founder of the Catholic Action movement in Ireland and Professor of Church History and Lecturer in Sociology at the Jesuit College in Milltown Park. Cahill and Waters were members of An Ríoghacht, a Catholic social action group established in 1926. It may seem odd that Hobson, a former Quaker, should team up with two Catholic social activists, but there were similarities in their views. For instance, Catholic social thinking promoted the solidarity of community as an alternative to class struggle. Middle-class Hobson never had much time for class struggle. His Dungannon Club had put what it saw as the interests of the nation before the divisive interests of class or religion.[69] In 1937 he even admitted that 'personally I don't care if there are a lot of rich people so long as there are none left in involuntary poverty'.[70]

An Ríoghacht hoped to influence the social and economic policy of the Irish government by making a submission to the Commission on Banking, Currency and Credit, which met between 1934–38. This commission, which was appointed by MacEntee, was directed to 'examine and report on the system in Saorstát Éireann of currency, banking, credit, public borrowing and lending' and 'to consider and report what changes, if any, are necessary or desirable to promote the social and economic welfare of the community and the interests of agriculture and industry'.[71] Hobson dismissed the commission as 'heavily loaded with partisans of the existing order'. Hobson, Waters and Cahill were keen to raise public awareness about the Banking Commission, so that matters 'of such vital importance to the whole community' would not be 'settled behind closed doors'.[72] Between July 1936 and October 1938 the trio tried to change the direction of the commission.[73]

In December 1936 Hobson, Cahill and Waters prepared a 16-page memorandum on behalf of the League for Social Justice, which they submitted to the commission on 14 January 1937. Unfortunately, it was delivered after the commission had finished hearing oral evidence and could not be considered. Hobson then sent the memorandum to two economists in England in order to gain feedback. Although John G. Smith, Professor of Finance and Dean of the Faculty of Commerce at the University of Birmingham, and James E. Meade, a Fellow and Lecturer in Economics at Hertford College, Oxford and future Nobel Laureate in Economics, criticised certain parts of the document, they were generally positive. Cahill forwarded the economists' opinions to de Valera.[74] In addition, Cahill, Hobson and Waters sent de Valera a 'first and tentative draft of the form which a minority report might possibly take' in September 1937.[75] In writing their draft, the trio had had access to parts of the draft majority report,[76] which recommended maintaining the economic status quo, thus following the policy of the previous Cumann na nGaedheal government.

De Valera had suggested to his friend Eoin O'Keefe, who was a member of An Ríoghacht, that members of the commission who favoured a more progressive economic policy should submit a minority report. O'Keefe initially approached a member of the commission, Alfred O'Rahilly, Professor of Mathematical Physics at University College Cork, about preparing a minority report, but he was too busy. The job then fell to Hobson, Cahill and Waters.[77] Finín O'Driscoll has argued that de Valera, in instigating the production of a report, 'was attempting to ensure that the more radical element within Fianna Fáil could find solace in one of the minority reports and that those elements could not accuse him of losing the ideology of self-sufficiency that had brought Fianna Fáil to power'.[78]

The document written by Hobson, Cahill and Waters was presented as the Third Minority Report[79] in March 1938 by Peadar O'Loghlen, a Fianna Fáil politician from Ballyvaughan, County Clare, who had been appointed to the commission ostensibly to represent the interests of the rural community. O'Loghlen, though he had diligently attended meetings, remained silent throughout the proceedings. It later emerged that he had been appointed not only as de Valera's watchdog,[80] but also 'to hold a watching brief for a group' within An Ríoghacht.[81] The Third Minority Report enraged MacEntee and the Secretary of the Department of Finance, J.J. McElligott, neither of whom appear to have realised that a civil servant was partially responsible for the document. They did not believe that O'Loghlen was the author and recognised that excerpts of the report were similar to passages in the anonymously published pamphlet *National economic recovery* and in two documents produced by the League for Social Justice, its submission to the Banking Commission and a pamphlet called *The Achill Island tragedy*.[82]

The Third Minority Report also generated criticism from Fr Edward Coyne, SJ, an economist and future chairman of the Commission on Vocational Organisation. He was dismissive of Hobson's involvement, calling him a 'Quaker or Protestant' whose 'technique was well known': he 'gets a number of prominent or semi-prominent people to join forces and he then uses them as a means to propagate his fads'. Coyne viewed the scheme outlined in the report as 'quite untrue, most unwise, injurious to the encyclicals and would bring them into disrepute with educated Catholics, or would lead the uneducated to believe that the Third Minority Report really was a concrete remedy backed by the Pope'.[83]

The Third Minority Report disputed 'the validity of the link with sterling', the perceived need for a central bank, and the ability of 'the private sector to remedy unemployment or to provide any meaningful economic growth'. It recommended 'comprehensive government intervention in the provision of capital, capital development, and the provision of full employment', possibly through a state afforestation policy.[84] The report reflects views put forward in Hobson's previous economic publications. Although de Valera praised the Third Minority Report, the production of which he had indirectly encouraged, the document made no impact on the existing policy.[85]

The contents of the Third Minority Report, and thus Hobson's ideas, later influenced the economic thought of Seán MacBride, Clann na Poblachta leader and son of Maud Gonne and John MacBride.[86] In response to the British government's devaluation of sterling in September 1949, the cabinet of the Irish inter-party government decided to establish a committee on devaluation the following month. Hobson, by then in retirement, was appointed to the committee, but it does not appear to have functioned.[87]

After his involvement with the production of the Third Minority Report, Hobson continued to work with Waters, writing pamphlets for the *Towards a New Ireland* series, which she edited.[88] This pamphlet series, which was published by the Irish People Co-operative Society Ltd., supported 'a broadly-based policy of social and economic re-construction in Ireland appealing to all sections and interests in the life of the nation'.[89] In contrast to Hobson's own papers *Prosperity* and *Social Justice*, this pamphlet series apparently 'had a wide circulation'.[90]

In addressing the need for economic renewal in the West of Ireland, Hobson's tone became increasingly sarcastic. In 1937 he noted:

> Perhaps when the last inhabitant of the Gaeltacht has departed for an English slum or a Scottish 'bothy' the Government will appoint a commission to report on the wealth which would be produced from the Irish Highlands. The report will be very interesting, but by then the absence of any available labour in the western desert will prevent its recommendations being carried out.[91]

In a book review of *The hill lands of Britain* Hobson praised Professor R.G. Stapledon's suggestions for developing and improving the productivity of highland areas, commenting that his work 'would be very highly prized in a rational society, and there is much that we in Ireland could profitably learn from him, if we had one here'.[92]

Hobson's remarks eventually landed him in hot water at work. As a civil servant he was prohibited from making political comments in the public arena. Media coverage of an An Ríoghacht meeting in March 1938 at which he made suggestions for ways to alleviate slum housing provoked MacEntee to demand an explanation and apology from Hobson, who explained:

> In saying what I did I was endeavouring to make a contribution to the problem of slum clearance, on the necessity for which I thought there was complete unanimity of opinion among all classes and parties ... I thought the subject lay in a field of social effort which was completely outside politics, which civil servants could legitimately enter.

His defence did not satisfy MacEntee, at whose insistence Hobson gave 'an unqualified undertaking' that he would not publicly comment on politics in future.[93] MacEntee does not appear to have held a grudge, as he approved a rise in Hobson's salary scale later that year.

In any case, by the late 1930s it had become increasingly difficult for Hobson to produce any writing for publication. In September 1937 he revealed that 'every time I agree to review a book fate intervenes and either I cannot see to read it or cannot get time to write about it'.[94] His failing eyesight eventually forced him to abandon writing economic propaganda and book reviews altogether.[95]

Hobson complained that political separatists had turned out to be economic unionists, content to settle for British policies that did not meet Irish needs.[96] His economic views were connected to his belief that a strong economy in the twenty-six counties comprising the Irish Free State (later the Republic of Ireland) would lead to the eventual reunification of Ireland. He thought that the best way to bring unity was 'to make an Ireland so prosperous that Ulster cannot afford to stay out of it'.[97] Hobson's concern for Irish unity dates back to his admiration for the cause of Wolfe Tone and the United Irishmen, and his own early efforts in Belfast to promote Irish unity through the Protestant National Society, the ULT and the Dungannon clubs.

Like McCullough, McCartan, Blythe and Lester, Hobson reconciled himself to living and working in a twenty-six-county Ireland though he continued to hope for future unity. He maintained contact with family and friends in the North. For instance, he and his children vacationed at the home of Ada MacNeill in Cushendun in the 1930s.[98]

Retirement

The year 1947 brought changes to Hobson's life. It was the year that his mother, Mary, died.[99] It was also the year in which he began to look for a property close to the sea where he could spend his forthcoming retirement from the civil service. He wanted 'to start a new life, away from the city' in a place where he could swim daily.[100] He also wanted to be able to look at 'a far horizon', believing that this might help his eyesight.[101]

He settled on Roundstone in Connemara, where he hired a local man, Tom MacDonagh, to build him a house overlooking Goirtín Bay. True to his Sinn Féin roots, Hobson insisted that the house was built using local materials.[102] He moved there after his retirement in 1948, but did not sell his Rathfarnham residence until 1955.[103] He lived in Roundstone until about 1963, when ill-health forced him to move in with his daughter, Camilla Mitchell, and her family in Castleconnell, County Limerick.

Built before Roundstone took off as a tourist destination, Hobson's house 'stood remote [and] solitary' a mile or two outside of the village. Known as 'a man who liked his own company just as much as he liked that of others', he is reputed to have said 'that he welcomed the coming of friends and welcomed their departure'.[104] A young visitor to Hobson's home was struck by the notion that an elderly man who was nearly blind could possess so many books.[105] Although a doctor had told him around 1946 that it would be impossible for him to continue reading, Hobson took pleasure in proving the physician wrong. To help himself to read, Hobson rigged up a table-top contraption with a large magnifying glass. His poor eyesight also did not stop him from cycling in and out of the village.[106]

Hobson lived alone during his retirement years in Roundstone – his marriage to Claire Gregan, forged so romantically while on the run, having ended in separation, possibly during the late 1930s.[107] He never mentioned her to his new neighbours.[108] When his estranged wife died in 1958 at the age of seventy, he attended her funeral in Dublin.[109] His Roundstone years were, perhaps, a time of reflection and possibly regret.

Conclusion

Hobson's life after 1916 featured changes as well as continuities. The changes are perhaps more obvious. He was no longer a political activist in the public eye and footloose bachelor, whose beliefs and activities made it difficult to remain in paid employment. Instead he had a steady job as a civil servant and a wife and children to support.

In many ways there were more continuities than changes in his life. He was still employed in the field of printing and publishing. He still doggedly advocated ideas that only appealed to a minority. To achieve goals, he was still willing to work with strange bedfellows, such as Catholic social activists. His relationships still had a tendency to fall apart, his marriage being a case in point. Yet he maintained connections with many friends and colleagues, particularly from his Dungannon Club and IRB days, such as McCartan, McCullough, Blythe, Lester and O'Hegarty. Most of all, he remained committed to improving Ireland materially and culturally. This commitment was expressed through his publication of propaganda on economic issues and his involvement in cultural activities, such as theatre and book publishing. He may not have lived up to his early promise as a political leader, but he continued to make a contribution to an independent Ireland.

Notes

1 McCartan to Dr William Maloney, 18 and 28 Jan. 1924 (NLI, PMcC, MS 17,675 (5)).
2 Hobson to Eoin MacNeill, 3 June 1918 (NLI, BH, MS 13,174 (4)); Hobson to F.J. Bigger, 12 Aug. 1918, 24 Sept. 1918, 27 Sept. 1918 (Belfast Central Library, Bigger Collection, CA 14). For more on Ó Lochlainn's presses, see Chalmers Trench, 'The Three Candles Press in the 'thirties', *Long Room*, 41 (1996), pp. 35–6; Dermot McGuinne, 'Colm Ó Lochlainn and the Sign of the Three Candles', *Long Room*, 41 (1996), p. 44.
3 His sister Florence may have helped to finance the venture. In consideration for financial assistance that Florence had rendered to him in 1918, Hobson bequeathed her a life annuity of £40 per year in addition to her share of his estate (Will of John Bulmer Hobson, second codicil, 10 Dec. 1967).
4 Copy of Martin Lester Ltd. letterhead (NLI, BH, MS 13,161 (1)). The 1920 *Thom's Directory* listed the Candle Press and Martin Lester Ltd. at 44 Dawson Street while the 1923 directory listed the businesses at 78 Harcourt Street.
5 See Hobson to Bigger, 12 Aug. 1918, 24 Sept. 1918, 27 Sept. 1918 (Belfast Central Library, Bigger Collection, CA 14). Among the authors with whom Hobson corresponded were Alice Milligan and her brother William, Eimar O'Duffy, Eoin MacNeill, Alice Stopford Green, Douglas Hyde, Brinsley MacNamara and Susan L. Mitchell. See NLI, BH, MS 13,161 (1–9).
6 Bulmer Hobson (ed.), *The life of Wolfe Tone* (Dublin, 1919).
7 Bulmer Hobson (ed.), *The letters of Wolfe Tone* (Dublin, 1920), p. 6.
8 'Peeps into pamphlets', *Irish Book Lover*, Apr. 1920, p. 100.
9 'Current affairs', *IRPEAL*, 11 Nov. 1922, pp. 13–14.
10 'Current affairs', *IRPEAL*, 25 Nov. 1922, p. 26.
11 'Current affairs', *IRPEAL*, 28 Oct. 1922, p. 2.
12 Milligan to Hobson, n.d. (NLI, BH, MS 13,161 (1)).
13 Johnston, *Alice Milligan*, pp. 138–9.
14 Letter from J [John / Eoin MacNeill] to M [Margaret MacNeill], Dec. 1920 (UCDA, EMacN, LA1/G/331).
15 O'Duffy to Hobson, 20 June 1921, 6 Mar. 1922 (NLI, BH, MS 13,161 (8)).
16 O'Duffy to Hobson, 1 Feb. 1922, 9 Feb. 1922, 6 Mar. 1922 (NLI, BH, MS 13,161 (8)).

17 *Thom's Directory* first listed Hobson at the Mill House in 1920.
18 Conversation with Robina Chapman, a former classmate of Camilla Hobson, 23 Apr. 2003; Declan Hobson to William Glynn, 19 Aug. 1969 (FHLD, Box 3A, No. 85).
19 Pinpointing the timing of Martin Lester Ltd.'s demise is challenging. O'Duffy's 1923 change in publishers from Martin Lester Ltd. to the Talbot Press may have been due to the company's failure. The 1924 edition of *Thom's Directory* no longer listed Martin Lester Ltd. and Candle Press. The two companies were certainly defunct by 1926 when Ó Lochlainn re-launched his printing and publishing business at 6 Fleet Street as the Three Candles Press. See Trench, 'The Three Candles Press', p. 35.
20 Remuneration of higher posts in Stamping Branch (NAI, Dept. of Finance, FIN/E2/1/39); Ronan Fanning, *The Irish Department of Finance 1922–58* (Dublin, 1978), p. 39.
21 In Feb. 1923 the Irish government announced its plans to set up the Office of the Revenue Commissioners. By Apr. 1923 the office was established. (Seán Réamonn, *History of the Revenue Commissioners* (Dublin, 1981), pp. 56–8; Paddy Ryan (ed.), *Revenue over the years* (Dublin, 1998), pp. 8–11; conversations with Paddy Ryan, Assistant Principal, Communications Branch, Office of the Revenue Commissions, 25 and 29 Aug. 2006.)
22 Telephone conversation with Cormac O'Callaghan, 20 Sept. 2006. Mr O'Callaghan joined the Stamping Department as an Assistant Stamper in 1947 and later rose to the position of Director of Stamping.
23 Basil Chubb, *The government and politics of Ireland* (3rd edn, London, 1992), p. 230.
24 Telephone conversation with Cormac O'Callaghan, 20 Sept. 2006.
25 Bulmer Hobson, 'Report of the Inter-Departmental Committee on the Sugar Beet Industry', May 1933 (NLI, BH, MS 13,172).
26 Telephone conversation with Cormac O'Callaghan, 20 Sept. 2006.
27 W.D.J., 'The making of the theatre', in Bulmer Hobson (ed.), *The Gate Theatre* (Dublin, 1934), pp. 11–12.
28 Phyllis Ryan, *The company I kept* (Dublin, 1996), p. 134.
29 Mervyn Wall to Des Gunning, 16 Jan. 1995 (letter in possession of Des Gunning).
30 Micheál Mac Liammóir, *All for Hecuba* (Dublin, 1961), pp. 60–1.
31 Ibid., pp. 87–8.
32 Ibid., pp. 82–3; W.D.J. 'The making of the theatre', p. 15.
33 See Bulmer Hobson (ed.), *The Gate Theatre* (Dublin, 1934).
34 See Bulmer Hobson (ed.), *A book of Dublin* (2nd edn, Dublin, 1930).
35 Molua (Fr Timothy Corcoran, SJ), 'The last pose of Bulmer', *Catholic Bulletin*, Apr. 1932, p. 273. See also Cuana, 'Hobson's ascendancy pamphlet', *Catholic Bulletin*, Oct. 1930, pp. 929–33.
36 Bulmer Hobson (ed.), *Saorstát Éireann Official Handbook* (Dublin, 1932), p. 15.
37 Molua, 'The last pose of Bulmer', *Catholic Bulletin*, Apr. 1932, pp. 274–9.
38 Hobson, *IYT*, p. 111.

39 Ibid., p. 112.
40 Bulmer Hobson, *A national forestry policy* (Dublin, 1931), p. 4.
41 Review of *A national forestry policy*, *Dublin Magazine* (Apr.–June 1933), p. 91.
42 Hobson, *A national forestry policy*, p. 15.
43 Review of *A national forestry policy*, p. 92.
44 Bulmer Hobson, 'Forestry and the Gaeltacht', *Ireland To-day*, Aug. 1936, p. 33.
45 Ibid., p. 34.
46 Comment written on Hobson's draft economic recovery plan (NLI, BH, MS 13,172).
47 Hobson to de Valera, 23 Sept. 1933 (NLI, BH, MS 13,172).
48 Ibid.
49 See Bulmer Hobson, *National economic recovery: an outline plan* (Dublin, 1935). This pamphlet is reprinted in Hobson, *IYT*, pp. 128–70.
50 This pamphlet is reprinted in Hobson, *IYT*, pp. 115–27.
51 William Murphy, 'Cogging Berkeley?: *The querist* and the rhetoric of Fianna Fáil's economic policy', *Irish economic and social history*, xxxii (2005), pp. 63, 76.
52 Edward Bell, *Social classes and social credit in Alberta* (Montreal, 1993), pp. 37, 42–4.
53 Hobson, *The new querist*, reprinted in Hobson, *IYT*, p. 116.
54 Ibid., p. 123.
55 Hobson, *IYT*, p. 128.
56 Hobson to William Glynn, 4 June 1937 (NAI, Dept. of the Taoiseach, S12293).
57 Fanning, *Irish Department of Finance*, p. 357.
58 Hobson to Dr William Maloney, 31 July 1934 (NLI, JMcG, MS 17,604 (2)).
59 Bulmer Hobson, 'The League against Poverty', *Prosperity*, Nov. 1935, p. 1.
60 Finín O'Driscoll, 'Social Catholicism and the social question in independent Ireland: the challenge to the fiscal system', in Mike Cronin and John M. Regan, *Ireland: the politics of independence, 1922–49* (London, 2000), p. 134.
61 These pseudonyms included Rigel, Aldebaran, X, Altair and Corvus. Cathal O'Shannon, William Glynn, B. Berthon Waters, Olive Gibson and Dr Eamon O'Hogan were among the other contributors. The bound copy of *Prosperity/Social Justice* in the Special Collections Dept. at UCD was annotated by Hobson, who listed the authors of most of the articles in the paper.
62 O'Driscoll, 'Social Catholicism', p. 135.
63 Garda special branch report (NAI, Dept. of Justice, JUS/8/436).
64 Bulmer Hobson, 'The manifesto of the League for Social Justice', *Prosperity*, Aug. 1936, p. 74.
65 *Social Justice*, Nov. 1936, p. 104.
66 Hobson to Edward Cahill, 6 June 1936 (IJA, Cahill Papers), qtd. in Maurice Curtis, 'Catholic action as an organised campaign in Ireland, 1921–1947' (PhD thesis, UCD, 2000), p. 291.

67 In the June 1937 issue of *Social Justice* Hobson announced that the paper was going to 'suspend publication during the summer months' (p. 1). He never revived it.
68 Note in Hobson's handwriting written on a bound copy of *Prosperity/Social Justice* in the Special Collections Dept. at UCD.
69 See Hobson, *The manifesto of the Dungannon Club*, p. 7.
70 Hobson to Glynn, 4 June 1937 (NAI, Dept. of the Taoiseach, S12293).
71 *Commission of Inquiry into banking, currency and credit – Reports and Minutes of Evidence* (Dublin, 1938).
72 Hobson, *IYT*, p. 171.
73 O'Driscoll, 'Social Catholicism', p. 135.
74 Ibid., pp. 135–6.
75 Cahill to de Valera, 8 Sept. 1937 (NAI, Dept. of Taoiseach, S12293).
76 Ibid.
77 J. Anthony Gaughan, *Alfred O'Rahilly, II: public figure* (Dublin, 1989), pp. 312–13; Enda Delaney, 'Fr Denis Fahey, CSSp, and Maria Duce, 1945–1954' (MA thesis, NUI Maynooth, 1993), p. 31.
78 O'Driscoll, 'Social Catholicism', p. 136.
79 Hobson, *IYT*, p. 171; Enda Delaney, 'Denis Fahey', p. 29. 'Draft for a report – Banking Commission 1938' is reprinted in Hobson, *IYT*, pp. 172–243.
80 O'Driscoll, 'Social Catholicism', p. 133.
81 Gaughan, *Alfred O'Rahilly*, p. 310.
82 Annotated copy of the Third Minority Report (NAI, Dept. of Finance, FIN/F009/0018/38).
83 Edward Coyne to Provincial, 1 Sept. 1938 (IJA, Coyne Papers), qtd. in Curtis, 'Catholic action as an organised campaign in Ireland', p. 309.
84 Eithne MacDermott, *Clann na Poblachta* (Cork, 1998), p. 61.
85 Delaney, 'Denis Fahey', p. 31.
86 MacDermott, *Clann na Poblachta*, p. 61.
87 Gaughan, *Alfred O'Rahilly*, pp. 387–8. The committee consisted of 'the Taoiseach and ministers for finance, industry and commerce, agriculture and external affairs, officials from their respective departments, the governor of the Central Bank, three professors of economics, Bulmer Hobson and a nominee of the Irish Banks' Standing Committee' (p. 388).
88 Hobson and Waters co-wrote the first pamphlet in the series, which was entitled 'Forging new links of the Empire'. His other contributions to the series included 'Invisible empire', 'Afforestation', 'National monetary policy', and 'Full home market'. See Waters to Hobson, 21 May 1948 (NLI, BH, MS 13,161 (9)).
89 Flyer for the *Towards a New Ireland* pamphlet series (FHLD, William Glynn Papers).
90 Hobson, *IYT*, p. 171.
91 Bulmer Hobson, review of *The hill lands of Britain* by Professor R.G. Stapledon, in *Ireland To-day*, Oct. 1937, p. 84.
92 Ibid.

Building a new life

93 Correspondence regarding statements made by Bulmer Hobson at a meeting of An Ríoghacht (NAI, Dept. of Finance, FIN/E109/17/38).
94 Hobson to Mr Sheehy, 21 Sept. 1937 (NLI, James L. O'Donovan Papers, MS 21,987/vi).
95 Hobson, *IYT*, p. 114. Fanciful folklore within the Revenue alleged that Hobson's 'eyesight was impaired as a result of injuries received during the 1916 rising' (see Paddy Ryan, 'The old stamping ground', *An Rabhchán*, Feb. 1995, pp. 10–11). Hobson himself stated that he had had 'persistent' 'eye trouble' since the age of seventeen (Ó Lúing, 'Talking to Bulmer Hobson', *IT*, 6 May 1961, p. 10).
96 Hobson, *IYT*, p. 112.
97 Ibid., p. 91.
98 Jeffrey Dudgeon, *Roger Casement*, p. 536.
99 Principal Probate Registry Northern Ireland Calendar, 1948, p. 149.
100 Ó Lúing, 'Talking to Bulmer Hobson', *IT*, 6 May 1961, p. 10.
101 Mervyn Wall, 'The Godstone and the Blackymor [by] T.H. White', in Proinsias Ó Conluain (ed.), *Islands and authors* (London, 1959), p. 33.
102 Interviews with Roundstone residents Joe Rafferty, Tom MacDonagh and Joe MacDonagh, 9 Jan. 2003.
103 Brochure for the Mill House, Whitechurch Road, Rathfarnham, Dublin 14, published by Sherry FitzGerald, 2003.
104 'Burial at Gorteen Bay', *The Kerryman*, 16 Aug. 1969.
105 John Gageby (Sean Lester's grandson) to Marnie Hay, 24 Apr. 2003 (email in possession of the author). John Gageby was about ten years old when he was taken to visit Hobson. Sean and Elsie Lester had a retirement home in Recess, Connemara. See Douglas Gageby, *Sean Lester*, pp. 260–1.
106 William Glynn, graveside tribute to Bulmer Hobson, 11 Aug. 1969 (FHLD, MSS B. 3A-87); Interview with Joe Rafferty of Roundstone, Connemara, 9 Jan. 2003; Gunning, 'Bulmer Hobson', *History Ireland*, Spring 2002, pp. 5–6; Wall to Gunning, 16 Jan. 1995.
107 I was unable to obtain access to documents outlining the terms of the Hobsons' separation due to the private and confidential nature of such information. In the Irish Free State in the 1930s there were two ways of separating. A couple might draw up a separation agreement with the assistance of a solicitor. Alternatively, they could seek a judicial separation if the grounds for this decree were adultery, cruelty or unnatural practices. (Dr Paul Ward, UCD School of Law, to Marnie Hay, 20 Aug. 2007; email in possession of author.)
108 Interview with Joe Rafferty of Roundstone, Connemara, 9 Jan. 2003.
109 Wall to Gunning, 16 Jan. 1995.

10

Remembering 1916

In 1924 Hobson confessed to McCartan that he found the period surrounding 1916 'too intense a personal tragedy', adding 'I have spent most of the intervening years trying to forget it'. The only way he could continue to live in Ireland, and in the Irish Free State in particular, was 'by assuming an indifference that I was far from feeling'.[1] Although Hobson lived a full and varied life after he left the nationalist movement, the rest of his days were haunted by what he considered the personal and political tragedy of Easter 1916.

As much as Hobson had wanted to forget 1916, he found himself compelled throughout the rest of his life to comment on the past in order to defend himself and friends like Casement, to contribute his intimate knowledge of the Irish nationalist movement to the historical record, and to promote his interpretation of the Irish revolutionary period. He was a vociferous advocate of the view that Casement's sexually explicit 'Black Diaries' were forged at the request of the British government. Hobson's various accounts of his involvement with the nationalist movement, combined with the documents that he managed to save and later donated to the National Library of Ireland, contributed greatly to the re-assessment of the Easter Rising and its prelude, begun by F.X. Martin in the 1960s.[2] This chapter will examine Hobson's responses to the 1916 rising in the years after the event.

1917 to 1959

After the rising, Hobson hoped to salvage his reputation, which had been damaged by rumours circulating about him as a result of his opposition to the insurrection and his failure to be arrested. While on the run from the authorities, he began writing *A short history of the Irish Volunteers*, only the first volume of which was completed and later published by Ó Lochlainn's Candle Press in 1918. Both he and McCartan hoped that this book would help to vindicate his position.[3]

Hobson was extremely disappointed with the introduction to the book, written by MacNeill. In a draft letter to MacNeill, dated 3 June 1918, Hobson wrote:

> I thought you would have written something that would have helped to lay the calumnies of the last two years and have made it clear that in acting as I did in 1916 I acted with you in everything. Instead you have carefully refrained from saying anything that could not be said equally appropriately in an introduction to any other book on modern Ireland.

Hobson pointed out that Griffith and others had defended MacNeill at the Sinn Féin convention in October 1917, but nobody – not even MacNeill himself – had defended those who had stood by the Volunteer leader. Considering Hobson's previous relations with Griffith, the chances of the Sinn Féin leader defending Hobson were slim to non-existent. Hobson added:

> You may possibly think that I attach too much importance to my personal position in the matter but it should be remembered that I have been denied any opportunity to have things cleared up in any other way – first by your failure to summon the old General Council last year and then by the refusal of de Valera to admit the members of the executive to the Volunteer Convention. In consequence my book is the only means left to me to clear up a matter of which I cannot take the detached view so easy for those who are not concerned.

Hobson wanted it made plain that, in acting as he and his colleagues did, they had been supporting 'honour against deceit'.[4]

MacNeill countered that it was 'not the time for clearing up that situation', and that Hobson should disregard 'slander and injustice for the time'. He added: 'It may be that the publication of the first part of your history will cause the tortoise to put out its head. Meanwhile, there will be little satisfaction in peppering it on the shell.'[5] In any case, the book did not succeed in rehabilitating Hobson's reputation, which may be why he did not finish the planned subsequent volumes. O'Shannon surmised that further volumes were not published because the publisher or the author did not want to antagonise the re-organised Volunteer movement.[6]

Hobson promoted his view of the rising as a *coup d'état* when Martin Lester Ltd. published his former Volunteer colleague Eimar O'Duffy's first novel, *The wasted island*. The plot follows the fortunes of a young nationalist in the years leading up to the Easter Rising. First published in 1919, the novel refers to public figures by name and features some characters who resemble real people. For instance, Hobson is thinly disguised as a character called Stephen Ward who agrees to the acceptance of Redmond's nominees in order to avoid splitting the Volunteer movement and calls the rising 'a piece of lunacy' that will 'be the ruin of the country'.[7] A contemporary reviewer described the novel as 'strongly Sinn Féin', adding that 'much of the dialogue is devoted to argument in favour of that policy, yet never to the detriment of the story'. In the book, O'Duffy denounced 'the falsehood and treachery towards their comrades of the extremists who rushed into the rebellion'.[8] Mabel FitzGerald feared that the novel would do nothing for O'Duffy's employment prospects in Dublin.[9]

Hobson had intended to write a book about Casement, but admitted to McCartan that the personal tragedy of the 1916 period had made such a project too painful, though 'this was not fair to Roger'.[10] Hobson may have felt guilty that he had failed to help his friend while Casement was on trial for his life. Hobson had been in hiding during the summer of 1916 and thus unable to contribute to the efforts to lobby in Casement's favour or to counter the hostility unleashed by the circulation of excerpts from the 'Black Diaries'. In any case, support from a republican like Hobson was more likely to hinder than help Casement in 1916.

Too traumatised to write a book about Casement himself, Hobson instead supported the efforts of McCartan's associate Dr William Maloney to pen such a book. Hobson was slow to contribute to the project. Initially this was because, having read Maloney's previous writings on Casement, he feared that the doctor would not get his facts straight. Emotions caused a further delay. It took Hobson over a month to write a letter providing information for Maloney, because he disliked 'writing and thinking about some things so much that it was an effort to do it at all'.[11]

Hobson asserted that allegations of Casement's homosexuality were 'the dirtiest bit of English propaganda'. As Casement's 'intimate friend' from 1904 until his death, Hobson had not witnessed anything to suggest that Casement was homosexual:

> I lived with him for periods, went on walking tours and holidays with him and wherever he was we corresponded constantly. Of all the men I have ever known he was the most generous and open minded and the most free from meanness. He was good in the best sense and all this talk about vice makes me want to assault the people who say it.[12]

Hobson may not have been aware of Casement's homosexuality because he never had a reason to reveal his sexual orientation to his young friend.

Hobson contrasted Casement to MacDermott, who, Hobson claimed, not only accused both him and Casement of selling out over Redmond's

6 Roger Casement: Hobson was a vociferous advocate of the view that Casement's 'Black Diaries' were forged

nominees, but had written 'to that effect' to Devoy and McGarrity. Hobson asserted: 'Roger was as unlike the mob here as a man could well be – he was their superior in everything but complacency and they didn't like it. They distrusted what they could not understand – his fineness and chivalry.'[13] For Hobson, Casement was the real hero of

1916. Whether or not Hobson realised it, his defence of Casement was an indirect way of lashing out against MacDermott and Clarke.

Maloney's book, *The forged Casement diaries*, finally appeared in 1936.[14] Hobson played a major role in the production of this book. He provided Maloney with information, went to considerable trouble to find a copy of the Casement family pedigree, read a draft of the manuscript and negotiated its publication with the Talbot Press.[15] Maloney's book argued that the so-called 'Black Diaries' had been forged by British intelligence in order to blacken Casement's name. It brought the question of the diaries' authenticity to the attention of the Irish public and forged a conspiracy theory that survives to this day.

Maloney's argument rested on what W.J. McCormack has dubbed the 'Normand Defence'. During his investigation into atrocities against the aboriginal population forced to work in the rubber industry in the Putomayo area of South America, Casement transcribed the diary of Armando Normand, a sadistic manager who oversaw rubber collection. Normand worked for the Peruvian Arana brothers, who had floated their rubber company on the London Stock Exchange.[16] Normand's diary described the abuse, often sexual in nature, of native workers. Upon his return from Brazil, Casement had told Hobson of this 'shockingly indecent diary', which formed part of the evidence for Casement's report on his investigation.[17] Hobson concluded that the 'Black Diaries' were based upon Normand's journal.[18]

McCormack has accused McCartan, McGarrity, Hobson and O'Hegarty of using Maloney to engineer the creation of the forgery theory in the 1930s.[19] Hobson, however, was sincere in his belief in the theory. In addition to supporting the publication of Maloney's book, McCartan and his associates contributed to the development of a Casement archive that includes documents advocating the forgery theory. Hobson in particular wanted a Casement collection to be established in the National Library of Ireland so that papers relating to his friend would be easily accessible and well cared for.[20]

Hobson's defence of his late friend extended to providing information to researchers and writing to newspapers and magazines to comment on the resulting books. Not surprisingly, he described Maloney's book as 'a brilliant piece of work and completely reliable'. He considered Denis Gwynn's 1930 book, *The life and death of Roger Casement*, as a generally reliable account, despite a few minor inaccuracies.[21] Hobson praised Geoffrey Parmiter's *Roger Casement* and Robert Monteith's *Casement's last adventure* for their accuracy.[22] He provided information for René MacColl's 1956 biography, *Roger Casement: A new judgement*, but described the resulting book as 'mean and despicable' because it accepted the 'Black Diaries' as genuine. 'He [MacColl] even had the cheek to write me a second letter, to which I made no reply,' Hobson indignantly declared.[23]

He also had occasional opportunities to comment on his own nationalist past. For instance, on the recommendation of Blythe, the editors of *An t-Óglách*, the Irish army magazine, asked Hobson to contribute articles on the formation of the Irish Volunteers. They were published in March and June 1931.[24]

During the 1930s Hobson provided information to Louis Le Roux, the Breton journalist who wrote hagiographical biographies of Pearse and Clarke. In 1931 Le Roux asked Hobson to comment on the manuscript of his biography of Pearse, but, upon receiving Hobson's notes, Le Roux feared that he had gone down in Hobson's estimation.[25] Le Roux's books presented as fact the allegation that Hobson had been stripped of all his offices within the IRB at a court martial held after Redmond's nominees were admitted to the Provisional Committee of the Irish Volunteers.[26] The Clarke biography also stated erroneously that Hobson had deduced that a rising was imminent after overhearing a conversation between IRB members at a Volunteer executive meeting on the Wednesday of Holy Week 1916.[27]

In 1947 Diarmuid Lynch, a member of the IRB Supreme Council in 1916, presented both of these errors as fact in an article entitled 'The countermanding orders of Holy Week 1916', which was written for *An Cosantóir*, the re-named Irish army journal.[28] The editor of *An Cosantóir* sent the article to Hobson for verification. Hobson, due to his poor eyesight, claimed he was only able to read a quarter of the article. He asserted:

> In the part I did read I found several misstatements of fact and a very distorted picture of the events between 1913 and 1916. For thirty years I have been seeing similar misstatements in print, and I have no wish to deter Mr Lynch from getting his particular distortion published. If this country ever does produce a historian, his difficulties will have been made insuperable in advance. My comment is that Mr Lynch's statements about myself and about certain other matters just do not happen to be true.[29]

As a result of Hobson's letter, the editor postponed publication of the article. Lynch's account was later published in his book *The IRB and the 1916 insurrection*.[30]

In 1947 the Department of Defence set up the Bureau of Military History in order to 'assemble and co-ordinate material to form the basis for the compilation of the history of the movement for independence from the formation of the Irish Volunteers' in November 1913 to the truce between the Irish and British forces in July 1921.[31] Hobson was among the first survivors of the revolutionary period to be approached by the BMH in 1947. He provided the BMH with sixteen witness statements regarding his early involvement in the nationalist movement, in organisations such as the IRB, the Fianna and the Irish Volunteers, and on individuals like Pearse and Casement. Although the files of the bureau were only opened to the public in 2003, Hobson made the bulk of his statements available in the National Library shortly after he had dictated them to a BMH stenographer. As early as 1932, Hobson was already planning to leave his own papers to the National Library.[32]

Hobson gave his witness statements to the BMH during a transitional period in his life when he was not only retiring from the civil service, but shifting his home from Dublin to Roundstone. Among Hobson's summertime neighbours in Roundstone was the writer Mervyn Wall (1908–97), who is perhaps best known for his two comic novels about a medieval monk called Fursey.[33] Wall described Hobson's house as 'fortress-like' and 'a refuge from a troubled Dublin life'.[34] Sympathising with what he viewed as Hobson's loneliness, Wall went to visit his neighbour a few evenings a week.[35] Not sharing Wall's interest in local antiquities and superstitions, Hobson preferred to reminisce about the paradoxes of his nationalist past.[36] Such reminiscences may have been sparked by his statements to the BMH. According to Wall, Hobson 'once said to me that my generation was a far more tolerant and understanding one than the generation that had condemned and hounded him'. Hobson even hinted that he would like someone to ghost-write his autobiography, but Wall refused to rise to the bait.[37]

In the 1950s Hobson blew hot and cold when it came to talking or writing about the past. In responding to a query about MacDermott, he informed Michael J. Lennon that he answered questions with 'increasing reluctance', explaining that 'I do not often think of those old days and when I have to bring my mind back to them I do not trust my memory'.[38] Wall certainly would have disputed the assertion that Hobson rarely thought of the old days. Perhaps Hobson was reluctant to answer Lennon's questions because O'Connor and Ó Lochlainn had challenged the authenticity of a published memoir by Fitzgibbon that Lennon had edited.[39]

In 1953 Seumas O'Sullivan asked Hobson to write an appreciation of Alice Milligan for *Dublin Magazine*, even though he knew that Hobson had said he would not write any more, ostensibly because of his failing eyesight.[40] Hobson refused, confessing to McCullough: 'I cannot and will not write about the people and times when we were young for reasons that are long and complicated. Briefly the phoenix of our youth has fluttered to earth such a miserable old hen I have no heart for it and if I force my inclination what I would write would not be worth printing.'[41] However, in 1956 Hobson did try to do some writing: 'largely because I can see to write when I cannot see to read'.[42]

A year later O'Shannon recorded his impression that Hobson would not talk publicly about the rising unless the focus was on Casement.[43] Hobson had delivered a talk on Casement on Radio Éireann on 17 February 1956.[44] That same year Hobson informed Dr Roger McHugh that he would be glad to talk to him about Casement 'at any time', in either Dublin or Roundstone.[45]

1960 to 1969

Pádraig Ó Snodaigh has suggested that to most Irish people after 1916 Hobson 'was, with his erstwhile colleagues, dead'.[46] The realisation that he was still very much alive came in the early 1960s as a result of the publication of excerpts from his papers on the Irish Volunteer movement in the *Irish Times*,[47] and the numerous media interviews that he gave. The 1960s offered Hobson many opportunities to share his account of the period 1900–16. The historian F.X. Martin was engaged in taking a revisionist look at the period, using Hobson's papers in the National Library. Excerpts from Hobson's papers were included in books on the Irish Volunteers and the Howth gunrunning that Martin edited in 1963 and 1964 respectively. In the run-up to the fiftieth anniversary of the Easter Rising, the print and broadcast media took an interest in Martin's research as well as in survivors from the revolutionary period.

One of the first interviews that Hobson gave was in 1960 to *Sunday Press* reporter and future TD Ted Nealon. He described Hobson, at the age of seventy-seven, as 'a ruddy-faced man with a magnificent mop of white hair', who was 'still gifted with a good memory and methodical mind' and had a 'clear and cultured voice'. In this interview Hobson discussed his involvement in the IRB and the Irish Volunteers in the period from the co-option of Redmond's nominees to his kidnapping by the IRB on Good Friday 1916.[48]

As ever, Hobson provoked controversy. The 1916 veteran Cormac Turner responded with a letter to the editor, pointing out that the split in the Volunteers might as well have happened sooner rather than later, and that guerrilla warfare tactics went against the IRB constitution as much as an insurrection did. He also cited Lynch's (erroneous) statement regarding when Hobson first heard that a rising was imminent, and denied the existence of a Dublin Centre within the structure of the IRB.[49] Eamon Martin replied with a rebuttal of Turner's points.[50]

It may have been in response to Hobson's interview in the *Sunday Press* that Cork County Librarian Pádraig Ó Maidín accused Hobson of having a 'personal vendetta against Clarke and Mac Diarmada' that was 'wholly unjustifiable'. Ó Maidín informed McCullough that Hobson was 'not doing himself any good if he wishes to have himself measured against them'.[51] To question the hero status of Clarke and MacDermott was still controversial.

Although Hobson played no official part in the 1966 commemoration of the Easter Rising, he shared 'his trenchant opinions and calm humour' regarding the insurrection and its leaders in interviews that were included in RTÉ and BBC documentaries.[52] In more private moments his fury was less easy to hide. Political scientist Tom Garvin recalls seeing an angry old man glaring at the big posters of the 'heroes' of 1916 that decorated Hodges Figgis bookstore in 1966. The angry old man was Hobson.[53]

In 1961 Hobson informed Griffith's biographer, Seán Ó Lúing, that he would not write his memoirs for four main reasons. Firstly, he had already provided an extensive account of his connection with the Irish nationalist movement to the BMH and made his witness statements available in the National Library. Secondly, Hobson felt that the history of 1916 was 'being pretty well rounded out by the various books written on it'. A third reason was that his poor eyesight was an obstacle to writing his memoirs. Finally, he was 'not ambitious to be an author' at this advanced stage in his life. Hobson declared: 'No. I will not write any formal memoirs. I probably wouldn't have a peaceful old age if I did!'[54]

The 1966 commemoration of the rising appears to have changed Hobson's mind about producing some sort of memoir. In 1968 he published his final book, *Ireland yesterday and tomorrow*. The first section of the book, which is based on his BMH statements, details his involvement in the nationalist movement, while the final section reprints some of his economic writings from the 1930s. The inclusion of these two sections suggests that Hobson was as proud of his economic propaganda, despite its lack of impact, as he was of his contributions to the nationalist movement. The book, though useful, leaves the reader feeling somewhat unsatisfied.[55] It traces Hobson's nationalist career, explaining his actions and decisions, but leaves out the emotional impact that 1916 had on his personal and professional life. It remains, however, essential reading for any study of the advanced nationalist movement in the period 1900–16.

Hobson was one of the earliest revisionists of 1916.[56] In his view, the rising was unnecessary. He predicted that without the insurrection:

[Dublin] Castle was undoubtedly going to gaol all the Volunteer leaders at the particular moment. And there would have been a long period of in and out of gaol and increasing agitation. And then guerrilla war would have started. I was quite clear in my mind that the one way to get the English out of Ireland was a sort of passive resistance that would enter gradually into a guerrilla business.[57]

In his opinion, 'if there was going to be a fight, and we realised all along there was going to be a fight at one stage, ... a guerrilla fight gave you the opportunity of never coming to a decisive engagement, of keeping the thing going if necessary for years'. Hobson viewed a policy of insurrection as too much of a gamble: 'After ... seizing the public buildings in Dublin, you could do nothing but sit there until you were shot out of them and that process only took a very few days.' He conceded, however, that the gamble paid off because the British executed the leaders; otherwise 'it would have been a complete fiasco'.[58]

Over the years Hobson had taken comfort in the belief that, although he himself did not have a political future, a combination of Sinn Féin-style passive resistance and guerrilla warfare, which he had 'advocated through arduous years', did have a political future. In his opinion, these policies, not the Easter Rising, 'led to the downfall of British power in Ireland'.[59] He denied any suggestion that the insurrection sparked the subsequent guerrilla war against the British, instead asserting that the guerrilla war was the direct result of the spontaneous operations of Dan Breen and Seamus Robinson and the indirect result of Volunteer training under O'Connell and O'Duffy prior to the 1916 rising.[60]

In his study of the Irish War of Independence, Michael Hopkinson countered the second part of Hobson's interpretation of the origins of the guerrilla war. Hopkinson found no evidence to suggest that the defensive warfare tactics promulgated by Hobson and his hero, Lalor, were 'studied or consciously taken up'. Disregarding the instruction provided by the *Irish Volunteer* newspaper, Hopkinson noted that at the time 'there was no blueprint' for guerrilla methods of fighting.[61]

Hobson's death on 8 August 1969 at his daughter's home in Castleconnell, County Limerick merited a front-page mention in the *Irish Times* at a time when the rising 'troubles' in his ancestral Ulster had seized the headlines. At his funeral a family member noted that his example of breaking down sectarian barriers could be 'followed with advantage elsewhere'.[62] There was no flag on the coffin or guard of honour, though President de Valera and Taoiseach Jack Lynch sent military representatives to the funeral. The parish priest said a prayer and Quaker William Glynn gave an oration. Among the mourners were T.K. Whitaker, the former Secretary of the Department of Finance, Douglas Gageby, the editor of the *Irish Times* and son-in-law of Sean Lester, and representatives of the Belfast Fianna Éireann and Casement commemoration committees. With the permission of the local congregation, Hobson was buried in a Catholic graveyard at the foot of Errisbeg overlooking Goirtín Bay, just down the road from his former home.[63]

Hobson left an estate valued at £19,985 11s. The bulk of his estate was divided equally to provide an income to his children Declan and Camilla, his sister Florence, and his friend Olive Gibson of Belfast, who had been a contributor to *Social Justice* back in the 1930s. He also left £50 to Mary Daly, a former neighbour in Rathfarnham, and his copyright and any other interest in his book *Ireland yesterday and tomorrow* to his son-in-law John Mitchell.[64]

Conclusion

Easter 1916 was the tragedy of Hobson's life. His negative opinion of the rising and its leaders did not change over the years. The anger remained, though he tried to submerge it. He wrote the first volume of his history of the Irish Volunteers in a failed attempt to defend himself. He then turned to defending Casement and sharing his knowledge of the nationalist movement on request. Although he preferred not to think of the past, he recognised that he had an important contribution to make to the historical record. His next accounts of the period 1900–16 were in response to requests from the army that he had helped to establish, first from the magazine *An t-Óglách* and later from the BMH. Emotionally, he appears to have found it easier to help others publish accounts of the period. His involvement in the production of the books by O'Duffy and Maloney are two examples. In the 1950s he refused to speak publicly about 1916 unless the topic was Casement.

His attitude seems to have altered in the 1960s. F.X. Martin's interest in Hobson's papers in the National Library was probably instrumental in encouraging him to share his side of the Easter Rising story with the public. It is likely that Martin's re-assessment of the insurrection and the period leading up to it, combined with media interest, gave Hobson a psychological boost. He even reversed his decision not to publish his memoirs. Hobson had mellowed so much that by 1965 he could look back on his days in the nationalist movement and comment to his old comrade McCullough: 'I wonder how many people nowadays get so much fun as we did.'[65]

Notes

1 Hobson to McCartan, 13 Feb. 1924 (NLI, PMcC, MS 17,675 (5)).
2 For a discussion of the re-assessment of the Easter Rising from the 1960s onwards, see Laffan, 'Insular attitudes: the revisionists and their critics', in Ní Dhonnchadha and Dorgan (eds), *Revising the Rising*, pp. 106–21.
3 Padraic [McCartan] to Hobson, 18 Aug. 1916 (NLI, BH, MS 13,161 (2)).
4 Draft letter from Hobson to MacNeill, 3 June 1918 (NLI, BH, MS 13,174 (4)).
5 MacNeill to Hobson, 8 June 1918 (NLI, BH, MS 13,161 (1)).
6 O'Shannon, 'Bulmer Hobson – key republican figure', *IT*, 9 Aug. 1969, p. 10.
7 Eimar O'Duffy, *The wasted island* (Dublin, 1923), pp. 269, 460. For an assessment of O'Duffy's literary work, see Robert Hogan, *Eimar O'Duffy* (Lewisburg, 1972).
8 *Irish Book Lover*, Mar. 1920, p. 82.
9 O'Duffy to Hobson, 6 Mar. 1922 (NLI, BH, MS 13,161 (8)).
10 Hobson to McCartan, 13 Feb. 1924 (NLI, PMcC, MS 17,675 (5)).
11 Ibid.
12 Ibid.
13 Ibid.
14 W.J. Maloney, *The forged Casement diaries* (Dublin, 1936).
15 Hobson to Maloney, 29 Oct. 1931 (NLI, JMcG, 17,604 (2)); McCartan to Hobson, 3 Mar. 1936 (NLI, JMcG, MS 17,604 (3)). For a discussion of Hobson's contribution to the project, see W.J. McCormack, *Roger Casement in death: or haunting the Free State* (Dublin, 2002), pp. 52–62.
16 McCormack, *Roger Casement in death*, p. 4. Mitchell offers a brief discussion of Casement's investigation in *Casement*, pp. 60–4.
17 Hobson, *IYT*, p. 82.
18 Hobson, statement, 17 Feb. 1933 (NLI, JMcG, MS 17,601 (8)).
19 See McCormack, *Roger Casement in death*, pp. 44–62.
20 Ibid., pp. 44–6; Hobson to Maloney, 22 Sept. 1932 (NLI, JMcG, MS 17,604 (2)).
21 Hobson, witness statement, Jan. 1948 (NAI, BMH, WS 85). See Denis Gwynn, *The life and death of Roger Casement* (London, 1930).
22 See Geoffrey Parmiter, *Roger Casement* (London, 1936); Robert Monteith, *Casement's last adventure* (Chicago, 1932).
23 Ó Lúing, 'Talking to Bulmer Hobson', *IT*, 6 May 1961, p. 10.
24 Inspector General, Dept. of Defence, to Hobson, 18 Dec. 1930 (NLI, BH, MS 13,169).
25 Louis Le Roux to Hobson, 29 July, 6 Aug. 1931 (NLI, BH, MS 13,161 (9)).
26 Le Roux, *Patrick Pearse*, p. 287; Le Roux, *Tom Clarke*, p. 135.
27 Le Roux, *Tom Clarke*, p. 192.
28 Printer's proof of Diarmuid Lynch, 'The countermanding orders of Holy Week 1916' (NAI, BMH, WS 651).

29 Hobson to Col Bryan, 18 July 1947 (NAI, BMH, WS 652).
30 See Lynch, *The IRB and the 1916 insurrection*.
31 Note on BMH (UCDA, DMcC, P 120/24 (11)).
32 Hobson to Maloney, 22 Sept. 1932 (NLI, JMcG, MS 17,604 (2)).
33 Wall to Gunning, 16 Jan. 1995.
34 Wall, 'The Godstone and the Blackymor', p. 33.
35 Wall to Gunning, 16 Jan. 1995.
36 Wall, 'The Godstone and the Blackymor', p. 34.
37 Wall to Gunning, 16 Jan. 1995.
38 Hobson to Michael J. Lennon, 9 Nov. 1955 (NLI, Michael J. Lennon Papers, MS 22,288/iii).
39 See Michael J. Lennon, 'The Easter Rising from the inside', *IT*, 18 Apr. 1949, 19 Apr. 1949, p. 4; Seamus O'Connor to editor, *IT*, 20 Apr. 1949, p. 5; Colm Ó Lochlainn to editor, *IT*, 22 Apr. 1949, p. 5.
40 O'Shannon to McCullough, 29 Apr. 1953 (UCDA, DMcC, P 120/15 (1)).
41 Hobson to McCullough, 5 May 1953 (UCDA, DMcC, P 120/17 (1)).
42 Hobson to McCullough, 30 Apr. 1956 (UCDA, DMcC, P 120/17 (2)).
43 O'Shannon to McCullough, 18 Mar. 1957 (UCDA, DMcC, P 120/15 (2)).
44 Hobson, Casement broadcast transcript, 17 Feb. 1956 (NAI, BMH, WS 1365).
45 Hobson to Dr Roger McHugh, 2 Nov. 1956 (NLI, BH, MS 8638).
46 Ó Snodaigh, 'Bulmer Hobson: A man of great integrity', *The Kerryman*, 16 Aug. 1969 (clipping, FHLD).
47 These excerpts were published in Nov. 1963.
48 Nealon, 'Hobson throws new light on IRB caucus', *SP*, 1 May 1960, p. 4.
49 Cormac Turner, 'Bulmer Hobson and the rising', *SP*, 8 May 1960, p. 10.
50 Martin, 'Bulmer Hobson and Redmondites – "This is a bitter pill – but one we must swallow"', *SP*, 15 May 1960, p. 10.
51 Ó Maidín to McCullough, 23 May 1960 (UCDA, DMcC, P 120/23).
52 Ó Snodaigh, 'Bulmer Hobson: a man of great integrity', *The Kerryman*, 16 Aug. 1969.
53 In conversations with Prof. Tom Garvin, UCD, 2003–4.
54 Ó Lúing, 'Talking to Bulmer Hobson', *IT*, 6 May 1961, p. 10.
55 In a positive review of the book, an *Irish Sword* critic voiced his suspicion that Hobson knew more than he revealed. See P.J.H., 'Ireland yesterday and tomorrow', *Irish Sword*, viii (1967–8), pp. 312–13.
56 Des Gunning suggests that a study of Hobson's writings bears out 'the claim that "revisionism" can be dated to at least a day or so *before* the 1916 rising'. See Gunning, 'Bulmer Hobson', *History Ireland*, Spring 2002, p. 5.
57 Transcript, *Old Ireland Free*, 24 Apr. 1966 (BBC Written Archives, Reading; UCDA, DMcC, P 120/36).
58 Hobson, TV interview, 5 Dec. 1963 (RTÉ Libraries and Archives).
59 Hobson, *IYT*, p. 78.
60 Ó Lúing, 'Talking to Bulmer Hobson', *IT*, 6 May 1961, p. 10.
61 Michael Hopkinson, *The Irish War of Independence* (Dublin, 2004), p. 15.
62 *IT*, 12 Aug. 1969, p. 5.

63 'Burial at Gorteen Bay', *The Kerryman*, 16 Aug. 1969 (clipping, FHLD); Glynn, 'The Quaker in Bulmer Hobson', *Irish Young Friend*, Aug. 1972 (clipping, Cork Archives Institute).
64 Will of John Bulmer Hobson, 11 Jan. 1963; Third codicil, 20 Nov. 1968.
65 Hobson to McCullough, 1 Sept. 1965 (UCDA, DMcC, P 120/17 (4)).

Conclusion

Like so many participants in late nineteenth- and early twentieth-century 'political movements of an often visionary and romantic character', Hobson was middle class, well educated by the standards of the time and frustrated in terms of career advancement.[1] What sets him apart from most of his contemporaries in the Irish nationalist movement is that he was an Ulster Protestant. What makes him even more unusual is that he was a Quaker – albeit a Quaker with an ambivalent attitude toward the use of violence to achieve political ends.

Yet the Ulster community in which he was raised exposed him to influences that led to his unusually active involvement in the advanced nationalist movement and helped to shape his republican ideology. Both of his parents took an active interest in politics. His father, a Gladstonian Home Ruler, taught him to fight injustice and to have the moral courage to uphold his convictions even when they clashed with mainstream opinion. His mother was a suffragist. His neighbours Milligan and Johnston shared their enthusiasm for Irish cultural and political nationalism with him. Their newspaper, the *Shan Van Vocht*, and its coverage of the centenary of the 1798 rebellion, inspired him to learn more about Wolfe Tone and the United Irishmen, whose ideology provided him with a political objective. His research into Irish history led him to Lalor's policy of moral insurrection, which offered him the means to pursue that political objective. His Quaker upbringing taught him to 'live his own truth',[2] as he pursued his 'concern' for the cultural, political and economic renewal of Ireland.[3]

During the period 1900–7 Hobson's energy, precocity and involvement in a wide and varied range of activities is impressive. His earliest propagandist enterprises involved adapting the endeavours of his elders so that they would appeal to young people like him. In some cases he gave the efforts of Dublin nationalists a northern spin in order to appeal to an Ulster audience. The derivative nature of his work suggests that he was a populariser, not an originator. His genius was not in conceiving new ideas, but in re-packaging the ideas of others in order to appeal to new audiences. These audiences, however, tended to have latent nationalist sympathies which were waiting to be activated by a fiery, persuasive preacher like Hobson. His efforts might not have succeeded in converting Ulster en masse to cultural or political nationalism, but they did foster the nationalism of individuals such as MacDermott, Blythe, O'Shannon and Lester.

Hobson, like so many other Ulstermen who held dissenting viewpoints, was forced to build a career outside his native province. Yet, his move to Dublin in 1908 allowed him to shift his focus to an all-Ireland stage with a larger and potentially more receptive audience for his nationalist message. A Dublin base facilitated his rise within the IRB, as well as his involvement in the foundation of the militarised, second incarnation of Na Fianna Éireann and later the Irish Volunteers.

It is ironic that, though Hobson opposed the Easter Rising, he provided the means to make the event possible. Even more than The O'Rahilly, he 'wound the clock'. He helped to establish two military organisations which participated in the insurrection, encouraged the mental and physical training of members of those organisations and co-ordinated the landing of guns and ammunition at Howth. As a leading member of the governing body of the Irish Volunteers, Hobson facilitated the placement of IRB members in strategic positions within that body and succeeded in postponing a potentially disastrous split in the Volunteer movement. The postponement of the split ensured the successful importation of arms and ammunition later used in the Easter Rising and provided members with more time to train with men who had military experience. Hobson even facilitated initial contact with Germany. Without manpower, training and weapons the IRB Military Council could not have implemented its insurrection strategy.

Whether in politics or religion, Hobson was a man who went his own way, acting in response to his own understanding of the truth. He defied IRB orders when they ran counter to what he believed were the best interests of the Irish Volunteers in particular and the nationalist movement in general. He also favoured a policy of guerrilla warfare over insurrection because, in his view, it had more chance of military success. His commitment to the struggle for Irish freedom could not be reconciled with the pacifist principles of his ancestral faith. Therefore, he resigned from the Society of Friends.

For Hobson, Easter 1916 was a political and personal tragedy. Yet, despite facing social ostracism and allegations that he was a traitor and a coward, he remained in Ireland, built a career as a Free State civil servant and wrote extensively on how key challenges for the new state, such as poverty, unemployment and emigration, could be combated. Even though there were times when he found thinking about or discussing the past emotionally painful, he recognised that his intimate knowledge of the Irish nationalist movement was historically significant, and he therefore shared this knowledge with the BMH, academics, journalists and later the general public. As a result, Hobson has contributed to and will continue to contribute to a deeper and more inclusive understanding of the Irish nationalist movement in the early twentieth century. He is a man who can provoke a variety of interpretations. This book represents only one.

Notes

1 Tom Garvin, 'Great hatred, little room: social background and political sentiment among revolutionary activists in Ireland, 1890–1922', in D.G. Boyce, *The revolution in Ireland, 1879–1923* (London, 1988), pp. 92–3.
2 Glynn, graveside tribute to Hobson, 11 Aug. 1969 (FHLD, MSS B. 3A-87).
3 Harrison, *Dictionary*, p. 17.

Bibliography

Manuscript sources

BBC Written Archive, Reading
Scripts for radio documentaries *Old Ireland Free* and *Easter 1916*

Belfast Central Library
Francis Joseph Bigger Papers

Historical Library of the Religious Society of Friends in Ireland
Genealogical Files
William Glynn Papers

National Archives of Ireland
Bureau of Military History witness statements
Department of Finance Files
Department of Justice Files
Department of the Taoiseach Files
Will of John Bulmer Hobson

National Archives of the UK, London
Inspector General's and County Inspectors' monthly confidential reports, CO 904/99–104
Nationalist organisations, CO 904/20
Postal censorship, CO 904/164
Précis of information received in Crime Special Branch, CO 904/117–120
Précis of information received relative to secret societies in the DMP district, CO 904/11–14

National Library of Ireland
Alice Milligan Papers

Bulmer Hobson Papers
Col Maurice Moore, 'History of the Irish Volunteers'
James L. O'Donovan Papers
Joseph McGarrity Papers
Mary Ann Bulmer Hobson, 'Bulmer family chronicle from before 1050 to 1936'
Michael J. Lennon Papers
Patrick McCartan Papers
Roger Casement Papers
Sheehy Skeffington Papers

Public Record Office of Northern Ireland
Birth register of Lisburn Monthly Meeting of the Society of Friends
Hobson – Bulmer Family Papers
Will of Mary Ann Hobson

RTÉ Libraries and Archives, Dublin
Interview with Bulmer Hobson, by John O'Donoghue, and featured in 'Thursday Topics', broadcast on Telefís Éireann, 5 Dec. 1963

University College Dublin Archives
Denis McCullough Papers
Eoin MacNeill Papers

Newspapers and periodicals

Bean na hÉireann
Belfast Evening Telegraph
Belfast Naturalists' Field Club Proceedings
Belfast Newsletter
Boston Post
Boston Sunday Post
Chicago Daily Tribune
An Claidheamh Soluis
Cleveland Plain Dealer
An Cosantóir
County Louth Archaeological Society Journal
Dana
Dublin Magazine
Éire
Evening Press
Fianna
Freeman's Journal

Gaelic American
Ireland To-day
Irish Book Lover
Irish Citizen
Irish Freedom
Irish Independent
Irish Nation
Irish Nation and the Peasant
Irish Naturalist
Irish News
Irish Press
Irish Review
Irish Review of Politics, Economics, Art and Literature
Irish Sword
Irish Times
Irish Volunteer
Irish Young Friend
Kerryman
National Democrat
Nationist
New York Times
Northern Whig
An t-Óglách
Peasant
Police Gazette
Prosperity
Republic
Shan Van Vocht
Sinn Féin
Social Justice
Sunday Press
Uladh
Ulster Journal of Archaeology
United Irishman

Interviews

Joe McCullough, Dublin, 20 June 2002.
Tom and Joe MacDonagh, Roundstone, Connemara, 9 Jan. 2003.
Joe Rafferty, Roundstone, Connemara, 9 Jan. 2003.
Paddy Ryan, Office of the Revenue Commissioners, Dublin, 29 Aug. 2006.

Books, articles and pamphlets

Bartlett, Thomas, 'The burden of the present: Theobald Wolfe Tone, republican and separatist', in David Dickson, Dáire Keogh and Kevin Whelan (eds), *The United Irishmen: republicanism, radicalism and rebellion* (Dublin, 1993), pp. 1–15.

Bell, Edward, *Social classes and social credit in Alberta* (Montreal, 1993).

Bell, Sam Hanna, *The theatre in Ulster* (Dublin, 1972).

——, et al. (eds), *The arts in Ulster* (London, 1951).

de Blaghd, Earnán, *Gaeil á múscailt* (Dublin, 1973).

Brady, Ciaran (ed.), *Worsted in the game: losers in Irish history* (Dublin, 1989).

Brown, Terence, *Northern voices: poets from Ulster* (Dublin, 1975).

Buckley, David N., *James Fintan Lalor: radical* (Cork, 1990).

de Búrca, Marcus, *The GAA: a history* (Dublin, 1980).

Campbell, Flann, *The dissenting voice: Protestant democracy in Ulster from plantation to partition* (Belfast, 1991).

Carroll, F.M., *American opinion and the Irish question, 1910–23* (Dublin, 1978).

Chubb, Basil, *The government and politics of Ireland* (3rd edn, London, 1992).

Clarke, Kathleen, *Revolutionary woman: Kathleen Clarke, 1878–1972: an autobiography*, ed. Helen Litton (Dublin 1991).

Coffey, Thomas M., *Agony at Easter* (London, 1970).

Cronin, Sean, *The McGarrity papers* (Tralee, 1972).

Czira, Sydney, *The years flew by* (Dublin, 1974).

Davis, Richard, *Arthur Griffith and non-violent Sinn Féin* (Dublin, 1974).

——, *Arthur Griffith* (Dundalk, 1976).

Denman, Terence, '"The red livery of shame": the campaign against army recruitment in Ireland, 1899–1914', *IHS*, xxix (1994), pp. 208–33.

Devoy, John, *Recollections of an Irish rebel* (New York, 1929).

Dublin Students' Dungannon Club, *Manifesto to the whole students of Ireland* (Dublin, 1906).

Dudgeon, Jeffrey, *Roger Casement: the Black Diaries with a study of his background, sexuality, and Irish political life* (Belfast, 2002).

Dudley Edwards, Owen, and Fergus Pyle (eds), *1916: the Easter Rising* (Dublin, 1968).

Dudley Edwards, Ruth, *Patrick Pearse: the triumph of failure* (London, 1977).

Elliott, Marianne, *Wolfe Tone: prophet of Irish independence* (New Haven and London, 1989).

Fanning, Ronan, *The Irish Department of Finance, 1922–58* (Dublin, 1978).
FitzGerald, Desmond, *Memoirs of Desmond FitzGerald*, ed. Fergus FitzGerald (London, 1968).
Foster, R.F., *Modern Ireland, 1600–1972* (London, 1989).
——, *W.B. Yeats: the apprentice mage, 1865–1914* (Oxford, 1997).
Fox, R.M., *Rebel Irishwomen* (Dublin, 1935).
Foy, Michael, and Brian Barton, *The Easter Rising* (2nd edn, Gloucestershire, 2004).
Fryer, Jonathan (ed.), *George Fox and the Children of Light* (London, 1991).
Gageby, Douglas, *The last secretary general: Sean Lester and the League of Nations* (Dublin, 1999).
Garvin, Tom, *Nationalist revolutionaries in Ireland, 1859–1928* (Oxford, 1987).
——, 'Great hatred, little room: social background and political sentiment among revolutionary activists in Ireland, 1890–1922', in D. George Boyce (ed.), *The revolution in Ireland, 1879–1923* (London, 1988), pp. 91–114.
Gaughan, J. Anthony, *Alfred O'Rahilly: public figure* (Dublin, 1989).
Glandon, Virginia E., *Arthur Griffith and the advanced nationalist press in Ireland, 1900–1922* (New York, 1985).
Gray, John, *City in revolt: James Larkin and the Belfast dock strike of 1907* (Belfast, 1985).
Greaves, C. Desmond, *Liam Mellows and the Irish revolution* (London, 1971; reprinted 1988).
Griffith, Arthur, *The resurrection of Hungary: a study in nationalism* (Dublin, 1904).
Gunning, Des, 'Bulmer Hobson, "the most dangerous man in Ireland"', *History Ireland*, no. 10 (Spring 2002), pp. 5–6.
Gwynn, Denis, *The life and death of Roger Casement* (London, 1930).
——, *The life of John Redmond* (London, 1932).
Hart, Peter, *Mick: the real Michael Collins* (London, 2005).
Haverty, Anne, *Constance Markievicz: an independent life* (London, 1988).
Hay, Marnie, 'Explaining *Uladh*: cultural nationalism in Ulster', in Betsey Taylor FitzSimon and James H. Murphy (eds), *The Irish revival reappraised* (Dublin, 2004), pp. 119–31.
——, 'This treasured island: Irish nationalist propaganda aimed at children and youth, 1910–16', in Mary Shine Thompson and Celia Keenan (eds), *Treasure islands: studies in children's literature* (Dublin, 2006), pp. 33–42.

——, 'The foundation and development of Na Fianna Éireann, 1909–16', *IHS*, xxxvi (2008), pp. 53–71.
Hewitt, John, *Art in Ulster* (2 vols, Belfast, 1977), i.
Hobson, Bulmer, *The flowing tide* (No place of publication, n.d.).
——, *To the whole people of Ireland: the manifesto of the Dungannon Club* (Belfast, 1905).
——, *The creed of the republic* (Belfast, 1907).
——, *Ireland or Westminster! Sinn Féin v. parliamentarianism: a debate in Glasgow between Mr Bulmer Hobson, Belfast and Mr J.J. O'Neill, Glasgow* (Dublin, 1908).
——, *Defensive warfare: a handbook for Irish nationalists* (Belfast, 1909).
——, *A short history of the Irish Volunteers* (Dublin, 1918).
—— (ed.), *The life of Wolfe Tone* (Dublin, 1919).
—— (ed.), *The letters of Wolfe Tone* (Dublin, 1920).
—— (ed.), *A book of Dublin* (Dublin, 1929, 1930).
——, *A national forestry policy* (Dublin, 1931).
—— (ed.), *Saorstát Éireann official handbook* (Dublin, 1932).
——, *The new querist* (Dublin, 1933).
——, *The Gate Theatre* (Dublin, 1934).
——, *National economic recovery: an outline plan* (Dublin, 1935).
——, *Ireland yesterday and tomorrow* (Tralee, 1968).
——, and P.S. O'Hegarty (eds), *The voice of freedom* (Dublin, 1913).
Hobson, Mary Ann Bulmer, *Memoirs of six generations* (Belfast, 1947).
Hogan, Robert, *Eimar O'Duffy* (Lewisburg, 1972).
——, *Mervyn Wall* (Lewisburg, 1972).
——, and James Kilroy, *The modern Irish drama* (2 vols, Dublin, 1976), ii.
Holland, Robert, *A short history of Fianna Éireann* (Dublin, n.d.).
Hopkinson, Michael, *The Irish war of independence* (Dublin, 2004).
Irish Unionist Alliance, *The Dungannon Clubs and a separate Ireland: a view of what 'Young Ireland' is doing* (Dublin, 1905).
Jamieson, John, *The history of the Royal Belfast Academical Institution, 1810–1960* (Belfast, 1959).
Johnston, Sheila Turner, *Alice: a life of Alice Milligan* (Omagh, 1994).
Jordan, Alison, *Who cared? Charity in Victorian and Edwardian Belfast* (Belfast, 1992).
Kennedy, David, 'Ulster unionism and the new nationalism', in Kevin B. Nowlan (ed.), *The making of 1916* (Dublin, 1969), pp. 71–95.
King, Sandra, *History of the Religious Society of Friends, Frederick Street, Belfast* (Belfast, 1999).

Krause, David (ed.), *The letters of Sean O'Casey, 1910–41* (4 vols, London, 1975), i.
——, *The letters of Sean O'Casey, 1942–54* (4 vols, New York, 1980), ii.
Laffan, Michael, 'Insular attitudes: the revisionists and their critics', in Máirín Ní Dhonnchadha and Theo Dorgan (eds), *Revising the rising* (Derry, 1991), pp. 106–21.
——, *The resurrection of Ireland: the Sinn Féin party, 1916–1923* (Cambridge, 1999).
Lalor, James Fintan, *The writings of James Fintan Lalor* (Dublin, 1895).
Le Roux, Louis, *Patrick H. Pearse* (Dublin, 1932).
——, *Tom Clarke and the Irish freedom movement* (Dublin, 1936).
Luddy, Maria, 'Isabella M.S. Tod', in Mary Cullen and Maria Luddy (eds), *Women, power and consciousness in 19th century Ireland* (Dublin, 1995), pp. 197–230.
Lynch, Diarmuid, *The IRB and the 1916 insurrection*, ed. Florence O'Donoghue (Cork, 1957).
Lynd, Robert, *Irish and English: portraits and impressions* (London, 1908).
MacAtasney, Gerard, *Seán MacDiarmada: the mind of the revolution* (Manorhamilton, 2004).
MacColl, René, *Roger Casement* (London, 1956).
MacDermott, Eithne, *Clann na Poblachta* (Cork, 1998).
MacFhloinn, Pádraig, 'The history and tradition of Fianna Éireann', in *Fianna Éireann Handbook* (Dublin, 1988), pp. 7–21.
MacLiammóir, Micheál, *All for Hecuba* (Dublin, 1961).
Maloney, W.J., *The forged Casement diaries* (Dublin, 1936).
Marreco, Anne, *The rebel countess* (London, 1967).
Martin, F.X. (ed.), 'Eoin MacNeill on the 1916 rising', *IHS*, xii (1961), pp. 226–71.
—— (ed.), *The Irish Volunteers, 1913–1915: recollections and documents* (Dublin, 1963).
—— (ed.), *The Howth gun-running and the Kilcoole gun-running, 1914* (Dublin, 1964).
—— (ed.), *Leaders and men of the Easter Rising: Dublin 1916* (London, 1967).
——, 'McCullough, Hobson and republican Ulster', in Martin (ed.), *Leaders and men of the Easter Rising*, pp. 95–108.
——, '1916 – myth, fact and mystery', *Studia Hibernica*, no. 7 (1967), pp. 7–126.
——, 'The 1916 rising – a coup d'état or a "bloody protest"?', *Studia Hibernica*, no. 8 (1968), pp. 106–37.

Maye, Brian, *Arthur Griffith* (Dublin, 1997).
McCartan, Patrick, 'Extracts from the papers of Dr Patrick McCartan', *Clogher Record* (1963), pp. 30–45; *Clogher Record* (1964), pp. 184–212.
McCormick, W.J., *Roger Casement in death: or haunting the Free State* (Dublin, 2002).
McCullough, Denis, 'The events in Belfast', *Capuchin Annual* (1966), pp. 381–4.
McGee, Owen, *The IRB* (Dublin, 2005).
McGuinne, Dermot, 'Colm Ó Lochlainn and the Sign of the Three Candles', *Long Room*, no. 41 (1996), pp. 43–51.
Mengel, Hagal, 'A lost heritage', *Theatre Ireland*, no. 1 (Sept.–Dec. 1982), pp. 18–19.
Meredith, Robbie, 'The *Shan Van Vocht*: notes from the North', in Alan A. Gillis and Aaron Kelly (eds), *Critical Ireland: new essays in literature and culture* (Dublin, 2001), pp. 173–80.
Mitchell, Angus, *Casement* (London, 2003).
Monteith, Robert, *Casement's last adventure* (Chicago, 1932).
Moore, Maurice, *Tús agus fás, óglách na hÉireann, 1913–1917* (Dublin, 1936).
Morash, Christopher, *A history of Irish theatre, 1601–2000* (Cambridge, 2002).
Morris, Catherine, 'Becoming Irish?: Alice Milligan and the revival', *Irish University Review*, no. 33 (Spring/Summer 2003), pp. 79–98.
——, 'In the enemy's camp: Alice Milligan and *fin de siècle* Belfast', in Nicholas Allen and Aaron Kelly (eds), *The cities of Belfast* (Dublin, 2003), pp. 62–73
Murphy, William, 'Cogging Berkeley?: *The querist* and the rhetoric of Fianna Fáil's economic policy', *Irish Economic and Social History*, xxxii (2005), pp. 63–82.
Newhouse, Neville H., *A history of the Friends' School, Lisburn* (Lisburn, 1974).
Novick, Ben, 'Postal censorship in Ireland, 1914–16', *IHS*, xxxi (1999), pp. 343–56.
——, 'The arming of Ireland: gun-running and the Great War, 1914–16', in Adrian Gregory and Senia Pašeta (eds), *Ireland and the Great War* (Manchester, 2002), pp. 94–112.
Nowlan, Kevin B., 'Tom Clarke, MacDermott and the IRB', in Martin (ed.), *Leaders and men of the Easter Rising*, pp. 109–21.
O'Brien, William, and Desmond Ryan (eds), *Devoy's post bag, 1871–1928* (2 vols, Dublin, 1953), ii.
Ó Broin, León, *Revolutionary underground: the story of the IRB, 1884–1924* (Dublin, 1984).

——, *Protestant nationalists in revolutionary Ireland: the Stopford connection* (Dublin, 1985).
O'Casey, Sean, *Drums under the windows* (London, 1945).
Ó Ceallaigh, Séamus, *Gleanings from Ulster history* (Draperstown, 1994).
O'Doherty, Michael Kevin, *My parents and other rebels* (Dublin, 1999).
O'Driscoll, Finín, 'Social Catholicism and the social question in independent Ireland: the challenge to the fiscal system', in Mike Cronin and John M. Regan (eds), *Ireland: the politics of independence, 1922–49* (London, 2000), pp. 121–43.
O'Duffy, Eimar, *The wasted island* (Dublin, 1923).
Ó Duibhir, Ciarán, *Sinn Féin: the first election, 1908* (Manorhamilton, 1993).
O'Faolain, Sean, *Constance Markievicz* (2nd edn, London, 1987).
O'Halpin, Eunan, 'British intelligence in Ireland, 1914–1921', in Christopher Andrew and David Dilks (eds), *The missing dimension: governments and intelligence communities in the twentieth century* (London, 1984), pp. 54–77.
O'Hegarty, P.S., *A history of Ireland under the Union, 1801–1922* (London, 1952).
O'Keefe, Timothy J., 'The 1898 efforts to celebrate the United Irishmen: the '98 centennial', *Éire-Ireland*, no. 23 (Summer 1988), pp. 51–73.
O'Kelly, Seán T., *Seán T.*, ed. Proinsias Ó Conluain (Dublin, 1963).
O'Rahilly, Aodogán, *Winding the clock: O'Rahilly and the 1916 rising* (Dublin, 1991).
O'Rahilly, The (Michael), *The secret history of the Irish Volunteers* (Dublin, 1915).
Ó Snodaigh, Pádraig, *Hidden Ulster: Protestants and the Irish language* (Belfast, 1995).
Parmiter, Geoffrey, *Roger Casement* (London, 1936).
Pyle, Hilary (ed.), *Cesca's diary, 1913–1916* (Dublin, 2005).
Réamonn, Seán, *History of the Revenue Commissioners* (Dublin, 1981).
Regan, Nell, 'Helena Molony', in Mary Cullen and Maria Luddy (eds), *Female activists: Irish women and change, 1900–1960* (Dublin, 2001), pp. 141–68.
Royal Commission of inquiry into the circumstances connected with the landing of arms at Howth on July 26th, 1914, *Report of commission and minutes of evidence* (London, 1914).
Royal Commission on the Rebellion in Ireland, *Report of commission* (London, 1916).
Royal Commission on the Rebellion in Ireland, *Minutes of evidence and appendix of documents* (London, 1916).

Ryan, Desmond, *The rising: the complete story of Easter Week* (Dublin, 1949).

Ryan, Paddy (ed.), *Revenue over the years* (Dublin, 1998).

Ryan, Phyllis, *The company I kept* (Dublin, 1996).

Saunders, Norah, and A.A. Kelly, *Joseph Campbell, poet and nationalist, 1879–1944: a critical biography* (Dublin, 1988).

Short, Con, *The Ulster GAA story, 1884–1984* (Rassan, 1984).

Tierney, Michael, *Eoin MacNeill: scholar and man of action, 1867–1945* (Oxford, 1980).

Townshend, Charles, *Easter 1916: the Irish rebellion* (London, 2005).

Trench, Chalmers, 'The Three Candles Press in the 'thirties', *Long Room*, no. 41 (1996), pp. 35–42.

Urquhart, Diane, *Women in Ulster politics, 1890–1940* (Dublin, 2000).

Van Voris, Jacqueline, *Constance de Markievicz in the cause of Ireland* (Amherst, Massachusetts, 1967).

Wall, Mervyn, 'The Godstone and the Blackymor [by] T.H. White', in Proinsias Ó Conluain (ed.), *Islands and authors* (London, 1959), pp. 33–43.

Ward, Margaret, *Unmanageable revolutionaries: women and Irish nationalism* (London, 1995).

Wigham, Maurice J., *The Irish Quakers* (Dublin, 1992).

Theses

Curtis, Maurice, 'Catholic action as an organised campaign in Ireland, 1921–1947' (PhD thesis, UCD, 2000).

Delaney, Enda, 'Fr Denis Fahey, CSSp, and Maria Duce, 1945–1954' (MA thesis, National University of Ireland, Maynooth, 1993).

Hannon, Charles, 'The Irish Volunteers and the concept of military service and defence, 1913–1924' (PhD thesis, UCD, 1989).

Hay, Marnie, 'Explaining *Uladh*: the promotion of nationalism and regionalism in Ulster' (MA thesis, QUB, 1999).

——, 'Bulmer Hobson: the rise and fall of an Irish nationalist, 1900–16' (PhD thesis, UCD, 2004).

Hynes, Sandra, '"Walk according to the gospel order": theology and discipline in the Quaker meeting system, 1650–1700' (PhD thesis, TCD, Dublin, 2002).

McHenry, Margaret, 'The Ulster Theatre in Ireland' (PhD thesis, University of Pennsylvania, 1931).

Phelan, Mark, 'The rise and fall of the Ulster Literary Theatre' (MPhil thesis, TCD, 1998).

Reference books

Belfast and Ulster Directory
Connolly, S.J. (ed.), *The Oxford companion to Irish history* (Oxford, 1999).
Harrison, Richard S., *A biographical dictionary of Irish Quakers* (Dublin, 1997).
Newmann, Kate, *Dictionary of Ulster biography* (Belfast, 1993).

Thom's Directory
Welch, Robert (ed.), *The Oxford companion to Irish literature* (Oxford, 1996).

Index

Note: literary works can be found under authors' names and page numbers in *italic* refer to illustrations.

abstention from parliament 31, 46, 84
agricultural commune 79–82, 86, 217
alcohol 43–4, 48, 66
All-for-Ireland League 83
Allan, Fred 96–7, 100–2
American tour 67–71, 94
amnesty campaign 20
Ancient Order of Hibernians (AOH) 48, 52, 82–3, 106, 112, 121, 124–5, 128
Anglo-Irish Treaty 217, 221
Anglo-Irish War *see* War of Independence
anti-military recruitment / enlistment campaign 45, 48–9, 58–9, 93
Antrim, County 28, 35
Antrim Road, Belfast 7–9, 11, 15, 18, 20
AOH *see* Ancient Order of Hibernians
Ardboe 50
Ardrigh 15
Armagh, County 99
Asgard 160
Asquith, H.H. 134–5, 201
Atkinson, F.M. 35
Aud 192, 194
Austria 46

Bachelor's Walk shootings (1914) 162
Baden-Powell, Robert 79
Bailey, Daniel 192
Banking, Currency and Credit, Commission on (1934–8) 226–8

Third Minority Report 227–8
Banna Strand 192
Bartholomew Teeling Literary and Debating Society 101
Barton, Brian 122, 189
BBC *see* British Broadcasting Corporation
Bean na hÉireann 77–8
Béaslaí, Piaras 97, 120, 123, 149, 152, 180, 196
Belcamp Park, Raheny 80–1
Belfast Association for the Employment of the Blind 19
Belfast dock strike (1907) 55–6
Belfast Evening Telegraph 33
Belfast Naturalists' Field Club 10, 25, 38
Belfast Newsletter 48
Belfast School of Art 31
Belfast Workhouse 10
Bell, Sam Hanna 30
Beltaine 34
Benington, Charles 6, 8–9
Berkeley, George 223
 querist, The 223
Bigger, Francis Joseph 15, 18, 51, 74, 81–2
Black and Tans 207
Black Diaries 236, 238–41
Blythe, Ernest (Earnán de Blaghd) 47, 52, 60–1, 81, 97, 103, 168, 171, 197–8, 200, 202, 219, 229, 231, 241, 251
BMH *see* Bureau of Military History

Index

Bodenstown 100, 102–3
Boer War 27, 60
Bonner, Richard 81
Boru, Brian 23–4, 30
Boston 68–70
Boundary Commission 200, 208, 217
Boy Scout movement 79
Boys' Brigade 28, 39
Bracken, Peadar 185
Brady, Ciaran 4
Brady, James 84
Brady, Sean 225
Branniff, Dan 50
Breen, Dan 215, 245
Britain 15, 45–6, 113, 154, 183, 221
British Army 28, 130, 144, 156, 158, 162, 170, 185
British Association for the Advancement of Science 10
British Broadcasting Corporation (BBC) 244
British Empire 114
Brooklyn 68
Brown, Terence 12, 24
Brugha, Cathal 103
Bulmer, Ann 7, 141
Bulmer family chronicle 10
Bureau of Military History (BMH) 1, 190, 241–2, 244, 246, 252
Burke, Martin 151
Burns, Peter 55
Byrne, L.P. 187

Cabra Park, Dublin 193, 196
Cahill, Edward 226–7
Camden Street, Dublin 29, 78
Campbell, Flann 55, 65
Campbell, John 24, 30, 34–5, 54
Campbell, Joseph 30, 55, 65, 120
Candle Press 216, 231–2, 236
Carbery, Ethna *see* Johnston, Anna
Carbery, Patrick 48
Carrickmore 14, 50, 52, 81–2, 98, 100
Carson, Edward 4, 109, 135
cartoons 30, 49, 51, 54
Casement, Roger 2, 15, 50–1, 55–8, 74, 80–3, 109, 113–16, 125, 129–30, 133–5, 140, 144–5, 148–9, 154, 159–60, 163, 166–7, 192, 236, 238–40, 239, 242–3, 246

Castleconnell 230, 245
Castle Document 187, 192, 194–5
Catholic Action movement 226
Catholic Bulletin 220–1
Cave Hill 13, 15
Cave Hill Road, Belfast 7, 18
Ceannt, Áine 103, 121, 195
Ceannt, Éamonn 103, 111, 120–1, 133, 143, 149, 152, 165–6, 169–71, 174, 180, 185, 189, 194–5, 206, 210
censorship 140, 187–8
Chicago 68–9
Childers, Erskine 144, 159, 160
Childers, Molly 144
Chotah 162
Christian Brothers 14, 24
civil service 216, 218–19, 221, 229, 251
Civil War *see* Irish Civil War
Claidheamh Soluis, An 37, 111, 216
Clan na Gael 14, 67, 70, 96, 100, 108, 114–15, 140, 163
Clann na Poblachta 228
Clarke, Daly 95
Clarke, Kathleen 94–6, 108–9, 113, 189, 205, 214
Clarke, Stephen 58
Clarke, Tom 2, 75, 84, 93–6, 95, 99, 100–2, 104–10, 113, 115–16, 122, 125, 133–4, 136–40, 145–6, 160, 163, 166, 172, 177, 189, 190, 193, 195, 197, 206, 240–1, 244
Cleveland 68
Cogley, Daisy Bannard ('Toto') 220
Colbert, Con 110, 120, 149, 152, 180, 190, 204
Cole, W.L. 71
Colivet, Michael 184
Collins, Maurice 194, 196–7
Collins, Michael 204
Colum, Padraic 47
commemoration
    1798 centenary 13, 27, 250
    Easter Rising 243
    Manchester Martyrs 98
    Robert Emmet 100, 115
    Wolfe Tone 100, 102
commission agent 74, 89
concern 9, 18, 250

Conlon, Martin 193, 196–7, 210
Conlon, Mrs Martin 194
Connolly, James 4, 104–5, 166, 174–5, 184, 190, 194–7
Connolly, Joseph 211
Connolly, Nora 104
conscription 173, 185, 206
co-operative movement 56–7, 59
Corcoran, Timothy 220–1
Cormackan, Thomas 99
Cosantóir, An 241
Cosgrave, William 206, 221
countermanding order 195, 206, 211, 241
court martial 100, 204, 206, 241
Cotter, Edmond 10, 156, 158–9, 163, 176
Cotton, Alf 171
County Dublin Observer 74
Cousins, James 24, 29, 33
   Ben Madigan and other poems 24
   Racing Lug, The 29
   Sleep of the King, The 33
Cowley, Michael 102
Coyne, Edward 227
Craig, E.T. 79, 217
   history of Ralahine, A 79
   Irish commune, An 217
Craig, James 217
Cromwellian settlement of Ireland 6
Cumann Cosanta, An 76, 168
Cumann na Cailíní 49, 53, 81
Cumann na mBan 186, 188, 194
Cumann na nGaedheal (political party) 221, 227
Cumann na nGaedheal (umbrella organisation) 2, 31–2, 42–3, 45–6, 50, 55, 67, 71–2, 77
Cushendall 57–8, 74
Cushendall Poultry Society 57–8, 82
Cushendun 51, 229
Czira, Sydney 78

Daly, John 94, 102, 117
Daly, Mary 246
Daly, Ned 197, 210
Daly, Paddy 190
Daly, P.T. 45, 72–3, 84, 96, 117
Dana 35
dancing 26, 53, 81

Darlington 7–8
Davis, Richard P. 12, 72, 207
Davitt, Michael 140, 148
DCWTCC *see* Dublin Central Wolfe Tone Clubs Committee
Deakin, Seamus 105, 120, 137–8, 150
de Búrca, Marcus 27
Defence, Department of 241
Defence of the Realm Act (DORA) 140, 168, 171, 185
de Lacey, Laurence 155
de Loughrey, Peter 188
Dempsey, Patrick 98
Derry 49
Derry, County 35
de Valera, Eamon 189, 205–6, 210, 217, 221–3, 226–8, 237, 245
Devlin, Joseph 128, 141, 148
Devolution Crisis (1904–5) 37
Devoy, John 67, 78, 80, 110, 112, 114, 134, 140, 150, 163, 239
Digges, Dudley 29
Dillon, Geraldine 180
Dillon, John 128
Divis Street, Belfast 43
Dobbs, St Clair 57
Dolan, Charles J. 55, 72–3
dominion status 167
Donegal, County 98
Donovan, J.T. 151
DORA *see* Defence of the Realm Act
Douglas, C.H. 224
Downey, William 55
Doyle, S. 71
dual monarchy 46, 71, 77, 85
Dublin Castle 27, 44–5, 100, 140, 160, 162, 187–8, 192, 195, 198, 219
Dublin Central Wolfe Tone Clubs Committee (DCWTCC) 96, 100, 102–3
Dublin Civic Week 220
Dublin Corporation 47, 188, 220
Dublin Magazine 242
Dundalk 55, 71–2
Dungannon 50
Dungannon clubs 2, 42, 45, 46–56, 58–60, 67, 71–2, 75, 81, 85, 91, 108, 226, 229, 231
Dungannon Convention (1782) 47, 104

Durham University 10
Easter Rising 1–5, 75, 87, 106, 119, 145, 153, 163, 166, 170, 172, 175, 177, 183–199, 202–4, 206–8, 220, 236–8, 241, 243–6, 248, 251
Economic Recovery Commission 223
Edmondson, William 7
Edward VII 31, 46
Edwards, Hilton 219–20
Egypt 54, 76
Elwood, John 50
Emergency *see* Second World War
emigration 51, 221, 223, 252
Emmet, Robert 70, 97, 100
Emmet, Robert Temple 69
Emmet, Thomas Addis 69
employment 25–6, 56–8, 74, 83, 155, 218, 222, 224
England 6–7, 15, 124, 217
External Affairs, Department of 219

Falls Road, Belfast 14, 26, 37, 44, 51
Famine, Great 2
farming 82–3, 86
Fay brothers 29
Feis of the Nine Glens 51
Feis Uladh 25–6
Fenians *see* Irish Republican Brotherhood
Ferguson, Samuel 24
ffrench-Mullen, Madeleine 78
Fianna Éireann, Na 2, 28–9, 37, 48, 59, 77–80, 85, 91, 101, 103–4, 109–10, 116, 123, 134, 145, 156, 161–2, 169, 171, 190, 204, 214, 242, 246, 251
Fianna Fáil 221, 223, 225, 227
Figgis, Darrell 159, 161, 172
Filgate, Harry 94
Finance, Department of 219, 224, 245
Finea 66
First World War 113–14, 143–5, 154, 163–4, 166, 169, 172, 177, 183, 224
FitzGerald, Desmond 154, 166–9, 177, 186, 194, 196, 199
FitzGerald, Mabel 167, 198, 238
Fitzgibbon, Sean 120–1, 125, 143, 149, 151–2, 156, 158, 162, 165, 167, 180, 185, 189, 194–6, 198, 205, 211, 242
Foy, Michael 122, 189
Freedom Clubs 85, 103, 116, 171
Friend, L.W. 187
Friends *see* Religious Society of Friends
Friends' School, Lisburn 6, 8–9, 12, 18, 203
funeral 245–6

GAA *see* Gaelic Athletic Association
Gaelic American 67, 70, 114–15, 121, 140, 150
Gaelic Athletic Association (GAA) 2, 27–8, 36
Gaelic football 28–9
Gaelic League 2, 11, 14, 18, 25–6, 34, 36, 48, 50, 58, 60, 101, 103–4, 111, 187, 194
Gaeltacht 103, 222, 228
Gageby, Douglas 245
Gageby, John 230, 235
Galway 103
gardaí *see* police
Garvin, Tom 244
Gavan Duffy, George 50
Gate Theatre 216, 219–20
General Post Office (GPO) 189, 197, 199
George V 100
Germany 113–16, 153–4, 163, 166–7, 173–4, 188–9, 192, 251
Gibson, Olive 233, 246
Ginnell, Laurence 66
Gladstone, William Ewart 1, 9, 250
Glasgow 74–5
Glynn, William 174, 200, 233, 245
G men 44–5
    see also police, Royal Irish Constabulary
Gogan, Liam 121, 127, 149, 152, 180
Gonne, Maud 20, 23, 25, 29, 30, 45, 78, 228
Good, James Winder 33–4, 54, 65
Gordon, John 35
Gore, John 121, 148–9, 151
GPO *see* General Post Office
Gratton, Henry 31
Greaves, C. Desmond 108, 200, 203, 214

Index

Gregan, Claire *see* Hobson, Claire
Gregory, Lady Augusta 32
Griffith, Arthur 2, 16, 27, 31, 36, 43, 45, 46–7, 54, 59, 67, 68, 70–3, 77–8, 81, 83–7, 100, 139, 195, 205, 207, 211, 237, 244
   resurrection of Hungary, The 45–6
guerrilla warfare 2, 16–17, 153, 169, 170–1, 173, 177, 184, 243, 245, 251
Gunning, Des 153, 176, 248
gunrunning 154, 189
   Howth 135, 142, 145, 151, 157, 159, 160–3, 172, 176–7, 179, 243, 251
   Kilcoole 135, 145, 162–3, 176, 189
   Larne 128
Gwynn, Denis 240
   life and death of Roger Casement, The 240

Hall, Reginald 193
Hannigan, Donald 80
Hannon, Charles 128–9, 131, 142, 163–4, 171
Harrel, William Vesey 161–2
Harrison, Henry 159
Hart, Peter 204
Healy, T.M. 84
Henry Joy McCracken Literary Society 12, 24
Henry, Paul 65
Heuston, Sean 204
Hobson, Benjamin 7
Hobson Jr, Benjamin 7, 9, 14–15, 17, 82, 250
Hobson, Bulmer 3, 77
   book of Dublin, A 220
   Brian of Banba 23, 29, 33–5
   Defensive warfare 75–6
   flowing tide, The 103
   Gate Theatre, The 220
   Ireland or Westminster! 75
   Ireland yesterday and tomorrow 1, 244, 246
   letters of Wolfe Tone, The 217
   life of Wolfe Tone, The 217
   National economic recovery: an outline plan 223–4, 227
   national forestry policy, A 222
   new querist, The 223–4
   Saorstát Éireann official handbook 220–1
   short history of the Irish Volunteers, A 236–7
   voice of freedom, The 103
Hobson, Camilla *see* Mitchell, Camilla
Hobson, Claire (née Gregan) 159, 188, 194–6, 198–9, 201, 203, 216, 218–20
Hobson, Declan 5, 159, 216, 218, 246
Hobson, Florence 7, 9–10, 14–15, 159, 197–8, 203, 246
Hobson, Francis 7
Hobson, Harold 7
Hobson, Laurence 7
Hobson, Mary Ann (née Bulmer) 7, 10–11, 14–15, 17, 19, 24–5, 144, 203, 229, 250
Hogan, Seán 207
Holohan, Garry 162, 190
Home Rule 11, 17, 51, 53, 83, 98, 109, 124, 134, 143, 163, 166, 250
   bills (1886, 1893, 1912) 1, 9, 24, 27, 109, 129
Hopefield Avenue, Belfast 7
Hopkinson, Michael 245
housing 223–4, 228–9
Hughes, Herbert 65
Hungary 46
hurling 26–9, 36
Hutton, Mary 24, 201, 213
Hyde, Douglas 25, 31, 231

Independent Orange Order 50, 60
India 54, 69, 76
Indianapolis 68–9
Inghinidhe na hÉireann 23, 29, 32, 36, 76–7, 100
Ingoldsby, A. 71
insurance 52, 57–8, 73, 75–6, 168
IRA *see* Irish Republican Army
IRB *see* Irish Republican Brotherhood
Irish Agricultural Organisation Society 56
Irish Book Lover 217
Irish Brigade 166, 192
Irish Citizen 78, 126
Irish Citizen Army 174
Irish Civil War 207, 217, 221

Irish Felon 16
Irish Freedom 2, 78, 85, 96–8, 100–6, 108, 114, 116–17, 137–8, 140, 151
Irish Free State 200, 207, 218, 220–1, 223, 225–6, 229, 235, 251
Irish Hospitals' Sweepstakes 50
Irish Independent 75
Irish language 26, 29, 36, 53, 81, 103, 222
  see also Gaelic League
Irish Literary Revival 23, 29, 36
Irish Literary Theatre 32
Irish mythology 12, 28, 35, 54
Irish Nation 202
Irish Nation and the Peasant 74, 80
Irish National Dramatic Company 29, 32
Irish National Theatre Society 32, 78
Irish News 27, 33, 37, 48
Irish Parliamentary Party 2, 13, 24, 27, 51, 69–70, 72, 74, 83–4, 109, 112, 121–4, 129, 131, 202
Irish People Co-operative Society Ltd. 228
Irish Republican Army (IRA) 207
Irish Republican Brotherhood (IRB) 2, 15, 20, 42–5, 47–50, 52, 72, 75, 79, 84, 87, 93, 95, 97–102, 105–8, 111–12, 115, 117, 120–1, 123–7, 129–30, 135–6, 140–1, 153, 155, 160, 164–5, 172, 196–7, 203, 206, 213, 231, 242, 251
  constitution 94, 117, 163, 177, 191, 199, 206, 208, 243
  Dublin Centres Board 102, 110, 137, 138, 146, 183, 190, 193, 243
  Fianna circle 102, 116, 190
  Leinster Executive 102, 137, 138, 193, 210
  Military Council 166–7, 170, 174–5, 177, 180, 183, 187–9, 193, 195, 208, 251
  Supreme Council 2, 44–5, 94, 96–8, 101, 103, 106, 108, 111, 113–14, 116, 120, 122, 132–4, 137–9, 143, 146, 150, 154, 163, 166, 174, 176, 183, 202, 204, 208, 241

  Teeling circle 101–3, 138
Irish Review of Politics, Economics, Art and Literature 217
Irish Times 243, 245
Irish Transvaal Committee 59–60
Irish Unionist Alliance 51
Irish Volunteer 111, 155–6, 169, 171–2, 184–6, 245
Irish Volunteers 2, 79, 87, 109, 110–11, 115, 127, 130, 137–8, 141, 151, 166, 176, 183, 185–7, 191–2, 196, 200, 202–3, 206–8, 236, 241–3, 245–6, 251
  arms and equipment 154, 156–7, 159, 160–4, 170, 177, 192, 195
  see also gunrunning
  Central Executive 165, 174–5, 184, 188–9, 193, 195
  Executive Committee 164–5, 168–70, 205
  fundraising 154, 159, 161, 167, 214
  General Council 164–5, 168–9, 205, 237
  military organisation 154, 156–8, 163–4, 169, 171–2, 177
  see also military training
  Provisional Committee 2, 112–13, 115–16, 119–29, 131–6, 139, 141–4, 146, 149, 153, 155, 157–8, 160
  split 144–5, 164, 177, 251
Irish Women's Association 11
Irish Worker 105

Jackson, Valentine 204
Johnson, Fred 225
Johnson, Tom 225
Johnston, Anna (Ethna Carbery) 1, 11, 13–15, 17, 20, 25, 30, 36–7, 54, 250
Johnston, Robert 11, 20, 44
Joshi, S.L. 69
Judge, Michael J. 121, 125–8, 130, 136, 147, 149, 151–2, 155–8, 161, 165, 170, 177, 179–80, 202–3
Justice, Department of 225

Kearney, Peadar 105
Kelly, Tom 85, 121, 188, 198

Kelpie 162
Kettle, Laurence J. 112, 121, 123, 148–9, 151
Kettle, Thomas 70, 112, 149
Keynes, John Maynard 224
  general theory of employment, interest and money, A 224
Keynesianism 224
kidnapping 149, 187, 191, 193–6, 212, 243
Kimmage 187, 194

labour movement 55–6, 105, 197
lace-making 53
Laffan, Michael 3, 72, 86
Lalor, James Fintan 2, 15–18, 46, 59, 67, 245, 250
Lalor, Patrick 16
land drainage 223–4
Larkin, Jim 49, 55, 105
League against Poverty 225
League for Social Justice 225, 227
Lenahan, James 121, 149
Lennon, Michael J. 180, 242
Le Roux, Louis 108–9, 138, 189, 202, 241
Lester, Sean 47, 61, 103, 175, 194, 198–9, 206, 229, 231, 235, 246, 251
Liberal Party and government 53, 60, 124, 134, 193
Liberty Hall 195
Lisburn 6, 8–9
List, Friedrich 46
Little, Patrick J. 187–8, 209
Little Theatre, The 220
Lloyd George, David 84
Lockout (1913) 105, 110, 174
Logue, Michael 187
London 50, 53, 71, 74
Lonergan, Michael 79, 110, 120
Lurgan 7, 99
Lynch, Diarmuid 95, 174, 189, 196, 241, 243
  IRB and the 1916 insurrection, The 241
Lynch, Jack 245
Lynch, Michael 194, 196
Lynd, Robert 49–50, 54, 65, 67, 74
Lyttle, Richard 24

Macardle, Dorothy 32
MacAtasney, Gerard 106
MacBride, John 45, 101, 108, 228
MacBride, Seán 228
McCartan, Patrick 13–14, 49–50, 53, 55, 60, 67, 71, 73, 78, 81, 95–7, 100–2, 106, 117, 119, 143, 145, 183, 201–2, 216, 220, 225, 229, 231, 236, 240
McCaw, Stevenson and Orr 25
MacColl, René 240–1
  Roger Casement: a new judgement 240
McCormack, W.J. 240
McCracken, Henry Joy 13, 43, 105
McCullough, Denis 14–15, 18, 25–6, 36, 42–53, 55, 60, 67, 71, 80–1, 85, 94–6, 98, 100, 103, 106–7, 115, 138–9, 150, 183, 186–7, 202, 208, 211, 220, 229, 231, 242, 244, 246
McCullough, Domhnall 25
MacDare, Curoi (Bulmer Hobson) 54, 97
MacDermott, Sean 3, 42, 48–9, 52, 61, 73, 75, 95–7, 101, 105–10, 107, 113, 116, 119–20, 122, 124–6, 133–4, 136–8, 143, 145–6, 149, 151–2, 156, 160, 163, 166, 172, 174–5, 180, 184, 187–8, 190, 192–7, 202–3, 206, 238, 240, 242, 244, 251
MacDonagh, Joe 213
MacDonagh, Thomas 121, 151, 161, 165–6, 169–72, 174, 176, 180, 184, 192, 194–6, 206, 210
MacDonagh, Tom 207, 213, 230
McDonald, William 30–1
McDonnell, Barbara 57–9
McDonnell, William *see* McDonald, William
McElligott, J.J. 227
MacEntee, Sean 225–7, 229
McGarrity, Joseph 14, 42, 53–4, 56, 58–9, 69–70, 75, 82, 139, 142, 150, 197, 202, 205, 208, 239–40
McGarry, Sean 51, 55, 78, 80, 95–7, 136, 202, 206

McGee, Owen 94, 96
Mac Giollarna, Seán 216
McHugh, Roger 243
Macken, Peadar 120, 149, 152, 156, 180
MacLeda, Fergus (Bulmer Hobson) 54, 97
Mac Liammóir, Micheál 220
  Ford of the Hurdles, The 220
MacManus, Seumas 24, 30–1, 38
MacNamara, Brinsley 231
Macnamara, Gerald *see* Morrow, Harry
MacNeill, Ada 51, 144, 229
MacNeill, Eoin 2, 111–12, 120–1, 123, 125, 127, 129–30, 133–6, 139, 141–2, 144–5, 148–9, 151, 154, 157, 159–62, 164–6, 169–75, 177, 180, 184– 208, 211, 216, 218, 231, 237
MacNeill, James 185, 199, 201, 216
MacNeill, Margaret 199, 218
MacNeill, Niall 196, 204
MacRory, Joseph 197
MacSwiney, Thomas 97
Magazine Fort 190
Magdala Street, Belfast 7
Maloney, William 238, 240, 246
  forged Casement diaries, The 240
Manchester Martyrs 81, 91, 98
Marino 104, 201
Markievicz, Count Casimir 80, 81, 217
Markievicz, Countess Constance 2–3, 37, 76, 77–81, 84–6, 91, 98, 100–1, 109, 141, 204–5, 217
Marreco, Anne 141
marriage 199, 201–2, 230–1, 235
Martin, Eamon 110, 120, 145, 149, 152, 180, 189–90, 202–3, 243
Martin, F.X. 4, 42, 104, 145, 172, 206, 236, 243, 246
Martin Lester Ltd. 216–18, 231–2, 237
Martyn, Edward 84
Maryborough (Port Laoise) 16, 103
Maxwell, John 199–201
Meade, James E. 226
Meehan, F.E. 72
Megahy, Kate 10
Mellows, Barney 127, 204
Mellows, Liam 120, 127, 133, 149, 152, 164, 167, 174, 180, 189, 200

Meredith, James Creed 142, 151
military training 79, 110, 127, 156–7, 162, 170–3, 245
Mill House, Rathfarnham 218, 230
Milligan, Alice 1, 11, 13, 15, 17, 20, 24, 30, 33, 36–7, 54, 218, 231, 242, 250
  Last Feast of the Fianna, The 33
Milligan, Seaton F. 11, 20
Milligan, William 218, 231
  Dynamite Drummer, The 218
Milroy, Seán 205
Minister and Secretaries Act (1924) 218
Mitchel, John 14, 95, 97
Mitchell, Camilla (née Hobson) 5, 218, 230, 245–6
Mitchell, John 246
Mitchell, Susan L. 231
Molony, Frank 78
Molony, Helena 76–9, 81, 100, 159, 205
Molony, Mrs M. 77
Monaghan, Alf 171
Monasterevin 7
monetary policy 223, 226–7
Monteagle, Lord 225
Monteith, Robert 192, 240
  Casement's last adventure 240
Moore, George 124
Moore, Maurice 121, 124, 126–30, 133–5, 147–9, 151, 153, 155–8, 164, 176
moral insurrection 2, 15, 17–18, 67, 250
Moran, D.P. 120
Morash, Christopher 33, 35–6
Morris, Catherine 11
Morrow brothers 49, 54
Morrow, Edwin 30
Morrow, Fred 33–4
Morrow, George 30
Morrow, Harry (Gerald Macnamara) 30, 32
Morrow, Jack 30, 33–4, 53
Morrow, Norman 30
Moy 6, 99
Mulcahy, Richard 211
Murphy, Peter 26
Murphy, William 223
Myles, Thomas 162

Nathan, Matthew 140
Nation, The 16
National Council 2, 31, 46, 55, 60, 67, 71–3
National Democrat 55
National Library of Ireland 1, 236, 240, 242–4, 246
National Volunteers 144–5, 164, 187
naval intelligence 192–3
Nealon, Ted 243
Neilson, Samuel 13
Newcastle-upon-Tyne 50
New Departure 140
Newry 98–9
Newtown School, Waterford 9, 218
New York 67, 69–70, 114, 121, 163, 171
non-sectarianism 13, 44, 47
Normand, Armando 240
North Leitrim by-election (1908) 55, 72, 106–7
Northern Ireland 217–18, 229, 245
Northern Literary Revival *see* Ulster Literary Revival
Northern Patriot 12
Northern Whig 33, 54
Nugent, J.D. 151

O'Boyle, Neil John 44
Ó Briain, Liam 196, 211
O'Brien, Conor 159, 162
O'Brien, P. 71
O'Brien, William 83–4
O'Callaghan, Cormac 232
O'Callaghan, John 70
O'Casey, Sean 104–6
Ó Ceallaigh, Séamus 187–8, 195–6, 209, 211
O'Connell, Daniel 16
O'Connell, J.J. ('Ginger') 169, 171–2, 174, 184–5, 188–92, 205–6, 245
O'Connell, Mortimer 211
O'Connor, Rory 187
O'Connor, Seamus 102, 105, 112, 114, 120, 123, 136, 149, 152, 157, 165, 174, 180, 187, 194, 211, 242
O'Doherty, Seamus 211
O'Driscoll, Finín 227

O'Duffy, Eimar 127, 167, 169, 190–1, 211, 218, 231–2, 237–8, 245–6
Wasted Island, The 237
O'Faolain, Sean 80–1
Óglách, An t- 241, 246
O'Grady, Standish 12, 14, 18
O'Growney, Eugene 25–6, 222
O'Halpin, Eunan 193
O'Hanlon, Jack 96–7, 101
O'Hanrahan, Michael 168
O'Hegarty, P.S. 50, 54, 73–4, 85, 95–7, 101, 103, 106, 113, 117, 119, 122, 137–9, 202, 231, 240
voice of freedom, The 103
O'Hogan, Eamon 233
O'Keefe, Eoin 227
O'Keeffe, Pádraig 211
O'Kelly, Seamus 25
O'Kelly, Seán T. 193, 197, 211
O'Leary, John 25, 97
Ó Lochlainn, Colm 121, 149, 152, 180, 187, 194, 211, 216, 232, 236, 242
Ó Lochlainn, Gearóid 220
O'Loghlen, Peadar 227
Ó Lúing, Seán 244
Omagh 99
Ó Maidín, Pádraig 208, 244
O'Neill, J.J. 74–5
O'Neill Crowley, Peter 43
O'Rahilly, Alfred 227
O'Rahilly, Aodogán 111–12, 161, 179, 212
O'Rahilly, The (Michael) 111, 120–1, 125, 128, 135, 141–2, 148–9, 157, 159, 161, 165, 169, 171, 174, 179–80, 185, 188–9, 194, 196, 198, 211, 251
Orangemen 73, 124
see also Independent Orange Order
O'Reilly, Myles ('The Slasher') 66
O'Reilly, Peter 121, 149
Ó Riain, Pádraig 110, 114, 120, 136, 149, 152, 156–7, 161, 165, 169, 172, 180, 190
Orr, William 81
O'Shannon, Cathal 35, 37, 54, 61, 75, 81, 103, 202, 233, 237, 243, 251
O'Shea, P.J. 25

O'Sheehan, Jack 50
Ó Snodaigh, Pádraig 243
O'Sullivan, Seamus 29, 242
Owen, Robert 79

pacifism 2, 12, 16, 31, 154, 176, 203, 208
Page, Robert 120, 149
papal encyclicals 225, 227
Parkhill, David (Lewis Purcell) 29–30, 33–4
 Enthusiast, The 34–5
 Reformers, The 33
Parmiter, Geoffrey 240
 Roger Casement 240
Parnell, Charles Stewart 13, 24, 27, 80, 140
partition 218
passive resistance 16–17, 46, 67, 69, 76, 173, 245
Patterson, Florence *see* Hobson, Florence
Pearse, Patrick 2, 100, 108, 110, 114–15, 120–1, 123, 140–3, 145, 149, 152, 155, 165, 169–70, 172, 174–5, 180, 184–6, 189–92, 195–7, 202, 206, 241–2
Peasant, The 54–5, 60, 74, 77, 221
Philadelphia 50, 68, 70, 75, 115, 121
Plunkett, George 187
Plunkett, Horace 56
Plunkett, Joseph Mary 121, 149, 151, 165–7, 169–70, 172, 174–5, 180, 184–5, 187, 194–5, 206
poetry 30–1, 35–7, 54
Poland 80
police 27–8, 44–5, 54, 81, 91, 93, 98, 100, 116, 138, 160–1, 185, 192, 198, 200–1, 205, 225
 see also G men, Royal Irish Constabulary
Poor Law Guardian 10
Port Laoise *see* Maryborough
poverty 221–3, 225–6, 252
Price, Ivor 140, 198, 212
prison 102, 104, 202–3, 245
propaganda 23–4, 36–8, 42, 46, 49, 54, 59–61, 86, 93, 154–6, 159, 168–9, 176, 216, 218, 221–9, 231, 250

Prosperity 225, 228
Protestant National Society (or Association) 30–2, 36–7, 40, 42, 47, 77, 229
Provisional Government of the Irish Republic 189
Purcell, Lewis *see* Parkhill, David

Quakers *see* Religious Society of Friends
Queen's College 7
Quin, Máire 29

Radio Telefís Éireann (RTÉ) 243–4
Radley, Joseph 8, 12
Rafferty, Joe 213
Raheny 79–82, 86, 217
Ralahine 79, 217
Raphoe 98
Rathfarnham Castle 201
re-afforestation 222, 224, 228
Rebellion (1798) 13, 17–18, 25
Redmond, John 2, 4, 51, 109, 111–12, 115, 119, 122–3, 128–37, 139–46, 148, 150–1, 158, 163–4, 187, 238, 243
Redmond, William 141–2, 151
Reid, Forrest 35
Reilly, Thomas Devin 97
Religious Society of Friends 6–10, 16, 18–19, 31, 43, 49, 153–4, 173–6, 197, 199–200, 203, 208, 226–7, 245, 250–1
rent strike 16
Repeal League 202
Republic, The 2, 49, 53–5, 59, 70–2, 75, 96–7, 221
republicanism 13–4, 47, 54, 71, 85, 250
retirement 229–30
Revenue Commissioners, Office of 218, 221, 235
 Stamping Department 218–19, 232
Reynolds, Joseph 214
Reynolds, W.B. 33–4
RIC *see* Royal Irish Constabulary
Ríoghacht, An 226–8
Roberts, George 32
Robinson, Seamus 245
Roundstone, Connemara 201, 207, 213, 230, 242–3

Royal Belfast Academical Institution 82
Royal Commission on the Rebellion in Ireland 198, 212
Royal Irish Academy 11
Royal Irish Constabulary (RIC) 44–5, 100, 192, 201, 207
  see also G men, police
royal visits
  Edward VII 31, 46
  George V and Mary 100
RTÉ see Radio Telefís Éireann
Russell, George (Æ) 29, 32, 35, 81, 217
  Deirdre 32
Russell, Thomas 13
Ryan, Agnes 211
Ryan, Desmond 114, 189
Ryan, Fred 29
Ryan, James 211
Ryan, Máire (Min) 211
Ryan, Phyllis 211
Ryan, W.J. 120
Ryan, W.P. 55, 74

St Enda's School 110, 114, 191, 202
St Louis 68
Salvation Army 73
Samhain 34
Sarsfield, Patrick 97
Sawyer, Roger 153, 176
Scannell, J.J. 151
Scottish nationalism 15
Second World War 220
sectarianism 32
secular education, 74–5
separatism 13–14, 17, 78, 85
Shan Van Vocht 9, 12–13, 18, 46, 54, 250
Shannon hydro-electric scheme 221
Sheehan, Dan 50
Sheehan, T.J. 71
Sheehy Skeffington, Francis 55, 126, 176, 187
Sherlock, Lorcan 123, 141
Sinn Féin 2, 16, 43, 45, 47, 52, 54–8, 60, 67–75, 77, 83–7, 93, 98–100, 105, 108, 115, 117, 168, 187–8, 205, 230, 237–8, 245
  amalgamation 71–3
  policies 46, 66, 173

Sinn Féin 67, 77–8, 84–5
Sinn Féin League 55, 60, 67, 72–3
Sligo Champion 73
Smith, Eugene 187
Smith, John G. 226
social credit 223–4
Social Justice 225, 228, 234, 246
Southwell, John 99
Stapledon, R.G. 228
Stationery Office 218
Stopford Green, Alice 15, 168, 231
Strangford Lough 58, 81
suffrage 10, 78, 126, 250
sugar beet industry 219
Sunday Press 190, 243–4
Sweetman, John 84

tableaux vivants 25, 36
Táin Bó Cúailnge 24, 201
Talbot Press 223, 232, 240
theatre 7, 29, 32–4, 231
Three Candles Press 232
Tierney, Michael 139, 145, 200, 213
Tithe War 16
Tobin, Sean 193
Toomebridge 34–5
Towards a new Ireland series 225, 228, 234
Townawilly 98
Townshend, Charles 3, 187, 193, 210
Trench, Cesca Chenevix 198
Turner, Cormac 243
Tyrone, County 6, 11, 98

UCD see University College Dublin
UIL see United Irish League
Uladh 34–7, 47, 55, 59
Ulster Arts Club 30
Ulster Branch of the Irish Literary Theatre 29–30, 32, 78
Ulster Debating Club 24–5, 31, 36–7
Ulster Debating Society 25, 36, 38
Ulster Journal of Archaeology 15
Ulster Literary Revival 23–4, 36
Ulster Literary Theatre (ULT) 2, 29, 33–5, 37–8, 47, 219, 229
Ulster Volunteer Force 109, 124, 128–30, 143
ULT see Ulster Literary Theatre
unemployment 221, 223, 228, 252

United Irish League (UIL) 70, 73–4, 112, 121, 124
United Irishman 25–8, 30–1, 33, 35–7, 46
United Irishmen 1, 13–14, 18, 24, 30–1, 47, 81, 96, 105, 229, 250
United States 2, 45, 54, 67–71, 73, 78, 110, 114, 121, 140, 154
University College Dublin (UCD) 187
university education 74

Vandeleur, John Scott 79
Vikings 23, 220
Von Bernstorff, Count 114, 116, 140, 154, 163

Wall, Mervyn 220, 242
Walsh, George 121, 149
Walsh, Paul 211
Walsh, Roisín 225
Walsh, William 187, 194, 199
War of Independence 207, 245
Waters, B. Berthon 226–8, 233

Welsh nationalism 15
Whately, Richard 222
Whitaker, T.K. 245
White, Peadar 121, 152, 180
Wolfe Tone, Theobald 1, 11, 13–14, 18, 30–1, 54, 100, 102, 105, 217, 229, 250
Wolfe Tone and United Irishmen Memorial Association 102
Wolfe Tone Clubs 96
women's rights 10
Woodtown Park, Rathfarnham 185, 191, 194, 198, 200–1
Workers' Republic 174
Wyse Power, Jenny 188

Yeats, W.B. 23, 29–30, 32–5
  Cathleen Ni Houlihan 29, 32
  King's Threshold, The 34
Young Ireland movement 16
Young Republican Party 104
youth 24–6, 28–9, 36, 48, 78–9, 95, 98–9, 110, 204